HOW
THE IRISH
INVENTED
SLANG

THE SECRET LANGUAGE OF THE CROSSROADS

HOW THE IRISH INVENTED SLANG

THE SECRET LANGUAGE OF THE CROSSROADS

DANIEL CASSIDY

INTRODUCTION BY PETER QUINN

CounterPunch
PETROLIA

PRESS

First published by
CounterPunch and AK Press 2007
© *CounterPunch* 2007
All rights reserved.

CounterPunch
PO Box 228 Petrolia, California, 95558

AK Press
674-A 23rd St, Oakland, California 94612-1163

ISBN 978-1-904859604

A catalog record for this book is available from the Library of Congress.
Library of Congress Control Number: 2006933530

Typeset in *Tyfa*, designed by František Štorm for The Storm Type Foundry, and
Stainless, Designed by Cyrus Highsmith for The Font Bureau, Inc.; the cover
uses *Amplitude* designed by Christian Schwartz for The Font Bureau, Inc.

Printed and bound in Canada.

Index by Jeffrey St. Clair.

Editing by Alevtina Rea.

Cover design by Tiffany Wardle.

Design and typography by Tiffany Wardle.

Contents

Dedication

This book is dedicated to my wife Clare Cassidy,
my mother Doris Cassidy,
and the memory of my father Daniel Patrick Cassidy.

Acknowledgements

I am deeply grateful to New College of California and An Léann Éireannach, the Irish Studies Program.

This project would not have been born without the Foclóir Póca (pocket dictionary) given to me by the late Kevin O'Dowd. I also want to thank: Peter Quinn, Michael Cassidy, Martin Hamilton, Alexander Cockburn, Esther O'Hara, Terry Golway, David Meltzer, Eamonn McCann, Kathleen Sullivan, T.J. English, Karen Ellis, Michael Patrick MacDonald, Bobby and Susanna Lavery, Margaret McPeake, Danny Schechter, Maureen Dezell, Patricia Harty, Gloria McIntyre, Eddie Stack, Deborah Dagg, Hillary Flynn, Peter Gabel, Micheál Ó hAodha, Karen Prescher, my grandmother, the late Muriel Ferris, and a special acknowledgement to the faculty, staff, and students of NYU's Glucksman Ireland House.

A special thanks must be extended to three people who helped in the making of this book: Tiffany Wardle, who tackled the unique typographic design challenges posed by an etymological dictionary; Alevtina Rea for copyediting a book written in three languages; and Kimberly Willson-St. Clair for giving the kind of sharp editorial and bibliographical advice that is the secret language of librarians.

INTRODUCTION

Lost and Found
By Peter Quinn

I N 1799, TROOPS WITH NAPOLEON'S ARMY IN EGYPT UNEARTHED AN ANCIENT tablet inscribed with a tribute to the Pharaoh in demotic script as well as Greek and hieroglyphs. As a result of this discovery outside the town of Rashid (Rosetta), the Egyptologist and linguist Jean-François Champollion was eventually able to reveal the meanings of a once-indecipherable language. What had been lost was found, and historians and scholars gained a new understanding of the past. Working with a pen (or, more likely, a computer) rather than a spade, and serving both as digger and decoder, Daniel Cassidy presents us with revelations that are, for etymologists in general and Irish-Americans in particular, every bit as momentous as those Champollion extracted from the Rosetta stone.

The discoveries that Cassidy has gathered into *How the Irish Invented Slang: the Secret Language of the Crossroads* represent a hugely significant breakthrough in our ability to understand the origins of vital parts of the American vernacular. He has solved the mystery of how, after centuries of intense interaction, a people as verbally agile and inventive as the Irish could seemingly have made almost no impression on English, a fact that H.L. Mencken, among other students of the language, found baffling. What was missing, it turns out, wasn't a steady penetration of Irish into English, but someone equipped with Cassidy's genius—a unique combination of street smarts and scholarship, of memory, intuition, and intellect—who could discern and decipher the evidence.

Like the Frenchmen who uncovered the Rosetta stone, Cassidy's discovery began with a serendipitous dig, a solitary stroke of the spade into the fertile earth of his own family's history, at the spot where a piece of the past jutted above the layers of time forgotten or obscured in the form of a single word, "Boliver" (*bailbhe, balbhán*, mute, inarticulate, a silent person), the semi-affectionate, semi-sarcastic nickname used to refer to his taciturn grandfather.

Beginning with that key, à la Champollion, Cassidy unlocks the secret of a centuries-long infiltration of Irish into English, exactly where it would be most expected, amid the playfully subversive, syncretic, open-ended olio of slang. "We were not *balbh* (mute) in Irish," writes Cassidy:

> The slang and accent of five generations and one hundred years in the tenements, working-class neighborhoods, and old *breac-Ghaeltachta* (Irish-English speaking districts) slums (*'s lom*, is a bleak exposed place) of Brooklyn and New York City held within it the hard-edged spiel (*speal*, cutting language) and vivid cant (*caint*, speech) of a hundred generations and a thousand years in Ireland: Gaeilge, the Irish language.

Cassidy's ability to see clearly what others—including myself—had missed entirely, his originality and eagle-eyed insight in locating what was hidden in plain view, brings to mind Edgar Allan Poe's famous short story "The Purloined Letter." At the outset of the story, C. Auguste Dupin is informed by the Prefect of Police that his men are nonplussed because the case they are trying to crack, which seemed simple at the outset, has proved unsolvable. "Perhaps it is the very simplicity of the thing which puts you at fault," replies Dupin. Later, he explains to his companion the underlying reason why the police, equipped with microscopes and following the rules of evidentiary logic, overlooked what was right before their eyes:

> Had the purloined letter been hidden anywhere within the limits of the Prefect's examination—in other words, had the principle of its concealment been comprehended within the principles of the Prefect—its discovery would have been a matter altogether beyond question.

Dupin's axiom—that while the obvious is often found in obvious places, locating it can require abandoning the safe harbor of theory for the open waters of reality and experience—underlies Cassidy's work. Take, for example, his explication of the word "crony," which *Merriam-Webster's Collegiate Dictionary* (Tenth Edition) speculates is perhaps from the Greek *chronios* (long-lasting) and was first recorded in English usage in 1663. The dating to 1663, the early days of the Restoration, with returning Irish exiles and refugees from the Cromwellian settlement abounding in English cities and towns, is a clue to the true origin of crony. More direct and, it seems to me, altogether beyond question, is the unadorned fact that the Irish word *comh-roghna*, pronounced co-rony, means, Cassidy tells us, "fellow favorites, mutual sweethearts, fellow chosen ones, figuratively, mutual pals."

The story of the Irish language's survival and its transatlantic impact is inseparable from the course of Irish history. Beginning with the dissolution of the Irish monasteries under Henry VIII through the Elizabethan conquest, the Flight of the Earls, and the aftermath of the Williamite victory, the old Gaelic order was gradually toppled and destroyed. Educated Irish-speaking monks, poets, musicians, genealogists, scholars, and brehons were driven from the scriptora, schools, castles, and courts where they had enjoyed the patronage of chieftains and, in some cases, of the Irish-Norman ("old English") nobility outside the Pale.

By the beginning of the eighteenth century, Irish, the first literate vernacular in Europe, had become almost exclusively the language of vagabond storytellers and musicians, hedge-school teachers, peasants, and spalpeens, its purview the cabins, clachans, and crossroads of the countryside, the vast half-hidden world beneath the new Anglo-Irish colonial order, the territory of the 's lom, or slum. With the great scattering driven by the Famine, the insular, self-referential confines in which most Irish speakers existed was broken open. The language was carried by immigrants, navvies, miners, travelers, laborers, and domestics to the New World. (There was an earlier influx of largely Scots-Gaelic speakers whose settlements reached from Cape Breton and Newfoundland to the Carolinas. Their impact on regional dialects and slang was profound and, as Cassidy is the first to point out, deserves the full attention of linguistic scholars.)

Just as important as the sheer number of those who left during the Famine decade, is where they went. A sizeable chunk descended on the burgeoning cities of one of the world's most rapidly industrializing societies at the very moment that railroads and telegraphs were revolutionizing the speed and impact of communications. Almost overnight, port cities such as New York, Boston, and New Orleans became home to large Irish communities, and newly emerging metropolises such as Chicago, San Francisco, and Kansas City weren't far behind.

The exact proportion of Famine immigrants monolingual in Irish or bilingual in Irish and English will never be known. Estimates of primary Irish speakers vary, running as high as thirty-five per cent. In his masterfully written, deeply researched history of a single village's fate during the Famine, *The End of Hidden Ireland*, Robert Scally relates how large numbers of arrivees in Liverpool tried to pass as English speakers, knowing that "speaking Irish above a whisper outside the Irish wards instantly marked the emigrant to both the authorities and the swarms of predators." Though the precise numbers of Irish speakers will remain, at best, an educated guess, there's no doubt that the *breac-Ghaeltacht*, or Irish-English speaking district, seeded itself in American cities, towns, and rural areas.

Sometimes these settlements were in mill towns such as Augusta, Maine, where Nathaniel Hawthorne recorded in his *Notebooks* sighting improvised *cláchans*, "the board-built and turf-buttressed hovels of these wild Irish, scattered about as if they had sprung up like mushrooms in the dells and gorges, and along the banks of the river;" or near Walden Pond, outside Salem, Massachusetts, where he came upon "a little hamlet of huts or shanties inhabited by Irish people who work upon the railroad . . . habitations, the very rudest, I should imagine, that civilized men ever made for themselves . . ." Other times, the language was embedded among the tenement dwellers of the Five Points, in New York City, and in dockside communities along the East and Hudson rivers. Wherever Irish was found, it had an effect, spicing people's everyday speech and percolating through mongrel networks of saloons, theaters, political clubhouses, union halls, and precinct houses, its *spiel* full of pizzazz.

The concentration of the Irish in the hub cities of America's industrial coming-of-age made the Irish prime participants in the often intertwined professions of politics, entertainment, sports (along with its less reputable sister, gambling), as well as a major part of the local criminal underworld (which was not infrequently an ally of the local political machine). Cut off from the main avenues of social advancement and power—the elite universities, Wall Street, the familial and fraternal networks of the Protestant upper classes—the Irish traveled the back streets and alleyways becoming a formative ingredient in the swirling mix of a still inchoate national identity.

Irish was an everyday part of the immigrants' journey from mud-splattered outsiders to smooth-talking prototypes of urban cool, from the hard-fisted slugger (*slacaire*) of the Five Points to the streetwise ward heeler (*éilitheoir*) of the ubiquitous political clubhouses to the quintessential American con game, the scam (*'s cam*). The language was woven into the fabric of how they lived, labored, and relaxed. It melded into the musical productions of the prolific Edward Harrigan (whose plays were so popular that he had his own theater in which to house them), into the lingo of street gangs and the police forces created to control them, into hobo camps and circus trains, into folk songs of east and west, into "Paddy Works on the Erie" and the cowboy anthem "Whoopie Ti Ti Yo," into the speakeasy shtick of Texas Guinan and the groundbreaking dramas of Eugene O'Neill.

As Ann Douglas points out in *Terrible Honesty*, her intriguing, often brilliant study of New York City in the 1920s, there was—and is—an underlying subversive dynamic to the American vernacular:

> The American language gained its distinctive character by its awareness of, and opposition to, correct British Standard English; white slang was played against conventional middle-class speak, and the Negro version of the language worked self-consciously against the white one. In both cases, the surprise came from the awareness of conventions being flouted.

The Irish-American vernacular was a ready-made alternative to "conventional middle-class Anglo-American speak." It provided a vocabulary that wasn't used in the classrooms or drawing rooms of the "respectable classes," but that reeked of the lower classes (or "the dangerous classes," as nineteenth century social reformer Charles Loring Brace referred to slum dwellers in general and the Irish in particular).

The infusion of Irish-American vernacular into popular usage involved, as well, the usefulness of words, their quotidian and demotic ability to get a point across, to lubricate the conversation of the streets, which has always—and will always—value "snazz" (*snas*, polish, gloss) and speed over technological precision or highfalutin airs. It's not an accident, I think, that slang words such as "lulu," "snazzy," "ballyhoo"—Cassidy's list of Irish derivatives is long and enlightening—have an onomatopoeic resonance similar to that of Yiddish, which explains in part why the two together probably account for so much of American slang.

The evolution of Irish into American vernacular was a gradual vanishing act. The words became such familiar parts of everyday speech that many seemed simply to belong to the way Americans talked, natural ingredients of popular speech. Most were entered into dictionaries as "origin unknown," or received far-fetched etymologies. In some measure, this reflected a growing paucity of native Irish speakers—a process accelerated by assimilation, economic mobility, and access to higher education. (Few if any of the Catholic universities or colleges in the U.S., the great majority founded in the wake of the Famine, had Irish studies or Irish language courses until very recently.)

Ignorance of Irish wasn't the sole culprit, however. There was also the active and aggressive "racial pride" of an immensely influential pan-Atlantic "Anglo-Saxonist" movement that fueled U.S. imperial expansion at the end of the nineteenth century, found widespread expression in the nativist-populist activities of the Ku Klux Klan, and helped drive the highbrow, bio-racist paranoia of the eugenics movement. As seen by Anglo-Saxon supremacists, Irish was the tongue of grooms and hod carriers, a provincial vestige of a failed culture, a primitive artifact, and to credit it as influencing the language of America's predominantly Anglo-Saxon civilization was as preposterous as it was insulting.

Time and again, whether the oversight was caused by passive neglect or active disdain, Professor Cassidy wields Occam's razor (the theory that the simplest of competing explanations is always to be preferred to the most complex) to shred the frail guesses of dictionary makers and reveal a self-evident Irish root. Take, for example, good solid slang words like "slugger," which Webster first finds in print in 1877 and traces to a Scandinavian root meaning "to walk sluggishly," "fluke," and "nincompoop," which are all listed as "origin unknown." Cassidy will have none of it. "Slugger," he points out, is almost a homonym for the Irish *slacaire*, "a mauler or bruiser." "Scam" fits the same pattern, sounding like a resonant echo of the Irish *'s cam (é)*, "(it) is a trick, (it) is a fraud." "Fluke?" How about *fo-luach*, pronounced fu-look, Irish for "rare reward or occurrence." "Nincompoop?" The Irish is *naioidhean ar chuma bub*, pronounced neeyan [er] ċumə boob, meaning "baby in the shape of a blubbering boob." Think this is all a lot of baloney? Then consider the Irish *béal ónna*, pronounced bael ona, meaning "foolish talk."

While the substance of Irish's lexical presence was ignored or forgotten, there has never been any question of Irish-Americans' impact on the American vernacular style. The rapid-fire, hardboiled, cynical, wise-guy banter that remains a defining characteristic of slangdom was perfected and popularized by a slew (from the Irish *slua*, a multitude) of great Irish-American character actors such as James Gleason (see his role as a Brooklyn detective in *Arsenic and Old Lace*); William Frawley (as a Tammany boss in *Miracle on 34th Street*); Brian Donlevy and William Demarest (together in Preston Sturges'—himself the son of an eccentric Canadian-Irish mother—*The Great McGinty*); Eddy Brophy (fittingly cast in his final film, *The Last Hurrah*, as "Ditto" Boland); and the nonpareil big city Irish-American tough guy sharpster, Jimmy Cagney, whose influence continues right down to today's gangsta rappers. Like the words themselves, the Irish-American vernacular style is in the very bloodstream of who we are as a people.

For me personally, the "secret knowledge" that Professor Cassidy exposes to public view has resolved some of my own ruminations over the argot of turn-of-the-century New York's underworld, which I encountered in researching my novel *Banished Children of Eve*. I suspected there was something going on under the always vivid, if often arcane slang, but was at a loss to explain what. Thanks to Cassidy's work, I've come to grasp not just the words beneath the words but also to see clearer than ever before that I wasn't as far removed from the Irish language as I once imagined.

In my own case, my mother's father had been born in Macroom, in County Cork, in the 1860s, which was an Irish-speaking area into the twentieth century. He said his prayers in Irish throughout his life, my mother informed me, a passing comment I filed away without much thought as to its significance. My father's maternal grandparents came to America during the Famine, in 1847, exactly a century before I was born. The urban *breac-Ghaeltachts* were still within living memory, a penumbra whose presence that, even if we felt, we weren't equipped to understand.

As kids in the Bronx, when we skedaddled or lollygagged or made a racket, we had no idea the descriptives we used were direct echoes of the Irish language. We didn't hear it in our speech. The Irish past was hidden from us. It was there, of course, a determining factor in how we worshipped, socialized, and worked, in the framework of our dreams and expectations. But we didn't know the Irish part of ourselves in any conscious way. As Irish-Americans, we put the stress on the second part of the identity, and while proudly acknowledging our Irish legacy, our eyes were trained on the future. The Irish language, we imagined, belonged exclusively to the old country and, like the place itself, was quaint, irrelevant, useless for making headway in the concrete and competitive precincts of urban America.

We weren't totally dumb, however, to the living elasticity of language, to its porousness and powers of infiltration. In the Bronx of the 1960s, we listened to and sometimes adopted the Spanish of the emergent Puerto Rican diaspora, referring to beer as *cerveza* and pretty girls as *muchachas*. Puerto Ricans, in turn, began to blend Spanish and English into a patois known as "Spanglish." Looking back, what's most notable for me isn't the pervasive existence of hybridity—the genetic, cultural, and linguistic mixing that is everywhere part of the crossroads (and isn't that what America is, after all, a great global crossroads?)—but the widespread obliviousness to the inevitability of such mixing and, sillier and more dangerous, the fanatic's quest for an imaginary "purity" of race and tongue.

Cassidy's ground-shifting thesis should transform and enrich much of the scholarly discourse about multiculturalism and the dialectic that drives and defines American society. Words and concepts like "jazz," "poker," "square," "scam," "sucker," "slum," "brag," "knack," etc., are as central to American culture and history as the language itself. What will people make of Cassidy's strongly convincing argument that an Irish derivative—jazz—now identifies America's most powerful and original art form, a creative achievement rooted in the hearts, history, and souls of black folks? Will it help add to our recognition that, despite our differences, we Americans are hopelessly (and hopefully) entwined with one another, our histories, ancestries, stories, songs, dreams, lives wrapped around each other like dual strands of DNA?

This revolutionary challenge to long-standing orthodoxies embedded in the dictionaries of Webster and the monumental *Oxford English Dictionary* of Charles Murray and his followers will undoubtedly lead to Cassidy being dismissed by some as heretic or dreamer. Great reappraisals, as Hubert Butler pointed out, are always threatening, especially to those who've helped build and maintain the status quo. But, as Nietzsche (a professional philologist, let's remember) once put it, what we need most times is not the courage of our convictions but the courage to question our convictions. The willingness to see the world afresh, to throw over old presumptions and consider new possibilities, to abandon routine and renew a sense of wonder, is as important to the scholar as the artist. Like the purloined letter in the short story by Poe (whose paternal ancestors were from County Cavan), the persistence of the Irish language was missed, in part, because it couldn't be comprehended through the narrow focus of conventional principles.

It is not just historians, I think, who come to grasp the proximity of the past, to pierce the illusion of the present's novelty, and perceive in our midst, in our loves, fears, and expectations, on our very tongues, what has gone before. Whether consciously or unconsciously, the further we move away in time from where we began, the more our journey seems—in the spectacularly inventive, polyglot vernacular of James Joyce—"a commodius vicus of recirculation," until we understand the extent to which today entails yesterday and how much the future is mortgaged to the past. Eventually, perhaps, whether as individuals or a society, we must inevitably come upon our own purloined letters, truths that we failed to see or successfully disregarded but that were always there, at the center of who we are.

The explorations that Cassidy undertakes in *How the Irish Invented Slang: the Secret Language of the Crossroads* have a distinctly personal element, about which he is forthright and upfront. He starts with his Irish-American family and New York Irish upbringing. But in good American fashion, and following in the footsteps of Walt Whitman, who lived not too far from Cassidy's ancestors in Brooklyn's dockside Irishtown, Cassidy celebrates more than self or a single family and embraces an experience far wider than Irish or Irish-American, penetrating to the dynamic of language-making itself, the most uniquely human of all our species' endeavors.

What Cassidy has done is nothing short of the miraculous: he has brought back to life that which was considered dead and settled. Roll over, Webster and Murray! In place of time-worn proprieties and stale assumptions, Cassidy gives us heat, passion, and excitement of a past rediscovered and made new. And ain't that the real jazz!

CHAPTER 1

Foclóir Póca: a Pocket Dictionary

> The Irish ... gave American, indeed, very few new words; perhaps speakeasy, shillelah and smithereens exhaust the list.—H.L. Mencken, *The American Language*, 1937.

> *A Dictionary of Hiberno-English* ... corroborates the well-known but puzzling fact that so few Irish words have been absorbed into Standard English.—Terence Patrick Dolan, *A Dictionary of Hiberno-English*, 1999.

IN DECEMBER 2000, I WAS GIVEN MY FIRST IRISH DICTIONARY. IT WAS NOT A happy occasion. A dear friend, Kevin O'Dowd, had died at the age of 37 and left me some Irish books in his will. It was the first thing I had ever inherited and it was heartbreaking.

I took the box of Kevin's Irish books home with me and showed them to my wife Clare. One of them was an old *Foclóir Póca*, a pocket Irish dictionary. I held up the little dictionary for Clare to see.

"I think I'll toss this," I said. "The college library won't take it, and I sure don't need it. I'm too old to learn Irish." Even though I taught courses in Irish and Irish-American history at New College of California in San Francisco, I had never owned an Irish dictionary.

"You can't throw that book out, Danny," Clare said, with a serious look on her face. "It's a gift from Kevin. Why don't you put it on your nightstand and look up a word a night?"

I glanced at the dictionary. "You're right," I said, and thought to myself, "It would be bad luck." I put Kevin's *Foclóir Póca* next to my bed.

A few nights later, I looked through the little pocket dictionary for the first time. The print was miniscule and I had to hold it up close to my eyes to read. But it was more impressive than it looked, divided into English-Irish and Irish-English sections, and containing 16,000 Irish headwords with pronunciations, definitions, and examples in Irish. Over the next few weeks I began looking up a few words every night before I turned out the light.

Then a light went on. I had a hunch. Was it possible that some of the slang words and phrases that I had learned as a kid in New York in the 1940s and '50s—like "in **dutch**" (**duais**, *pron*. dush, trouble), "say **uncle**" (**anacal**, mercy, quarter), "**dukin'** (**tuargain**, hammering, thumping, pounding) it out," **snazz** (**snas**, polish, gloss, lustre), **snazzy** (**snasach**, *pron*. snasah, polished, glossy, elegant), **glom** (**glám**, grab), and **dude** (**dúdach, dúd**, *pron*. dood, a foolish-looking person, a dolt)—were derived from the Irish language? How could that be possible?

Unlike Italians, Jews, Hispanics, French, Dutch, Germans, Scandinavians, African-Americans, Native Americans, Asians, and almost every ethnic group in North America, it was a well known but "puzzling" linguistic fact that the Irish had contributed almost no words or phrases to the English language. Not even in Ireland itself or the great crossroads cities of the Irish diaspora, like London, Liverpool, New York, New Orleans, Boston, Chicago, San Francisco, Melbourne, and Sydney—where millions of Irish speakers had emigrated over hundreds of years—have scholars uncovered *any* evidence of Irish-language influence on English, or its vernaculars and dialects. It was a mystery. But it was a mystery that was confirmed by every major English dictionary editor since Noah Webster and James Murray. In their rapid movement from Irish to English, Irish speakers, and their children and grandchildren, had lost the Irish language completely, utterly, without a whisper or a trace.

While researching our own family history, my brother Michael and I discovered that my father's family was speaking Irish in Greenpoint, Brooklyn, in the 1920s, just two decades before we were born. And Irish had certainly left no trace in our speech. The only Irish words I knew as a kid were **pugga mahone** (**póg mo thóin**, *pron*. pogue mə hone, kiss my ass) and **Erin go bragh** (**Éirinn go brágh**, Ireland forever).

It was a mystery. A mystery I set out to solve.

One thing I did know was that I was a "native speaker" of the old New York-Irish working-class dialect. I didn't have to look into slang dictionaries, or watch old Jimmy Cagney movies, or read *Gangs of New York*, to learn its vivid, hard-edged vocabulary and idiosyncratic accent. It was my family's speech, a language I had been taught assiduously to unlearn in school and at college. Could this despised and discarded old dialect be secretly **snazzed** up with Irish words and phrases?

Snazz, *al.* **snaz,** *n.,* *v.,* polish, gloss, elegance, style, "class," to polish, gloss, make elegant, stylish, flashy, glossy; attractive, "classy." **Snazzy,** *adj.,* stylish, flashy, glossy; attractive, elegant, classy. ("Origin unknown," *OED.*)

Snas, *n.,* polish, gloss, elegance, style, wealth, "class." **Snas,** *v.,* to polish, gloss; to make elegant, stylish, "classy;" *al.* **snasaigh. Snasach** (*pron.* snasać, snasah), *adj.,* glossed, polished, neat, elegant, wealthy, classy, stylish. (Patrick S. Dineen, *Foclóir Gaedhilge agus Béarla,* 1927, 1074; Niall Ó Dónaill, *Foclóir Gaeilge-Béarla,* 1977, 1124.)

Did Irish-Americans remember the Irish language without knowing it?

CHAPTER 2

Boliver of Brooklyn

There is nothing ... so hidden that we cannot discover it, provided only we abstain from accepting the false for the true.—René Descartes

MY GRANDFATHER "POP" WAS BORN IN 1895 IN BROOKLYN'S OLD FIFTH Ward, known as "Irishtown," a once legendary, long forgotten, dockside **breac-Ghaeltacht** (*pron.* brak-gaeltaċt; mixed Irish-English speaking district), next to the Brooklyn Navy Yard and across the big bend of the East River from Corlears Hook and the piers and river wards of lower Manhattan.

Pop was the grandson of Irish immigrants who had fled the mass death of *An Gorta Mór*, the Great Hunger of Ireland, fifty years before and settled with thousands of other dispossessed Gaels into the riverside streets, alleys, and tenements of Irishtown.

Irishtown was one of the lips of the big **gob** (**gob**, beak, mouth) of the Port of New York, an East River crossroad neighborhood of more than 20,000 inhabitants, with a core population of Irish and Irish-Americans intertwined like a Celtic triple-spiral into an ethnic, cultural, and linguistic **slew** (**slua**, a multitude, a throng) of dazzling complexity. Italians, Jews, Scandinavians, and nationalities **galore** (**go leor**, in abundance), as well as an historic African-American community, all lived in the midst of the **clamour** (**glam mór**, mighty shout, great howl) of Irishtown, sharing tenement, **shack** (**teach**, *pron.* chaċ, house) and **shanty** (**seantigh**, *pron.* shan-tí, old house) with newly arrived Irish immigrant families. (Ronald Bayor & Timothy Meagher, ed., *The New York Irish*, 1996, 559.)

Pop's mother, Loretta O'Brien, who we called **Nana** (**Nain**, grandmother) Number Two, was raised in the 1880s on Irishtown's Green Lane with her father and mother, famine immigrants Thomas and Catherine O'Brien, and her five brothers and sisters. Back then, Green Lane was as Irish as Donegal and as African as New Orleans' Congo Square. For most of Nana Number Two's childhood her next-door neighbors were African-American. The *Brooklyn Eagle* of Nana's youth is filled with lurid crime stories, racist cartoons, and even songs and poems about Irishtown's infamous Green Lane, and its "wild" Irish and African-American inhabitants. (U.S. Federal Census, Kings County, 5th Ward, 1850, 1860, 1870, 1880, 1900.)

Irishtown's ethnic hybridity, as well as its Irishness, mirrored most of New York's slum neighborhoods in the 19th and early-20th centuries. Even the most Irish of the city's wards—like Brooklyn's Irishtown and New York's 4th, 7th, and 14th—were only fifty to sixty per cent Irish.

Rather than being concentrated in cultural and linguistic ghettos, the Irish were scattered all across the Port of New York, in the same way that they had been scattered into a global Diaspora: a Gaelic **holler** (**oll-bhúir**, *pron.* holl-oor, a terrific yell) of **loingseoir** (*pron.* longshor, mariner, seaman, sailor, ship worker) port cities from Brooklyn to the Big Easy to the Barbary Coast. (Bayor and Meagher, Appendix I, 552–559.)

Pop had an unusual moniker—"Boliver."

When I was a kid in the late 1940s and 1950s, Pop's nickname of "Boliver" was mainly used by the older generation, like Nanny and my Aunt Tootsie, and usually when my grandfather wasn't around. Nanny and Aunt Tootsie were first cousins married to brothers, Pop and my Uncle Ranny. Their families were also out of Ireland, but by way of the Bowery and Chatham Square in New York City, five blocks from the old Five Points.

"I better get home and cook 'Boliver' his supper," Nanny would say to Aunt Tootsie. And even as a kid, "Boliver" sounded to me like the name of an English Duke or some Park Avenue **swell** (**sóúil**, luxurious, rich, prosperous; *fig.* a wealthy person), the kind of **dude** (**dúd**, *pron.* dood, a dolt, a numbskull, a foolish looking person) that went "slumming" in the slum instead of the moniker of a guy born in one—like Pop.

There were plenty of nicknames in my family. But most of them made sense to me as a kid. Uncle Ranny was "Smoky." That was easy. He smoked Lucky Strikes. My Uncle **"Dukie"** (**Tuarga**, *pron.* duarkə, a pounder, a solid block of a man) was "Dukie" because he had made his living **dukin'** (**tuargain, tuargaint**, *pron.* duarkin, pounding, battering, thumping, hammering) it out in the ring with another **slugger** (**slacaire**, a mauler, a bruiser), as a professional prizefighter. They called my Uncle Johnny "the Night Lifeguard," because he sunbathed on the same barstool every night in my Uncle Matty's joint in Rockaway Beach. Matty had made his **jack** (**tiach**, *pron.* jaċ, small purse or wallet; *fig.* money) as a local bootlegger. Aunt Tootsie didn't need a nickname. Her nickname became her name.

I had a few monikers as a kid. My mother called me the **Glom** (**glám**, to grab, **glámaire**, a grabber, a snatcher), because I was always **glommin'** on to other kid's stuff. **Mommy** (**Mamaí**, *pron.* mammy, mother) affectionately called my father "skinny ba-link." **Daddy** (**Daidí**, *dim.*, father) was the orphaned son of Irish-speaking immigrants from the north of Ireland and a hustling "skinny ba-link" when my mother met him in Rockaway during the Depression. Nanny didn't have a nickname, they just called her Francie. But "Boliver?" It was a mystery.

It was a family mystery that lasted for more than half a century, until a night in early April 2001, when I stumbled onto the Irish words **balbh** (*pron.* baləv, inarticulate, mute), **bailbhe** (*pron.* baləvə, muteness) and **balbhán** (*pron.* baləvan, baləvar, a silent or mute person) in the tiny *Foclóir Póca* (pocket dictionary) I had been studying for months. The Irish words were like the whisper of **sanas** (a hint, a whisper, secret knowledge, etymology) in my ear.

It wasn't **Boliver**, as in the "Duke of Irishtown," it was **Bailbhe** (*pron.* baləvə) or **Balbhán** (*pron.* baləvan, baləvar), meaning "a mute, silent, inarticulate person." And that was Pop, Nana Number Two's middle-son, squeezed between my great uncles, Matty and Ranny, who could both talk the head off a keg of beer with their Brooklyn-Irish **baloney** (**béal ónna**, *pron.* bæl óna' foolish, humorous talk). Pop was a man of very few words.

And in that moment, I remembered something that I had never known. We had never stopped speaking Irish in my family. The slang and accent of five generations and one hundred years in the tenements, working-class neighborhoods, and old *breac-Ghaeltacht* East River slums of Brooklyn and New York City had held within it the hard edged **spiel** (**speal**, cutting satiric words) and vivid **cant** (**caint**, speech) of a hundred generations and of a thousand years in Ireland: Gaeilge, the Irish language.

It was from these crossroad dockside neighborhoods like Irishtown that the banished, penalized tongue of the Irish was scattered across North America and became a key strand in the slang of back alleys and slums, a demotic dialect of the dispossessed Irish-American vernacular.

Irishtown, the home of the Brooklyn cattle drives—where the children of the famine Irish leaned out of tenement windows to watch the **longshore** (**loingseoir**, *pron.* longshor, sailor, ship worker) Brooklyn Irish cowboys drive the **dogies** (**do-thóigthe**, *pron.* do'hogǝ, hard-to-raise, hard-to-fatten calves) off the cattle boats and up Hudson Avenue to the slaughterhouses on Tillary and Adams streets—was one of those crossroads.

In 1850 the young poet Walt Whitman lived with his parents and siblings in a **swell** (**sóúil**, comfortable, prosperous) middle-class neighborhood only a few blocks from Irishtown. Whitman, the wandering **lollygag** (**leath-luighe géag**, *pron.* l'a-liɣ g'íōg, a reclining, leaning, lolling youth), strolled along the streets and docks of Irishtown every day on his way to the Fulton Street Ferry to Manhattan. The **racket** (**raic ard**, loud ruction and violent melee) of Brooklyn's old Fifth Ward was a chorus of the Great American Opera and working-class **shindig** (**seinnt-theach**, *pron.* shent-aċ, house party, musical celebration) that Walt Whitman heard and celebrated in his poetry.

Biddy Hoolahan, the Belle of Irishtown

There's a charming buxom damsel who resides in Irishtown,
Her name is Biddy Hoolahan, she weights two hundred pounds,
She came from dear old Gran-u-ail, and well it's understood
She's the boss of all the **shindigs** in that famous neighborhood.

She has no use for fol de role; she dresses plain and neat;
She wears her skirts just long enough, but not to sweep the street.
When going to church on Sundays she wears an old plaid shawl,
A relic from her native spot—the County Donegal.
(Michael J. Shay, *Brooklyn Eagle*, Dec. 15, 1901, 42.)

Irishtown was at the center of North America's greatest port city and the Irish-American vernacular spoken on its blocks, streets, alleys, piers, and docks became a key, anonymous, linguistic strand of the American language we speak today. The illiterate, despised slang of the Irish-American poor and immigrant working classes of the vast East River slums of New York City was in fact descended from the first *literate* tongue in Europe, after Greek and Latin: Irish.

The Irish had invented slang by remembering the Irish language without knowing it.

Willie Sutton and Yank

Willie Sutton was born and raised in Irishtown's old St. Ann's Parish, where Pop (in 1895) and Nana Number Two (in 1872) were baptized. Known as Willie "the Actor," a moniker given to him because he used elaborate disguises and the art of **finagle** (**fionna aclaí**, agile contrivance, adroit invention), rather than violence, when pulling off a sting, Willie Sutton said he robbed banks "because that's where the money was." (Willie Sutton with Edward Linn, *Where the Money Was: The Memoirs of a Bank Robber*, 1976, 17.)

> I was born on June 30, 1901 ... in a section along the Brooklyn docks known as Irishtown... It was a tough neighborhood, but it was toughness without any strut or swagger... There was constant warfare for control of the docks, because to control the docks meant that you controlled the gambling, the loan-sharking, the pilfering, and the kickbacks. Plus the loading racket, which was the sweetest racket of all. A flat rate, otherwise known as extortion, was levied against the importer ... for every crate they loaded...
>
> Lead pipes and brass knuckles were standard equipment. Murder was commonplace. No one was ever convicted. A code of silence was observed in Irishtown more faithfully than *omerta* is observed by the Mafia ... Nobody ever talked in Irishtown..." (Sutton, 1976, 18, 19.)

It was on the Brooklyn waterfront that Willie "the Actor" learned the *Single Commandment* of Irishtown: "Thou shalt not **squeal** (**scaoil**, *pron.* skŭ~eel; divulge, inform, reveal, publish, broadcast, snitch)."

Everyone was "Boliver" in Irishtown

The playwright Eugene O'Neill, whose famine immigrant father, James O'Neill, was raised in the dockside slums of Buffalo, captured the distinctive vivid slang and accent of early-20th century New York Irish-American vernacular in the voice of "Yank," a ship's coal stoker who is the protagonist of O'Neill's 1922 Pulitzer prize-winning play, *The Hairy Ape*. O'Neill's "Yank" was born and raised on the Brooklyn docks around the same time as my grandfather, Pop.

> YANK: Come on youse guys! (*He is turning to get some coal when the whistle sounds... This drives him into a sudden fury.*) Toin off dat whistle! Come down outa dere, yuh **yellow** brass-buttoned, Belfast bum, yuh! Come down and I'll knock your brains out! Yuh lousy, stinkin', **yellow** mut of a Catholic-moiderin' bastard!...I'll moider yuh!...I'll drive yer teet' down yer troat!...yuh lousy **boob**... (O'Neill, *The Hairy Ape*, 1922.)

> YANK: Choich, huh? I useter go to choich onct—sure—when I was a kid. My old man and woman dey made me. Dey never went demselves, dough.

Always got too big a head on Sunday mornin', dat was dem. (*With a grin*.) Dey was scrappers **for fair**, bot' of dem...I run away when me old lady **croaked** wit de tremens...Den I shipped in de stoke hole... De Brooklyn waterfront, dat was where I was dragged up. (O'Neill, *The Hairy Ape*, 1922.)

The *Slum*

Slum is an ugly and depressing word in any language, covered in shame, poverty, and trauma. It is the place where the phrase "fuh'ged it" (forget it) was born. But the slum is also the crossroad where millions of Irish immigrants and their children first put down roots in America. Perhaps, if we turn back to this forgotten crossroad, we will discover the **sanas** (whisper, secret knowledge, glossary, etymology) of the **slum?**

CHAPTER 3

The Sanas
(Etymology, Secret Knowledge)
of Slum

LL Anglo-American dictionaries agree that the origin of the word "slum" is a mystery.

> Slum, *n.*, a "section in a city where the poorest people live... (1825), origi-nally a cant or slang word meaning a room ... of unknown origin." (*Barnhart Dictionary of Etymology*, 1988.)

'S lom (é), meaning "it is an exposed vulnerable place, it is poverty," is the simple Irish solution to the mystery of the word **slum.**

'S (*contraction*), is (*copula; pron.* iss), is. Lom (*pron.* lum), *n.*, a bare place or thing; an unprotected or vulnerable place; poverty, distress. (Dineen, 1927; Ó Dónaill, 1977.)

A **slum** (**'s lom**) is not just poor; it is naked poverty and distress, stripped and laid open to the elements, like Brooklyn's Irishtown and the Five Points of New York in the 19th century, and the Gaza Strip today.

'S **lom** an seomra é. (*pron.* s' lum en shomra ay); it is a bare bleak room. 'S **lom** an áit é (*pron.* s'lum an átch ay); it is an impoverished place. 'S **lom** an saol é (*pron.* s'lum an sæl ay); it is a poor life, it is a barren life." This is a **slum.**

Mo *lom!* Alas! My ruin!

In 1842, the future communist leader Frederick Engels was sent to England by his father to work for the family textile business of Ermen and Engels. In Manchester, Engels met Mary Burns, a young working-class Irish woman, and her sister Lizzie. It was the Burns sisters who introduced Engels to the Manchester slums.

> It has been calculated that more than a million (Irish) have already immi-grated...nearly all of whom enter the industrial districts, especially the great cities, and there form the lowest class of the population...These people have

grown up almost without civilization, accustomed from youth to every sort of privation, rough, intemperate, and improvident. They bring all their brutal habits with them...

The worst dwellings are good enough for them; their clothing causes them little trouble, so long as it holds together by a single thread; shoes they know not; their food consists of potatoes and potatoes only; whatever they earn beyond these needs they spend upon drink. What does such a race want with higher wages? The worst quarters of all the large towns are inhabited by Irishmen. Whenever a district is distinguished for especial filth and especial ruinousness, the explorer may safely count upon meeting chiefly those Celtic faces which one recognizes at the first glance as different from the Saxon physiognomy of the native, and the singing, aspirate brogue which the true Irishman never loses. I have occasionally heard the Irish-Celtic language spoken in the most thickly populated parts of Manchester. (Frederich Engels, *The Condition of the English Working Class*, 1842.)

Despite Fred Engels' disgust with the Irish, the upper-class German revolutionary fell in love with Mary Burns' clever Irish **puss** (**pus**, mouth, lips; *fig.* face). Mary Burns became Engels' mistress and lived with him secretly for more than thirty years. On her death in 1878, Engels began a relationship with her sister, Lizzie, whom he would finally marry on her deathbed, when he was in his sixties. Under the influence of the two Burns sisters, Engels' fear and loathing of the Irish slum had been transformed into its opposite. He saw its power!

What people! They haven't a penny to lose, more than half of them have not a shirt to their back, they are real proletarians and sans culottes, and Irish besides—wild ungovernable fanatical Gaels... If I had two hundred thousand Irish I could overturn the whole British monarchy. (Engels.)

In the last decade of his life, Frederich Engels was teaching himself the Irish language and working on *A History of Ireland*. He had learned from the Burns' sisters that slums give birth to revolutions.

James Connolly and James Larkin were children of the slum. Connolly was born in 1868 in The Cowgate, Edinburgh's most notorious slum. His parents were Irish emigrants from Monaghan. Jim Larkin was born in 1874 in a Liverpool slum. By his early twenties, he had become a leader of the militant Liverpool dock workers. In 1907, Larkin moved to Ireland and founded the Irish Transport and General Workers Union, leading the Irish working-class out of the Dublin slums during the Lockout of 1913. Three years later, Connolly was shot by a British firing squad for his leading role in the Easter Rising of 1916.

The first and most infamous English slum was the Seven Dials and St. Giles.

> The Seven Dials—the core of the evil apple that has been so repeatedly pared—remains still intact... how it passed so completely into the hands of the Irish, history sayeth not... but when one sees nobody but Irish people, never Scotch, never Welsh, the sole inhabitants of localities given over to filth and squalor, one is almost brought to entertain the question—is it the Irish that make wretchedness and depravity, or is it wretchedness and depravity that make people Irish? Let it be how it may, one thing is certain, the Irish have got hold of Seven Dials beyond redemption. The Seven Dials and the Irish are identical... (James Greenwood, *Unsentimental Journeys; or Byways of the Modern Babylon*, 1867.)

Slum first appears in print in English in the early-19th century as a "cant" word for a room. **Cant** (**caint**, speech, talk, spoken word) was a name for the vernacular of the slum. "Slum, a room." (J.H. Vaux, *Flash Dictionary*, 1812.)

A room, a tenement, or entire district that is a slum, **'s lom** é (it is an exposed place; it is poverty) in Irish **caint** (speech).

This is no linguistic **scam** (**'s cam** é, it is a deceit, it is a trick), Irish talk (**caint**) was a tongue (**teanga**, language) of the slum.

> But the worst was when we got out into the street; the whole district had become alarmed, and hundreds came pouring down upon us... they tore up the very pavement to hurl at us, sticks rang about our ears, stones, and Irish—I liked the Irish worst of all, it sounded so horrid, especially as I did not understand it. It's a bad language. (George Borrow, *Lavengro*, 1851, in Peter Linebaugh, *The London Hanged*, 1993.)

This room is a **slum**. **'S lom** an seomra é (*pron.* s' lum en shomrə ay), the room is bare, bleak, poor.

> In the first room, the windows of which were filled with tins, wood, rags, etc., we found a middle-aged Irishman mending the trowsers of a lad about eight years of age, whom he was going to dispatch to "worruk, to get his living, God help him." The room above presented a scene of still greater destitu-tion...There was not a single piece of furniture in it; three beds were rolled up on the ground. (George Godwin, *London Shadows*, 1854.)

This building is a **slum**. **'S lom** an teach é (*pron.* s'lum en chaċ ay), the build-ing is bare, bleak, poor.

> Few would suppose that these dilapidated buildings were inhabited, and that too in the midst of winter, by human beings. In some parts the glass and framing have been entirely removed, and vain attempts made to stop out the wind and snow by sacking and other matter. The basement is occupied by donkeys and dogs. In one of the rooms we found a very old Irish woman (who said she was more than five score years of age), crouching over a little fire; her son, a man about thirty years of age, lives with her. There was no

bedstead or other furniture in the room; the ceiling was cracked and rotten, and the window destroyed. The rent of this room is 6d. per week. (George Godwin, *London Shadows*, 1854.)

The neighborhood called the Five Points was a **slum**.

The first and most famous American **slum** was the Five Points: 91 per cent of its residents were born in Ireland. (Tyler Anbinder, *The Five Points*, 2004.)

To the *New York Times* the children of the Irish **slum** were frightening.

They are human children, ragged, dirty, premature, horrible, delighting in idleness, ignorant of decency; prone hurrying to perdition...We cannot kill twenty thousand intending burglars, murderers, thieves, and vagabonds who swarm in the back slums and the alleys of our gorgeous capital. Can we do nothing else with them?" (*New York Times*, May 25, 1857, 4.)

But to some newspapers in the 1890s, the Irish **slum** was fun.

One hundred and eight years ago this week, on May 5, 1895, readers of the *New York World* found a new addition to their usual spread of Sunday cartoons. "Hogan's Alley," widely recognized as the first American comic strip, debuted that day.

Set in the Irish slum wards of New York City, it centered on the humorous exploits and observations of a pack of street urchins and a host of neighborhood characters. Chief among them was Mickey Dugan, soon to be known as the "Yellow Kid," a bald, toothless boy dressed only in a yellow nightshirt. (Edward T. O'Donnell, *Irish Echo*, July 11, 2006, 27.)

In 1896, William Randolph Hearst lured cartoonist R.F. Outcault away from Joseph Pulitzer's *New York World*. The "Yellow Kid" and his gang moved out of "Hogan's Alley" and into a new color comic strip (and slum) in the *New York Journal* called "McFadden's Row of Flats."

SAY!

Hogan's Alley Has Ben Condemed
By De Board of Helt
An We Was Gittin Tired of it Anyway

No Sentiment About Us—We
Are Outer de Dough—Keep De Change

A Foxy Move—Be Gee!

From de Alley now we go
Down into McFadden's Row
Mickey Dugan—Molly Brogan an de rest
But we'll be de same ole crowd

Where no quiet ain't allowed
An te make ye laff we'll allus do our best

Fur de alleys on de bum
An its got ter be a **slum**
An we ought te have a better place te stay
So we geddered up our traps
Our hats, an shoes an wraps
An we're glad to say we're goin te move away.
(By) Chimmie de Laureate

ARE YE WIT US?

Next Sunday come an see us in
McFadden's Row of Flats

(R.F. Outcault, E.W. Townsend, "Mc Fadden's Row of Flats,"
New York Journal, Dec. 13, 1896.)

Mickey Dugan was a wise-cracking little **dork** (**dorc**, a small person, a dwarf) from the slums of New York who became the most famous cartoon character in America. He was tiny; he was a cartoon; but he wasn't a **twerp** (**duirb**, **doirb**, a worm, an insect, a spineless person.)

The Yellow Kid never cried **"uncle"** (**anacal**, mercy, quarter).

Eugene O'Neill's father, James O'Neill, was born in Kilkenny, Ireland, in October 1845, during the first week of the Great Hunger. Fleeing starvation, the O'Neill family emigrated in 1852 to New York and the notorious dockside **slum** of Buffalo's First Ward.

By the time he was in his late-twenties, James O'Neill had risen from the **slum** to become one of the most famous actors in America. But like so many others raised up in a **slum**, he could never escape its psychological grip.

In Eugene O'Neill's *Long Day's Journey into Night*, the character Tyrone is based on his father James.

> TYRONE: My mother was left a stranger in a strange land, with four small children, me and a sister a little older and two younger than me. My two older brothers had moved to other parts. They couldn't help. They were hard put to keep themselves alive. There was no damn romance in our poverty. Twice we were evicted from the miserable hovel we called home, with my mother's few sticks of furniture thrown out into the street, and my mother and sisters crying. I cried, too, though I tried hard not to, because I was the man of the family. At ten years old! (O'Neill, *Long Day's Journey Into Night*, 1939.)

In 2006, PBS presented a documentary on the life of Eugene O'Neill, son and grandson of Irish famine immigrants, and the child of an immigrant child of the slum. The PBS documentary barely mentioned O'Neill's Irish heritage, or the brutal poverty of his father's life in the **slum**.

One could understand, then, why O'Neill had once complained to his son and namesake that "the critics have missed the most important thing about me and my work—the fact that I am Irish." (Edward Shaughnessey, *The Eugene O'Neill Review*, 1998.)

O'Neill's first play, *The Web*, and his greatest plays, *The Hairy Ape, Anna Christy, The Iceman Cometh*, and *Long Day's Journey into Night*, are filled with the Irish voices of the colony and the slum.

The upper-class cultural gatekeepers and **dude** (**dúd**, *pron.* dood, dolt, long-necked eavesdropper, numbskull) scholars of the English-speaking empire will never understand the language of a slum, whether it is Irish, African, or Arab.

> EMILINE: ...Oh, Aunty, the slumming party will soon be here.
> LAVINIA: Yes, but we shan't start before eight...
> PERCY: Miss Gale, the gentleman who is to be our guide is Officer Moran. He will protect us from all harm.
> LAVINIA: Yes, there's danger in the slums.
> EMILINE: Slumming is an English fad.
> LAVINIA: Dear old England.
> (Edward Harrigan, *Reilly and the 400*, 1890.)

The **slum** called the Gaza Strip **'s lom** (is poverty, is nakedness, is distress) in Irish and in Arabic.

The language of the slum will always be a mystery to the Anglo-American dudes of empire, because it is the many-tongued **caint** (speech) of the colony. The slang of the slum is a language of liberation.

CHAPTER 4

The Gangs of New York Talk Back—In Irish

I think it cannot be maintained by any candid person that the African races have ever occupied...any very high place in the human family...The Irish cannot. The Chinese cannot. The American Indian cannot. Before the energy of the Caucasian race, all other races have quailed and done obeisance.—Ralph Waldo Emerson, 1855.

N JULY 1857, THE RAGTAG IRISH STREET GANGS AND VOLUNTEER MILITIA companies of New York City's Five Points slum—called "**Dead Rabbits**" by the press—fought a two-day running gun battle with the Bowery Boys, a powerful gang allied with the virulently anti-Catholic, anti-immigrant American Republican Party, or "Know Nothings."

The headlines of the *New York Times* blared:

THE CITY UNDER ARMS...
RIOTING AND BLOODSHED;
THE FIGHT AT COW BAY.
Metropolitans Driven from the 6th Ward.
Chimneys Hurled Down Upon the Populace.
"**Dead Rabbits**" Against the "Bowery Boys"
ORDER RESTORED AT MIDNIGHT.
Riots in the 6th, 7th and 13th Wards.
THE STREETS BARRICADED.
THREE REGIMENTS CALLED OUT.
THE 4TH AND 5TH OF JULY.
Six Men Killed and Over One Hundred Wounded.
(*New York Daily Times*, July 6, 1857, 1.)

"The 'Bowery crowd' were finally forced to retreat and the 'Five Points,' alias '**Dead Rabbits**,' alias 'Roach Guards,' then retired...They lived below Elizabeth street, in Mulberry street and the Points." (*New York Daily Times*, July 6, 1857, 1.)

In other words, the Irish immigrants of the Five Points had beaten back the nativist gangs from the gates of the Five Points.

Churches of Fire

The Irish-Americans of the Five Points had good reason to defend themselves in the hot summer of 1857. Over the previous two years, Irish neighborhoods had been regularly attacked and Catholic churches dynamited and burned, all across the United States. More than a score of Irish immigrants had been murdered and hundreds wounded. (John B. Boles, *Religion in Antebellum Kentucky*, 1976; Carleton Beals, *Brass Knuckle Crusade*, 1960.)

The "Dead Rabbits" of New York had delivered a **Sunday** (**Sonnda**, vigorous, powerful) punch to the nativist gangsters and their police department allies.

The "Bowery Boy" **sluggers** (**slacaire**, slacairí, bruisers, maulers), Know Nothing bigots, and so-called "True Americans," had been **"86'd"** (**éiteachas aíochta**, *pron.* ayt'aas eektə, denial or refusal of hospitality; *fig.* barred or expelled) from the Five Points by the newest Americans.

> **Eighty-six**, *n.*, to be barred from a saloon (*or any place*); to be denied hospitality.
> **Éiteachas aíocht, Éiteachas aíochta** (*pron.* ayt'aas eektə), denial of hospitality; refusal of lodging (for a night); refusal of service; *fig.*, to be barred or expelled. (Ó Dónaill, 1977.)

Bloody Rabbits

One of the mysteries of *The Gangs of New York* concerns the origin of the name "Dead Rabbits," the mythic, supposedly ultra-violent, Irish-American gang that plays a central role in both Martin Scorsese's film and the 1927 book by Herbert Asbury on which it is based.

Asbury wrote that the Dead Rabbits were originally part of the Roach Guards... [and] at one of the gang's stormy meetings, someone threw a dead rabbit into the center of the room. One of the factions accepted it as an omen... and called themselves Dead Rabbits." (Herbert Asbury, *Gangs of New York*, 1927, 21.)

Regrettably, Martin Scorsese hung his epic Irish-American film on Asbury's "Dead Rabbit" yarn. Scorsese was born to an Italian immigrant family in Little Italy, just a short distance from the old Five Points, and should have known better. But the talented director off the block swallowed Herbert Asbury's "Dead Rabbit" baloney.

One of the key scenes in *The Gangs of New York* portrays the Irish-American defenders of the Five Points in July 1857, marching proudly behind the carcass of a bloody bunny impaled on the end of a stick! Less than a year later, these same Irish-Americans from the Sixth Ward and Five Points would found Clann na Gael, the American wing of the republican Fenian Movement, with a Gaelic harp of gold on a field of green as their standard.

I always had a **hunch (aithint**, *pron.* ahənch, to know, discern, intuit; an inference, a perception) that Herbert Asbury's "Dead Rabbit" tale was a **scam ('s cam**, is a deceit, is a trick, is an error). If some **loogin (leath-dhuine**, *pron.* l'ah-ginə, a half-wit, a fool, an idiot) had thrown a dead rabbit into a joint **teeming (taomanna**, *pron.* tæmŭn, flooding, overflowing) with Irish famine immigrants, they would have skinned it, cooked it, and fed it to the family in a stew.

So what is the origin of the moniker "Dead Rabbit?"

At the end of Herbert Asbury's book is a list of several hundred words and phrases called "The Slang of the Early Gangsters," excerpted from a larger underworld dictionary, *Vocabulum: Or, the Rogue's Lexicon*, compiled by former New York City Top **Cop (ceap**, a protector, a leader), Big **Shot (seád, seód**, *pron.* shod, a jewel; *fig.* a big chief) and Warden of the Tombs Prison, George W. Matsell. Matsell was not an Irish **cop** or Tammany ward **heeler (éilitheoir**, *pron.* h-élό'r, claimsman, petitioner, advocate), but was of English Protestant background. Irish-American Big Shots would not lead Tammany Hall or the New York City Police Department until the late 1880s.

Cop, *n.*, a police officer.
Ceap (*pron.* k'ap) *n.*, a protector, a leader, a chief. (Dineen, 178.)

(Big) **Shot**, *n.*, a very influential or important person.
(Big) **Seód** (*Gaelic*), **Séad, Seád** (*pron.* shod), a jewel; *fig.* a big chief, a warrior, a
   hero, a valiant person. (Dwelly, *Gaelic-English Dictionary*, 1901.)

Heeler, a ward heeler, *n.*, a ward-level political party operative.
Éilitheoir (*pron.* élό'r, h- élό'r), *n.*, one who demands or charges; a petitioner;
   a claimer; a friendly petitioner, a claimsman, an advocate; one who makes
   friendly inquires about; one who visits in a friendly manner. (Dineen, 1927;
   Ó Dónaill, 1977.)

Matsell's *Vocabulum* was first published by *The Police Gazette* in New York City in 1859 and is descended from a long line of English underworld dictionaries dating back to the 16th century. It is especially indebted to a *Classical Dictionary of the Vulgar Tongue* compiled by Captain Francis Grose in London in 1785.

In George Matsell's slang dictionary, a **rabbit** is defined as a "rowdy" and a **dead rabbit** is "a very athletic fellow." (George Matsell, *Vocabulum*, 1859, [1997].)

In Niall Ó Dónaill's modern *Foclóir Gaeilge-Béarla, Irish-English Dictionary*, published in Dublin in 1977, the word **ráibéad** (*pron.* rábæd) is defined as a "big hulking person" and a **ráibéardaí** is "an athletic, dashing fellow."

> **Ráibéad** (*pron.* rábæd), *n.*, a hulking person; a big man. **Ráibéardaí,** *n.*, a loose-limbed, active person; an athletic person; a dashing fellow.
> **Ráib,** *n.*, a hero, a valiant man. (Ó Dónaill, *Foclóir Gaeilge-Béarla, Irish-English Dictionary*, 1977, 981; An Seabhac, *Foclóir Gaeilge-Béarla*, 1958, 108.)

It is this Irish word **ráibéad** (*pron.* rábæd), along with the English slang intensifier *dead*, meaning "very," that provides the simple solution to the 150-year-old mystery of the origin of the term **Dead Rabbit**.

In mid-19th century Irish-American vernacular, a **Dead Rabbit** (**ráibéad**, a hulking person, a broad-shouldered muscular man) was a "big lug."

It was a New York nativist police sergeant named Van Orden who first popularized the "shaggy dog story" of the dead rabbit in the pages of the *New York Times*.

> VAN ORDEN: About five years ago … one night while they were holding a meeting, a dead rabbit was thrown into the room, and the circumstance gave the seceders the title of "Dead Rabbits." Becoming proud of the name, a Club was formed called "The Dead Rabbit Club," which became popular in that quarter. It is regularly organized, has a President, Secretary, and other offices, and the printed notices which are sent out to members are embellished at one corner with the cut of a dead rabbit hanging by the heels. The members, or those who are known as "Dead Rabbits," are eighteen to twenty-five years of age, and they number from one to two hundred members. Their numbers were increased however, on Saturday … by the circulation of an idle and vicious report that the Know Nothings and Black Republicans were coming down to destroy a Catholic Church in Mott street. (*New York Times,* July 7, 1857.)

But the old slang word **rabbit** (**ráibéad** *pron.* rábæd, a hulking, broad-shouldered person) for a husky young "sport" did not originate in New York's Five Points or in Matsell's slang dictionary in the late 1850s. The 1785 edition of Francis Grose's *Dictionary* records the slang term **rabbit sucker** as a moniker for a wild, free-spending young **buck** (**boc**, playboy, rogue) in the hip "flash talk" of late-18th century London.

> **Rabbit sucker,** Young spendthrifts, fast young men. (Grose, *Classical Dictionary of the Vulgar Tongue*, 1785; Matsell, *Vocabulum*, 1859.)
> **Ráibéad sách úr** (*pron.* rábæd sawċ úr), a dashing young sport; a fresh, young, wealthy buck.

Ráibéad (*pron.* rábæd), *n.*, a hulking person; a muscular person. **Ráibéardaí** (*pron.* rábærdi), an athletic person; a dashing fellow, a sport. **Sách** (*pron.* sawċ), *n.*, *adj.*, a well-fed, prosperous, wealthy person; *fig.* a fat cat; sated, well-fed, prosperous. **Úr**, *adj.*, new, green, fresh, young. (Ó Dónaill, 1977.)

Sucker, A term applied by gamblers to any person who can be cheated at cards. (Matsell, 1859.)

Sách úr (*pron.* sawċ úr), a fresh "fat cat;" a new well-fed fellow.

The slang of the early-19th century London underground was first popularized by the Irish-born boxing journalist Pierce Egan in best-selling books like *Boxiana* and his "Tom and Jerry" stories. Egan's flash prose dazzled the upper-class aristos, college boho swells, and dude-ish literati with its pitch-perfect evocation of the vibrant vernacular of London's underworld. The slummers descended into the slum to watch the poor at play, and on display, and to mimic their colorful secret **cant** (**caint**, speech). It was at the crossroads where the swells and rabbit suckers of the fancy rubbed shoulders with "milling coves" and "blowens" of the poor.

Pierce Egan was fluent in both Standard English and the hybrid slang of the boxing ring and boozing ken. Not surprisingly, given the overwhelmingly Irish population of the Seven Dials and St. Giles in this period, much of the so-called cant, flash talk, and slang that emerged from its back streets and lanes was as Irish as Egan himself.

Many of the early English slang dictionaries, some dating back to the 1560s, are akin to lexical archeological sites, preserving the times, places, and contexts where the Irish language—Europe's first literate vernacular in the 5th-century—began entering the English language as thieves' cant, argot, jargon, flash talk, Pedlar's French, St. Giles' Greek and slang.

For instance, in Grose's *Vulgar Tongue* a **fawney** is defined as a "ring."

In Patrick S. Dineen's *Foclóir Gaedhilge Béarla: Irish-English Dictionary*, published in Dublin in 1927, a **fáinne** (*pron.* fá-nĭ) is also defined as "a ring."

An ancient Irish **fáinne** and an English slang word **fawney** both mean the same thing—"a ring."

In *Barnhart's Dictionary of English Etymology* and the *Oxford English Dictionary*, the English **phoney** is defined as "a fake" or "a sham" and is traced back by the editors to the Irish word **fáinne**, meaning "a ring."

Phony or phoney, *adj.*, not genuine, fake, sham. 1900 phoney... American English, perhaps an alteration of an earlier English slang **fawney**, a gilt brass ring used by swindlers (1781), borrowed from the Irish **fáinne**, ring.—*n.*, fake, pretender, 1902, phony, American English probably from the adjective." (*Barnhart Dictionary of English Etymology.*)

The Irish word **fáinne** was transformed by English dictionaries into a vulgar flash word "fawney," meaning "a fake gold ring" used in a trickster's scam, and then into the American slang "phoney," meaning a fake or a sham.

In the same way, the Irish language was transformed from an ancient, classical language of old Europe—and the Atlantic world—into a cant and slang of thieves and vagabonds, and then into a secret strand of the American language we speak today.

Here are a few examples of the Irish words and word-phrases, hidden beneath English phonetic "overcoats," found in Grose's *Vulgar Tongue* and Matsell's *Rogue's Dictionary.* Many of these old slang words like "rabbit," "blowen," and "Patrico" have become obsolete, while others—like the world-famous "sucker"—are still current in contemporary vernacular. A few have even climbed out of the lexical slum of slang and joined the **swank** (**somhaoineach**, *pron.* suhwainaċ, valuable, rich, wealthy, classy, ritzy) ranks of Standard English.

Bloss, the pretended wife of a bully or shoplifter. (Obsolete; Grose, Matsell.)
Blás (*pron.* blás), a bloom, a beauty; *fig.* a pretty girl.

Blowen, a mistress or whore of a gentleman of the scamp. (Obsolete; Grose, Matsell.)
Bláthán (*pron.* bláhán), a bloom, a blossom, a small flower. A term of endearment for a young girl.

Crony, an intimate companion, a comrade, also a confederate in a robbery.
Comh-róghna (*pron.* ko-ronə, co-rony), fellow-favorites, fellow chosen ones, mutual sweethearts, fellow-pals.

Cull, a man; sometimes a partner. (Obsolete; Matsell.)
Comhall (*pron.* cowall), *al.* coall, *n.*, companionship; a companion, a partner.

Doodle, a silly fellow. (Matsell, Grose.)
Dúdalaí, a fool.

Farmer, an alderman. (Obsolete; Matsell.)
Fear mór (*pron.* f'ar mor), a big man, an important man.

Gallore, golore, galore, plenty. (Grose.)
Gilyore, Plenty. (Matsell.)
Go leor, enough, plenty, a sufficiency.

Gigger, a latch or a door. (Obsolete; appears in 16th century English cant dictionaries.)
Gíogaire, a squeaker; *fig.* a squeaky latch or door.

Giggle, to suppress a laugh. (**Giggle** has become Standard English.)
Gíog gheal, a happy squeak, a merry squeal.

Ground sweat, a grave. (Obsolete; Grose, Matsell.)
Grian-suite (*pron.* griŏn sŭĭt'), a sunny site, a sunny spot; *fig.* a gravesite.

Hanker, to hanker after any thing; to have a longing after or for it. (Grose.)
An-ghá (*pron.* an-ċá), *n.*, a great need, a great want; intense need, intense desire, great longing.

Helter Skelter, to run helter skelter, hand over head, in defiance of order.
Áilteoir scaoilte (*pron.* ál't'or' scailt'ïh), a run-amuck clown; a wild prankster; a loose limbed trickster; (like) a joker running amuck.

Lib, libbeg, libegge, a bed. (Cant, 16th century, Grose.)
Leab (*pron.* l'ab), a bed. **Leapacha** (*pron* lapaċa), beds.

Lick, to beat.
Leag, to knock down (with a blow); to beat down; throw down; to defeat.

Miller, a fighter, a prizefighter or boxer. (Matsell, Grose, Egan.)
Míle (*pron.* míl'ə), a warrior, a champion, a hero.

Nicknacks, toys, baubles, curiosities.
Neamh-ghnách (*pron.* n'ah-ċnack), unusual, extraordinary, exotic; a curiosity, an unusual extraordinary thing,

Nincompoop or **nickumpoop**, a foolish fellow. (Grose.)
Naoidhean (ar) **chuma búb** (*pron.* neeyan ċumə boob), a baby in the form of a bellowing fool. **Naoi** (ər) **chuma búb** (*pron.* nee ċumə boob), an infant in the form of a blubbering boob.

Oliver, the moon. (Obsolete cant word, dates to 16th century; Grose, Matsell.)
Oll ubh óir, oll uibh óir (*pron.* olluvór, ollivór), great egg of gold.

Patrico, strolling priests that marry people under a hedge, without a common prayer book. Also any minister or parson. (Cant, 16th-century; Grose.)
Paidreachán (*pron.* pa-draċán, pa-draċár), one given to prayers and praying, a praying person, a prayer-monger. **Paidreacha** (*pron.* pa-draċa), a prayer.

Pigeons, sharpers, confederates of a thief. (Grose, Matsell.)
Béideán (*pron.* beeján), *al.* béadán, a calumniator, a slanderer, a stool pigeon.

Queer or **quire**, base, roguish, bad, odd, uncommon. (Cant, 16th century; Grose.)
Corr, *adj.*, odd, occasional; queer, peculiar, eccentric, strange; dismal, unusual.

Scrag (*slang*), *v.*, to hang on the gallows, to get your neck stretched; *fig.* to kill a person. **Scragged**, hanged. **Scraggy**, lean, bony. (Grose, Matsell.)

Scrog, *al.* **scroig,** a neck; especially a small, narrow, or thin neck; a long stretched neck; *fig.* a neck that has been stretched thin on the gallows; a hanged neck. **Scrogach,** long-necked, thin-necked. What a hangman's noose does to a neck.

Slug, to drink a dram. (Grose.)
Slog, a sudden swallow, a gulp.

Smack, to **smack.** To kiss. (Grose, Matsell.)
Smeach (*pron.* sma'ċ), a kiss. **Smeachaire** (*pron.* smaċirə), a kiss.

Sneak, a pilferer. (Grose, Matsell.)
Snag, a creeping thing or person. **Snagaire,** a sneak, a creeper.

Spree, a frolic, fun; a drinking bout, a party of pleasure. (Grose.)
Spraoi (*pron.* spree), fun, sport; a drinking bout. Dul ar an **spraoi**, to go on a drinking bout.

Spunk, rotten touchwood, or a kind of fungus prepared for tinder; *fig.,* spirit, courage. (Grose.)
Sponc, sponnc, tinder, coltsfoot used as tinder, touchwood; spirit, courage, energy, passion; a spark, a spark of life. **Sponcán,** a spark; a flare up of passion. *Cf.* French *éponge.* Cuir **sponc** éigin ionnat féin, be more energetic, look alive.

Square, honest, upright, not roguish. (Matsell, Grose.)
'S cóir (é) (*pron.* s'có'r), (it) is honesty, (it) is fair play.

Swell, a gentleman. (Grose, Matsell, Egan.)
Sóúil, (*someone*) comfortable, luxurious, prosperous, wealthy; *fig.* a wealthy person or a gentleman; (*someone or something*) grand, superb, elegant, splendid, deluxe, fancy, opulent, plush, swank, ritzy, classy.

Irish-American Vernacular

My family once spoke the Irish-American vernacular of the old *breac-Ghaeltachta* (Irish-English speaking districts) and dockside neighborhoods of New York City and Brooklyn. My mother's grandmother "Mamie" Byrnes and her six siblings were raised in Chatham Square on the Bowery, five blocks from the old Five Points, in the 1870s and '80s. The Irish language—spoken continuously in New York City and Brooklyn since the 17th century—was the secret source of their vivid slang and accent.

Americans speak Irish every day, but they do not **dig** (**tuig,** understand, comprehend, have a feeling for) it. The words and phrases of Ireland are as woven into the **clamour** (**glam mór,** great howl, shout, and roar) and **racket** (**raic ard,** loud melee) of American life as the hot **jazz** (**teas,** *pron.* j'as, ch'as, heat, passion, excitement) of New Orleans, the mighty baseball **slugger** (**slacaire**, batter) of Yankee Stadium, Southern **cracker** (**cracaire**, boaster, jester, windy talker) of Georgia, Arkansas **Bubba** (**Bobaire**, trickster, joker), crossroads **poker** (**póca**, pocket) game card sharp, **natty** (**néata**, neat, dapper) Chicago bootleg **racketeer** (**racadóir**, sportive character, dealer), Tammany ward **heeler** (**éilitheoir**, *pron.* éló'r, friendly claimsman or advocate), New York Irish **cop** (**ceap**, *pron.* k'ap, a chief, a protector), Texas **buckaroo** (**bocaí rua**, *pron.* buckæ roo, wild playboy, rough rogue), carny barker's **ballyhoo** (**bailiú**, *pron.* balihoo, gathering, assembling, enticing a crowd) ... and the eternal **sucker** (**sách úr**, *pron.* sawċúr, fresh new "fat cat"), who is born every minute, pipe-dreaming of the Mountains of Sponduliks and the mythical hills of **Moolah** (**moll óir**, a heap of gold and money) at the end of a **scam** (**'s cam**, is a trick) rainbow.

CHAPTER 5

Songs of the Crossroads
Paddy Works on the Erie

> In eighteen hundred and forty-wan,
> I put me cord'roy breeches on,
> I put me cord'roy breeches on,
> To work upon the railway.
>
> Fil-i-me-oo-re-i-re-ay
> Fil-i-me-oo-re-i-re-ay
> Fil-i-me-oo-re-i-re-ay
> To work upon the railway.

THE SONG "PADDY WORKS ON THE ERIE," ALSO KNOWN AS, "PADDY WORKS on the Railway," and "Poor Paddy Works on the Railroad" is the seventh song in the 1934 collection, *American Ballads and Folk Songs*, by John A. and Alan Lomax. With its rousing tune and 6/8 jig time, it is one of the most popular and widely known American folk songs. But "Paddy Works on the Erie" is also a **sanas-laoi** (*pron.* sanas læ, a secret song) of the crossroads. (John A. and Alan Lomax, *American Ballads and Folk Songs*, 1934, [1994].)

> In eighteen hundred and forty-two,
> I left the old world for the new,
> Bad cess to the luck that brought me through,
> To work upon the railway.
>
> Fil-i-me-oo-re-i-re-ay
> Fil-i-me-oo-re-i-re-ay
> Fil-i-me-oo-re-i-re-ay
> To work upon the railway.

Alan and John Lomax traced the origin of "Paddy Works on the Erie" to an "old newspaper clipping" and cite the poet Carl Sandburg's 1927 book, *American Songbag*. Sandburg claimed he found "Paddy Works on the Erie" on sheet music published in 1850; but no copy has ever been found. The earliest printed version of the song is dated 1864. (Lomax, 1934, [1994]; Sandburg, *American Songbag*, 1927.)

> When we left Ireland to come here,
> And spend out latter days in cheer,
> Our bosses they did drink strong beer,
> And Pat worked on the railway.
> Fil-i-me-oo-re-i-re-ay
> Fil-i-me-oo-re-i-re-ay
> Fil-i-me-oo-re-i-re-ay
> To work upon the railway.

The lyrics vary widely, with local versions scattered all across the mid-19th century Irish diaspora, New York, Liverpool, San Francisco, Melbourne, wherever Paddy bent his back and laid a track. In Pennsylvania in the 19th century, it was said that every mile of railroad was an Irish grave. Recently, lost cemeteries have been found along the old northeastern railroad lines, hurried mass burials in improvised gravesites, often involving typhus, cholera, smallpox and other infectious diseases that plagued poor Paddy, working on the railway.

> Our contractor's name it was Tom King,
> He kept a store to rob the men,
> A Yankee clerk with ink and pen,
> To cheat Pat on the railroad.

> Fil-i-me-oo-re-i-re-ay
> Fil-i-me-oo-re-i-re-ay
> Fil-i-me-oo-re-i-re-ay
> To work upon the railway.

> It's "Pat, do this" and "Pat, do that,"
> Without a stocking or cravat,
> And nothing but an old straw hat,
> While Pat works on the railroad.

From the 17th century to the 1920s, seven million Irish people emigrated to North America. "This vast flow was of great historical significance," historian Kerby Miller wrote. "The Irish played an important role in the commercial and industrial revolutions that transformed the North Atlantic World." (Kerby Miller, *Emigrants and Exiles*, 1985, 3.)

In other words, Paddy was a workin' **stiff**.

Stiff, *n.*, a worker, the common working man or woman, especially a manual laborer or factory worker, a fellow, a regular Joe or Jane; a migratory worker; a hobo, a bindle-stiff. *Also*, a dead person.

Staf, staif, *pl. n.*, a burly person, a strong, husky, muscular person, a broad-shouldered person, a "big lug." Also, **staf** an bais (*pron.* staf ən bash), the stiffness caused by death; *fig.* "a stiff," a corpse. (Dineen, 1927.)

Ex-hobo, circus roustabout, boxer, PR man, writer, and novelist, Jim Tully, described his Irish Famine immigrant father in his 1928 memoir *Shanty Irish*.

My father was a gorilla-built man. His arms were long and crooked. The ends of a carrot-shaped mustache touched his shoulder blades. It gave his mouth an appearance of ferocity not in the heart. Squat, agile and muscular, he weighed nearly one hundred and ninety pounds. His shoulders were early stooped, as from carrying the inherited burdens of a thousand dead Irish peasants... A man of some imagination, he loved the tingle of warm liquor in his blood. He was for fifty years a ditch digger. (Jim Tully, *Shanty Irish*, 1928, 34.)

Fil-i-me-oo-re-i-re-ay
Fil-i-me-oo-re-i-re-ay
Fil-i-me-oo-re-i-re-ay
To work upon the railway.

The song "Paddy Works on the Erie" journeys year by year through the decade of the 1840s, when millions of Irish people, nearly half of them women and girls, scattered to the port cities and rural crossroads of America.

There was no food to eat so the pizzants ate grass and seaweed and potaties that were rotted—A million av the poor devils died with the achin' pain in their guts... (Tully, *Shanty Irish*, 1928, 34.)

Fil-i-me-oo-re-i-re-ay
Fil-i-me-oo-re-i-re-ay
Fil-i-me-oo-re-i-re-ay
To work upon the railway.

During the famine period, Miller has estimated that as many as 500,000 Irish speakers immigrated to the United States, "representing between one-quarter and one-third of total Irish immigration." (Kerby Miller, *Emigrants and Exiles*, 1985; Thomas Idhe, *Irish Language in United States*, 1994.)

In eighteen hundred and forty-three,
'Twas then I met sweet Biddy Magee,
And an illygant wife she's been to me,
While workin' on the railway.

Fil-i-me-oo-re-i-re-ay
Fil-i-me-oo-re-i-re-ay
Fil-i-me-oo-re-i-re-ay,

>To work upon the railroad.

More than one hundred and fifty years later, at the beginning of the 21st century, the U.S. Federal Census recorded 25,000 native Irish-speakers in the United States.

>In eighteen hundred and forty-six,
>A gang pelted me with stones and bricks.
>Oh, I was in a helluva fix,
>While workin' on the railroad.

>Fil-i-me-oo-re-i-re-ay
>Fil-i-me-oo-re-i-re-ay
>Fil-i-me-oo-re-i-re-ay
>To work upon the railway.

Yet, despite the immigration of millions of Irish speaking people to North America over three centuries, scholars have "minimized the significance of the use of Irish or have failed to uncover evidence of it." (Idhe, *Irish Language in United States*, 1994.)

>In eighteen hundred and forty-seven,
>Sweet Biddy Magee, she went to heaven,
>If she left one child, she left eleven,
>To work upon the railroad.

"Paddy Works on the Erie" is an Irish **sanas-laoi** (*pron.* sanas-lay, secret song) of immigrant **spalpeens** (**spailpíní**, laborers, migratory workers, working stiffs; bold lads, rogues, bucks) and **colleens** (**cailíní**, girls, maids, working girls, spirited gals) who came to America searching for work and freedom.

>Fil-i-me-oo-re-i-re-ay
>Fil-i-me-oo-re-i-re-ay
>Fil-i-me-oo-re-i-re-ay
>To work upon the railway.

The lilting chorus of **fil-i-me-oo-re-i-re-ay** has always been characterized as macaronic, or nonsense syllables.

In fact, **fil-i-me-oo-re-i-re-ay** is a hidden litany of labor sung in Paddy's other tongue: Irish.

>In eighteen hundred and forty-eight,
>I learned to take my whiskey straight,
>'Tis an illygant drink and can't be bate,
>For working on a railway.

Fil-i-me-oo-re-i-re-ay
Fil-i-me-oo-re-i-re-ay
Fil-i-me-oo-re-i-re-ay
To work upon the railway.

Fil-i-me-oo-re-i-re-ay is the English phonetic spelling of the Irish phrase **fill-fidh mé uair éirithe** (*pron.* fill'ih mæ úĕr í-ríhǝ), meaning "time to get up, I'll go back."

Fil-i-me-oo-re-i-re-ay,
Fillfidh mé uair éirithe (*pron.* fill'ih mæ úĕr í-ríhǝ),
Time to get up, I'll go back,
To work upon the railway.

Fillfidh (*pron.* fill'ih), *v.* (*future*), will return, will go back. **Mé** (*pron.* mæ, may), *pers. pron.*, I, me. **Uair** (*pron.* oo-er, úĕr), *n.*, hour, time, occasion. **Éirithe** (*pron.* í-ríhǝ) *adj.*, rising, ascending, getting up. **Éirí** (*pron.* í-rí), *v.*, to rise up, to get up, to ascend. (Ó Dónaill, 492, 489; Dineen, 403, 404.)

Fillfidh mé uair éirithe (*pron.* fill'ih mæ úĕr í-ríhǝ, time to get up, I'll go back), is the hidden refrain of working and rising, rising and working, that is the **sanas-laoi** (secret song) of Paddy and Colleen and all immigrant workin' stiffs to North America.

Fil-i-me-oo-re-i-re-ay,
Fillfidh mé uair éirithe (*pron.* fill'ih mæ úĕr í-ríhǝ),
Time to get up, I'll go back,
To work...

"The Gila Monster Route"

"The Gila Monster Route" is song eight in the Lomax collection, *American Ballads and Folk Songs*. It was written by L.F. Post and Glenn Norton in the old vernacular of migratory workers, hobos, ginks, blanket stiffs, bindle stiffs, gay cats, dingbats, yeggs, "Johnsons," Wobblies, and the vast army of the unemployed, who rode the rails and wandered the roads of late-19th and early-20th century America, looking for work and food.

"Gila Monster Route"

The lingering sunset across the plain,
Kissed the rear-end door of an east-bound train,
And shone on a passing track close by,
Where a **dingbat** sat on a rotten tie.

He was **ditched** by a **shack** and a cruel fate,

> The con high-balled, and the manifest freight,
> Pulled out on the stem behind the mail,
> And she hit the **ball** on a sanded rail.
>
> He was **ditched** on the Gila Monster Route...
> Nothing in sight but sand and space
> No chance for a **gink** to feed his face;
> Not even a **shack** to beg for a lump,
> Or a hen-house to frisk for a single **gump**...
>
> In a hostile **burg** on the Nickel Plate.

Dingbat, *n.*, a beggar, a vagabond, a hobo; a stupid person.
Duine bocht (*pron.* din'ə boċt), *n.*, a poor person, a pitiful wretched person.

Ditch, to be put off a train; abandon or discard a person or thing; displace someone or something.
De áit (*pron.* d'atch, de'atch), off a place or spot; from a place or spot; *fig.* (slang), to put off or displace; to off-place. **De**, *prep.*, from, off; off of (denoting removal or separation). **Áit** (*pron.* atch), *n.*, a place, a position.

"I had the young road kid's terrible aversion against walking the track for any man. My law was—to stay with the train, to allow no man to **ditch** me." (Tully, *Circus Parade*, 1927, 243.)

Shack (1), *n.*, a brakeman; any employee of the railroad; named for the shack or the caboose on the train.

Shack (2), *n.*, a shanty; a shed; a house.
Teach (*pron.* chaċ), *n.*, a house.

Ball, *n.*, a spot; a place.

Gink, *n.*, a fellow, a man, a hobo (*frequently pejorative*).
Geanc, geannc, *n.*, a surly lout; a snub-nosed, short-faced, surly person; a crooked, dumpy-looking person. (Dineen, 526; Dwelly, 485; Ó Dónaill, 621.)

Burg, *n.*, a town, a village, a city.
Buirg, *n.*, a borough, a district; *fig.* a town or city.

Gump, *n.*, a chicken.
Colm (*pron.* kŭləm), *n.*, a dove, a pigeon; *fig.* a chicken, an edible "boid."

Though hidden until now, the Irish language is a key linguistic strand of the **cant** (**caint**, speech) of the American crossroads—from the Erie Railroad to the Gila Monster Route and the Old Chisholm Trail.

"Git Along Little Dogies"

In 1910 John Lomax concluded the first edition of *Cowboy Songs and Frontier Ballads* with a song he called "the quintessential cowboy song, unlike others known to have been imported and adapted in the West," "Whoopie Ti Yi Yo, Git Along Little Dogies."

> As I was a-walking one morning for pleasure,
> I spied a cow-puncher a-riding along.
> His hat was throwed back and his spurs were a-jinglin',
> As he approached me a-singin' this song.
>
> Whoopie ti yi yo, git along, little **dogies**,
> It's your misfortune and none of my own;
> Whoopie ti yi yo, git along, little **dogies**,
> You know Wyoming will be your new home.

Lomax wrote that "the tune of this song was given to me at the Texas Cattleman's Convention, Fort Worth, Texas, 1910, by Mrs. Trantham, a wandering gypsy minstrel." In a later expanded edition of *Cowboy Songs*, John Lomax characterized the enigmatic lyrics and haunting air of the song he named "Git Along Little Dogies" as being "touched by the style of the Irish traveling folk."

> Early in the springtime we'll round up the **dogies**,
> Slap on their brands, and bob off their tails;
> Round up the horses, load up the chuck wagon
> Then throw those doggies upon the trail.
>
> Whoopie ti yi yo, git along, little **dogies**,
> It's your misfortune and none of my own;
> Whoopie ti yi yo, gut along, little **dogies**,
> You know Wyoming will be your new home.

The "gypsy" minstrel, Mrs. Trantham, was not a Romany Gypsy, but an American-Irish Traveller, a scattered diaspora of Irish Cant or Gammon speaking people that have lived and flourished in the United States for more than 250 years. They are the "cousins" of the Irish Travellers of Ireland and the most invisible of invisible Irish America. (Lomax, *Cowboy Songs and Frontier Ballads*, 1910, [1986].)

Mrs. Trantham's version of "Git Along Little Dogies" soon became an American roots classic. The quintessential American cowboy song of the old West had musical and linguistic roots in Ireland.

> When the night comes on and we hold them on the bed-ground
> These little **dogies** that roll on so slow;
> Roll up the herd and cut out the strays
> And roll out the **dogies** that never rolled before.
>
> Whoopie ti yi yo, git along, little **dogies**,
> It's your misfortune and none of my own;
> Whoopie ti yi yo, gut along, little **dogies**,
> You know Wyoming will be your new home.

One of the mysteries of "Git Along Little Dogies" is the origin of the word **dogie** for an orphaned calf. Both John and Alan Lomax searched for the source of this enigmatic word throughout their lives.

> **Dogie**—A scrubby calf that has not wintered well and is anemic from the scant food of the cold weather ... also a dogey. It is in the language of the cowboy "a calf who has lost his mammy and whose daddy has run off with another cow." (Ramon F. Adams, *Dictionary of the American West*, 1968.)

Some scholars have speculated that **dogie** derives from the Mexican word *dogal* for a calves' halter, while others claim that **dogie**, said to be pronounced more like "doughy" by the cowboys, may have derived from the phrase "dough-guts," and describes the bloated look of the hard to feed calves, too young or anemic to eat scrub grass. But all scholars seem to agree that the cowboys themselves defined a **dogie** as a runty orphan calf.

In a lifelong quest for the song's origins, Alan Lomax found a number of similar tunes—"a Dakota cowboy version with the image of an old man rocking a baby, alternating with verses about the little **dogies** ... a Michigan lumberjack ballad about a man rocking a baby that was none of his own..." and finally, in Dublin, Seamus Ennis sang him the full-blown comic ballad about an old man married to a younger woman, sitting home and rocking his son, while his wife gads about to balls and parties.

Further research by Alan Lomax uncovered the Irish song "Lament of the Old Cuckold," but "even that was not the end of the trail." He finally found ninety-year-old Mrs. Cronin, "deep in the countryside" of Ireland, who sang an Irish-language lullaby, set to the same air as "Git Along Little Dogies," and other songs of motherless infants and orphan calves. Mrs. Cronin told Alan Lomax, "Now that's the oldest song in all this world, for you see, it's the lullaby that Joseph sang to the baby Jesus." (Lomax, 1910, [1986].)

But, the haunting unforgettable air is not the only Irish influence on this classic Gaelic song of the American West. The source of the mysterious word

dogie, for a sickly hard-to-fatten, hard-to-feed, orphan calf (or motherless child), is also Irish.

> **Dogie**, *n.*, a scrubby calf that has not wintered well and is anemic from the scant food of the cold weather; an orphan calf.
>
> **Do-thóigthe** (*pron.* dohóg'ə), hard to rear, hard to fatten (as a calf); *fig.* a sickly orphan calf or child, without a mother to nurse them. (Dineen, 1927.)

In the introduction to *Cowboy Songs and Other Ballads*, John Lomax and Joshua Barrett describe how the cowboys would raise up the weakest **dogies** onto the pommels of their saddles, to hand-feed them and rest them for the long journey ahead. "Git Along Little Dogies" is the cow puncher's lament for the hard-to-feed orphan **dogie** (**do-thóigthe**, *pron.* dohóg'ə, hard-to-fatten calf) at the end of a trail so full of misfortune.

> Whoopie ti yi yo, git along, little **dogies**,
> It's your misfortune and none of my own;
> Whoopie ti yi yo, git along, little **dogies**,
> You know Wyoming will be your new home.

"Doney Gal"

There are several version of the old cowboy song "**Doney** Gal"; all of them musical tributes to another much abused and much loved creature of the old West, the cow puncher's faithful **nag** (**n-each**, *pron.* n'aċ, horse).

The origin of the word **doney**—like the origin of **dogie**—is said to be "unknown." (John and Alan Lomax, *Cowboy Songs and Other Frontier Ballads*, 1910, [1986], 8–11.)

> "Doney Gal"
>
> We're alone **Doney** Gal, in the rain and hail
> Got to drive these **dogies** down the trail
>
> We'll ride the range, from sun to sun,
> For a cowboy's work is never done;
> He's up and gone at the break of day,
> Drivin' in the **dogies** on their weary way.
>
> We're alone **Doney** Gal, in the rain and hail
> Got to drive these **dogies** down the trail...
>
> Get along, little **dogie**, on your way.

> **Dona**, *adj.*, poor, unfortunate, unlucky; wretched, miserable, sad, sickly, of ill-health. (Dineen, 1927; Ó Dónaill, 1977.)

The cowboy rides his **doney** (**Dona**, poor, unfortunate) Gal from "sun to sun," until sad old **Doney** (**dona**, unlucky) Gal's race is run.

"Take Me Out to the Ball Game"

Jack Norworth, a vaudeville hoofer and songwriter, wrote the 1908 classic song "Take Me Out to the Ball Game" on some scrap paper on a trainride to Manhattan. In 1927, Norworth changed the lyrics and a second version appeared. The original song features a baseball-mad Katie Casey—instead of Nellie Kelly—as the "**rooter.**"

> "Take Me Out to the Ball Game"
>
> Katie Casey was base ball mad.
> Had the fever and had it bad;
> Just to **root** for the home town crew,
> Ev'ry sou Katie blew.
> On a Saturday, her young beau
> Called to see if she'd like to go,
> To see a show, but Miss Kate said,
>
> "No, I'll tell you what you can do."
>
> Take me out to the ball game,
> Take me out with the crowd.
> Buy me some peanuts and cracker jack,
> I don't care if I never get back,
> Let me **root**, **root**, **root** for the home team,
> If they don't win it's a shame.
> For it's one, two, three strikes, you're out,
> At the old ball game.
>
> by Jack Norworth and Albert Von Tilzer, 1908

The words **root**, meaning to cheer wildly for a team, and **rooter**, for a loudly cheering fan, do not enter American English until the late 1890s, only a few years before the chorus of "Take Me Out to the Ball Game" knocked every baseball **rooter** (**radaire**, *pron.* rod-ïre, ranter, raver, bellower) in the bleachers for a loop.

Root, *v.*, to cheer wildly, to yell, harangue, rant, rave; to give support and encouragement for someone or something (like a team or a political candidate); to cheer enthusiastically for a baseball team.
Rooter (*orig. U.S.*), *n.*, a person who loudly and vociferously cheers and "roots" for a sports team; (*Baseball*), a loud, passionate fan.

Rad (*pron.* rod), *v.*, **radadh** (*pron.* rodhă), *vn.*, rant, rave, harangue, yell, bellow; ranting, raving, yelling, talking at random, reveling. **Rabhd** (*Scots-Gaelic*; *pron.* raud), *n.*, a rant; a boast; coarse, unbecoming language; a harangue. *Cf.* **rabhairt** (*pron.* rauairt'), **rabhait** (*pron.* rouait'), *n.*, a bout of revelry and riotous behavior.

Radaire (*pron.* rodh-ĭre), *n.*, ranter, yeller, coarse bellower, comical shouter, prattler. **Rabhdair** (*Gaelic*; *pron.* roud-ər), *n.*, a boaster; verbose talker, prater, coarse jester; someone who uses coarse or unbecoming language. (Dwelly, 1901, [1994]; Ó Dónaill, 1977; Dineen, 1927.)

Most Anglo-American dictionaries derive the cheering, ranting, raving slang word **rooter** from the English language rooting of a pig's snout in the muck.

In the East River neighborhoods of Brooklyn in the 1920s and 1930s, the U.S. Federal Census recorded both Irish and Scots-Gaelic speakers living and **rooting** in the same family. Their **root** was not the English "rooting" of a pig's nose in mud, but was the wild **racket** (**raic ard**, loud ruckus) and raucous **root** (**rabhd**, *pron.* raud, coarse language and harangue) of the Brooklyn Gaelic **rooter** (**radaire**, *pron.* rodire, yeller, bellower), ranting and raving fuh' "Dem Bums"—the one and only Brooklyn Dodgers. (14th U.S. Federal Census, 1920, Ward 17, ED 910–912, Precincts 48–50; Precinct 52; Precinct 150–161, Kings County, Brooklyn, New York.)

> Let me **root**, **root**, **root** for the home team,
> If they don't win it's a shame.
> For it's one, two, three strikes, you're out,
> At the old ball game.

"Thou Swell"

Most Anglo-American dictionaries derive the cheerful, luxurious, comfortable, prosperous, delicious, slang word "swell" from the painful, protuberant, swollen Standard English "swell," from Old English *swellen*. (Barnhart, 1988.)

Swell (*slang*), *adj.*, joyful, cheerful, pleasing; excellent; grand, fine, stylish, elegant, luxurious; enjoyable; delicious, sumptuous.

But **swell** ain't swollen; it's grand!

"Thou **Swell**"

> Thou sweet! Thou grand!
> Wouldst hold my hand?
> Both thine eyes are cute too...
> And Thou **swell**! Thou Witty! Thou Grand!
> (Lorenz Hart and Richard Rodgers, 1927.)

The Irish-American vernacular **swell** is neither painful nor swollen. The American slang **"swell"** is derived from the snazzy old Irish **sóúil** (*pron.* sowul), meaning "cheerful, joyful, enjoyable, happy; grand, prosperous, wealthy, comfortable, luxurious, superb, elegant, splendid, deluxe, fancy, snazzy, swank, ritzy, classy; satisfying, delicious, appetizing, delectable, scrumptious, tasty, exquisite, and delightful."

> I can't give you anything but love, baby...
> Gee, I'd sure like to see you lookin **swell**, baby.
> (Dorothy Fields, Jimmy McHugh, "I Can't Give You Anything But Love, Baby," 1928.)

Ain't dat *sóúil?*

Sóúil (*pron.* sówul), *adj.*, cheerful, joyful, enjoyable, happy, glad; prosperous, wealthy, (*someone or something*) comfortable, luxurious, grand, superb, elegant, splendid, deluxe, fancy, opulent, plush, swank, ritzy, classy; *fig.* a wealthy person; (*of food*) satisfying, delicious, appetizing, delectable, delightful, scrumptious, tasty, exquisite. *Al.* **sóghmháil**; (*Scots-Gaelic*) **sòghail**. (Dineen, 1927; Ó Dónaill, 1977; Dwelly, 1901, [1994].)

CHAPTER 6

The Sanas of Faro and Poker

There's a **sucker** (**sách úr**, *pron.* sawċúr, a fresh new "fat cat") born every minute.—Michael Cassius McDonald, Chicago, 1839–1907.

There isn't any such person as an honest gambler.—Richard Canfield. (Donald Henderson Clarke, *In the Reign of Rothstein*, 1929.)

THE IRISH LANGUAGE IN AMERICA IS A LOST, LIVING TONGUE, HIDDEN beneath quirky phonetic orthographic overcoats and mangled American pronunciations. Irish words and phrases are scattered all across American language, regional and class dialects, colloquialism, slang, and specialized jargons like gambling, in the same way Irish-Americans have been scattered across the crossroads of North America for four hundred years.

Irish was transformed by English cultural imperialism from the first literate vernacular of Europe in the 5th century, into the underworld **cant** (**caint**, speech) of thieves and "vagaboundes" by the 16th, and then into the countless number of anonymous Irish words and phrases in American Standard English, vernacular, slang, and popular speech today.

From the early-19th century to the mid-twentieth century, Irish-Americans played a key role in the development of professional gambling and casinos in the United States. With a political base made up of millions of Irish immigrants and their American-born children, in cities as geographically scattered as New Orleans, Chicago, New York, Boston, Hot Springs, Dallas, and San Francisco, Irish-Americans built powerful urban political machines fueled by the cash flow generated by the gambling underworld. (T.J. English, *Paddy Whacked: The Untold Story of the Irish-American Gangster*, 2005; Kerby Miller, *Emigrants and Exiles: Ireland and the Irish Exodus to North America*, 1985, 315, 329.)

There were sure-thing tricksters and professional gamblers of all nationalities from the earliest days of the American Republic. French, Scottish, English, and Creole gamblers and gambling syndicates were augmented in the late-19th century by waves of impoverished southern Italians and Sicilians, as well as Jews from the shtetls of Eastern Europe and Russia. But from the early 1800s until the 1930s, Irish urban street gangs, and the political machines that grew out of them, controlled the tiger's share of the profits from illegal gambling in the United States.

Irish-American big shots Price McGrath, Jimmy Fitzgerald, and Pat Herne were the leading faro bankers in the wide-open city of New Orleans in the first decades of the 19th century. When the political fix curdled in the Big Easy in 1830, clans of sure-thing tricksters fled up the Mississippi River and scattered to a hundred towns and cities. Price McGrath opened up a faro "rug joint" in New York City, at 5 West 24th street, with former heavyweight boxing champion, John Morrissey, as a partner. The two men couldn't have been more different: McGrath was a sporty **swell (sóúil, sóghamhail,** *pron.* sówul, comfortable, prosperous; *fig.* a wealthy gentleman) and Morrissey a world-class **slugger (slacaire,** mauler, bruiser). But they both spoke the same language. (T.J. English, *Paddy Whacked,* 2005; Asbury, *Sucker's Progress,* 1938.)

Secret Flash Words of the Secret Brotherhood of Gamblers

In the 1840s, a former professional gambler, faro mechanic, and card sharp, Jonathan Harrington Greene, announced in the press that he had become a born-again evangelical Christian, whose new mission in life was exposing the **scams ('s cam** [é],(it) is a fraud, a deceit) and **gimmicks (camóg, camag,** camóga, crooked devices, tricks) of a vast, secret "brotherhood of gamblers," ruled by a mysterious underground hierarchy of Grand Masters. Like all successful con men, Jonathan Harrington Greene was a master of the **ballyhoo (bailiú,** (*act of*) gathering and enticing a crowd) and took his **slick (slíocach,** cunning, sleek) **spiel (speal,** sharp, cutting, satiric speech) on the road, adding some pizzazz to his born-again **baloney (béal ónna,** *pron.* bæl owny, silly talk) with fancy card tricks and elaborate demonstrations of ingenious cheating devices, for overflow audiences of zealous Christian reformers and middle-class curiosity seekers.

In two best-selling autobiographical books, Green claimed that this brotherhood of faro tricksters even communicated in a secret language. The few examples Green gave of this underworld lingo of "the Brethren" were, in fact, neither "flash" nor secret, but the American-English phonetic spelling of fairly common Irish words.

In a chapter entitled "Flash Words of the Secret Brotherhood of Gamblers," Green wrote: "The Grand Master shall be fully invested with power to give out the following catalogue of useful flash words. The six words of quality are highly beneficial in conversation and must, in all cases, be used when one is present who is not known to be a member. By this means can be found out strange Brethren, who are ever ready for any sound so familiar to their own ears." (Jonathan Harrington Greene, *The Secret Band of Brothers*, 1841.)

Below is a list of the Gambling Brotherhood's so-called secret words, spelled first in Green's phonetic English and then in Irish, with matching definitions. It is not surprising that the Irish gambler's secret cant was as Gaelic as the gamblers themselves.

Huska, good, bold, intrepid.
Oscar (*pron.* h-uscar), a champion or hero; a bold intrepid hero. **Oscartha** (*pron.* h-uscarha), martial, heroic, strong, powerful; nimble.

Cady, a highway man.
Gadaí (*pron.* gadí), a thief, a robber. **Gadaí** bóthair, a highway man.

Maugh, profession.
Modh (*pron.* moh), mode of employment.

Caugh, quarrelsome, treacherous.
Cath (*pron.* cah), battle, fight, conflict. **Cathaitheoir** (*pron.* cah-ih'or), a mischief-maker, a troublemaker.

Cully, a pal, a confederate, a fellow thief.
Cuallaidhe (*pron.* cullía), companion, an associate, a comrade, a partner.

Gaugh, manner of speech
Guth (*pron* guh), voice, manner of speech.

Haugh, sick.
Othar (*pron.* ohar), sickness. Fear **othair** (*pron.* f'ar hohar), a sick man.

Glim, a light.
Gealaim (*pron.* galim): I light or brighten. **Geal-laom** (*pron.* **g'al læm**), a bright blaze of fire, a bright flash, a bright white flame, a bright blaze, a bright shining, a gleam; *fig.* a bright light.

Geister, an extra thief.
Gastaire, a tricky cunning fellow; a person with artifice, skill, ingenuity.

In fact, Jonathan Green was no **huska** (**oscar**, hero) of Christian rectitude, but a **caugh** (**cath**, *pron.* cah, warrring, quarrelsome) **geister** (**gastaire**, tricky cunning fellow; thief), whose new **maugh** (**modh**, *pron.* moh, profession) involved a smooth **gaugh** (**guth**, *pron.* guh, manner of speech). "Doc" Greene put the **glim** (**geal laom**, bright light) on his former **cullys** (**cuallaidhe**, cuallaidhthe, *pron.*cullíə, companions, associates, comrades) and **cronies** (**comhroghna**, *pron.* cuh-rony, fellow-favorites, mutual-sweethearts), while keeping it off of himself. Green's secret lexicon demonstrates the early and pervasive influence of the Irish language on the argot of American gamblers—a fact as secret today as it was in the 1840s.

The Irish-American Big Shot

> **Seód, séad, seád,** *pron.* shod, a jewel; *fig.* a chief, a warrior, a powerful person.
> (Dwelly, 1901; Dineen, 1927.)

The **Ard Rí** (High King) of faro and professional gambling in America after the Civil War was the head **Dead Rabbit** (**ráibéad**, a hulking person, a big galoot) of the Five Points, former World Heavyweight Boxing Champ, congressman, and Tammany Hall big **shot**, John Morrissey, who owned the **swank** (**somhaoineach**, suwænać, valuable, wealthy) gambling casino, 18 Barclay Street, near the New York Stock Exchange, where he plucked only the fattest **suckers**, bankers, stockbrokers, and merchants. But the jewel in "Old Smoke" Morrissey's big **shot** crown was Saratoga, in upstate New York, where he founded the world-famous racetrack and gambling casino in the early 1870s—at the dawn of the Gilded Age. (English, 2005; Kenny, 2000; Asbury, *Sucker's Progress*.)

In the 1880s, Mike McDonald was king of **Slab** (**Slab**, Mud) Town's gamblers and popularized the famous aphorism "there's a **sucker** (**sách úr**, *pron.* sawć úr, fresh new "fat cat") born every minute." McDonald reigned over Chicago's **faro** dealers, **grifters** (**grafadóir**), and crooked gambling joints, with the aid of ward **heelers** (**éilitheoira**, *pron.* él'rə, h-éló'rə, advocates, friendly claimsmen; *fig.* local political operators) Silver Bill Riley and Big Jim O'Leary, until his middle-aged wife ran off to Europe with a handsome young priest. King Mike converted to Protestantism, got divorced, and shacked up in his mansion with a showgirl half his age. The world-class big shot had turned into a world-class sucker and became the proof of his own axiom. Mike McDonald was succeeded by the master **grafter** (**grafadóir**, grubber, scrounger, hoer) and legendary diminutive boss of Chicago's wide open First Ward and its infamous Levee District, "Hinky Dink" Kenna, and his hulking, dapper partner, "Bathhouse" John Coughlin. "Hinky Dink" and "Bathhouse" ruled over Chicago's underworld for more than three decades with iron hands that were always palms up. (Asbury, *Chicago, Gem of The Prairie*, 1940; Kenny, 1995; English, *Paddy Whacked*, 2005.)

From his bailiwick on New York City's Bowery, Big Tim Sullivan, the High-King of the Tammany Ward, replaced "Old Smoke" Morrissey as the big shot of New York's underworld from the 1880s to the first decades of the 20th century. Whether five-cent "Policy" banks, floating crap games in the East Side tenement districts, or uptown "rug joints" and **snazzy** (**snasach**, *pron.* snasa; glossy, polished, elegant, classy) faro palaces a short **block** (**bealach**, *pron.* b'alaċ, a path, a road) from Wall Street, the Sullivan Machine controlled New York City gambling. The teetotal Big Tim was a world-class gambler himself, losing vast amounts of **moolah** (**moll óir**, a pile of gold) during his lifetime. (Leo Katcher, *The Big Bankroll*, 1959.)

The first decades of the 20th century saw the rise of New York City's powerful **Gopher** (**Comhbhá**, *pron.* cofa, Alliance) Gang and its leader, Owney "the Killer" Madden. In the decades leading up to Prohibition, Madden took a motley crew of Hell's Kitchen Irish street gangs and transformed them into a West Side alliance that became an international underworld corporation. With the end of Prohibition—and the defeat of the Irish bootleg **racketeers** (**racadóir**, a dealer, a seller, a sportive character) in the war between the "Guineas" and the "Micks"—Madden "retired" and married the postmaster's daughter in Hot Springs, Arkansas, a gambling town once controlled by the Flynn brothers' southern-Irish political machine. Owney "the Killer" became Owney "the Businessman" and managed his considerable assets in bookmaking operations, wire services, and racetracks, throughout the Northeast and the South, until his death in Bubbles (Hot Springs) in 1965. (Richard J. Butler, Joseph Driscoll, *Dock Walloper: The Story of "Big Dick" Butler*, 1933; Yablonsky, *George Raft*; Bayor and Meagher,1996; English, 2005.)

In January 1947, Benny Binion, an illiterate Irish-American road gambler, "policy" wheel operator, dice "fader," and triggerman—who had been a top player in Texas gambling and political circles for more than two decades—decided it was high time to **boogaloo** (**bogadh luath**, *pron.* bug'ah lŭŏ, move quickly). The Fix had shifted in Dallas and the Chicago Outfit and Jack Ruby had invaded Binion's old turf. Benny went on the **lam** (**léim**, jump), scramming to Vegas with two million dollars in the trunk of his maroon Cadillac. Benny Binion opened up the Horseshoe Casino in 1951, with Meyer Lansky as a silent partner, and in 1970 founded the World Series of Poker. He remained a major figure in Las Vegas until his death at the age of eighty-five in 1989. (Mary Ellen Glass, *Lester Ben "Benny" Binion: Some Recollections of a Texas and Las Vegas Gaming Operator*, 1976; Ed Reid and Ovid Demaris, *Green Felt Curtain*, 1963.)

But while it may have been Irish-Americans like Price McGrath, "Old Smoke" Morrissey, King Mike McDonald, Hinky Dink Kenna, and Big Tim Sullivan who laid the foundation for today's multi-billion dollar American gaming industry, the foundation itself was the now-forgotten gambling game called **faro**.

The Sanas (etymology, secret knowledge) of Faro

Conventional wisdom on the history of the banking card game of faro is that it was derived from the Italian card game *Bassetta* and first appeared in France sometime in the 17th century under the mysterious name of **pharaon**, where it was transformed into a fast-paced gambling game called **faro**.

Pharaon and **faro** are said to be derived from the word pharaoh for an Egyptian monarch, supposedly a common image on the backs of 16th and 17th century French card decks, which were later imported to England. However, no evidence of Pharaoh face cards in France or England in 17th, 18th, or 19th centuries has ever been documented. What is certain is that by the 1700s, faro had spread from France to England and was all the rage among the slave-owing, slave-trading English aristocrats and nouveau riche merchant classes. (Asbury, *Sucker's Progress*, *The French Quarter*.)

In **pharaon** and **faro** the main move is called "the turn" and occurs when the faro dealer turns out *two cards together* from the card shoe and places them face up on the faro layout. The first card is a loser, and all wagers on it are collected by the bank; the second card is a winner for the gambler who has bet on it and pays two to one. The Irish and Scots-Gaelic verbal phrase **fiar araon** means precisely "to turn both; to turn each of two; to turn both together" and is the source of the mysterious word **pharaon**.

> **Pharaon**, an early name for faro.
> **Fiar araon**, to turn both; to turn two together.

Fiar is an Irish transitive verb and means "to turn, twist, coil, or bend; the adverb **araon**, means "together, both, each of two." The verbal nominative of the Irish verb **fiar**, "to turn," is **fiaradh** (*pron.* fiəroo or fïŏroh) and is defined as "the act of turning, twisting, or coiling." **Fiaradh** (*pron.* fiəroo, turning) is the Irish name for the "turning" game of **faro.**

Faro, a banking card game where the main move is called "a turn."

Fiaradh (*pron.* fiəroo), *vn.*, turning, a turn; (*act of*) turning, coiling, twisting.

The Fiaradh (*pron.* fiəroo, turning) of the Wild Geese

From a historical perspective, it is not surprising that Irish words found their way into 17th and 18th century French gambling slang and the Paris underworld. In the two hundred years between the Flight of the Irish Earls in 1607 and the unsuccessful United Irish Societies' rising of 1798, hundreds of thousands of Irish-speaking soldiers, rebels, refugees, and Gaelic aristocrats fled to France in the largest protracted Irish continental emigration in the early modern period. In 1691 alone, 11,000 Irish soldiers sailed to France after the Treaty of Limerick. This multi-generational, mass Irish emigration to France, Spain, and Catholic Europe is known in Irish history as the Flight of the Wild Geese.

The negative impact of this long Irish exile in France and Spain has been highlighted by the historians Maurice Hennessey and David Bracke, who traced the pervasive crime and destitution in the ranks of the Irish Regiments in France to cuts in troop levels by Louis XIV, following the Treaty of Riswick in 1697. "A good many of (the Irish) became highwaymen and robbers ... formed themselves into gangs and roamed the roads and farmlands in search of prey." The Irish Wild Geese had shape-shifted into highwaymen, gamblers, smugglers, and **buccaneers** (**boc aniar**, rogue(s) from the west, playboy(s) of the western world) of imperial France and Spain and their North and South American colonies. (Maurice N. Hennessey, *The Wild Geese: Irish Soldiers in Exile*, 1973; Thomas O'Connor, ed., *The Irish in Europe, 1585–1815*.)

Gaelic New Orleans: 1717–1769

The Gaelic influence on the port city of New Orleans was present from the very moment of its birth. In September 1717, the world-class Scottish **faro** (**fiaradh**) banker, con man and financial wizard, John Law, and his Company of the West, popularly known as The Mississippi Company, obtained control of the entire French province of Louisiana by royal grant.

A former high-stakes faro "mechanic" (crooked dealer) and sure-thing trickster, John Law worked fast. He initiated a land and stock selling campaign that swept France into a frenzy of financial speculation. The French national currency was floated, and the Mississippi Bubble was inflated into the most massive financial swindle in early modern European history, bringing the country to the brink of economic ruin.

Colonists willing to immigrate to Louisiana were needed to create the illusion of success, so John Law's underworld operatives ransacked French jails and hospitals to find them: "Disorderly soldiers, black sheep of distinguished families, paupers, prostitutes, political suspects, friendless strangers, unsophisticated peasants, were all kidnapped, herded, and shipped under guard to fill the emptiness of Louisiana." The city of New Orleans was founded a year later, in 1718, and by the 1740s had become a prosperous port city with 2,000 inhabitants, including 300 French soldiers and 300 African slaves.

The new French royal colony came to a sudden end in August 1769, when Don Alexander O'Reilly, an Irish soldier of fortune and one of the most celebrated of Ireland's **Na Géanna Fiáine** (the Wild Geese), landed at New Orleans with twenty-four Spanish warships and 3,000 soldiers—many of them the Irish-speaking **buccaneers** of the Spanish crown's Irish brigades—and took possession of the city for the King of Spain. The turbulent rule of Admiral O'Reilly and his Irish mercenaries set an early pattern of Irish immigration to the Crescent City that was to persist and grow for more than a hundred years.

In 1860, the United States Federal Census reported that 14 per cent of the citizens of New Orleans were Irish-born, equaling exactly the per centage of African-Americans (7 per cent *gens de coleur libre*, free people of color, 7 per cent slaves) in the city's burgeoning population. If we add second, third, and even fourth-generation Irish-Americans, whose families had lived in the port city since the mid-18th century, on the eve of the Civil War, twenty to twenty-five per cent of the population of New Orleans was of Irish or hybrid-Irish descent. (English, 47–55; Asbury, *Sucker's Progress*, 44–50; U. S. VIII Federal Census, 1860, Louisiana.)

By the 1820s, New Orleans had also become the premier gambling city in the United States, and **faro** was its **tiger** (**diaga**, holy, divine) god of the odds. From 1830 to the Civil War, the underworld historian Herbert Asbury estimated that between six to eight hundred gamblers and sure-thing tricksters, most of them Irish-Americans, regularly worked the steamboats that ran between New Orleans and St. Louis. Famous faro sharpers like Jimmy Fitzgerald, Gib Cohern, Jim McClane, Tom Mackay, Charles Cassidy, Pat Herne, and Price McGrath were all leading members of the loosely organized, hybrid-Gaelic gambling clans of

New Orleans, who scattered throughout the south and northeastern United States in the 1830s.

In New York City, the Big Easy Irishman Pat Herne teamed up with the top faro banker **Henry Colton**, who "was regarded as a sort of supreme tribunal of gaming ... and in gambling circles throughout the United States his decisions were binding." **Henry Colton's** moniker (alias or underworld name) in Irish is **An Rí Ghealltáin** (*pron.* ən-ree ċaltán), which means "the King of Wagers, Bets, and Promises."

From **Henry Colton** in the 1840s, to the panel-house operator and gambler **Shang** (**Seang**, *pron.* shang, slim) **Draper** (**dribire**, one who lays snares) in the 1880s, to the **Yellow** (**Éalú**, secretly absconding, escaping, sneaking away) **Kid**, the nickname of both a famous newspaper cartoon character and Chicago con man in the early-1900s, to Owney Madden's old underworld ally, **Tanner** (**dána**, bold, intrepid) Smith, at the dawn of the **Jazz** Age, underworld monikers were often as Irish as the **racketeers** (**racadóir**, racadóirí; dealers, sporty characters) themselves. (Asbury, *Sucker's Progress*, 170; 235; English, *Paddy Whacked*, 47-55.)

By the mid-19th century the faro "tiger" was on the prowl from the prairies and wide-open cow towns of Texas to San Francisco of the Gold Rush era. "Faro was the mainstay of every important gambling house north of the Rio Grande River ... No other card game or dice game, not even poker or craps, has ever achieved the popularity in this country that faro once enjoyed."

Faro also became the "first medium of extensive card cheating seen in the United States," and was the crooked foundation on which the world-famous gambling casinos of New York City and Saratoga, and today's multi-billion-dollar, multinational, legal gambling empires, were built. (Asbury, *French Quarter*, 205; *Sucker's Progress*, 6; English, *Paddy Whacked*, 54, 55.)

Rules of the Faro Game

Faro was one of the simplest gambling games ever devised. Players bet against "the bank," or "the house," rather than against one another's **póca** (pocket or purse) as in a **poker** game. Punters (gamblers) placed their bets on a green baize layout called a **sweat** (**suite**, set, fixed, site) cloth, with the images of a suit of cards painted on it, representing all thirteen denominations from Ace to King. Once a **faro** (**fiaradh**) banker set out his "sweat cloth" and "case keeper" in a saloon or gambling joint, he was in business. (Albert H. Morehead, *Official Rules of Gambling*, 285; John O'Connor, 60–66; Asbury, *Sucker's Progress*, 7–19.)

Sweat cloth
Suite cloth, a set, fixed, site (cloth).

Unique to faro was the **case** (**cas**, turn) keeper, an abacus-like device, set within a wooden cabinet with miniature cards painted on to it, matching those on the layout. A thin wire ran from each card picture on which four button-shaped discs were hung, which another dealer's assistant, also called a **case** keeper, manipulated like a miniature billiard counter, recording each of the cards as they were turned out two at a time from the tell box. The **case** keeper allowed the bettors to determine which card denominations had been turned out of the deck.

"Keepin' cases" in a faro game took a sharp eye and became a popular slang term for keeping a close watch on someone or something. A variation of "keeping cases," which still survives today, is the term "to **case** a joint," meaning to check a place out carefully with the vigilance of a **case** keeper.

In *Hughie*, Eugene O'Neill's last play, set in a crummy hotel near Times Square in 1928, a year before the Age of **Jazz** became Age of the Wall Street **Sucker**, a small-time **grifter** (**grafadóir**, grubber, scrounger) and gambler named "Erie" Smith complained about his dead pal Hughie's wary wife.

> ERIE SMITH: In all the years I knew him, he never bet... on nothin'. But it ain't his fault. He'd have took a chance, but how could he with his wife **keepin' cases** on every nickel of his salary? I showed him lots of ways he could **cross** her up, but he was too scared. (Eugene O'Neill, *Hughie*, 1942.)

Case Keeper.
Cas (Turn) Keeper.

Cas, *v.*, to turn, to twist, wind, coil.
Casadh (*pron.* casah), *vn*, act of turning, twisting, coiling.

Cas is an Irish verb meaning "to turn, twist, or wind," and its verbal nominative **casadh** (*pron.* casah) is translated as "the act of turning, twisting, winding, or coiling." Cartaí a **chasadh** (*pron.* cartí a casah) means "to **turn** the cards."

The Case Keeper is the Cas (Turn) Keeper

Two Irish and Scots-Gaelic words, **fiaradh** (*pron.* fiəroo) and **cas**, both mean "turning and twisting" in a gambling game whose main move was called "the turn"—in English.

For gamblers in an honest faro game, the ideal time to wager was after three cards of the same denomination have been turned out. The house or bank had absolutely no advantage then, so smart players could **buck** the **tiger** if the odds turned in their favor.

Like any successful gambling game, whether in a swank rug joint or the back lot of a carnival, faro appeared to be a game that could be beat.

But there was no such thing as **square** (**'s coir** é, it is fair play) faro. Every **faro** game was a **scam** (**'s cam**, is a trick). (David Brittland and Gazzo, *Phantoms of the Card Table*, 2003, 21–35; Donald Henderson Clarke, *In the Reign of Rothstein*, 1929, 34.)

Square
'S cóir, *contraction* of **is cóir** (é), (It) is fair play.
Cóir, *n.*, justice, equity, honesty, fairness, fair play.

Scam
'S cam. *contraction of* **is cam** (é), (It) is a trick; (it) is a deceit; (it) is a fraud.
Cam, *n.*, crookedness, a deceit, a trick, a fraud.

The turns, coils, bends, and twists of the "turning" game of **faro** mirrored the Celtic triple-spirals sculpted onto the massive lintel stones of megalithic monuments in the Boyne Valley, fifteen hundred years before a Pharaoh built the first pyramid. The **tiger** was the faro gambler's god of the odds, and the **sweat** cloth was his altar.

The Tiger God of the Odds

Diaga, holy, **diagaire**, divine, and **diagacht**, a god, are all modern Irish words descended from the Old Irish word **dea**, meaning "a pagan divinity," and **deacht**, "a pagan god." (*MacBain's Gaelic Etymological Dictionary*, 1982; John Strachan, *Old Irish Paradigms & Selections from Old Irish Glosses*, 1949.)

The American-Gaelic tricksters of the 19th and early-20th centuries worshipped a god who gambled with the universe.

In a faro game ruled by the **tiger** and dealt by a "mechanic" (crooked dealer), a **sucker (sách úr**, a fresh new "fat cat") or **mark (marc**, target) out on a **spree (spraoi**, fun, sport, frolic, drinking bout) was lured by a **roper** into a faro **joint (díonta**, *pron.* jíntə, shelter; *fig.* a house), where a skilled **shill (síol**, *pron.* sheel, to seed) seeded the game with the house's **moolah (moll óir**, a pile of gold or money), while the **capper (ciapaire**, a goader) goaded the **swell (sóúil**) to **guzzle (gus óil**, drink vigorously) and **slug (slog**, swallow, gulp) the high-class **whiskey (uisce**) and wager his **jack (tiach**, *pron.* j'aċ, a wallet or small purse; *fig.* money) with abandon.

The premier faro rug joint of 19th century New York City was the Tapis Franc, where the organization put the screw to the slumming **dude** (**dúd,** *pron.* dood, numbskull) and fleeced the **flush** (**flúirse,** *pron.* flursho, abundant, plentiful) pockets of the super-sucker known as a **Mark Antony** (**marc andána,** a rash and reckless mark) who foolishly tried to buck the faro "tiger."

The Sanas (etymology, secret knowledge) of Poker

The *American Heritage Dictionary* sums up contemporary scholarly opinion on the history and origin of the word poker: "etymology [and] origin unknown." *The Oxford English Dictionary* is equally "uncertain" and traces one of the earliest appearances of the word **poker** in the American-English language to an 1836 quote from Hildreth's *Campaigns in the Rocky Mountains.* "M—lost some cool hundreds last night at **poker**." (*OED.*)

By the 1870s, poker was the most widely played short card game in the United States and was said to be based on the ancient Persian game of *As Nas*, which had been imported into France sometime in the 18th century. According to most gambling historians, *As Nas* evolved into a French three-card bluffing game called **poque,** another word of mysterious origin. As the story goes, **poque,** like faro, was carried to New Orleans in the early-19th century by French and European gamblers, where it ultimately emerged as the game we know today as **poker.**

Poker was described by Herbert Asbury as a hybrid short card game "formed by superimposing two important American innovations—Jackpots and Stud... on the **bragging** (**bréag,** to lie or exaggerate) or bluffing found in many English, French, and Italian games like Brag, Primero ... Poque and Amigu." (Dineen, 1927, 851; Asbury, *Sucker's Progress*, 1935, 20–23.)

Some dictionaries suggest that the word **poque** might be related to the German gambling game *pochspiel*, or the "pounding game," which contains an element of bluffing. But pounding on the table is never an effective poker bluff—even in a German beer hall.

In his book, *Fifth Street*, the Irish-American novelist and poker champion, James McManus, speculates that the word **poque** might be derived from the Irish word **póg** (*pron.* pogue), meaning a "kiss." However, Patrick S. Dineen in his *Foclóir Gaedhilge agus Béarla: Irish-English Dictionary* derives the Irish word **póg** (kiss) from the Latin word *pax*, meaning "peace," and the early medieval

Christian practice of greeting people with the word pax and a **póg** (kiss) on the cheek. Kissing and peace are incompatible with poker.

It is possible McManus might be subconsciously referring to the loud **póg** heard in poker games in his birthplace of the Bronx after a bad **beat** (**béad**, an injury, or a loss), in the NY-Irish phrase **póg mo thóin** (*pron.* pogue ma hone), meaning "kiss my ass," which turns the early medieval Irish-Christian practice on its head.

Perhaps, we should turn conventional wisdom on its head and—as in a **poker** game—go for the pocket?

Poker is a short card game that is played out of your **póca** (pocket) and against the other gambler's **póca** (pocket or purse.) There is no bank or "house" in poker. A **faro** (**fiaradh**, *pron.* fiəroo, turning) game needs a skilled dealer (a mechanic), an assistant dealer, and a **case** (**cas**, turn) keeper, as well as **cappers**, **ropers**, and **shills**, to seed the game with the house's **jack**, work the **marks**, and feed a constant supply of fresh **suckers** to the faro **tiger**. Faro also requires a large amount of money for a house bank.

Raising the **nut** (**neart**, *pron.* n'art, a sufficiency, enough) for the bank and transporting the cumbersome faro paraphernalia, was difficult for the itinerant gamblers of the 19th century American frontier. In a **poker** game the gambler carried all his paraphernalia, a deck of cards and a bankroll, in his back **póca** (pocket). There was a fresh pocket to be plucked in each new hand of poker. The possibilities of new pockets were as limitless as the endless supply of suckers.

The Irish word **póca** means "a pocket, bag, pouch, or purse" in English and is said by Anglo-American dictionaries to be derived from the Middle English word *poke*, the Anglo Saxon *poca*, and the English *pocket*. The German language scholar Kuno Meyer, however, takes the Irish word **póca** from the Norse *pok*. Norwegian and Danish Vikings founded Dublin, Waterford, and other Irish port cities in the 8th and 9th centuries and left a considerable lexical imprint on the Irish language. (O'Donovan, ed., *Annals of The Four Masters*, 1632, [1851]; *MacBain's Gaelic Etymological Dictionary*, 1982.)

Exactly when the transition in America from **poque** to **poker** occurred is unknown. Irish-American writer (and poker champion) James McManus also speculated that the southern pronunciation of **poque** was **pokuh**, which is precisely how you pronounce **póca** (pocket) in Irish. What we do know is that old **poque** game evolved into the modern **poker** game on the fingertips of the professional card sharps, as the rules were changed and the game was sped up and modernized.

The twenty-card deck was replaced with fifty-two cards to accommodate as many as ten players. Flushes and straights were introduced, and a draw of up to three cards was permitted, producing more rounds of betting. This in turn produced bigger payoffs and a larger pot for the gamblers, as well as more opportunities to cheat. The old **poque** game of New Orleans became the new **poker** (**póca**, pocket) game we play today: the hybrid short card game with the hybrid Irish and American name.

Poker (game)
Póca (game)
Pocket (game)

The English word **pocket** is a key term in modern No-Limit Texas Hold 'Em Poker. The two "hole" cards each gambler is dealt down are called pocket cards. Two pocket aces are "pocket rockets" and two pair in the hole is a "pocket pair."

In a **faro** game all bets paid two to one, except the "last turn" of the final three cards, which paid four to one. In a **poker** (**póca**, pocket) game the limit to the pot is the amount of the **jack** in the other person's pocket. There is a new pot for every hand in a **póca** (pocket) game and a new player can add his or her pocket of fresh **jack** to the pot at any time. The poker bank is as inexhaustible as the pockets of the players.

In the new democratic **poker** (**póca**, pocket) game, unlike aristocratic **faro**—where the bank or "house" totally controls the deal—there is always a "new deal." The **button** (**beart t-aon**, one dealing) rotates to all players.

In the 1870s, a new poker game called **stud** poker became popular. In **stud** (**stad**, stop) poker the deal does not rotate from player to player, but stops (**stad**, stop; *fig.* stays) with the house dealer. It is a one-**button** game.

If a **poker** game is **square** (**'s cóir**, is fair play) any smart lucky "punter" (gambler) can be a winner. But if the **button** is **snakin'** (**snoíochan**, *pron.* sníóčán, marking, clipping, cutting, meddling with) the deck, putting in the **gaff** (**gaf**, a trick or deceit, a crooked device), or **ringing** (*pron.* rinn, to deal) in a crooked deck, every gambler is a loser. Cheating is as easy in **poker** as it is in **faro.**

When a poker game is a **scam** (**'s cam** é, it is a fraud, a trick), the **river** (**ríofa**, calculator, computer, enumerator, reckoning) card always runs into the **póca** (pocket) of the dealer. No matter how many times a **mark** (**marc**, a target) shuffles and cuts the deck, Fifth Street is always **Beat** (**Béad**, Loss, Crime, Injury, Sorrow) Street.

A **mark** in a **snaked** game might as well **muck** (**múch**, *pron*. múċ, turn over and smother) a **nut** (**neart**, *pron*. n'art, power, strength) hand; the pot always winds up in the pocket of the dealer with the **gimmick** (**camóg**, **camag**, a crooked device, a trick).

The **poker** (**póca**, pocket) game is the ideal name for the premier short card game of the American crossroad. There is no house bank. It is one pocket against another.

CHAPTER 7

How the Irish Invented Dudes

Dude, *n.* a dapper dandy; a swell, an affected, fastidious fop; a city slicker at a dude ranch. "Origin unknown." (*Barnhart Dictionary of English Etymology*, 305.)

Dúd, dúd(a) (*pron.* dood), *al.* **dúid**, *n.*, a foolish-looking fellow; a dolt, a numbskull; a clown; an idiot; a rubbernecker; a long-necked eavesdropper. **Dúdach** (*pron.* doodah), *adj.*, rubber-necked; foolish-looking, queer. **Dúdaire**, *n.*, a clown, an idiot (*Kerry*); a long-necked person; a dolt; an eavesdropper. **Dúdálaí**, *n.*, a stupid person; an idiot; a self-conscious person. (Dineen, 377, 378; Ó Dónaill, 459, 460; *Foclóir Póca*, 349, 350.)

DÚD WAS A MONIKER IRISH-AMERICANS SLAPPED ON SLUMMING, DAPPER, wealthy, young swells out on a **spree** (**spraoi**, fun, sport, frolic, a drinking bout) in the concert saloons, dance halls, and theaters of old New York.

On February 25th, 1883, the *Brooklyn Eagle* defined the new word **dude** on the front page.

> A new word has been coined. It is **d-u-d-e** or **d-o-o-d**. The spelling does not seem to be distinctly settled yet... Just where the word came from nobody knows, but it has sprung into popularity in the last two weeks, so that now everybody is using it... A **dude** cannot be old; he must be young, and to be properly termed a **dude** he should be of a certain class who affect Metropolitan theaters. The **dude** is from 19 to 28 years of age, wears trousers of extreme tightness, is hollow chested, effeminate in his ways, apes the English and distinguishes himself among his fellowmen as a lover of actresses. The badge of his office is the paper cigarette, and his bell crown English opera hat is his chiefest (*sic*) joy... As a rule they are rich men's sons, and very proud of the unlimited cash at their command ... .They are a harmless lot of men in one way ... but they are sometimes offensive. No **dude** is a real **dude** who does not talk to a fellow **dude** in a loud voice during the play ... The most eminent **dude** in New York is the son of a Wall Street broker of considerable wealth ... and his name has been muddied up with half a dozen dirty scandals. (*Brooklyn Eagle*, Feb. 28, 1883, 1.)

The **dudes** of the *Oxford English Dictionary* believe **dude** is an *artificial* "slang" word, connected to the English aesthetic movement of the late-19th century.

> DUDE: A factitious slang term which came into vogue in New York about the beginning of 1883, in connexion with the "æsthetic" craze of that day. Actual origin not recorded. (*OED*, July 23, 2006.)

This is a word-perfect example of an English-dictionary **dúd** (*pron.* dood, numbskull) etymology, which allows for no Irish influence on the imperial English lingo, dude!

Oscar Wilde was the most famous dude in the world. But he was actually a brilliant **corr** (queer, odd, peculiar) literary Irish **dúd** (*pron.* dood, a long-necked, foolish-looking fellow).

THE DUDE

> "Everybody has expressed a desire to define the **dude**, and yet there can be no better definition than this, that he is one who should be fined for appearing on the streets in men's clothes. He is a result of Oscar Wilde, and is as much the furniture of nature and art as is the slim neckedstork... (*Brooklyn Eagle*, Aug. 16, 1885, 6.)

The **dude** was an early stage-door Johnny.

DUDES DID DINE

With Some of the Girls of the Gaiety Company
Waylaying Their Guests at the Theater Door—
Rude Young Men Who Took
The Everett Assembly Rooms Gallery by Storm...

> The New York morning papers were never more mistaken in their lives than when they said that the Gaiety girls did not go to the ball at Everett Hall last evening. They did go or, at least, enough of them went to make the **dudes** who invited them and who put up $25 each for the entertainment happy. (*Brooklyn Eagle*, Jan. 22, 1889, 4.)

In the 1880s, the average daily wage for textile workers for a ten-hour day was $2.00 for men and $1.17 for women; if you were lucky enough to have a job. (Philip Foner, *A History of the Labor Movement in the United States*, Vol. I, 1947, 1972, 442.)

At one point, there was a fear that the **dude** would become extinct.

ALL THE DUDES ON HAND

What Came of Answering a Newspaper "Personal"
A South Brooklyn Young Man Made the Victim of a Party of Jokers—

> A few days ago sundry South Brooklyn youths ... had noticed with sorrow the gradual disappearance of the genuine **dude**, and feared ... it would disappear like the dodo. It was resolved to see if any of the species still existed. (*Brooklyn Eagle*, Aug. 17, 1884, 12.)

But, by the 1890s, the **dudes** were dancing in the streets. The hit song "Sidewalks of New York" even featured a waltzing **dude**.

> Little Nelly Shannon, with a **dude** as light as cork, learned to do the waltz-step on the sidewalks of New York. (James W. Blake, Charles E. Lawlor, "The Sidewalks of New York," 1890.)

Soon the Irish word **dúd** (*pron.* dood, a dolt, a numbskull), spelled **dude**, was being applied to all dapper young sports, whether they were swells or not. "Big Dick" Butler was an Irish Hell's Kitchen **slugger** (**slacaire**, mauler, bruiser) who styled himself a teenage **dude** in the 1890s.

> My hair was slicked back from the right side, semi-pompadour ... Oh, I was a **dude**, all right, a regular Jim Dandy. (Butler, Driscoll, *Dock Walloper*, 1934, 78.)

Some **dudes** scrammed out west.

> I'm a coyote of the prairie **dude**, hear me zip; in the company of gentleman I'm rude with my lip... (J. Lomax, *Cowboy Songs and Frontier Ballads*, "The Bad Man from the Brazos," *ca.* 1884, 1910, 1938, 138.)

But, at the end of the day, **"dude"** could also be an angry epithet. In Eugene O'Neill's early play, *Abortion*, written in 1914, Joe Murray is an Irish-American mechanic from the other side of the tracks, whose sister has just died in a botched abortion. Murray confronts the Yale **dúd**, who dumped her with just enough money to pay for a back-alley abortionist.

> MURRAY: ...Yuh think yuh c'n get away with that stuff and then marry some goil of your own kind... I've always hated yuh since yuh first come to the house. I've always hated your kind. Yuh come here to school and yuh think yuh c'n do as yuh please with us town people. Yuh treat us like servants, an' what are you, I'd like to know? A lot of lazy no-good **dudes** spongin' on your old men; and the goils, our goils, think yuh're grand! (Eugene O'Neill, *Abortion*, 1914, 217.)

But the last "woid" on "de **dood**" goes to the 1890s' cartoon character Mickey Dugan, the Yellow Kid of "Hogan's Alley" and "McFadden's Row of Flats," whose Irish-American vernacular speech became "woild" famous in Joseph Pulitzer's *New York World* and William Randolph Hearst's *New York Journal*. It was the Yellow Kid who gave his moniker to the Yellow Press.

The Yellow Kid's Diary

I seen me friend Mrs. Gould in one uv der boxes ... But some of dem **doods** wot wuz sittin' around Mrs. Astor comes fer me ... De wimmin down stairs had dere hats off, as if dey wuz afraid de **doods** in de boxes wuz goin' t' t'row paperballs on dere heads... de **doods** wuz all dressed up. (Richard Outcault, cartoon, *The Yellow Kid's Diary*, "He Goes to the Opera," *New York Journal*, Nov. 18, 1898.)

Dude is Irish, **dúd**. (Unless you are an English Dictionary **dúd**.)

What's Not in the News

In Praise of "Jazz," a Futurist Word Which Has Just Joined the Language.

THIS COLUMN is entitled "What's not in the news," but occasionally a few things that are in the news, leak in. We have been trying for some time to keep one of those things out, but hereby acknowledge ourselves powerless and surrender.

• • •

THIS THING IS a word. It has recently become current in The Bulletin office, through some means which we cannot discover but would stop up if we could. There should be every precaution taken to avoid the possibility of any more such words leaking in to disturb our vocabularies.

• • •

. **THIS WORD IS** "JAZ." It is also spelt "Jazz," and as they both sound the same and mean the same, there seems to be no way of settling the controversy. The office staff is divided into two sharp factions, one of which upholds the single z and the other the double z. To keep them from coming to blows, much Christianity is required.

• • •

"JAZZ" (WE CHANGE the spelling each time so as not to offend either faction) can be defined, but it cannot be synonymized. If there were another word that exactly expressed the meaning of "jaz," "jazz" would never have been born. A new word, like a new muscle, only comes into being when it has been long needed.

This remarkable and satisfactory-sounding word, however, means something like life, vigor, energy, efferves-

prizefight stories, in the tale of action

Justin Fitzgerald, the Santa Clara Lightning Bolt as a "Futurist" Sees Him

BY BRETON

Ducks' Roster Is Like Page From "Blue Book"

You Could Save Time by Calling Up the Undertaker First : : By Breton

CHAPTER 8

The Sanas of Jazz

A Supplement to the Oxford English Dictionary (1972, 1976) examples first printing of the word "jazz" in relation to music to *The Bulletin*, San Francisco,
March 6, 1913, "Its members trained on ragtime and **jazz**."[1]

What is the "**jazz?**" Why, it's a little of that "old life," the "gin-i-ker," the "pep,"
otherwise known as the enthusiasalum.—Edward Scoop Gleeson, *San
Francisco Bulletin*, March 6, 1913.[2]

Spell it **Jass, Jas, Jaz,** or **Jazz**—nothing can spoil a **Jass** band. Some say the
Jass band originated in Chicago. Chicago says it came from San Francisco—
San Francisco being away across the continent.—*Victor Record Review*, March
7, 1917.[3]

BORN IN THE **SLUM** AND DOCKSIDE STREETS OF THE PORT CITY OF NEW
Orleans, and at the rural crossroads of the American South, and popularized in the dance halls and cabarets of Chicago in the years before
the Great World War, the roots and origins of the African-American music
called "Jazz" have been researched and documented for almost a century in a
slew (slua, a multitude) of scholarly articles, popular magazines, books, newspapers, plays, radio shows, television documentaries, and Hollywood films.[4]
Condemned and vilified as a "cultural plague" by the **yackin' (éagcaoin,**
pron. y-éag-keen, complaining, lamenting) upper-middle class **swells (sóúil,**
comfortable, wealthy) and cultural gatekeepers of the early-20th century, today,
at the beginning of the 21st, jazz music is now enshrined at the highest level of
American culture.

Jazz music has jazzed up High Society.
But dat ol' woid "**jazz**" is still a motherless child.

.The *Oxford English Dictionary*, the *Barnhart Dictionary of Etymology*, the *Merriam-
Webster Dictionary*, and the *American Heritage Dictionary* all agree that the origin of
the word **jazz** is "not known."

> **Jazz,** *n.* 1913, American English, a kind of ragtime dance (*sic*), perhaps related
> to earlier **jasm,** energy, drive (1860), apparently of African origin...The source
> of jazz in English is not known. By 1922 jazz was applied to the music (*sic*)...
> originating among American Blacks. The meaning of energy, excitement,
> pep is first recorded in 1913, again perhaps influenced by the earlier jasm.[5]

Writers, crackpots, and scholars have proposed a mind-boggling variety of etymologies for the word **jazz**: the name of a dancing slave named "Jasper," the moniker of the mythical musician "Jasbo Brown;" the French word *chasse* for the gliding dance step that gave us the American word *sashay*; the Creole French *jaser*, meaning "useless talk;" a New Orleans perfume called "jasmine;" and the Arabic *jazib*, meaning "one who allures."[6]

John Philip Sousa, American march composer and band leader, believed the word **jazz** came into American speech through jazzbo, 1890s vaudeville slang for the rousing **rollick** (**ramhallach,** *pron.* rawəlaċ, raving, rambling, cavorting) of the finale, when performers would come back out on stage to gad about and cavort for the audience.[7]

The birth of the music called jazz within African-American culture has led others to look for an origin in African languages, such as the Mandingo *jasi* and the Wolof *yees*, meaning to "step out of character." These etymologies have been rejected by American and African language scholars.

There is no evidence of the words **jass** or **jazz** in any African-American slave narratives, oral histories, folk songs, or recorded vernacular speech, prior to 1913. The late Alan P. Merriam, professor of Anthropology, wrote in 1974: "I have never found the word in Africa."[8]

Jesse Sheidlower, editor at large for the *Oxford American English Dictionary*, wrote in *Slate* magazine in December 2004: "The African etymology of jazz was fabricated by a New York press agent in 1917."[9]

The press agent was the glib master of **baloney** and **hoopla,** Walter Kingsley, whose tongue-in-cheek article on the new word **jass,** "Whence Comes Jass?" was published in August 1917 in the *NY Sun*. Kingsley's **phoney** African etymology of jazz was first exposed as a **scam** ('s cam é, it is a trick, a deceit, an error) by the writer and researcher Dick Holbrooke, who reprinted it in full in *Storyville* jazz magazine in January 1974.[10]

"Variously spelled Jas, Jass, Jaz, Jazz, Jasz, and Jascz. The word is African in origin. It is common on the Gold Coast of Africa and in the hinterland of Cape Castle ... In his studies of the Creole patois and idiom of New Orleans Lafcadio Hearn reported the word 'jaz,' meaning to speed things up was common among blacks of the South and had been applied by the Creoles (*sic*) as a term to be applied to music of the syncopated type... No doubt the witch doctors and medicine men on the Congo used the same term at those jungle "parties" when the tom-toms throbbed and their sturdy warriors gave their pep an extra kick ...My own personal idea of jazz and its origin is told in this stanza by Vachel Lindsay: 'Fat black bucks in a wine barrel room...With a silk umbrella and the handle of a broom. Boomlay, Boomlay, Boomlay BOOM.' Lindsay is then transported to the Congo and its feats and revels and he hears, as I have heard, a 'thigh bone beating on a tin pan gong.' Mumbo Jumbo is the god of jazz. Be careful how you write of jazz else he will **hoodoo** you." [11]

If so, a **hoodoo** (**uath dubh**, *pron.* uəh doo, h-uəh doo, dark specter, malevolent phantom) haunts the slick hack Walter Kingsley's **ground sweat** (**grian suite**, sunny site; *fig.* grave) for writing such racist tripe. Kingsley's faux-linguistic treatment of the word **jass** has been quoted in the academic echo chambers by **dude** (**dúd, numbskull**) scholars, historians, lexicographers, and etymologists **galore** (**go leor**, plenty, abundant, enough.) His facile, literate mullarkey on the word **jass** was nothing more than a **cute** (**ciúta**, a clever quip, an ingenious trick) publicity **gimmick** (**camóg, camag**, a crooked device; an equivocation, a trick) to boost his big **shot** (**séad, seád**, *pron.* shod, a jewel; *fig.* a big chief) client Florenz Ziegfeld's summer musical spectacular *Midnight Frolic*, which featured the new hot music called **jass** on the cool **snazzy** (**snasach**, *pron.* snasah, elegant) roof of the **swank** (**somhaoineach**, *pron.* sowĭnaċ, wealthy, ritzy, profitable) New Amsterdam hotel in midtown Manhattan. The *NY Sun*'s editors got the joke and Flo Ziegfeld's advertising **moolah** (**moll óir**, pile of gold or money), humorously entitling Kingsley's piece: "Whence Comes Jazz?—Facts from the Great Authority on the Subject."[12]

Kingsley's putative source, the writer Lafcadio Hearn, never used the word jazz or jass or jaz in any of his books, articles, or letters, a fact confirmed by Richard Holbrooke and Hearn's biographers. But the Hearn **bunkum** (**buanchumadh**, *pron.* buan-kumah, perpetual invention, long made-up tale; *fig.* shaggy dog story) and Kingsley's outrageously racist *NY Sun* article continue to be cited by American and English dictionaries.[13]

African-American Musicians' Hatred for the Word "Jazz"

The words **jass** or **jazz** were not used by any of the early African-American New Orleans musicians—from Buddy Bolden and Bunk Johnson to Joe "King"

Oliver, Sidney Bechet, and Louis Armstrong—prior to the release of the first **jass** record in history, "Dixieland **Jass** One Step and Livery Stable Blues," in New York City, in March 1917.[14]

Louis Armstrong wrote in 1944: "I moved back home with my mother (in 1918). I was working at Tom Anderson's Cabaret—located on Rampart ... Lots of big shots from Lulu White's used to come there ... And I was playing the cornet. We played all sorts of arrangements... T'wasn't called **jazz** back there in those days... They played a whole lot of ragtime music. We called it Dixie-**Jazz**, in the later years." [15]

The influential New Orleans Creole reedman Sidney Bechet, who was a native speaker of French-Creole vernacular, called the music ragtime all his life. In his autobiography, *Treat It Gentle*, Bechet set the tone for succeeding generations of African-American musicians, who have expressed contempt and even hatred for the name **jazz** for their music: "What does **jazz** mean to you when I come up behind you: '**jazz**,' I say, 'what does that do to you? That doesn't explain the music." [16]

Bechet wrote: *"But let me tell you one thing: Jazz, that's a name the white people have given to the music* [my italics]. There's two kinds of music. There's classic and there's ragtime. When I tell you ragtime, you can feel it, there's a spirit right in the word ... But **jazz**—**jazz** could mean any damn' thing: high times, screwing, ballroom. It used to be spelled **jass**..." [17]

In 1968, at the height of the Black Nationalist movement, in back-to-back newspaper columns by San Francisco music critics Ralph Gleason of the *Chronicle* and Philip Elwood of the *Examiner*, the Chicago bandleader and drummer "Big Black" got right to the point: "We should kill jazz, wipe jazz out... **Jazz** is not the proper name for anybody's music ... The truth is that **jazz** as a word is vulgar and profane and we should tear it down and then there won't be any **jazz** clubs, there will be music houses. The **jazz** image is a funky image. We ought to get a coffin and have a parade and bury it.... It got the name through sarcasm, through misunderstanding ... and **jazz** is no title for this music."

"They slapped that **jazz** on the black man's music to make sure everyone would treat it as an inferior kind of artistry." [18]

Chico Hamilton was interviewed by Les Tomkins in 1972: "The fact is music is a multi billion-dollar business now; it's come a long way. They've got away from using the word **jazz**, in many cases, and as a matter of fact, it's not a good word anyway. Originally, it didn't have anything to do with music. That's Mr. Ellington's bone of contention also, that it should be called something else." [19]

Duke Ellington said naming African-American music **jazz** was equivalent to calling it a "four letter word." At a meeting of the California Arts Commission in Monterey in the 1960s, when one of the Commission members said that the word jazz came from New Orleans, Duke Ellington said: "They didn't learn it there..." Ellington later added, "By and large, **jazz** always has been like the kind of man you wouldn't want your daughter to associate with. The word **jazz** has been part of the problem. In the 1920s I used to try to convince Fletcher Henderson that we ought to call what we were doing 'Negro music.' But it's too late for that now. This music has become so integrated you can't tell one part from the other so far as color is concerned." [20]

In 2003, pianist and composer Billy Taylor confirmed that the negative attitude of African-American musicians towards the word **jazz** hasn't changed since Sidney Bechet's day. He spoke to Ben Wattenberg on the PBS program *Think Tank*.

> BEN WATTENBERG: Is it true that Ellington never said that he played jazz; that's not a word he used?
> BILLY TAYLOR: He hated the term, as many jazz musicians do. We're saddled with it. But the music was always called something by someone that had nothing to do with the music itself. So the [term] ragtime came from other sources. The term Dixieland, swing, almost all of the categories that jazz is divided or subdivided into were named by people who didn't have nothing to do with the music. *And all of the musicians hated the term* [my italics] because they felt that the terms were too confining... So the terms, we're saddled with them. (Duke Ellington) called jazz Negro music, because he was trying to write music that reflected the thoughts and feeling and the expressions and emotions of the African-American race...

***

"Actually (Ellington) was an international musician ... **jazz** was created by African slaves and it came out of the spiritual, it came out of some of the work songs... They were not allowed to bring any cultural supports ... as people who were a part of this country. And so that's why African music is African-American, and it's what happened when people of African descent had to refashion their cultural expressions to fit a new situation." [21]

San Francisco "Jazz"—1913

In a series of groundbreaking articles exploring the origin of the word **jazz**, written between 1938 and 1981, the world-class San Francisco **sanasán** (vocabularist, etymologist), researcher, archivist, and folklore collector, Peter Tamony, shocked **jazz** scholars when he revealed that the word **jazz** burst into print for the first time in the history of the American language in the spring of 1913, in the sports pages of the *San Francisco Bulletin* in the prose of a **natty** (**néata**, neat, dapper) 27-year-old San Francisco Irish-American baseball scribe with the snazzy moniker of Scoop Gleeson.

It is a testament to the strength of Peter Tamony's pre-cyber age grassroots scholarship that since the 1938 publication of his first article on the 1913 birth of the word jazz in San Francisco, only one earlier published example of jazz has been discovered by countless researchers, scouring thousands of published sources with the aid of computers. In 2004, using a historical newspaper data-base and computer search engine, New York University librarian George Thompson found the word jazz in an anonymously written sports snippet in the *Los Angeles Times*, published on April 2, 1912, entitled "Ben's **Jazz** Curve." Curiously, the jazz fizzled out in the *Times* after this single appearance. But, less than a year later, the word jazz sizzled into print in San Francisco forever. [22]

In a series of "Special Dispatches" written from the San Francisco Seals baseball team's spring training camp at Boyes Hot Springs, Sonoma County, forty miles north of the city, and from Recreation Park Stadium in the heart of the old Mission District, sports reporter Scoop Gleeson used the new word **jazz** more than forty times in March and April 1913. This hot word **jazz** soon spread like verbal wildfire to the *Bulletin* sports headlines, other reporters, feature stories, and even the cartoons.[23]

Gleeson's first use of the word **jazz** was on March 3, 1913: "McCarl has been heralded all along the line as a 'busher,' but now it all develops that this dope is very much to the '**jazz.**'" [24]

What Scoop Gleeson was saying here, in early-20th century vernacular, was that local baseball experts, fans, and sportswriters had put out the skinny that the new Seals rookie George McCarl was an inexperienced bush leaguer, or rural amateur league player. But all this bad talk and gossip (dope) was nothing but the jazz, meaning a lot of hot air and **baloney** (**béal ónna**, *pron.* bæl óna, foolish talk). Young George McCall, Scoop wrote, was an "experienced player" with six years in professional baseball.[25]

Then three days later on March 6, 1913, under a full-page banner headline, "Seals Return From the Spa to Tackle the Famous White Sox," the *Bulletin* editors gave Scoop Gleeson a full front-page **ballyhoo**, a four-paragraph, two-column-wide lead, set in boldface type, to define the hot new word **jazz** to San Francisco baseball fans.

> Come on there, Professor, string up the big harp and give us all a tune ... Everybody has come back to the old town full of the old "**jazz**" and they promise to knock the fans off their feet with their playing.
>
> What is the "**jazz**?" Why, it's a little of that "old life," the "**gin-i-ker**," the "pep," otherwise known as the enthusiasalum. A grain of "**jazz**" and you feel like going out and eating your way through Twin Peaks. It's that spirit which makes ordinary players step around like Lajoies and (Ty) Cobbs...
>
> "Hap" Hogan gave his men a couple of shots of "near-**jazz**" last season and look what happened—the Tigers became the most ferocious set of tossers in the league. Now the Seals have happened upon great quantities of it in the quiet valley of Sonoma and they're setting the countryside on fire. [26]

What did this hot new word **Jazz** mean to Scoop Gleeson in March 1913? The synonyms he used for **jazz** were "pep," "enthusiasalum," the "gin-i-ker," and "spirit."

"Pep" is "hot" like pepper, from which it is derived, and is defined by *Roget's Thesaurus* as "energy," "spirit," "fire," and "vim." While Scoop's marvelous invented word "enthusiasalum" showed that the young Scoop Gleeson had linguistic pizzazz.[27]

But what did the mysterious synonym **gin-i-ker** mean? And how were great quantities of **jazz** setting the Sonoma countryside on fire?

The answer is Irish.

The **gin-i-ker** is the phonetic spelling of the Irish word-phrase **tine caor** (*pron.* jin-i-kær) and means "raging fire and lightning." It is the **gin-i-ker** (**tine caor**, a thunderbolt of fire) that produces **jazz** (**teas**, *pron.* jass, j'as, heat).[28]

Gin-i-ker Tine caor (*pron.* jin-i-ker), raging fire, lightning.

Tine, *al.* **Teine** (*pron.* jin-ih, chin-eh), fire; conflagration, incandescence; luminosity, flash.[29]

Caor (*pron.* kær), a thunderbolt, a meteor, a round mass of flame, a glowing object.[30]

Jazz is the phonetic spelling of the Irish and Gaelic word **teas**," meaning "heat, passion, excitement, and highest temperature."

Jazz

Teas (*pron.* j'as, jass, or ch'as), *n.*, heat, warmth, passion, excitement, fervor, ardor, zeal, enthusiasm, anger, and highest temperature.[31]

The ancient Irish word **teas** (*pron.* j'as, heat) was reborn in a 20th century Irish-American **gob** (**gob**, beak, mouth) as **jazz**: the hottest American word of the 20th century.

Teas, spelled **jazz** by Scoop Gleeson, holds within it the divine **racket (raic ard**, loud ruckus) and **clamor (glam mór**, great howl) of the "**jazz**" (**teas**, *pron.* jass, heat, passion, excitement, fervor) of Irish-American vernacular and African-American music.

Jazz is always **jazzy** (**teasaí**, *pron.* j'así, hot, exciting, and passionate).

Jazzy

Teasaí (*pron.* j'así, ch'así), *adj.*, hot, warm, passionate, exciting, fervent, enthusiastic, feverish, angry.[32]

But how does an Irish word spelled **teas**, which looks like it sounds like the English word **tease**, become pronounced **jass** or **jazz** in an Irish or American **puss** (**pus**, a mouth, lips; *fig.* a face)?

The *Jazz* (Teas, *pron.* j'as, heat) of the Affricate

"The Rule of Tír" (**tír**, land, country) states that the Irish word **tír** can be correctly pronounced *jeer, cheer,* or *tear* in the Irish language. So, too, the Irish word **teas**, meaning "heat," can also be pronounced *j'as* in Ulster and North Mayo, *ch'as* in Connaught, or *t'as* in Munster, the three living dialects of the Irish language.

In Ulster and Connaught Irish, and in the languages of Scots-Gaelic and Manx, the word **teas**, meaning "heat," is pronounced *j'as* or *ch'as* and is called an affricate, which is a speech sound consisting of a *stop* and a *fricative* articulated at the same point.

The sound of the slender consonant "t" in the Irish word **teas** (*pron* .j'as or ch'as), meaning "heat," is created by blocking the air and then releasing it with friction against the palate. The sound produced resembles the "j" in the English word *joy* or the "ch" in *chair*. [33]

The fricative friction of the affricate produces the heat of **teas** (*pron.* j'as or ch'as, heat, highest temperature), which is itself a word that is in a constant state of **jazz** both in its meaning and in the natural physical law embodied in its articulation.

Dig it or not (**Tuig** é nó ná, *pron.* **dig** ay no ná, understand it or not), **jazz** is an Irish and American word with naturally **jazzy** (**teasaí**, *pron.* j'así, hot) onomatopoeia.

The Waters of Boyes Hot Springs, California

On March 8, 1913, Scoop Gleeson wrote that the San Francisco Seals baseball team kept their **jazz** (**teas**, *pron.* j'as, ch'as, heat, passion, excitement) in a can. "Spence the catcher zipped the old pill around the infield. He opened a can of '**jazz**' at the tap of the gong. Henley the pitcher put a little more of the old '**jazz**' on the pill." [34]

On March 14th, Scoop told his readers precisely where to find the **jazz** (**teas**, *pron.* j'as, heat). It was in the **jazzy** (**teasaí**, *pron.* j'así, hot) waters of Boyes Hot Springs where, he wrote: "there's **jazz** in the morning dew, **jazz** in the daily bath, and **jazz** in the natural spring water..." [35]

It was the **jazz** of the **gin-i-ker** at the earth's core that caused the **jazzy** spring water of Boyes Hot Springs to bubble up and effervesce with 135 degrees Fahrenheit of natural **jazz.**

Almost ninety years later, the Mission Springs Hotel in Boyes Hot Springs, California, in Sonoma's Valley of the Moon, is still extolling the heat and healing properties of the natural spring water on its website: "Paradise found—where Mother Nature has generously combined health enhancing water and minerals heated to 135 degrees of perfection, 1,100 feet within the earth's core."

It is the earth's water in a sizzle that is the hydrothermal womb where the "old **jazz**" became "life." [36]

By March 29, 1913, the San Francisco Seals were a lifeless fizzle; though Scoop's snazzy prose still had pizzazz. Scoop used the hot new word **jazz** more than ten times in this single story.[37]

Under the headline, "Now the Local Players Have Lost the **Jazz** and Don't Know Where to Find It," Scoop lamented:

> The poor old Seals have lost their "**jazz**" and don't know where to find it. It's a fact, gentle reader, that the "**jazz**," the pepper, the old life, has either been lost or stolen, and that the San Francisco club of today is made up of "**jazzless**" Seals.
>
> There is a chance that the old "**jazz**" was sent by parcel post, which may account for its failure to arrive yesterday...
>
> The Seals pitcher, "Cac" Henley will need a gallon of **jazz**... From the way the White Sox stacked up, one might have suspected that they were inocu-

lated with the "jazz" during their stay in the Valley of the Moon ... Suffice it to say that the Seals were without the "jazz" and they played in last season's faulty style... Manager Del had better send for the "jazz" wagon—Quick! Quick! Bring on the old "jazz!"

Then on April 10, 1913, the word **jazz** brought its Irish-American verbal heat and excitement to the comics for the first time in history. In a five-column wide *Bulletin* sports page cartoon headlined, "Justin Fitzgerald, the Santa Clara Lightning Bolt," the speedy Fitzgerald was drawn by the cartoonist Breton as the personification of the **gin-i-ker** with the head of a man and a lightning bolt for a body.[38]

In the cartoon the hapless Seals' infielders lurch and stumble, while the young **slugger** (**slacaire**, batter) zaps around the bases like a "blue streak." In the cartoon's foreground, a fan in a slouch hat cracks to three **cronies** (**comhróghna**, *pron.* co-ronə, cuh-rony, fellow-favorites, mutual-sweethearts) in the stands: "He's full of the '**old jazz**.'"

In the background of the cartoon, beyond the left-field fence of Recreation Park at 15th and Valencia, in the Mission District's old Irishtown neighborhood, Breton has sketched in the steeple of Mission Dolores Cathedral and the hills of San Francisco's Twin Peaks.

In the hot spring of 1913, on the eve of World Ward I, there were thousands of native Irish speakers and their first-generation Irish-American children living in the *breac-Ghaeltachta* parishes and neighborhoods surrounding the old Seals' stadium. Their old Mission District **spiel** (**speal**, cutting satiric speech) was peppered with the phonetic **jazz** of the Irish language.[39]

In 1920, the U.S. Federal Census recorded hundreds of *breac-Ghaeltachta*, containing thousands of Irish speakers in American cities as geographically diverse as San Francisco, Boston, New York City, Springfield, Illinois, Butte, Montana, and Portland, Maine.[40]

By mid-April 1913, the word **jazz** had become so hot in San Francisco that *Bulletin* columnist Ernest Hopkins devoted an entire feature story to this local verbal phenomenon. Hopkins' jazzy column was a lulu, illustrated with a cartoon of a **dude** (**dúd**, a dolt, a numbskull) in a swell three-piece suit, presumably Hopkins himself, precariously balancing the letters **J-A-Z-Z** on the tip of his middle-class **snoot** (**snua ard**, lofty visage.)[41]

In Praise of "Jazz" A Futurist Word Which Has Just Joined the Language
By Ernest Hopkins, April 5, 1913, *San Francisco Bulletin*

This column is entitled "What's Not in the News" but occasionally a few things that are in the news leak in. We have been trying for some time to keep these things out, but hereby acknowledge ourselves powerless and surrender.

This thing is a word. It has recently become current in the *Bulletin* office through some means which we cannot discover but would stop up if we could. There should be every precaution taken to avoid the possibility of any more such words leaking in to disturb our vocabulary.

This word is "JAZ." It is also spelt "**Jazz**," and as they both sound the same and mean the same, there is no way of settling the controversy. The office staff is divided into two sharp factions, one of which upholds the single z and the other the double z. To keep them from coming to blows much Christianity is required.

"JAZZ" (We change the spelling each time so as not to offend either faction) can be defined, but it cannot be synonymized. If there were another word that exactly expressed the meaning of jaz, Jazz would never have been born. A new word like a new muscle only comes into being when it has been long needed.

This remarkable and satisfactory-sounding word, however, means something like life, vigor, energy, effervescence of spirit, joy, pep, magnetism, verve, virility, ebulliency, courage, happiness—oh, what's the use?—JAZZ.

Nothing else can express it.

You can go on flinging the new word all over the world, like a boy with a new jack-knife. It is "jazz" when you run for your train; "jaz" when you soak an umpire; "jazz" when you demand a raise; "jaz" when you hike thirty-five miles of a Sunday; "jazz" when you simply sit around and beam so that all who look beam on you. Anything that takes manliness or effort or energy or activity or strength of soul is "jaz."

We would not have you apprehend that this new word is slang. It is merely futurist language, which as everybody knows is more than mere cartooning.

"Jazz" is a nice word, a classic word, easy on the tongue and pleasant to the ears, profoundly expressive of the idea it conveys—as when you say a home-run hitter is "full of the old jaz." (Credit Scoop.) There is and always has been an art of genial strength; to this art we now give the splendid title of "jazz."

The sheer musical quality of the word, that delightful sound like the crackling of an electric spark, commends it. It belongs to the class of onomatopoeia. It was important that this vacancy in our language should have been filled with a word of proper sound, because "jaz" is a quality often celebrated in epic poetry, in prizefight stories, in the tale of action or the meditative sonnet; it is a universal word, and must appear well in all society.

That is why "pep," which tried to mean the same but never could, failed; it was a rough-neck from the first, and could not wear evening clothes. "Jazz" is at home in bar or ballroom; it is a true American. " (Ernest Hopkins, *San Francisco Bulletin*, April 19, 1913.)

Less than a week later, on April 25, Scoop spelled out the Irish definition of the American word **jazz** for his San Francisco readers:

H.E.A.T. is a staple product of Los Angeles and Manager Dillon must have had some of it expressed to Oakland for use in the third game. However, the Seals invoked the aid of "jazz" which keeps equally in hot or cold weather and were thus able to win out on a 3 to 2 score. [42]

By May 1st Scoop Gleeson was writing poems to the elusive "**jazz.**"

The old Wolf sat in the clubhouse door,
Hoping that his team might score.
The game rolled on, but he WOULD not go,
Because he loved those umpires so.
(Help! The old "jazz" is out again!). [43]

By the end of May 1913, the Seals were 9-13 and totally out of **jazz**—in last place. On June 5, Scoop Gleeson blamed the loss of the old **jazz** on an old Irish jinx: "Too long have the Oaks proved to be the **hoodoo** ... for the Seals." [44]

Then on July 7 in another large Breton cartoon on the front page of the sports section, a distraught father rushes about, frantically searching for a bottle of **jazz** water to revive his sick baby (the San Francisco Seals.) But, in store after store, he is unable to find the life-giving **Jazz** to save his **kid** (**cuid**, a term of affection, a **chuid**, my dear, mo **chuid**, my darling). [45]

By July 24, the Seals were truly sick kids and had lost 15 of the last 16 games. In August, they were in the cellar of the Pacific Coast League without a drop of **jazz**. At the end of the 1913 baseball season, the San Francisco Seals had finished fifth out of 6 teams. [46]

But that "futurist" San Francisco Irish-American vernacular word **jazz** was just starting to sizzle into the consciousness and print of American speech and culture.

In early June 1913, the San Francisco **jazz** had already whizzed east into Indiana. In a feature story entitled "Best Sellers in City Slang," the *Fort Wayne Sentinel* reported that the "**old jazz**" was the "newest slang term in San Francisco." [47]

By the fall of 1913, **jazz** jumped like an electric spark from the baseball diamond to the boxing ring. In the *Oakland Tribune* on October 4, the **slugger** (**slacaire**, a batter; a mauler, a bruiser) in the story wasn't a Seal hitting a baseball with a **smack** (**smeach**, *pron.* smać, a whack) and a **wallop** (**bhuail leadhb**, *pron.* whual lob, a mighty blow), but two palookas **dukin'** (**tuargain**, hammering, slugging) it out in the ring: "The Sailor was off his feet last night, although Clabby handed him shots of the old ½-**jazz** which made the ex-sailor's knees sag." [48]

The **jazz** of Ireland and San Francisco was on its way to becoming the hottest new word of the 20th century.

1. Cited in Peter Tamony, *Jazz: The Word, And Its Extension To Music*, JEMF Quarterly, Spring 1981, 10.

2. Edward Scoop Gleeson, *San Francisco Bulletin*, March 6, 1913, 13.

3. *Victor Record Review*, March 7, 1917; cited in Peter Tamony, *Jazz: The Word, And Its Extension To Music*, JEMF Quarterly, Spring 1981, 10.

4. Louis Armstrong, *Louis Armstrong: In His Own Words*, ed. Thomas Brothers, Oxford, 1999, 23–24, 38, 83: "T'wasn't called Jazz back there in those days," 218–219; Sidney Bechet, *Treat It Gentle: An Autobiography*, 1960, 1978, 1–5; 62–67; Alan Lomax, *Mr. Jelly Roll: The Fortunes of Jelly Roll Morton, New Orleans Creole and "Inventor of Jazz,"* 1950, 1973, 2001, x, 124–126.

5. *Barnhart Dictionary of Etymology*, 1988, 551; OED, "Jazz...origin unknown."

6. Peter Tamony, *Origin of Words, San Francisco Wasp*, March 17, 1938, 5; Tamony, *Jazz, The Word, Jazz: A Quarterly of American Music*, ed. Ralph Gleason, Phillip Elwood, October 1958, 34–45 ; Tamony, JEMF Quarterly, Spring 1981, 9–11; Dick Holbrooke, *Our Word Jazz, Storyville* magazine, January, 1974, 58.

7. Tamony, *Jazz, The Word, Jazz: A Quarterly of American Music*, 35; OED.

8. *Barnhart Dictionary of Etymology*, 551; Tammony, *Jazz, The Word*, 46; Holbrooke, *Our Word Jazz*, 58; Fradley H. Garner, Alan P. Merriam, *The Word Jazz, The Jazz Review*, Vol. 3, No. 3, March–April 1960, 39–40. David Meltzer, *Writing Jazz*, 1996, 3.

9. Jesse Sheidlower, *MSN Slate Magazine Online*, http://slate.msn.com, December 11, 2004.

10. *Barnhart Dictionary of Etymology*, 789, "Phony or phoney, *adj.*, not genuine, fake, sham. 1900...American English; perhaps an alteration of earlier English slang fawney, a gilt brass ring used by swindlers (1781), borrowed from the Irish fáinne, ring."

11. Holbrooke, "Our Word Jazz," *Storyville* magazine, 56–58.

12. Tamony, JEMF Quarterly, 11: "Merriam-Garner material ... lays to rest the alleged Arabic-African roots of the word. It details failure to find the word 'jaz' in the literary work of Lafcadio Hearn," Holbrooke, 58, citing Lafcadio Hearn biographers Bisland, Krehbiel, Brenner, Thomas, Tinker, Hutson, et al.

13. *OED* quotes the August 1917, Kingsley *New York Sun* article and quotes a Dr. Bender, quoted in the *New York Times* in 1950, who cites Lafcadio-Hearn bogus Creole dialect jazz meaning "to hurry up."

14. *Louis Armstrong, In His Own Words*, 1999, 83, 218, 175.

15. *Louis Armstrong, In His Own Words*, 33, 83. Big Shot: "Seód, *al.* seud, [Irish, séad], a jewel, *often used figuratively*; hero, valiant man, chief or warrior." *Faclair Gaidhlig Bu Beurla Le Dealbhan, Illustrated Gaelic-English Dictionary*, 1901, 1994, 808; see also Robert Goffin, *Horn of Plenty: The Story of Louis Armstrong*, 1947, 109, 111: "(In 1917) Joe Oliver...showed Louis a letter from Freddie Keppard. In it Freddie reported that the new music known as ragtime in New Orleans was called Jazz in Chicago and it was creating a torm."

16. Sidney Bechet, *Treat It Gentle, An Autobiography*, 3; Martin Williams, *Jazz Masters of New Orleans*, 1967.

17. Bechet, 3.

18. Philip Elwood, *San Francisco Examiner-Chronicle*, November 10; B4/1-2; Ralph Gleason, *San Francisco Chronicle*, November 1, 1968, 47.

19. Transcript of 1972 interview: Chico Hamilton with Les Tomkins, http://www.jazz-professional.com/interviews/Chicoper cent20Hamilton_1.htm

20. Tamony, *JEMF Quarterly*, 13; Ralph J. Gleason, *San Francisco Chronicle*, November 1, 1968, 47.

21. PBS Online, *Think Tank with Ben Wattenberg*, official transcript of interview with Dr. Billy Taylor, 2003.

22. Peter Tamony, *Origin of Words, San Francisco Wasp*, March 17, 1938; Tamony, *Jazz, The Word, Jazz: A Quarterly of American Music*, ed. Ralph Gleason, Phillip Elwood, October 1958: Scoop Gleeson 1938 article "*I Remember: The Birth of Jazz*" in *San Francisco Call-Bulletin*, Sept,. 3, 1938, reprinted in full, 40; Tamony, *JEMF Quarterly*, Spring 1981. NYU librarian, George Thompson, using a computer search engine discovered one earlier baseball "jazz" on April 2, 1912 in anonymously written article in *Los Angeles Times*, part III, 2, "Ben's Jazz Curve." However, the old "jazz" fizzled in *Los Angeles Times* and did not appear again until 1917-1918.

23. *San Francisco Bulletin*: see especially March 3, 6, 8, 14, 24, 29, April 2, 9, 10 (also Breton cartoon), 14, 25, May 1, 1913.

24. *San Francisco Bulletin*, March 3, 1913, 13.

25. *Ónna*, a., simple, silly, Dineen, 821.

26. *San Francisco Bulletin*, March 6, 1913, 16.

27. *The Original Roget's Thesaurus*, 1852, 1965, 102.

28. *Teine caor, al.* tine caor, a raging fire, lightning, Dineen, 1200.

29. *Teine*, Dineen, 1200; tine, Ó Dónaill, 1235; teine, Dwelly, 943.

30. *Caor*, Dineen, 163; Ó Dónaill, 189.

31. *Teas*, Dineen, 1194-95; Ó Dónaill, 1221-22; Dwelly, 942. *Teas*, heat, passion; Irish synonyms: *ainmhian, an-suim, díochracht, díograis, grá, paisean, teasaíocht. Corpas Comhthreomhar Gaeilge-Béarla*, Kevin P. Scannell, 2004, http://borel.slu.edu/cgi-bin/cc.cgi .

32. *Teasaí*, Dineen, 1194-95; Ó Dónaill, 1221-22; Dwelly, 942.

33. Mícheál Ó Siadhail, *Learning Irish*, 2-4, Sec. 4, 5, 6. The realization of the slender consonants varies somewhat from dialect to dialect; for example [t´] is an affricate [tʃ] in Ulster, a palatalized [tj] in Connacht, and an apical postalveolar [t] in Munster.— Eamonn Mhac an Fhailigh, "*The Irish of Erris, Co. Mayo.*" Notes on affricates: The slender T and D. *Daltaí Boards*: The Irish pronunciation rule of the slender T. The Rule of Tír. Daltaí Board, Padraig, January 28, 2005. http://www.daltai.com/discus/messages/board-topics.html. "Taunt...of **uncertain** origin." (Barnhart, 1118.)

34. *San Francisco Bulletin*, March 8, 1913, 12.

35. *San Francisco Bulletin*, March 14, 1913, 20. See also "jazzers."

36. History of Mission Springs Hotel, Sonoma County, California. Online.

37. *San Francisco Bulletin*, March 29, 1913, 26. See also March 14, 1913.

38. *San Francisco Bulletin*, April 10, 1913, 14 . See also: April 2, 1913, 17.

39. *Fourteenth Census of the United States*, San Francisco: Assembly District 22, see examples: 508—534 Connecticut Street; 605-665 Arkansas Street; Precinct 27, SD4; Dolores Street; Assembly Dist. 25, Precinct 28, SD4: see 2688, 2690 24 Street,1069-1081 Dolores Street; Precinct 88, 1061-1065 Dolores St.; Precinct 48-50; Precinct 52; Precinct 150-159.

40. *14th Census*, Kings County, NY (Brooklyn), see examples: ED 910-912 (Greenpoint); *14th Census*, Springfield, Illinois. See ED 119-120; Portland, Maine.

41. Holbrooke, *Storyville*, Hopkins' article reprinted, 52-55; *San Francisco Bulletin*, April 5, 1913, back page number illegible.

42. *San Francisco Bulletin*, April 25, 1913, 19. "Seals Sizzle ... H.E.A.T."

43. *San Francisco Bulletin*, May 1, 1913, 16.

44. *San Francisco Bulletin*, May 1-31, 1913. May 1, 1913, subhead, 16. "Hoodoo," May 29, 1913, "Seals in Last Place."

45. *San Francisco Bulletin*, July 7, 1913, Breton cartoon: "You Could Save Time by Calling Up the Undertaker First," 14.

46. *San Francisco Bulletin*, July 24, 15, "Seals Lose 15 of 16 games;" July 31, 1913, "Seals in cellar."

47. *Fort Wayne Sentinel*, Box: Best Sellers in City Slang, June 4, 1913, 8.

48. *Oakland Tribune*, October 4th, 1913, 8, (illegible) col. 7.

A Dictionary of
Irish-American Vernacular

Bibliographic note on abbreviations.

Patrick S. Dineen, *Foclóir Gaedhilge agus Béarla—Irish-English Dictionary*, 1927: Dineen.

Niall Ó Dónaill, *Foclóir Gaeilge-Béarla*, 1977: Ó Dónaill.

Tomás de Bhaldraithe, *English-Irish Dictionary*, 1959: de Bhaldraithe.

Edward Dwelly, *Faclair Gaidhlig Gu Beurla Le Dealbhan: The Illustrated Gaelic-English Dictionary*, 1901, 1994: Dwelly.

An Etymological Dictionary of the Gaelic Language, Alexander MacBain, 1896, 1982, online edition, Gairm Publications, (www.ceantar.org/Dicts/MB2/), MacBain.

Oxford English Dictionary, (http://www.oed.com/): OED.

Oxford Dictionary of English Etymology, 1966, 1978: ODEE.

Robert K. Barnhart, *The Barnhart Dictionary of Etymology*, 1988: Barnhart.

Harold K. Wentworth and Stuart Berg Flexner, *Dictionary of American Slang*, 1960: *DAS*.

Robert L. Chapman, *American Slang*, 1987: Chapman.

A

Acushla, a term of endearment and affection.
A chúisle (*pron.* a ċushla), *voc.*, my pulse; cúisle mo croí (*pron.* ċushla macree), my heart's pulse, my darling. Cúisle (*pron.* cushla), *n.*, a vein, a pulse.

"**Macushla**" is the nickname for the female prizefighter played by actress Hilary Swank in the film *Million Dollar Baby*. Clint Eastwood portrays her hard-bitten manager, who teaches himself Irish with a foclóir póca (pocket dictionary) in his spare time. (See: **macushla**.)

Agrah, a term of endearment.
A ghrá, my love, my dear.

"A Stór, A Stór, **A Ghrá**" (my darling, my darling, my love) is an Irish tradition-al song found in the repertoires of many Irish-American musicians. Stór, *n.*, store, abundance, wealth, treasure, riches; a term of endearment. A stór! Darling! Mo mhíle stór (*pron.* mo vílə stór), my dearest love.

"Siúl Siúl **A Ghrá**" (*pron.* shool, shool a ghrá), "Walk, Walk, My Love," is a song that recounts the sadness of a young woman as she bids farewell to her soldier sweetheart, who is sailing from Ireland in 1691 to fight with the Irish brigades ("The Wild Geese") in Spain and France. The song, often written phonetically as "Shool, Shool, **A Graah**," first became popular during the American Revolution and was known as "Johnny's Gone for a Soldier."

Siúl (*pron.* shool), *n.*, walk; travel, journey; movement, speed. **Grá**, *n.*, love, beloved person.

Alanna, *n.*, a term of endearment; a name.
A leanbh (*pron.* a'lanəw), *voc.*, my baby, my child; my fair lady.

The song "Eileen **Alannah**" was composed by John Rogers Thomas and recorded by the legendary Irish tenor John McCormack. **Alanna** is a woman's name in Ireland and Irish-America.

Andána, rash; foolhardy, reckless, given to taking unnecessary risks.

Andána is still used in Hiberno-English. "That fellow is only **andána** (only a fool)." The word survives in Irish-American vernacular as part of the gambling slang term a "Mark **Antony**" or "Mark **Anthony**" for a reckless mark.. (Dineen, 45; Ó Dónaill, 46; Dolan, *Dictionary of Hiberno-English*, 1998, 9.) (see: **Mark Anthony**.)

A nail, *n.*, a sexually transmitted disease, gonorrhea, syphilis. "Pick up **a nail**," catch the clap, become infected with gonorrhea. (*Urban Dictionary Online*, 2006.)

Ainfheoil (*pron.* an'ól, an~ĭÿ-il), *n.*, corrupt flesh, gross flesh, granulations; *fig.* STD. (Dineen, 19; Dwelly, 15.)

HICKEY: I picked up **a nail** from some tart in Altoona." (Eugene O'Neill, *The Iceman Cometh*, 1939, [1954], 712.)

A noogy, to give someone a noogy is to grab them and rub them on the head with your knuckles, or give them light taps or whacks on the noggin; also common in Australia.

Aonóg (*pron.* ænóg, *dim.* ænóg + y), *n.*, a nip, a pinch, a little whack; *fig.* affectionate, rough-house play. (Dineen, 53; Ciarán Ó Duibhín, *Foclóir Oirthear Uladh, Consolidated Glossary of East Ulster Gaelic; American Australian Slang Dictionary* online edition, 2006.)

An Gorta Mór, the Great Hunger.

An, *art.*, the. **Gorta**, *m.*, hunger; scarcity; famine; destitution. **Mór**, *adj.*, big, great, large. Fuair sé bás den **ghorta** (*pron.* fuər shay bás den ghorta), he died of hunger.

There was no "famine" in Ireland in the mid-19th century. Only one crop failed—the potato. Ireland's colonial landlords exported grain and foodstuffs throughout the famine period of 1845-1852. More than one million Irish people died in five years and another million fled. It has been estimated that 500,000 Irish speakers emigrated during the "famine." (Miller, *Emigrants and Exiles*, 1985, 297; Thomas Idhe, *The Irish Language in the United States*, 1994, 29.)

Aroon, a term of affection found in Irish love songs.
A rúin, my love, my sweetheart; *voc.* **rún**, a secret, a secret treasure, a love. **A rúin** is often written phonetically as "**aroon**."

"**Shool Aroon**" (**siúl a rún**, walk, depart, my darling), is one of many Irish songs in North American roots music in which the phonetically written Irish language lyrics are often treated as macaronic or nonsense syllables. (See: "Pat Works on the Railway.")

Is go dté tú a mhuirnín slán,
(*pron.* iss guh day tú avirnín slán),
May you go safely darling,
Siúl a rún siúl a rún
(*pron.* shool aroon, shool aroon),
walk my darling, walk my darling.

Arrah na Pogue, a popular mid-19th century play by Irish playwright Dion Boucicault, which is still performed in America today.
Ara na bpóg, Arrah of the Kiss.

The word *póg* means "kiss" and is often written phonetically in English as *pogue*; hence the name of the popular Irish band, the Pogues. In New York City, **póg mo thóin** (*pron.* pogue mahown) was often pronounced "pugga mahone" and means "kiss my ass." The Irish sanasánaí (etymologist, vocabularist, lexicographer), Patrick S. Dineen, derives the Irish word **póg** from the Latin word *pax*. (Dineen, 56.)

Astore, *al.* **asthore**, a term of endearment.
A stóir, a term of endearment, my treasure, my darling, my love, *voc.* **stóir**, store, treasure. **A Stóir Mo Chroí**, "Treasure of My Heart."

Avoorneen, a term of endearment.

A mhuirnín (*pron.* avirnín), my little darling; **a mhuirnín dílis** (*pron.* avirnín d'ílish), my own love. (Dineen, 772.)

B

Babe, *n.*, a girl, a sexually attractive young woman; a term of affection. Uncertain origin. (Barnhart, 70.)

Báb (*gen.* báibe, *pl.* bába), *n.*, baby; a maiden, a young woman; a term of affection; *dim.* **báibín**, **bábán**, a baby, a maiden, a young woman. (Dineen, 66; Ó Dónaill, 73.)

Babe is most often used as a term for a pretty young woman; but can be used affectionately for any gender. *Babe Gordon* was touted in 1930 as "Mae West's novel of the New York underworld."

"**Babe** was eighteen and a prizefighter's tart, picking up her living on their hard-earned winnings. Her acquaintances numbered trollops, murderers, bootleggers, and gambling den keepers." (Mae West, *The Constant Sinner*, 1930, 9.)

Mae West was a Brooklyn-Irish **báb**, born in Greenpoint on August 17, 1893. Her father John Patrick West was a prizefighter, bodyguard, and detective. Mae West wrote novels, hit Broadway plays, and the original screenplays for some of the most popular films in Hollywood.

"I'm class, **babe**. Just look at that figure." (Mae West, *Sex: A Comedy Drama*, 1926, [1997], 38.)

Bad Beat (*gambling slang*), *n.*, a bad "**beat**" occurs when a powerful poker hand is defeated by an even more powerful one. Any severe loss, theft, or injury. (See: **beat**.)

Béad, bad **béad**, (bad) loss; crime, robbery, injury; sorrow. To be robbed, or cheated badly. (Dineen, 85; Ó Dónaill, 93; Dwelly, 80.)

"They **beat** the sucker for a nice pocket-touch (proceeds of his pockets)." (Goldin, O'Leary, *Dictionary of American Underworld Lingo*, 1950, 24, 25.)

When a poker game is a **scam** (**'s cam**, is a fraud, is a trick) "Fifth Street" is always "**Beat** (**béad**, loss, crime, injury, sorrow) Street."

Bailiwick, *n.*, district of a bailiff; *fig.* a local area of personal influence.

Báille vicus (*pron.* bál'ə wicus; Irish/Gaelic-Latin compound), bailiff town, bailiff district.

Báille (*pron.* bál'ə), *n.*, a magistrate, a "baillie," or bailiff. **Vicus** (*Latin; pron.* vicus, wicus), *n.*, a town, a district. The English suffix *wick* is derived from Latin *vicus*. "Bàillidh, a magistrate, balie; Scottish *bailzie* English *bailiff*, French *bailli*." (*MacBain's Gaelic Etymological Dictionary*, 1896, [1982].)

Ball, *n.*, a dance, a party.

Ball (*Scots Gaelic*), *n.*, a dance; a spot, a place. Compare Italian *ballo*, dancing; Spanish *baile*. (Dwelly, 62; Dineen, 75.)

Bally (*carnival, circus*), *v., n.*, to ballyhoo, to spiel. A pitch or spiel that gathers a crowd to a circus or carnival sideshow; *fig.* publicity of any kind that draws or entices an audience. (Wentworth & Flexner, *Dictionary of American Slang*, 1960, 17.)

Bailigh (*pron.* bal'í), *v.*, to gather, to collect, to assemble (a crowd); to bring together; to entice. (Dineen, 70.)

"When Joe **ballys** the tip (crowd) the grifters sure go to town." (Goldin, O'Leary, *Dictionary of American Underworld Lingo*, 1950, 22.)

"Looks like some advance **bally**." (*Variety*, Aug. 25, 1948.)

Bally show (*carnival and circus*), *n.*, a carnival side-show having continuous or regularly scheduled performances; also called a grind show. **Bally stand** (*carnival and circus*), *n.*, the platform or stand in front of the sideshow tent where the barker gives his "spiel" to gather a crowd.

Ballyhoo, *n.*, the pitch, bally, spiel, or music used to attract a crowd; publicity; a short free exhibition or sample of a side-show, accompanied by a barker's spiel. **Ballyhoo**, *v.*, to pitch, spiel, or advertise a show or attraction. Origin unknown. (Chapman, *American Slang*, 1986, 14.)

Bailiú (*pron.* bal'iú), *vn.*, (*act of*) gathering, collecting, amassing; enticing, (*act of*) assembling a crowd; a gathering, an assemblage. Bhí an-**bhailiú** daoine ann, there was a great assemblage of people there.

The *Oxford Dictionary of Etymology* defines **ballyhoo** as an American word meaning "publicity (and) blarney," dating it to the 19th century; and deriving it "from the name of a Central American wood, of which some schooners were made that were failures..." (*ODEE*, 1966, 71.)

"Amid the boom of flashpoweder and the uproar of **ballyhoo**, William Randolph Hearst was elected to the Congress of the United States." (Harry J. Coleman, *Give Us a Little Smile, Baby*, 1943, 60.)

Ballyhoo truck. Clarence Williams was an African-American musician, composer, and music publisher in the first half of the 20th century. "When Sophie Tucker came to New Orleans in about 1910 or 1911, they would have a **ballyhoo truck**... and the bands would get on these trucks and wagons and ride all over town. Sophie Tucker and the Avon Four, who were playin' at the Orpheum Theatre, were on one of those trucks, and I followed them around all day." (Nat Shapiro, Nat Hentoff, *Hear Me Talkin' To Ya: The Story of Jazz as Told by the Men Who Made It*, 1955, 32, 33.)

Ballyrag, use of abusive language; variation of bullyrag (see below).

Bollaireacht (*pron.* bullairaċt) *n.*, (*act of*) bragging, prating, babbling, blustering. (Ó Dónaill, 124.)

Baloney, *al.* **boloney**, *n.*, nonsense, pretentious talk; bunk, worthless talk. (Chapman, 1986, 14; *DAS*, 1960, 51.)

Béal ónna (*pron.* bæl óna), silly loquacity, foolish talk; blather, blarney; stupid gossip. **Béal** (*pron.* bæl), *n.*, mouth, talk, speech, rumor, blather, talkativeness. **Ónna** (*pron.* óna), *indec. adj.*, silly, simple, foolish, stupid. (Dineen, 821.)

Barnhart's *Dictionary of English Etymology* derives verbal **baloney** from Italian *bologna*, "reputed to be stuffed with asses' meat from Bologna, a city in Italy where these sausages are made..." (Barnhart, 1988, 73.) This is a canard and an insult to the sausage makers of Bologna.

> ERIE SMITH: He liked to kid himself I'm mixed up with the rackets. He thought gangsters was romantic. So I fed him some **baloney** about a highjacking I done once... (Eugene O'Neill, *Hughie*, 1959, 283.)

(See: O'Rahilly, *óinmhid*, ***ónna***, *amaid*; *Ériu* 13, 1942, 149–52, 218. Notes, mainly etymological, #5; *Focail as Irisleabhair Éagsúla* 7rl, Seán Ua Súilleabháin; óinmhid; *Ériu* 13, 149, óinmhid, **ónna**, amaid, amadán.)

Banana *n.*, a comedian, especially in burlesque and vaudeville; the headlining comedian was called the "top **banana**," second billed the "second **banana**," etc. The *Dictionary of American Slang* suggests the term was derived from phallic-shaped bladder clubs used by the comedians to whack each other over the head. (*DAS*, 1960, 18.)

Baothán nathánach (*pron.* bíhán nahánəċh, bæhán nahánəh), a saucy fool, a witty simpleton, a fool fond of adages, epigrams, and retorts; a jester; *fig.* a comedian. **Baothán** (*pron.* bíhán), *n.*, a fool, a simpleton, a fop; **nathánach** (*pron.* nahánəċ), *adj.*, saucy, witty, aphoristic, fond of witty sayings. (Dineen, 79, 784; Ó Dónaill, 86, 87, 896, 897.)

"So they made me into a comedian, third **banana**." (Red Buttons, *New York Times Magazine*, Feb. 22, 1954.)

Bannock, *n.*, a homemade loaf or scone.
Bannach (*Irish*), *n.*, an oatmeal cake. **Bannag** (*Scots-Gaelic*), *n.*, a Yule cake. (Dineen, 77; Dwelly, 66.)

When I visit my Canadian mother-in-law on Vancouver Island for the holidays, she often makes **bannock** bread.

Banshee, *n.* an Irish female spirit whose howls and wailing often presage a death in a family.

Bean sí, *al.* **bean sidhe** (*pron.* b'an shee), a fairy woman; a woman from the fairy mound.

> MARY TYRONE: That foghorn! Isn't it awful...?
> CATHLEEN: It is indeed, Ma'am. It's like a **banshee**... bad cess to it.
> (Eugene O'Neill, *Long Day's Journey Into Night*, 1939, 21.)

Bard, *n.*, a poet.

Bárd, bard, *n.*, a poet, a bard, a rhymer; a scold.

> Professor MacBain the Gaelic etymologist derives Scots-Gaelic *bard* from "Irish *bárd*, Early Irish *bard*, cognate with Welsh *bardd*, Breton *barz*, Gaulish *bardos, bardo-s*... a poet." (*MacBain's Gaelic Etymological Dictionary*, 1896, [1982]; Dineen, 80; Dwelly, 69.)

Beak, *n.*, a judge, a magistrate.

Beachtaí, beachtaire, *n.*, a critic; a correcting, captious, judgmental person; *fig.* a judge. **Beacht**, *al.* **beachd** (*Gaelic*), *n.*, judgment, opinion.

> **Beak** as slang or cant for a judge was already hundreds of years old in 1859, when the Warden of New York City's Tombs (prison), George Matsell, published his underworld dictionary, *Vocabulum: the Rogue's Lexicon*. Much of Matsell's underworld dictionary is copied from older English slang and canting dictionaries like Francis Grose's late-18th century *Classical Dictionary of the Vulgar Tongue*.

Beat, to **beat**, *v.*, *n.*, to rob, cheat, or swindle someone; to be robbed or cheated. In poker a "bad **beat**" is a very bad loss. Also, a moocher, a loser, a cheat, a thief, a "**beat** artist." A "dead **beat**," is a worthless person; a loser; (*post-1945*) a hipster. (Goldin, O'Leary, 24, 25; *DAS*, 25.)

Béad, *n.*, loss, injury, robbery, crime; ill-deed; ill-doings, an injury; sorrow; robbed or cheated; flattery; trick; cunning. **Béadan**, *n.*, a forward, pushy person; a petulant, scurrilous, slanderous person; a gossip, a slanderer; *al.* slander; a crime. (Dineen, 85; Ó Dónaill, 93.)

In *The Adventures of Huckleberry Finn*, Mark Twain uses the word "**beat**" to describe the ill-doings, crimes, and sorrows of the world, as well as to describe the two **beat** artists known as the King and the Duke.

"I could swear they was **beats** and bummers..." (Mark Twain, *Huckleberry Finn*, 1885, [1994].)

"Then the people began to flock in, and the **beats** and the girls took seats in the front row at the head of the coffin..." (Twain, *Huckleberry Finn*, 1885, [1994].)

"If they wasn't the **beatenest** lot, them two frauds, that ever I struck." (Twain, *Huckleberry Finn*, 1885, [1994].)

In New York's Irish neighborhood of Hell's Kitchen, in the early-20th century, a "dead **beat**" was a total loser. "She folded the money in her kick, right off the reel. She was dumb struck, but not for long. 'Ah sure, and God bless you,' she said to me. 'I knew I'd get it back.' Which was a damn lie, because they had all been downing me as a dead **beat**." (Richard Butler and Joseph Driscoll, *Dock Walloper: The Story of "Big Dick" Butler*, 1935, 87.)

Herbert Huncke is said to have introduced the word **beat** to William Burroughs, Allen Ginsberg and Jack Kerouac in 1945. Huncke never intended the slang word **beat** to be transcendant. As he said, "I meant **beaten**... the world against me." Huncke's **beat** was the Irish **béad** of "loss, injury, robbery, crime, and sorrow." There was nothing "beatific" about it. (Gilbert Millstein, *New York Times*, Sept. 5, 1957; Steven Watson, *The Birth of the Beat Generation*, 1995; Allen Ginsberg, *Howl and Other Poems*, 1956.)

Beef, *v.*, to blame, to complain to the police or authorities; *n.*, a complaint. **Beefed**, *p.p.*, blamed, accused, complained. (Grose, *Classical Dictionary of the Vulgar Tongue*, 1785, [1811]; Goldin, O'Leary, 1950, 25.)

B'aifirt (*pron.* b'af'ərt), rebuked, blamed, accused, complained; reproached, "beefed." **Ba, b'**, *past & condit. forms of copula*, is. **Aifirt** (*pron.* af'ərt), *vn.*, rebuking, reproaching, blaming; complaining, "beefing."

"To cry **beef**; to give the alarm. They have cried **beef** on us." (Grose, *Classical Dictionary of the Vulgar Tongue*, 1785, [1811].)

Tɪᴍ: Shut up! I ain't got time to listen to your **beefin**." (Eugene O'Neill, *The Web*, 1913, [1988].)

Cʜᴜᴄᴋ: Den she **beefs** we won't be married a month before I'll trow it in her face she was a tart. (O'Neill, *The Iceman Cometh*, 1939, [1954], 616.)

Bees knees (*in phrase*), "it's the **bees knees**," *n.*, something outstanding or new; a fresh new style.

Béas núíosach (*pron.* bæs núísəċ, bæs núísəh), fresh new style, novel manner; *fig.* the new thing. **Béas**, *n.*, style, manner, custom, habit; **núíosach** (*pron.* núísəċ, núísə), *adj.*, new, unaccustomed, novel, fresh, strange. (O'Dónaill, 100, 101, 916.)

Bee's wax (*in phrase*), "mind your own **bee's wax**," meaning "mind your own business." Origin unknown. (*DAS*, 1960, 28.)

Béasmhaireacht (*pron.* beeswəraċt), *n.*, morality, manners, habits. (Ó Dónaill, 100, 101.)

Mind your own **bee's wax** (**béasmhaireacht**, *pron.* beeswəraċt, manners, habits, morality) first became popular in American slang and vernacular in the 1920s. There have been countless wacky tales told to account for its origin. "American women slathering their skin with bee's secretions might sound like a honey of an idea, (but) there's no evidence it ever happened." (*Merriam-Webster Online.*)

When you mind your own **bee's wax** (**béasmhaireacht** (*pron.* beeswəraċt, morality, manners), you are minding your own own *personal* business.

Benny, *n.*, a man's overcoat. **Ben**, *n.*, a vest, a jacket. "Archaic, underworld use." (*DAS*, 1960, 31.)

Báinín (*pron.* bánín), *n.*, a jacket or overcoat made of woolen cloth; any type of overcoat, or jacket.

Báinín was clipped in American vernacular to **benny** or **ben**. It was a common expression for an overcoat in many working class Irish-American families in the first half of the 20th century.

"He got his bit for boosting a **benny**." Also a "benjamin." (Goldin, O'Leary, 1950, 26; Asbury, *Gangs of New York*, 1927, [1998].)

Bicker, *n.*, a loud squabble; a noisy altercation; the sound of bickering; to quarrel loudly and constantly. **Bickerer**, *n.*, a loud quarreler, a screamer, a shouter.
Béicire (*pron.* békirə), *n.*, roarer, bawler, bellower, prater. **Béiceadh** (*pron.* békah), *vn.*, act of screaming, yelling, shouting; a bittern (bird), known for its loud cry. **Béic**, *n.*, yell, shout. **Beucaich** (*Gaelic*), *n.*, roaring, loud noise, roar; yelling, bellowing. (Dineen, 92; Ó Dónaill, 102; Dwelly, 88, 89.)

The *Oxford Dictionary of Etymology* derives **bicker** from Middle English *biker*, of "unknown origin." **Bicker** is (inexplicably) said to be formed in English from Middle Dutch *bicken* to slash. (*Oxford Dictionary of English Etymology*, 93; *Merriam-Webster Dictionary* Online.)

I do not want to be a **bickerer**, but deriving **bicker** from Middle Dutch *bicken*, to slash, is a scream.

"If thou sey nay we two shul have a **bekyr** [*v.r.* byker, biker, bekir, bikre, bykkyr]." (Chaucer, c1385; *OED*.)

Biddy, *n.*, a gossipy woman; a shrew; a name for an Irish servant girl, *ca.* 1858; said by most Anglo-American dictionaries to be from the name Bridget. (*DAS*, 1960, 33.)
Beadaí; beadaidhe (*pron.* b'ad-í), *adj.*, *n.*, saucy, impudent; a flatterer; an impertinent person; a goose. (Dineen, 85; Dwelly, 80.)

In my family an old biddy was an epithet for a gossipy old woman, who wouldn't mind her own beeswax.

Big-Bug, *n.*, a big man, a big buck, a big "shot."
(Big) **Boc**, *n.*, a (big) buck; wag, playboy, rogue, a dashing fellow.

"Starchy clothes—very. You think you're a good deal of a big-**bug**, don't you?" (Mark Twain, *Huckleberry Finn*, 1885, [1994].)

"(Chief Devery) called his party the **Bugs** and some people thought we were loco to buck the Tiger." (Butler, Driscoll, *Dock Walloper*, 1933, 49.)

"Irish *boc*, he-goat, Old Irish *bocc*, Welsh *bwch*, Cornish *boch*, Breton *bouc'h*, *bukko-s*; Sanskrit *bukka*, goat; cognates, Armenian *buc*, lamb, English *buck*, German *bock*." (*MacBain's Gaelic Etymological Dictionary*, 1896, [1982], Sec. 4.)

Big Onion, *n*., a moniker for New York City.
(Big) **Anonn** (*pron.* ə'non), *n*., (big) beyond, far side. (Dineen, 47, 48.)

NYC was the "big beyond" to millions of Irish immigrants, who journeyed **anonn** tar aigéan (*pron.* ə'non tar ag'én), across the ocean to the far side.

"**Big Onion** Walking Tours offers tours of New York City, including...Irish New York. Explore the former 'Little Ireland' district of the Lower East Side, between City Hall and Houston Street... Stops include: the founding site of the Ancient Order of Hibernians, Al Smith's childhood home, the former Five Points..." (http://www.bigonion.com/schedule/)

Big **Shot**, *n*., a very influential, important person, often used ironically.
(Big) **Seód** (*Gaelic*), **Séad**, **Seád** (*pron.* shód, sh'æd, sh'ád), *n*., a jewel; *fig.* a (big) chief, a warrior, a hero, a valiant person. (Dwelly, 808; Dineen, 998, 999.)

> Hughie: I told him I knew all the **big shots.** Well, so I do, most of 'em to say hello, and sometimes they hello back. (Eugene O'Neill, *Hughie*, 1940, 283.)

"I was working at Tom Anderson's Cabaret—located on Rampart... Lots of Big **Shots** from Lulu White's used to come there..." (*Louis Armstrong, In His Own Words*, 1999, 33.)

Billy, billy club, *n*., a policeman's club. In the early-19th century a **billy** was a highwayman's bludgeon; later it became a name for a cop's nightstick. Many Anglo-American dictionaries derive the word **billy** from the nickname for William.
Buille (*pron.* bil'ə), *n*., blow, stroke, hit, whack; **buille** de bhata (*pron.* bili de wata), blow of a club; **builleach**, *adj.*, striking, smiting, beating.

Bata **builleach** (*pron.* bata bil'əaċ, bata bil'əah) is a hitting club, a beating bat, a striking, smiting stick, a **billy** club.

"The foremost villain broke down her guard with a short iron crowbar, or '**billy**' as the burglars term it." (Ned Buntline, *Mysteries of New York*, 1848.)

"Eight men set upon a policeman this morning, taking his revolver and **billy** away from him." (*New York Times*, Sept. 11, 1903.)

Bird, a **bird**; the **bird**, *n.*, an excellent, extraordinary thing. "Anything admirable or excellent may be spoken of as a **bird**." (George Krapp, *Modern English: Its Growth and Present Use*, 1909.) This usage is rare today. Sadly, the once extraordinary **bird** (or **boid**) has been reduced to a mere "raspberry," or Bronx cheer.

Beart, *al.* **beirt** (*pron.* b'art, b'irt), *n.*, a great deed, an admirable feat, an exploit, an action, a plan; a prank, a trick, a joke, a gag, a spoof, sport. **Beartaire**, *n.*, a trickster, a prankster.

"The morning game was a '**bird**'—the best of the season, in fact. The Seals delivered the only tally in the twelfth round. The fans in the stand and bleachers were burning up with joy and excitement." (*San Francisco Call*, April 7, 1913.)

"Big Bill" Devery was a Tammany big shot who had been NYC's Chief of Police in the 1890s. Devery's top slugger was another big galoot named "Big Dick" Butler, who wrote about Devery in his 1932 autobiography, *Dock Walloper*.

In 1902, Chief Devery had broken ranks with his old cronies in Tammany Hall and ran for the Assembly as an independent in the Irish longshore neighborhoods along Manhattan's lower west side docks. "Big Bill" Devery had made a lot of money while chief of police and he spent it like a drunken sailor to win votes. Mammoth river excursions and beer barbecues were arranged at a cost of thousands of dollars. The biggest political excursion in the city's history left the foot of West Twenty-fifth street one hot July day (in 1902). There were nine boats in the fleet, two steam propeller boats... and six triple-deck hay barges and a noisy tug, all lashed together and loaded down with 18,000 women and children... The top heavy barges were linked together by gangplanks, forming a pontoon

flotilla five hundred feet wide. Talk about your Cleopatra's barges...
When "Big Bill" Devery was asked by reporters to comment on his grand
party, he said, "It certainly was a **bird**. Yes, it was a **lulu**."
(Richard Butler and Joseph Driscoll, *Dock Walloper: The Story of "Big Dick"
Butler*, 1933.)

The **bird** (**beart**) could be a trick or prank, as well as a great feat. In the 1880s,
actors like James O'Neill would say "the **bird** is there," if a noisy, heckling
prankster was in the audience.

"Give him the **boid**, feller—the raspberry!" (Eugene O'Neill, *The Hairy Ape*,
1921, [1954], 243.)

Block, *n.*, a city street, a city road.
Bealach (*pron.* b'alaċ), *n.*, a road, a path, a way, a passage, a thoroughfare.

If someone has "been around the block," it means they are street-smart.

Up until the mid-19th century most of New York's population lived below
Canal Street, where the **block** (bealach, *pron.* b'alaċ, a road, a path) was often
part of a tangled weave of paths and old Indian trails that had been paved
over and turned into the city's streets. There was nothing "blockish" about
them.

Blow, *n.*, The *Oxford Dictionary of Etymology* defines **blow** as "a hard stroke with
a fist or weapon" and traces its emergence in English to the 15th century.
Unknown origin. (*Oxford Dictionary of English Etymology*, 101,102.)

In American standard usage and slang, the word **blow** has a wide variety of
meanings. **Blow**, *n.*, a hard stroke with the fist; a shock or disaster; *v.*, to treat
someone to a drink or meal; to lose something in defeat; to spend or lose
money quickly or unnecessarily; to defeat; a command to leave, to depart;
to play a musical instrument; **blowing**, *vn.*, going away, departing, leaving;
treating; losing money; playing music. (*ODEE*, 102; *DAS*, 45.)

The Irish verbal noun **bualadh** (*pron.* búŏl-ŭ, striking, beating) is the origin
of both the Standard English and slang word **blow** and encompasses all of
its various definitions.

Bualadh (*pron.* búŏl-ŭ), *vn.*, (*act of*) striking, beating; starting; departing, going; strolling; proceeding, advancing; striking course; rushing; calling in; defeating, beating, winning (*as in a game of cards*); surpassing; clapping, laying or slapping down (*as money on a bar or table*); *fig.* treating; playing music. (Dineen, 134–35; Ó Dónaill, 151–54.)

In Eugene O'Neill's play *Anna Christy*, set in the dockside slums of lower Manhattan around 1910, Matt Burke, an Irish seaman, invokes the **blow** of a fist.

> Matt Burke: (*fiercely*) ...And each time I'd be hitting one a clout in the mug, it wasn't his face I'd be seeing, but yours, and me wanting to drive you a **blow** would knock you out of the world where I wouldn't be seeing or thinking of you. (O'Neill, *Anna Christie*, 1922, [1954], 70.)

Marthy is a street-wise old dame, who knows when it's time to **blow** (**bualadh**, *pron.* búŏl-ŭ, depart).

> Marthy: I'm gonna beat it down to the barge, pack up me duds, and **blow**. (O'Neill, *Anna Christie*, 1922, [1954], 19.)

In *The Iceman Cometh*, a "stool pigeon" named Parritt uses **blow** to mean "treating," as in "slapping down" money on a bar for drinks.

> Parritt: sNix! All you guys seem to think I am made of dough. Where would I get the coin to **blow** everyone? (O'Neill, *The Iceman Cometh*, 1939, [1954], 595.)

When a band hits it, the drummer, bass, and guitar player **blow** (bualadh, *pron.* búŏl-ŭ, play music) as much as the horns. You don't need breath to blow hot jazz. Ag **bualadh** ar an veidhlín agus ar an bpíb (*pron.* eg búŏl-ŭ ar an viɣlín agus ar an bíp) means "playing music on the violin and the pipes."

When millions of people were forced to **blow** Ireland, they took their ancient language with them and **blew** to the crossroads of the world.

In his *Gaelic Etymology of the Languages of the World*, published in Edinburgh in 1879, Charles Mackay derived the mysterious word *blow* from the Scots-Gaelic *buille* and the Irish verb *buail* and its verbal noun, *bualadh*. Mackay's Gaelic etymological dictionary was dedicated to the Duke of Edinburgh, who had sponsored and financed it. But, a few **blows** from the Irish Fenian movement in the 1880s, and Mackay's thesis of a substantial Irish and Gaelic influence on English was out of the question—like Irish Home Rule.

Blow (2), *v.*, to snitch, to inform on someone, to "squeal."
Béalú (*pron.* bæl-ú), *vn.*, (*act of*) speaking about; gossiping; *fig.* snitching.

Ni'l duine sa pharróiste ná go mbíonn sí ag **béalú** air (*pron.* ní'l din'ə su fŭr-ósh-tĭ ná gu mínn shí əg bæl-ú er'), there is no one in the parish about whom she does not gossip." (Dineen, 87, 88.)

"Blamed if I trust you. What if you was to **blow** on us..." (Mark Twain, *Huckleberry Finn*, 1885, [1994].)

Blowen, *n.*, the mistress of a thief; the sweetheart of a gangster.
Bláthán (*pron.* bláhán), *n.*, small flower, little blossom; *fig.* a pretty girl; a term of endearment for a young girl. Bláth bán na finne, the white blossom of fairness. *Al.* bláth, bláthanna. (Dineen, 101; Dwelly, 100.)

"**Blowen**, a prostitute; a woman who cohabits with a man without marriage." (J.H. Vaux, *Flash Dictionary*, 1812.)

"With black-eyed Sal (his **blowing**)." (Byron, *Don Juan*, 1823.)

Blowen as a word for a pretty girl first appears in Awdeley's cant dictionary in the 1560s and can be found in all major English and American slang dictionaries.

Blowhard, *n.*, a loudmouth; a loud speaking person.
Béalú h-ard (*pron.* bæl-ú hard), loud speaking; loud mouthing; *fig.* a loud mouth. **Bealú**, *n.*, act of speaking about, talking, gossiping. **Ard**, *adj.*, loud. A **blowhard** (**béalú h-ard**, loud talking) is a loud mouth personified.

Boiler room, *n.*, a collection agency
Bailitheoir (*pron.* bal'ihór), *n.*, collector; collection. **Bailitheoir** cánách (*pron.* bal'ihór cánáċ), tax collector, fiach **bailitheoir** (*pron.* fíẏċ bal'ilhór), debt collector.

A **boiler** room is an office of debt collectors, working the phones for a collection agency. The term *boiler room* today is applied to any high pressure phone solicitation or collection outfit.

"Legs" Diamond and his brother, Eddie, got their start working as teenage collectors for the **Boiler** (**bailitheoir**, *pron.* bal'ihór, collector) Gang in Philadelphia. (T.J. English, *Paddy Wacked: The Untold Story of the Irish-American Gangster*, 2005, 129.)

Boob, booby, *n.*, a nincompoop, a cry-baby, a loud-mouth dolt. Doubtful origin. (*OED.*)

Búb; búbaí, búbaire; búbán, búbail, *n.*, *vn.*, bellow, roar, yell; a person that blubbers, a booby, a coxcomb, a bittern bird; roaring, bellowing, blubbering, yelling. (Dineen, 136; Dwelly, 137; Ó Dónaill, 155.)

Chapman's *American Slang* derives the loud **boob** from a German dialect word *bubbi*, meaning a woman's breast. (Chapman, *American Slang*, 38.) But breasts do not blubber like boobs.

"Cry, you great **booby**." (Fletcher, *Customs of the Country*, 1616; *OED*.)

YANK: Shut up yuh lousy **boob**. (Eugene O'Neill, *The Hairy Ape*, 1921, 24.)

ERIE SMITH: ...and the poor **boob** never stood a chance. (Eugene O'Neill, *Hughie*, 1940, 278.)

"Only **boobs** and shitheads rooted for Nixon in his troubled time..." (William Kennedy, *Legs*, 1975, 216.)

Booby hatch, *n.*, a home for the insane; a lock-up or jail.

Búbaí háit (*pron.* búbí átch), a place of bellowing boobs; *fig.* an insane asylum. **Búbaí, búbaire**, *n.*, a booby, a person that blubbers and howls (*like a crazy person*). **Áit** (*pron.* átch), *n.*, a place, locality, site, room, locale. (Dwelly, 137; Ó Dónaill, 155; Dineen, 136.)

"If any of my friends heard you, they'd say you belonged in the **booby hatch**." (James T. Farrell, *Young Lonigan*, 1938, [2004], 167; *DAS*, 1960, 53.)

"At that time King Bolden cut hair in the **booby hatch**..." (S. Longstreet, *The Real Jazz Old and New*, 1956, 11.)

Boodle, boodling, *n.* bribe money; *vn.*, bartering votes, influence, and access for money. Boodle is also slang for counterfeit bills or misappropriated money. Origin and history obscure. (*OED*.)

Babhtáil (*pron.* baut'ál), *vn.*, (*act of*) swapping, bartering, exchanging; misappropriating; cúblaidhe (*pron.* coobliɣə), *n.*, a boodler, an intriguer. Cúblálaim, *v.*, I misappropriate, I pick up, I boodle. (Dineen, 280.)

"A CLEAN SWEEP—Wholesale Arrest of **Boodle** Alderman." (*Brooklyn Eagle*, April 13, 1886, 1.)

"**Boodle** at the Capitol (*Albany Journal*): '**Boodle** is the grease as makes bills slip through the legislature as smoothly as this elevator does through a shaft.'" (*Brooklyn Eagle*, April 1, 1883, 1.)

"He is our machine, tireless and fearless. He has X-ray eyes, and can look right through a candidate and see whether he is a **boodler** or not." (Wendt & Kogan, *Lords of the Levee*, 1943, 143.)

Boogaloo, *n. & v.*, a 1960s dance performed with fast swiveling shuffling movements of the body; to dance; to move fast. Origin uncertain. (*OED*.)

Bogadh luath (*pron.* bog'ah lúō or bug-ŭ lúō), moving fast; moving quick; fast rocking. **Bogadh** (*pron.* bug-ŭ, bog'ah), *vn.*, (*act of*) moving, stirring; loosening; rocking. **Luath** (*pron.* lúÿ), *adj.*, quick, fast, speedy; chomh **luath** le giorria, as fleet as a hare. Níl **bogadh luath** ann (*pron.* neel bug-ŭ lúÿ ann), he is unable to move fast. **Bogadh luath** as áit (*pron.* bug-ŭ lúÿ ass atch), to move fast out of a place; to boogaloo out of a joint.

"After a person has outfitted himself at one of the 27 psychedelic shops... he is ready to dance the **Boog-a-loo** at Cheetah, a New York nightspot. (*Dictionary of American Regional English*, 1967.)

"The fugitive dealer, who was the passenger in Frankie '**Boogaloo**' Mulholland's jeep when the (Belfast) cocaine dealer was lured into a UFF/LVF trap last December, had been on the run for over six months." (High Court of Justice in Northern Ireland, Nov. 2002.)

Boogy, *v.*, *n.*, to dance; to move, to shake. Boogy music. Origin unknown.
Bogadh (*pron.* bug-ŭ, bog'ah), moving, stirring, shaking, rocking.

Níl **bogadh** ann (*pron.* neel bog-ah ann), he can't boogie (move).

Cliabhán a **bhogadh** (*pron.* klĭŏ-wán a wogah), rocking a cradle.

The words **boogaloo** and **boogie** may be Irish; but the **boogie** (**bogadh**, *pron.* bog-ah, moving, shaking, rocking) is charged with African-American **jazz** (**teas**, *pron.* j'as, ch'as; heat, passion, excitement.)

Booly dog, *n.*, a policeman. (George Matsell, *Vocabulum*, 1859, [1997]; Herbert Asbury, *Gangs of New York*, 1927, [1998], 350.)
Buailteach (*pron.* búĕl-t'aċ), *adj.*, (*someone*) disposed or given to striking, whacking, or beating; *fig.* a policeman. (Dineen, 134.)

In Peter Quinn's novel, *Banished Children of Eve*, set in New York City in July 1863, a young reporter in search of a story needs a translator to understand the Irish-American vernacular of the time.

"Our guide spoke first: 'Now listen hear, I'm not out to **flog** (**fliuch**, *pron.* fl'uc, wet, rain; *fig.* piss on) old man Dunne's ground sweat (**grian suite**, sunny site; *fig.* a gravesite) let him and all the faithfully departed, as they sez, rest in peace, but to listen to all the talk you'd think it was some saint that died instead of a kiddie who stuffed the rhino (money) and set hisself up in business before the **booly dogs** could lay a hand on him.'" (Peter Quinn, *Banished Children of Eve*, 1994, 7.)

Boondoggle, *n.*, a trivial, useless, or unnecessary undertaking; wasteful expenditure. Origin uncertain. (Barnhart, 107.)
Buan-díchiall (*pron.* búōn-d'iċíŏll), *n.*, permanent-folly, perpetual-foolishness. **Buan-**, *pref.*, permanent-; perpetual-. **Díchiall** (*pron.* d'iċíŏll), *n.*, folly, lack of sense, foolishness, humbug; *al.* **dí-chéillidhe**, **díchéillí**, **díth-céille**.

"In the 1936 presidential election, **boondoggling** became the term for describing the waste…in New Deal government agencies and bureaus. Administrators of relief became **boondogglers** to the Republican press…" (*Amer. Speech XII*, 1937.)

"Nixon and the arms race: the bomber **boondoggle**." (*New York Review of Books*, Jan. 2, 1969.)

Boot, *n.*, what is given in exchange on terms of boot, swapping.

Babhta (*pron.* boutŭ), *n.*, what is given in exchange on terms of "boot;" swap, trade. Thing exchanged. (Dineen, 67; Ó Dónaill, 73.)

Booze, *n.*, whiskey, aqua vita. **Bowse, bouse**, *n., v.*, a drink; to drink. *Cant.* Uncertain origin.

Beath-uisce, beathuisce (*pron.* b'ah-ishkee; (*Eng.*) baewhisky), *n.*, aqua vita, whiskey. The word booze is derived from a contraction of **beathuis[ce]**, *pron.* b'ah-ish-, (*Eng.*) baewhis-, water of life, whiskey.

Most dictionaries derive the word **booze**, and the older **bouse, boose, booz, bowse**, etc., from a medieval Dutch word *busen*, meaning to drink to excess, which is related to an obscure German word *bausen*, with the same sense. There are no modern Dutch or German words resembling *busen* or *bausen*, except the German *busen*, a woman's bosom.

Booze, as **bouse, bowse, booz**, and **boose** meaning "to drink," begins to appear in the mid-16th century as a word of vagabond cant. In 1566 Crown magistrate Thomas Harmon published one of the earliest known cant dictionaries: *Caveat or Warening for Common Cursetors Vulgarely Called Vagabones*, a handbook for Counstables and Bayliffes that records the strange vernacular spoken by bands of itinerant vagabones, who had begun proliferating in great numbers across the English countryside. The Irish were identified by Harmon as forming a significant part of these vagabond groups. (Maurizio Gotti, *Lexicographica, The Language of Thieves and Vagabonds*, 17, 20, 2001.)

Boss, *n., adj.*, a person or thing regarded as the best. A chief, the person in charge. (Chapman, *American Slang*, 1987, 40, 41.)

Bas, *n.*, boss; best, very good. Is é **bas** é (*pron.* iss ay bas ay), it is the best; there is nothing to beat it. (Ó Dónaill, 90.)

Boss as a slang term for best or good became popular in the 1960s. But **boss** (**bas**, best) was old when the King and the Duke drifted down the Mississippi River with Huck Finn and Jim in the 1840s.

> "Good land, duke, lemme hug you!... Oh this is a **boss** dodge, ther' ain't no mistake 'bout it!" (Mark Twain, *Huckleberry Finn*, 1885, [1994].)

Bounce, *v.*, to remove someone from a premises; to eject someone. Uncertain origin. (*OED*.)

Bain as (*pron.* ban'as), *v.*, to extract out of; to remove from, to eject, to extract from.

> McGLOIN (*contemptuously*): They'd take one look at you and **bounce** us both out on our necks. (O'Neill, *The Iceman Cometh*, 1939, [1954], 681.)

"**Bounce**. To bully a man out of anything. To remove people from the premises." (Grose, *Classical Dictionary of the Vulgar Tongue*, 1785, [1811]; Matsell, *Vocabulum*, 1859, [1997].)

"The kiddie **bounced** the swell of the blowen." (Grose, *Classical Dictionary of the Vulgar Tongue*, 1785, [1811].)

Boyo, *n.*, a term of affection for a young man.

Boy Ó, *n.*, dear boy, a bi-lingual appellation and term of affection. **Ó**, a term of affection, a mhic ó (*pron.* a vic oh), my dear fellow. (Dineen, 802.) A boyo is a **bucko** (**boc ó**).

Bozark match (*carnival slang*), *n.*, a women's wrestling or boxing match.

Basóg, *n.*, a slap, a slight blow with the open hand. **Bas**, *n.*, hand, palm of hand; **-óg**, *diminutive suffix.*

Bozark matches in carnivals were an excuse for men to ogle female flesh, much like mud-wrestling contests. Today, women's boxing is no **bozark** match, but a dead serious business.

Brace joint, brace game, *n.*, a crooked gambling house; a "bust out" game.

Beir as (*pron.* b'er ass), make off, take off; *fig.* steal. In a crooked **brace** game you take off the mark and make off with the **moolah** (**moll óir**, pile of gold or money).

Brag, *v.*, to boast, exaggerate, or lie; *n.*, the name of an early card game related to poker. Origin uncertain. (*OED.*)

Bréag (*pron.* b'ríŏg), *n.*, a lie, an exaggeration, a deceit, a deception.

Bréag (*pron.* b'ríŏg) is the simple solution to the orgin of the word **brag**. **Brag** became popular in the early-19th century as the name for a short card game resembling poker. **Brag**'s influence on poker was so great that it was often called "the **brag** game." In the early forms of **brag**, the jack of clubs and the ace and nine of diamonds were wild and called **braggers**. The key endeavor of the **brag** game, as described in Seymour's *Court Gamester*, published in 1719, was " to impose on the judgment of the rest who play... by boasting or **bragging** of the cards in your hand."

The *Barnhart Dictionary of Etymology* speculates that the word **brag** might "possibly" have an Irish origin, though inexplicably links it to a Celtic word meaning trousers: "brag...of uncertain origin; possible sources include Gaullish or Celtic 'braca,' (a) kind of trousers..." Barnhart also cites Provencal, French (Swiss dialect), Scandinavian, and Old Icelandic as other possible sources of **brag**. (*Barnhart Dictionary of Etymology*, 1988, 112.)

Well into the late-19th century **brag** was considered slang in American English. The underworld slang lexicologist and warden of New York City's Tombs prison, George Matsell, included **brag** in his *Vocabulum: The Rogue's Lexicon*, defining it is a "boast." Professor MacBain, the Gaelic etymologist, derives the Irish word **bréag**, meaning "a lie, exaggeration, deceit, deception," from Old Irish *bréc*, and relates it to the Sanskrit *bhramca*, a deviation. (*MacBain's Gaelic Etymological Dictionary*; Matsell, *Vocabulum*, 1859, [1997].)

Bragger, *n.*, someone who brags, exaggerates, and lies.

Bréagóir, breagaire, *n.*, a liar, a wheedler, a deceiver, an exaggerator; "a narrator of untrue stories." (Dineen, 119; Ó Dónaill, 135, 136.)

Brat, *n.*, a mischievous young child.

Brat, *n.*, a rag, a garment, an article of outer clothing that may be laid aside; *fig.* an improvised diaper. **Bratóg**, *n.*, a small cloak, a covering, a swathe. (Dineen, 116, 117.)

The *OED* derives **brat** "from Old Irish *brat*(t)...a covering for the body, plaid, mantle, cloak." The Irish word **brat**, meaning "a rag, a garment," may have been applied to the torn raggedy diapers of poor young children. In my family, a favorite word for young children was "droopy drawers," as well as **brats**.

"Irsche brybour baird, wyle beggar with thy **brattis**." (Dunbar, *ca.* 1505; *OED*.)

Brisk, *adj.*, quick, active, lively.

Briosc, *adj.*, quick; crisp; brittle.

The word **brisk** appears in print in English at the end of the 16th century. Its derivation is uncertain.

"Welsh *brysg* (used of briskness of foot) occurs in a poem of the 14th century. This appears to answer in form to Old Irish *brisc*, Irish, *briosg*, Gaelic *brisg*, Breton *bresk*, 'brittle,' 'crumbly;' but it is not easy to connect the senses." (*OED*.)

"...then they waked up another fellow and told him, and laughed, but he didn't laugh; he ripped out something **brisk** and said let him alone." (Mark Twain, *Huckleberry Finn*, 1885, [1994].)

Bub, *n.*, one that is cheated; to bribe or cheat someone; an old slang word dating from the 17th century. Today **bub** is a familiar, jocular term of address for a young man or boy, short for "**bubba**."

Bob, *n.*, a trick; a confidence trick; an act of fraud; "bhuail sé bob orm (*pron.* wuail shay bub urm), he took me in, played me false. **Bobaire**, *n.*,

a trickster, practical-joker; *fig.* a "wise guy." (Dwelly, 102; Dineen, 104.)

"Well, I shall have to tear myself away from you, **bub**." (Mark Twain, *Roughing It*, 1872.)

Bubba, bubber, *n.*, a thief, a drinker, a trickster. (*Cant*, 17th century.)

Bobaire, *n.*, a trickster, a practical joker; *fig.* a wise guy. (Dineen, 104.)

"A **Bubber**…goes to the Alehouse, and steals there the Plate. (R. Head, *Canting Academy*, 1673.)

Bubba (**bobaire**) is a common nickname in the southern United States, where Irish and Scots-Gaelic have been spoken since the 17th century. Chapman's *American Slang* speculates that **bubba** is derived from the English word *brother*. (Chapman, 1987, 86.)

Buck, *n.*, a strong and spirited young man; a dashing fellow; also a dandy, a fop. Often used as a form of familiar address.

Boc, *n.*, a buck, a wag, a playboy, a dashing young fellow; a he-goat. (Dineen, 104.)

MacBain's dictionary derives **buck** from **boc**, and the Gaelic languages, and thence to a Sanskrit root: *"boc*, a buck, Irish *boc*, he-goat, Old Irish *bocc*, Welsh *bwch*, Cornish *boch*, Breton *bouc'h, bukko-s*; Sanskrit *bukka*, goat." (*MacBain's Gaelic Etymological Dictionary*, 1896, [1982].)

Bucking, buckin'; **bucking** the "tiger." To play against a faro game; to go up against, or defeat (*someone or something*). Origin obscure. (*OED*.)

Buachan, Buchan (ar) (*pron.* búŏċan', búŏċan'ar), *v.*, gain, winning (a victory), defeating, overcoming, going up against. **Buachan** ar dhuine (búŏċan' ar ghinə), to prevail over someone; **buachan** ar rud, to defeat something.

Buckin' or "**bucking** the Tiger" meant to play faro, or to go up against the "tiger" and defeat the house, or faro bank.

"I've been **bucking the tiger,** riding high on his back, and rode the monster into the dust." (Peter Quinn, *Banished Children of Eve*, 1995, 213.)

Bucking contests in late-19th and early-20th century New Orleans were described by Sidney Bechet in his autobiography, *Treat It Gentle*:

> Sometimes we'd have what they called in those days "**bucking contests**;" that was long before we talked about "cutting contests." One band would come right up in front of the other and play at it, and the first band would

play right back, until finally one band just had to give in. And the one that didn't give in, all the people, they'd rush up to it and give it drinks and food and holler for more..." (Sidney Bechet, *Treat It Gentle*, 1960, 63–65.)

But a faro game wasn't the only "tiger" in town to be **bucked**. In New York's Chelsea, Big Bill Devery **bucked** the Tammany Tiger.

"Devery revolted against Tammany and enlisted powerful independents, including myself, on his side. He called his party the Bugs (**boc, boic,** *pl.* playboys) and some people thought we were loco to **buck** the Tiger." (Butler & Driscoll, *Dock Walloper: the Story of "Big Dick" Butler*, 1934, 49.)

Buccaneer, *n.*, a pirate.

Boc aniar (*pron.* boc ĭnĭŏr, buc ĭnĭŏr), *n.*, western playboy or rogue, dashing young man from the west; a playboy of the western world.

Boc, *n.*, a buck, a wag, a playboy, a dashing young fellow. **Aniar** (*pron.* ĭnĭŏr), *adj.*, from the west; western; an ghaoth **aniar** (*pron.* en ghæ ĭnĭŏr), the west wind; an fear **aniar** (*pron.* an f'ar ĭnĭŏr), the man from the west. **Aniar** as Connachta, from Connaught in the west.

All Anglo-American dictionaries derive the word **buccaneer** from an obscure French word *boucanie* meaning "one who hunts wild oxen" and cooks their meat on a *boucan*, or a barbecue, said to be from an unidentified Caribbean Native-American word. (E.B. Taylor, *Early History of Man*, 261; *OED*.)

Buccaneer as **buckaneer** is first found in the canting dictionaries of the 1690s. "***Buckaneers***, West-Indian Pirates... also the Rude Rabble in Jamaica." (B.E.'s *The Canting Crew Dictionary*, London, 1690.)

In the two hundred years between the "Flight of the Irish Earls" in 1607 and the unsuccessful United Irish Uprising of 1798, hundreds of thousands of Irish-speaking soldiers, rebels, and Gaelic aristocrats fled to France and Spain in the largest protracted Irish continental immigration in the early modern period. This multi-generational, mass Irish emigration to France, Spain, and Catholic Europe is known in Irish history as the "Flight of the Wild Geese." The exiled Irish soldiers and sailors of the Wild Geese had shape shifted into **buccaneers** (**boic aniar**, western rogues) of the Atlantic world. The exiled **boc aniar** (**buccaneer**) of Ireland had been "blown" to the Americas on "an ghaoth **aniar**" (*pron.* en ghæ ïníŏr, the western wind) of Atlantic history.

Buckaroo, *n.*, a cowboy, a cattle drover, a roving, wild rogue of the western plains. Buckaroo is said by all Anglo-American dictionaries to be from *bakhara*, a "corruption" of *vaquero*.

Bocaí rua (*pron.* bucæ rúŏ), *n.*, a fierce buck, a rough wild rogue, a wild playboy. **Boc, bocaí,** *n.*, a playboy, a scamp, a buck, a rogue. **Rua,** *adj.*, red-haired, wild, fierce, tough, strong.

Bocaí rua were the wild Gaelic "bucks" of the American prairie. Many of the West's earliest cattle drovers and cowboys were Irish and Scottish.

In Francis Grose's 1785 slang dictionary, *Classical Dictionary of the Vulgar Tongue*, the word **bugaroch** means "comely and handsome" and is said to be "Irish;" perhaps derived from Irish **bocaí ruthagach** (*pron.* bucæ rúagaċ): a dashing, impulsive young buck. (Grose, *Classical Dictionary of the Vulgar Tongue*, 1785, [1811].)

Bud, *n.*, a nickname or form of address for a boy or man; friend, fellow, often used with hostile intent. (Chapman, *American Slang*, 1987, 48.)

Bod, *n.*, a churl, a lout; a lusty youth; **bod** an bhóthair (*pron.* bud en wohŏr), a vagrant, itinerant, tramp, hobo. As a prefix **bod-** in Irish means "big, ungainly; loutish, crude, and unskilled." (Ó Dónaill, 118.)

Buddy, *n.*, a friend, a chum, also a form of address to a boy or man, sometimes with a hostile intent. (Chapman, *American Slang*, 1987, 48.)

Bodach (*pron.* budŏċ, budah), *n.*, a clown, churl, a strong lusty youth.

In Irish a **bodach mór** is a big-wig or a big shot. As an adjective **bodach** in Irish means "strong and lusty;" márlach **bodach** is "a lusty youth." All Anglo-American dictionaries inexplicably derive the words "bud" and "buddy" from the English word *brother*.

Bullyrag, *al.* **ballyrag,** *n.,* bullying speech, loud prating. Etymology unknown.

Bollaireacht (pron. bullar'aċt), *n.,* act of bragging, prating, talking tripe. Bollaire, *n.,* a braggart. In Irish a related word, **bollscaire,** means "a boaster, a bully, a blusterer." (Dineen, 109; Ó Dónaill, 24.).

"Next day (Pap) was drunk, and he went to Judge Thatcher's and **bullyragged** him and tried to make him give up the money..." (Mark Twain, *Huckleberry Finn,* 1885, [1994].)

Bummer, *n.,* a moocher, a bum, a loafer; a loud mouth, a doofus.

Bumaire, bomaire, buimiléar, bumaireach; bum-báille, *n.,* a bum; a braggart; a stupid fellow; a bum; *vn., (act of)* bragging, boasting; a bum-bailiff. (Ó Dónaill, 159; Dineen, 140.)

Bumaire in Irish means a "bragging, loud-mouthed bum;" the kind of person that could "bum" anyone out.

"I could swear they was beats and **bummers...**" Huck here is referring to the King and the Duke, who were **bummers** (**bumaire, bumairí,** braggarts, boasters, bums), as well as loafers—like all kings and dukes. (Mark Twain, *Huckleberry Finn,* 1885, [1994].)

> McSweeney: Dan, he's a **bummer.** (Edward Harrigan, *The Mulligan Guard Nominee,* 1882.)

A **bum-báille** is a "bum-bailiff," or an evicting sheriff, and appears as a "devilish old **bum**" named David in an early-18th century poem by Seán na Ráithíneach.

> Maithim dhon bhás a ndearnaidh d'argain riamh
> Ó threascair an stráille Dáth an **seana-bhum diabhail.**
> I pardon Death all the ravage he ever made,
> Since he has tripped up the lout David, the **old devilish bum.**
> (Seán na Ráithíneach, in Daniel Corkery, *Hidden Ireland,* 1924.)

Bun, *n.,* light alcoholic buzz. A person's bottom or buttocks. Slang; origin unknown.

Bun, (*Irish*), *n.,* bottom, base, foundation.

"A **bun** is a light jag." (R. Connell, in *American Slang,* 52.)

A **bun** is a nice foundation. "Mary was in bed and not feeling so well herself when I staggered in with a nice **bun** on, and the champagne under my arms." (Butler and Driscoll, *Dock Walloper: The Story of "Big Dick" Butler*, 1933, 97.)

I'll grab Ron's or Alan's **buns** sometimes and they're firm and hard." (*American Slang*, 1987, 53.)

Bunk, *n*., contraction of **bunkum**, humbug, long-winded nonsense, a made-up story or tale. **Bunkum**, *al.* **bunk**: empty oratory, humbug, nonsense, tall tales.

Buanchumadh (*pron.* buən ċumə), *n.*, perpetual invention, endless composition (of a story, poem, or song), a long made-up story; *fig.* a shaggy dog tale.

Buan- (*pron.* buən), *prefix*, long-lasting, enduring, perpetual, endless. **Cumadh** (*pron.* kumə), *vn.*, (*act of*) contriving, composing, inventing, making-up; an invention, a made-up story.

"Is iontach an scéal so... nó mura **cumadóireacht** di féin é." "It is a wonderful story... or unless it was pretence and **invention** on her part." (Humphrey O'Sullivan, *Cin Lae Amhlaoibh*, 1827, [1970], 16.)

Níl ann ach **cumadh** (*pron.* neel ann aċ kumə), it is just a made-up story. (Ó Dónaill, 353.)

If it were a very long made-up story, one would say in Irish: níl ann ach **buan-chumadh**, it is just a "long, endless invention or tale." A similar Irish compound, **buanchuimhneach**, means "(*someone*) having a long memory."

The word **bunkum** is derived by all Anglo-American dictionaries from a shaggy-dog tale. As the yarn goes, during the 16th American Congress, a long-winded congressman from Buncombe County, North Carolina, spoke endlessly on a particular bill, while other members impatiently waited to vote. From then on, as the etymological **bunkum** goes, to talk "**bunkum**" meant to speak as endlessly as that long-forgotten politician from Buncombe County. (See: Bartlett, *American Dictionary*.)

Ironically the old congressman from Buncombe County may have been spieling Gaelic **buanchumadh** (*pron.* buən ċumə, a long made-up story, an endless invention) after all. North Carolina had an historic Scots-Gaelic and Irish-speaking population up until the beginning of the 20th century. The jazz musician Dizzy Gillespie's family were African-American Gaelic speakers from North Carolina and Alabama. So Buncombe County may have been the origin of **bunkum** as **buanchumadh** (*pron.* buən ċumə, a "shaggy dog tale"), after all.

"Under an enormous image of (Dizzy) Gillespie beamed on to a wall at Sprague (Hall), Yale music professor Willie Ruff salutes his old friend and explains to the audience how this musical journey began. 'Dizzy used to tell me tales of how the blacks near his home in Alabama and in the Carolinas had once spoken exclusively in Scots Gaelic. He spoke of his love for Scotland...'" (*The Scotsman*, Sept. 25, 2005.)

African-American Scots-Gaelic and Irish speakers were not limited to the American South. The Irish and Gaelic languages are hidden strands of both African- and Irish-American vernacular. Ya' **tuig** (*pron.* dig, understand, comprehend)? **Tuig é nó ná** (*pron.* dig ay no naa, understand it or not). According to both enumerations of the 1870 U.S. Federal census, a significant per centage of the African-American community in New York City was Irish-African-American. Despite all the academic "whiteness" **bunkum** today, at the dawning of the Gilded Age in just a single New York City ward there were hundreds of Irish-African-American families crammed together in the tenements and rookeries of Laurens (W. Broadway), Thompson, Sullivan, and Spring streets, in what is the **swank** (**somhaoineach**, *pron.* sŏ'wænaċ, wealthy, rich) neighborhood of Soho today.

In America the word **bunkum** has been slowly replaced by the abbreviated "**bunk**." But in modern Ireland, the word bunkum is still popular.

"Enough 'one-side-is-as- bad-as-the-other' **bunkum** ...The fact that this both-sides **bunkum** is offered by the great and the good, and the media, under the guise of balance and fairness, makes it all the more sickening. (Jude Collins, *Daily Ireland*, 11/05/2006, 1.)

> Pearl (*stiffly*): De old **Irish bunk**, huh? (O'Neill, *The Iceman Cometh*, 1939, [1954], 635.)

> Yank: You're de **bunk**. Yuh ain't got no noive, get me? Yuh're yellow, dat's what. (O'Neill, *The Hairy Ape*, 1923, [1954], 212.)

> Belle (*angrily*): Aw, can it! Give us a rest from that **bunk**! (O'Neill, *Ah, Wilderness!*, 1932, [1967], 73.)

Burg, *n.*, a town or city.

Buirg, *n.*, borough; *fig.* a town or small city. **Buirgéiseach**, *n.*, a burgess. (Ó Dónaill, 158)

The German word *burg* is derived from Late Latin *burgus*, which is also the source of the word *borough* in English. The Irish **buirg** and **buirgéiseach**, a burgess, may also be derived from *burgus*.

> ERIE SMITH: I don't remember much about Erie, P-a, you understand… Some punk **burg**! (O'Neill, *Hughie*, 1939, 269.)

Buster, *n.*, a fellow, a joker, a roisterer. (Chapman, 56.)

Pastaire (*pron.* pastïrï), *n.*, a joker, a trifler, a cheeky fellow, a brat. (Ó Dónaill, 943; Dineen, 833.)

"Tá **pastaire** mic ag Tadhg ná féachann d'aoinne;" (*pron.* tá pastïrï mic eg' Taig ná fæčann d'ænnə.) Tadhg has a **joker** of a son who cares for nobody. (Dineen, 833.)

Butter and Eggman a wealthy, small-town businessman who tries to act like a big shot when visiting the city. The term **Butter and Eggman** was popularized by the Irish-American nightclub queen Texas Guinan in New York City during the 1920s. (*DAS*, 1960, 81.)

Bodaire an aicme án (*pron.* budirə ən ak'mə án), a debauchee of the noble class; *fig.* a wild upperclass lout. Also, **bodair na aicme án**

Bodaire, *al.* **bodair**, *n.*, a debauchee; a churl, a lout. **Aicme**, *n.*, class; set, clique. **Án**, *adj.*, noble, upper-class, elegant, ritzy. (Ó Dónaill, 16, 43, 118; Dineen, 105; Dwelly, 104.)

In New York City's El Fey Club, in the Roaring 20s, "Texas" Guinan would throw a big **smacker** (**smeachaire**, *pron.* smačïrə, a kiss) to the crowd and holler out her trademark line of "Hello, Sucker!" to some big **butter and eggman** in the joint; while the playwright George S. Kaufman wrote a play in the **butter and eggman**'s name; and Louis Armstrong, the King of Jazz, sang out that fat-cat's moniker in a 1926 hit song.

> **Big Butter and Eggman**
> Transcribed from vocals by Louis Armstrong and May Alix, recorded Nov. 16, 1926.

MAY ALIX: I want my **butter and egg man**, from away out in the west...
LOUIS ARMSTRONG: Now, mama, I'm your big **butter and egg man**!... Now
listen, baby... I'll buy you all the pretty things that you think you need
'cause I'm your big **butter and egg man**
From 'way down in the South...

Button, the name for the dealer in poker. In casinos, where the house controls
the deal, the **button** is indicated by a rotating disc, also called the button.

Beart t-aon (*pron*. b'art æn), (the) one dealing (cards); a dealer. Beart, *al*. beirt
(*pron*. b'art, b'irt), a move, cast; brandish; deal (at cards, or dice). **Aon** (*pron*.
æn), *n*., one.

By Golly, an oath or exclamation.

Bíodh geall air (*pron*. bíÿh g'all er), I'll wager; I'm sure; I'll bet. Bíodh geall le
(go); I'll wager, I am sure that.

"The card-dealer calls upon him to return the 'ticket,' adding, '**By golly**, Sir,
you have beaten me this time...'" (William Fraser Rae, *Westward by Rail: A
Journey to San Francisco and Back and a Visit to the Mormons*, 1871, 187.)

> CHRIS (*eagerly, to Anna*): But ay gat place, Anna—nice place...You don't
> never have to work as nurse gel no more. You stay with me, **py** (*sic*) **golly**!
> (Eugene O'Neill, *Anna Christy*, 1922, [1954], 22.)

C

Caca, *n*., excrement, shit; often used as euphemism in presence of children.

Caca, *gen*. as *attrib. adj*. of **cac**, excrement, filth; *fig*. shit; rud caca, a dirty, shitty
thing. (Dineen, 145.)

The Irish **cac** and **caca** are probably derived from the Latin *caco*, to void
excrement. (*Cassell's Latin-English Dictionary*, 76.) Seamus an **Chaca** (Seamus
the Shit) was the moniker given to James II of England, a royal "chicken"
caca, who abandoned his beleaguered Irish army on the Boyne River in June
1690.

Cadger, *n.*, to go about as a cadger or pedlar, or on pretence of being one; to go about begging.
Caidéir (*pron.* ca'jér), *n.*, a cadger, an idler. **Ceaidé** (*pron.* c'ajé), *n.*, a rambler, a worthless fellow. (Ó Dónaill, 169; Dineen, 173.)

The cant word **cadger** first appeared in print in Scotland. It is also found in J.H. Vaux's 1812 *Flash Dictionary*, meaning "a good-for-nothing who begs," (*ODEE*, 134.)

"**Cadge** the swells. Beg the gentleman." (Grose, *The Dictionary of the Vulgar Tongue*, 1785, [1811].)

Cady, *n.*, a thief, a highway man.
Gadaí (*pron.* gadí), *n.*, a thief.

This old slang word "**cady**," for a highwayman or thief, first appears in print in Jonathan Harrington Greene's *Secret Band of Brothers: A Full and True Exposition of All the Various Crimes, Villanies, and Misdeeds of This Powerful Organization in the United States*, an alleged exposé of the New Orleans-based gambling clans of the early-19th century, published in 1858 in New York City. Greene claimed the secret brotherhood spoke a secret language, which was in fact merely the phonetic spelling of common Irish words like **gadaí**, meaning a "thief."

Cahoot, cahoots, in cahoot, in cahoots, *al* cohoot, *n.*, a company, or partnership; in league or partnership with; to act in partnership. **Cahoots** is also the name for a professional touring children's theatre company based in Belfast. Uncertain origin. (Barnhart, 134.)
Comh-údar (*pron.* cohúdər), *n.*, a co-author, co-originator, co-starter, co-instigator; *fig.* partner. **Comh-údarás** (*pron.* coh-údərás) *n.*, co-authority, co-responsibility, co-instigation; *fig.* partnership.

The *OED* speculates that cahoot might be from the French word *cahute* meaning "a cabin or a poor hut." (*OED*.)

"They all agree to **cahoot** with their claims against Nicaragua and Costa Rica." (*New York Herald*, May, 20 1857; *Bartlett's Quotations* online.)

Can (slang), *n.*, rear end; butt, the human rump.

Ceann (*pron.* k'an), *n.*, (*of person*) end, extremity; rear end.

"Wanting to see him turned out on his **can**..." (James T. Farrell, *Short Stories*, 1946; *DAS*, 86.).

"See this room...a toilet bowl in the corner with a scratched metal lid that freezes your **can** when you sit on it..." (J. McCormick, *Bravo*, 1965; *OED*.)

Cant, *n.*, "The secret language or jargon used by gipsies, thieves, professional beggars, etc." Any jargon used for the purpose of secrecy. (*OED*.)

Caint, *al.* **cainnt** (*pron.* ka'nt'), *n.*, speech, talk, conversation, act of talking, conversation; **cainteoir** (*pron.* ka'nt'ór), *n.*, a talker, a speaker. Ag **caint** Gaeilge, talking Irish; tá **caint** agat! it is easy for you to talk! An-**chaint**, back talk; deagh-**chaint**, wit, clever talk. (Dineen, 149.)

The *OED* derives the word **cant** from the Latin *cantus*, singing, song, but then concedes that "the details of the derivation and development of (this) sense are unknown... some have however conjectured that *cant* is the Irish and Gaelic *cainnt*." It also suggests that **cant** "may be derived from the name of Andrew **Cant** or his son Alexander Cant, Presbyterian ministers of the 17th century..."

Cantankerous, *adj.*, stubborn and quarrelsome (*person*), perverse, cranky; given to opposition, contrarious; difficult to deal with, intractable.

Ceanndánacht ársa (*pron.* k'an danánȧt'ársǝ), old obstinacy, aged willfulness, elderly stubbornness. **Ceanndánacht**, **ceann-dánacht**, *n.*, stubbornness, headstrong, obstinate, willfulness. **Ársa**, *adj.*, aged; old; *al.* an old person.

Cantankerous does not enter the printed English language till the late-1770s. The *Barnhart Dictionary* derives cantankerous "perhaps from the Old North French *contekier*, to touch, feel the hands..." (Barnhart, 140.)

"A crusty old bachelor or ... a **cantankerous** husband." (Livingstone, *Zambesi*, 1865, *OED*.)

Cap, *v.*, to act as an aggressive shill, goading and prodding marks to bet their money in a crooked or "braced" gambling game.

Ciap, *v.*, to harass, annoy, torment, goad.

"To **cap**...To assist a man in cheating. The file kidded the joskin with sham books, and his pall **capped**; the deep one cheated the countryman with false cards, and his confederate assisted in the fraud." (Grose, *Classical Dictionary of the Vulgar Tongue*, 1785, [1811].)

Capper, *n.*, an aggressive shill who goads a mark to bet aggressively; also, a dummy bidder at an auction, who drives the price up with his aggressive bids.

Ciapaire, *n.*, a goader, a teaser, a vexer.

"(Soapy Smith's) '**cappers**,' 'boosters,' and 'shills' fought with the yokels for a chance to get something for nothing and always beat them to the pieces of soap containing the money." (Jack Black, *You Can't Win*, 1926, [2000], 162.)

In a (crooked) **faro** game ruled by the Tiger, a skilled **shill** (**síol**, *pron.* sheel, to seed) seeds the game with the house's **moolah** (**moll óir**, pile of gold or money), while the **capper** (**ciapaire**, goader) goads the **swell** (**sóúil**, prosperous; *fig.* wealthy person) to **guzzle** (**gus óil**, *pron.* gus ól, drink vigorously) and **slug** (**slog**, swallow, gulp) the high class **whiskey** (**uisce beatha**, aqua vita), and **blow** (**buadladh**, *pron.* bŭÿl-oh, slap down, clap down) his **jack** (**tiach**, **tiag**, *pron.* jiaċ, chiag, purse; *fig.* money) with abandon.

Carrying the banner, carryin' a banner: to walk the streets all night for want of a place to sleep. (*DAS*, 89.)

Comhshaoránach bonnaire (*pron.* ko'æránċ bonnirə, ko'æránəh bonərə); fellow-citizen foot-man, fellow-citizen walker, fellow-citizen hobo. **Comhshaoránach** (*pron.* ko'æránəh), *n.*, fellow-citizen. **Bonnaire**, *n.*, a walker, a pedestrian, a foot-man; *fig.* an itinerant or hobo.

"I have '**carried the banner**' in infernal metropolises..." (Jack London, *The Road*, 1907.)

"Emmett looked at the outspoken girl across the table from him. Her eyes were a vivid blue, and her hair a beautiful shade of blonde... (She said), 'I know some of the boys there, and you can get a bed and two meals a day there anyhow. It beats sitting up, or **carrying the banner.**'" (Jim Tully, *Vivian*, 1922.)

Case, case keeper, keeping **cases** (*faro slang*); also, to **"case"** a joint.

Cas, *v.*, to turn, to twist, wind, coil. **Casadh** (*pron.* casah), *vn*, (*act of*) turning, twisting, coiling. Cartaí a **chasadh** (*pron.* cartí a casah), to turn the cards.

Unique to faro was the **case keeper**, an abacus-like device, set within a wooden cabinet with miniature cards painted on to it, matching those on the layout. The Case Keeper allowed the betters to keep track of which card denominations had already been turned out of the deck. It was manipulated by a dealer's assistant, also called a "Case Keeper."

Cas (turn) keeper.

Cas is an Irish verb meaning "to turn, twist, or wind," and its verbal nominative **casadh** (*pron.* casah) means "turning, twisting, winding, or coiling." Two Irish and Scots-Gaelic derived words, **faro** (**fiaradh**, *pron.* fiəroo, twisting, turning) and **case** (**cas**, turn) both mean "turning and twisting" in a faro game where the main move is called the **"turn"** in English. **"Keepin' cases"** in a faro game took a sharp eye and became a popular term for keeping a close watch on someone or something. A variation of **"keeping cases"** which still survives today is the term "to **case**," meaning to check a place out carefully with the vigilance of a "case keeper."

In Eugene O'Neill's first play, *The Web*, written in 1913, a detective **"keeps cases"** on a joint in the slum. "First Plain Cothes Man: ...I'll stay here and **keep cases** on the room. I'm sick of listenin' to that sob stuff." (O'Neill, *The Web*, 1913, [1988], 27.)

> SALESMAN: (*Getting up*) ...Say, I'll go **keep cases** on him—see he gets on the trolley all right, anway... (*He hurries out*). (Eugene O'Neill, *Ah, Wilderness!*, 1933, [1967].)

Keeping cases was shortened to "**case**," with the same meaning. "I began to **case** a place over at Eighth Avenue and Fourteenth Street, one of those scenic corners where there were three banks." (Willie Sutton & Edward Linn, *Where the Money Was: Memoirs of a Bank Robber*, 1976, 306.)

Cheese, "**cheese** it," *v.*, to shut up; to be quiet. *Also*, to run away, to "scram," to flee or escape. "Slang, thieves cant..." (*OED*.)

Téigh as (*pron.* chéy'as), go away from; flee from; get out of, escape. Ná **teigh as** láthair, don't absent yourself. Go out, extinguish, stifle (*as sound*); *fig.* "shut up." (Ó Dónaill, 1224, 1229; Dineen, 1187, 1198.)

In the opening scene of Edward Harrigan's 1878 hit musical comedy, *The Mulligan Guard*, teenage Tommy tells his father, Dan Mulligan, to "**cheese**" or "be quiet" and not bug him about Maggie O'Brien. Tommy secretly intends to elope with the German butcher's daughter, Katy Lochmuller.

> DAN: Maggie O'Brien loves the ground you walk on, Tommy.
> TOMMY: Oh, **cheese—cheese**!
> (Edward Harrigan, *The Mulligan Guard*, 1878, typescript.)

"**Cheese**" (**téigh as**, *pron.* chéy'as, escape) also means to "flee from." James Michael Curley "**cheesed**" the Irish slums of late-19th century Boston and made it to the Massachusetts governor's mansion.

"Ward Seventeen had its rough-and-tumble teen-age gangs who hung around the gashouse or in the square at the end of the street. '**Cheezit**, the cops!' still has a nostalgic ring to me. (James Michael Curley, *I'd Do It Again*, 1957, 35.)

Cheesy, *adj.*, cheap, of cheap material, second-rate; (*someone or something*) cheap, frugal, sparing, stingy.

Tiosach (*pron.* chísəċ, chísəh), *adj.*, thrifty, economical, sparing; *fig.* cheap. Ná bí chomh **tíosach** sin leis an im, don't be so "cheesy" with the butter. (Ó Dónaill, 1240.)

"For a man with 25,000,000 bucks, Wirts certainly lives in a **cheesy** neighborhood." (J.E. Evans, *Halo for Satan*, 1948; *DAS*, 96.)

Chicken; to play **chicken,** *n.*, *adj.*, *v.*, a cowardly person, cowardly; to run away, dodge, or flinch first. In a game of **chicken** two cars speed towards each other down the middle of a road and the first one to swerve out of the way is **chicken.**

Teith ar cheann (*pron.* chih'ər ċ'an): to flee first, to retreat first, to abscond; to run away ahead of (*someone or something*). Most dictionaries derive the slang word "**chicken**" from the feathered fowl.

"You would of been the first to **chicken.**" (Carson McCullers, *The Clock Without Hands*, 1961.)

"The Harvard Student Council... just plain **chickened** out..." (*Cornell Daily Sun*, 1950; *DAS.*)

Chuck, *v.*, **chucking,** *vn.*, to throw, especially to throw or pitch a ball; tossing, discarding. Uncertain origin or onamatopoeic. (Chapman, 71; *OED.*)

Teilg (*pron.* chel'əg), *v.*, to cast, throw, sling; **teilgean** (*pron.* ch'el'əgən), flinging, throwing, tossing, "chucking."

Teilg uait é (*pron.* chel'əg uətch ay), toss it away. **Teilgean** chrú capaill (*pron.* chel'əg'ən ċrú capəl), throwing a horseshoe.

The Irish **teilg** (*pron.* chel'əg, throw) is spelled "chock" when it gets tossed into English slang in the 16th century.

Chucker, *n.*, a pitcher, a tosser (*baseball slang*). Origin unknown.

Teilgeoir (*pron.* ch'el'əgór), *n.*, a thrower, a pitcher, a slinger. (Ó Dónaill, 1227.)

A **chucker** (**teilgeoir,** *pron.* ch'el'əgor, pitcher) slings to a **slugger** (**slacaire,** a batter) while we **root** (**rad, rabhd,** *pron.* rod, roud; rant, rave) for the home team.

"The pitching size-up will have to wait until the **chuckers** can throw a few innings." (Associated Press, April 16, 1956; *DAS*, 104.)

Clack, *n.*, the clapper of a mill; din of speech, senseless chatter; loud talk.

Clag, *v.*, clagadh, *vn.*, clack, clatter; clattering, rattling. **Clagaire,** *n.*, a clacker, a loud noisy talker. **Clagairt,** *vn.*, (*act of*) rattling away at.

Do chrom sé ar an mBéarla do **clagairt**; he began to rattle off English for me. (Dineen, 198.)

The origin often cited for "**clack**" is French *claque*, a clap or blow with the flat of the hand; also Dutch. *klak*, and Middle High German. *klac*, a crack. Perhaps to this Euro-chorus of *claque*, *klac*, *klak*, and *clack*, we can add the clattering **clag** of Ireland and its diaspora? "And the place was plumb full of farmers and farmer's wives... and such a **clack** a body never heard. Old Mrs. Hotchkiss was the worst; her tongue was agoing all the time." (Mark Twain, *Huckleberry Finn*, 1885, [1994].)

Clean a clock, clean his clock, *ph.*, to clobber someone; to defeat totally (in boxing or a fight); to beat with your fists; to knock someone out. (Chapman, *American Slang*, 72.)

Cling a clog, to ring his bell; to hit someone in his head. Cling, *v.*, to ring. A, *poss. pron.*, his, her. Clog, *n.*, bell.

When you **clean** (**cling**, ring) someone's **clock** (**clog**, bell), you clobber them in the head. Most dictionaries are clueless on the origin of this signature Irish-American vernacular phrase, though Chapman's *American Slang* gives it a shot: "probably from clock 'face' and the notion that chastisement is a sort of cleaning, as in clean up on someone." (Chapman, 1986, 72.)

A *Guardian* article by Simon Hoggart mourning the loss of the "Irish joke," due to political correctness, also provides readers with an etymology for the phrase *clean his clock*. "Shoo, or I'll **clean** your **clock**, buddy...'**Clean** his **clock**' means to defeat utterly, and comes from the world of clock-cleaning by way of boxing. It means to completely disassemble an opponent, like someone laying out the clock's component parts..." (*Guardian*, June 10, 2006.)

The "Irish joke" is on Mr. Hoggart, four out of seven words in the *Guardian* headline are derived from Irish. (See: **buddy, shoo, clean a clock**.)

Clinic Kid, *a moniker*. The **Clinic** Kid was one of the most famous confidence men of the early-20th century.

Claonach (*pron.* clǽnaċ), *adj.*, deceitful, perverse, crooked. **Claonach** (crooked) Kid.

David Maurer, linguistics professor and chronicler of the Big Con, derived the **Clinic** Kid's moniker from the Kid's practice of swindling wealthy patients at a "famous mid-western clinic." (Maurer, *The Big Con*, xix, 25.) Health spas and hot springs have always been prized locations for conmen and swindlers. But the **Clinic** (**Claonach**, *pron.* clænać, crooked) Kid's moniker simply means "crooked."

Clout, *v.*, *n.*, to hit or strike a person or object with force. To hit a baseball; steal; smack; influence, "juice," political power. (*DAS*, 111.)

Clabht (*pron.* klaut), **clabhta** (*pron.* klautə), *n.*, a blow with the open hand, a blow, a whack, a hit, a clout; *al.* a clodhopper, a lout. (Ó Dónaill, 236; Dineen 137.)

"Steve Bilko **clouted** a homer in the eighth." (*DAS*, 111.)

Cock-eyed, *adj.*, *n.*, squint-eyed, cross-eyed; also, blind drunk.

Caoch-eyed (*pron.* cæć-eyed), *adj.*, blind-eyed, dim-eyed, squint-eyed. **Caoch** (*pron.* cæć), *adj.*, blind, dim-eyed, squint-eyed; completely "blind," deceived, confused; fear **caoch** (*pron.* f'ar cæć), a squint eyed man, a blind man (*abusive*). **Caoch** (*pron.* cæć), *n.*, a blind, squinting, or one-eyed man. **Caoch-**, **caoich-**, *in compounds*: blind, empty, dim, closed up. (Ó Dónaill, 185, 186; Dineen, 159, 160.)

"**Cock**-eyed drunk" is said to originate in American slang. Bhí sé **caoch** ar meisce (*pron.* ví shay cæć er mesh'kə), he was blind drunk (Ó Dónaill, 185, 186.)

Cold turkey (*slang phrase*), to cut off a drug habit abruptly, without tapering off; applied to any habit which is cut off suddenly. (American slang, 20th century.)

Coillteoireacht, **coillteoireachta** (*pron.* kol'ə'ter'əkt [+ y]), *n.*, (*act of*) cutting off, expurgation; castration.

Conducer (*carny slang*), *n.*, the carnival boss who controls the gimmick or gaff on the crooked gambling wheels and games of chance. A **conducer** awards cheesy (cheap) come-on prizes or "slum" to keep the marks betting.

Ceann-duaiseoir, ceann-duasóir (*pron.* k'an-duəshór, *pron.* k'an-duəsór), *n.*, manager of prize winners. **Ceann-**, *prefix*, manager, head-, chief-, leader-. **Duasóir, duaiseoir**, *n.*, a prize winner, winner of a prize or gift. (Ó Dónaill, 455, 456.)

The **Conducer** controls the "Ikey Heyman" axle, the hidden foot pedal that manipulates and controls the Prize Wheel.

"That **conducer** has plenty of grift sense. He feeds out a lot of come-on prizes, and the suckers love it." (Goldin, O'Leary, *Dictonary of American Underworld Lingo*, 47.) (See: **Ikey Heyman** axle.)

Coon, *n.*, a racist term for an African-American from the middle 1800s; also, a dolt or stupid person, who can be swayed easily. (*DAS*, 1960, 122.)

Cúán, *n.*, a backward, quiet person; *fig.* a hick. (Dineen, 279.)

All Anglo-American dictionaries derive the racist term "**coon**" from the word *raccoon*. Wentworth and Flexner's *Dictionary of American Slang* elaborates with a quote from H.L. Mencken in the *Dictionary of American English*: "...originally from the name of the animal [raccoon] which Southern Negroes were supposed to enjoy eating." The word "**coon**" was used in the 19th century as a word for a simple-minded person of any ethnic group.

Cooze, cooz, coose, *n.*, an extremely vulgar term for a woman; the female genitals; a woman viewed solely as a sex-object.

Cuas, *anat. n.*, a cavity; an orifice, a hole; *fig.* a vagina. "**Cuas**" is an utterly neutral anatomical term in Irish.

In American slang **cuas** spelled "**cooze**" or "**coose**" is an obscene word for a woman or a vagina. Today **cooze** is used primarily as a come-on word for porn sites, which any quick search on Google will confirm.

Cooze was more acceptable in the early-20th century than it is today. The novelist James T. Farrell put "**coose**," in the big **gob** (**gob**, beak, mouth) of the blowhard McGinty in his early novel, *Gas-House McGinty*, set in Chicago in 1914.

"'**Coose** is darb,' McGinty said, roaring..." (James T. Farrell, *Gas-House McGinty*, 1933, [1950], 103.)

Coochie, *n.,* a coochie dancer, a hootchie-coochie dancer, a belly-dancer; also, a "cooch," a bold, promiscuous girl.

Geáitse, geáitsí (*pron.* g'aut'shí), *n.,* antics, unusual gestures, boldness in manner, bold provocative poses. (Dineen, 523.)

A **coochie** (**geáitsí,** *pron.*, g'aut'shí, bold poses and antics) dancer works the "cooch" show in a carnival.

Cop (*Slang*), *n.,* a police officer, a "copper." **Cop,** *v.,* to seize, to grab; to conceive, to think, to suspect.

Ceap (*pron.* k'ap), *n.,* a protector a leader, a chief.

Ceap (*pron.* k'ap), *v.,* to seize, to stop, to catch, to intercept, to grab, to put into stocks or custody; *fig.* to arrest. **Ceapaim,** *v.,* I stop, catch, seize, control; I conceive, think, imagine; I check, restrain, limit, put into stocks or custody; *fig.* I arrest. **Ceap** é (*pron.* k'ap ay), intercept him, catch him, seize him. **Ceapadh** (*pron.* k'ap'ah) *vn.,* (*act of*) seizing, controlling, stopping, catching, putting into stocks, jail, or custody; *fig.* a **copper**; *also,* (*act of*) thinking; thought, idea, notion; suspicion. (Dineen, 178; Ó Dónaill, 209, 210; Dwelly, 180.)

Ceap (*pron.* k'ap) is the simple Irish solution to the sanas (etymology) of the slang noun and verb **cop.** Most Anglo-American dictionaries derive the words "cop" and "copper" from the copper badges said to be worn by police officers in the United States in the 19th century. The main problem with this theory is that there is no evidence that police departments ever issued any copper badges to their cops. In fact, the slang word "copper" was first applied to thieves who **copped** (**ceaptha,** *pron.* k'ap'hə, grabbed) purses and valuables from victims. When a thief was apprehended by the police he was said to be "copped." The Irish verb **ceap** (*pron.* k'ap), means precisely "to seize, stop, catch, intercept, grab," as well as "to put into stocks or custody; *fig.* arrest"

"**Copped**. Arrested." (Matsell, *Vocabulum*, 1859, [1997], 31.)

The Irish noun **ceap** (*pron.* k'ap) means a "protector." Sometimes a **cop** (**ceap**, *pron.* k'ap, a leader, a chief, a protector) offers protection for a price to people who do not want to be **copped**.

"In addition to the big shots of Broadway, we had an off-color mob hanging out there sometimes. The **coppers** would come in and tip me off, and I would run the crooks out." (Butler & Driscoll, *Dock Walloper*, 1934, 93.)

> YANK (*blinking at them*): What the hell...oh, it's you Smitty the Duke. I was
> goin' to turn one loose on the jaw of any guy'd **cop** my dame, but seein'
> it's you—(*sentimentally*)—Pals is pals and any pal of mine c'n have anythin' I
> got, see? (O'Neill, *The Moon of the Caribees*, 1918, 540.)

To **cop** to something also means to think of something or arrive at a notion, idea, or suspicion. **Ceap** (*pron.* k'ap), (*act of*) thinking.

Cove, *n.*, a man, a fellow, a rogue, a fellow-rogue. Still used in Australia.
Caomh (*pron.* cæw, cæv), **caoimhe** (*pron.* civ'ə), *n.*, a friend, a relative; a beloved object. **Caomhach** (*pron.* cæw'aċ, cæv'əh), *n.*, friend, bosom-friend, associate, bed-fellow. (Dwelly, 164; Dineen, 162,163; An Seabhac, 1958, 19.)

Cove is one of the earliest cant words, dating to the mid-16th century. "Coue, or Cofe, or Cuffin signifies a Man, a Fellow, etc." (Thomas Dekker, *Lanthorne & Candle Light*, 1609; Gotti, *Lexicographica*, 29.)

Cuffin, *n.*, man, a fellow. (Grose, *Classical Dictionary of the Vulgar Tongue*, 1785, [1811].)
Caomhán, caomhan (*pron.* cæwán, cæván), *n.*, a friend, a friendly man, a companion, a gentle-person. (Dineen, 163; Dwelly, 164.)

"Queer-**cuffin**. A judge." (Grose, *Classical Dictionary of the Vulgar Tongue*, 1785, [1811].)

Crack, *v.*, *n.*, to boast and brag; exaggeration, lie; brisk conversation, news, fun, amusement, wisecrack.

Most dictionaries, whether English, Irish, or Gaelic, standard or slang, seem to agree that the origin of crack is in Scottish dialect with its ultimate origin obscure. The popular Irish word "crack" meaning "fun, amusement, and good times" is spelled **craic**, but is also said to originate in Scotland.

Edward Dwelly in his *Gaelic-English Dictionary* shows a possible evolution of the word **crack** from **cracaire** and **cnacair**.

"**Cracaire**, -an, *s.m.*, see Cnacair... Cnacair, *m.* Talker, (Scot., cracker.) 2. Cracker. 3. Cracker of a whip. 4. Knocker. Cracaireachd, *San Francisco* see Cnachaireachd, *San Francisco* Conversation, chat." (Dwelly, 216, 217, 259.)

Cracker, *n.*, a poor "white" person in the American South; said by some dictionaries to be short for "corn-cracker."
Cracaire, *n.*, a boaster, a jester, a talker. (Dineen, 255; Dwelly, 216, 217, 259.)

The Scots, Scots-Irish, and Irish of the rural south took pride in the name **cracker** (**cracaire**, a boaster, a jester), which soon became applied to any poor rural "white" person from the southern states. Many slang dictionaries derive the term **cracker** from the use of whips with a piece of buckskin at the end for cracking. It is interesting to note that the Gaelic **cracaire** means "a cracker of a whip," as well as a "jester" and "talker." (Chapman, *American Slang*, 1986, 85; Dwelly, 216, 259.)

"I should explain to your Lordship what is meant by *crackers*; a name they have got from being great boasters; they are a lawless set of rascalls on the frontiers of Virginia, Maryland, the Carolinas and Georgia, who often change their places of abode." (G. Cochrane, *Letter*, June 27, 1766.)

"A number of people called **Crackers**, who live above Augusta, in the province of Georgia, had gone in a hostile manner to...Okonee." (*New York Mercury*, Sept.21, 1767, cited in *Mag. Amer. Hist.* [1878]; *OED.*)

Crank (1), *n.*, a term for a baseball fan in late-19th and early-20th centuries.
Crancaire, (*cont.*. **cranc**[aire]), *n.*, a boaster, a jester, a talker.

"Freedman was the most hated man in the sport... Nobody could work for him. Davis was his fifteenth manager in sixteen years. Hardly any **cranks** (as fans were called till about this time) would travel up to Harlem to see Freedman's (Giants) team play." (Frank Deford, *The Old Ball Game*, 2005, 4, 5.)

The grouchy, cranky "**crank**" is said by Anglo-American dictionaries to be derived from the miserable, vexatious, fretful, peevish, and mysterious adjective "cranky."

Crank (2), *n.*, a cranky, crotchety, grouchy person; an eccentric, monomaniacal person, obsessed with some issue or idea, said by most dictionaries to be derived from "cranky."

Cranky, *adj.*, fretful, ill-natured, annoying, cross-tempered, vexing, very irritable, as in a "cranky" baby or old man, etc. Origin uncertain.

Crá aingí (*pron.* crá'angí): fretful vexing; angry misery, ill-natured torment. Is mór an **crá aingí** iad, they are a terrible ill-natured nuisance.

Crá, *al.* crádh, *vn.*, (*act of*) vexing, tormenting, anguishing, annoying, troubling. **Aingí**, *adj.*, fretful, peevish, cross, ill-natured; wicked, furious. Leanbh aingí (*pron.* lanuw angí), a peevish child; seanduine aingí (*pron.* sh'an'dinə angí), an ill-natured, fretful old man. (*MacBain's Gaelic Etymological Dictionary*, Section 10; Dineen, 255, 256.)

Most dictionaries agree that the adjective **cranky** is a "comparatively modern formation," which only enters the American English language in the early-1820s. (Barnhart, 231; *OED*.) **Cranky** is in fact a modern American word with ancient Irish roots.

Crap, **Crap** Game, **Craps**, *n.*, a dice game.

Crath abair (*pron.* crah' abər; *contraction* crah'ab-), shake say; shake! speak! **Crath** (*pron.* crah), *vn.*, *n.*, shake, shaking; sprinkle; scatter; **crathadh** (*pron.* crahah), *vn.*, (*act of*) shaking. **Abair** (*pron.* abər), *imper.* Speak! Say!

The word **crap** may be derived from the *contraction* of the Irish phrase **crath abair** (*cont. pron.* crah'ab[ər]), meaning "shake say!" In a **crap** game you shake and scatter the dice while shouting out your "point" (the number desired). The word **crap** or craps is a very late arrival in English, first appearing in 1843 in *An Exposure of the Arts and Miseries of Gambling* by the gambler, conman, and reform-huckster Jonathan Harrington Greene.

"The game of **craps** is a game lately introduced into New Orleans, and is fully equal to faro in its ruinous effects." (Jonathan Harrington Greene, *An Exposure of the Arts and Miseries of Gambling*, 1843, 88.)

Croak, *v.*, to murder, to kill; to die; to hang.
Croch (*pron.* croċ), *v.*, to hang, crucify; to execute; to destroy; *fig.* to kill. Duine a **chrochadh** (*pron.* dinə a ċroċə), to hang someone. **Croch**, *n.*, a cross, a gallows. Ar an **gcroch**, on the gallows. **Crocadh** ard chugat lá gaoithe (*pron.* croċə árd ċugat lá gíhə), may you hang high on a windy day. (Ó Dónaill, 320; Dwelly, 275 267.)

> STEVE: ...It ain't any of your business. She's my goil.
> TIM: ...Git outa' here before I **croak** yuh.
> (O'Neill, *The Web*, 1913, [1988], 20.)

"When asked why he did not apply at the County Hospital for aid, the old vagrant replied, 'I got a chance outside, but they'll **croak** me sure there.'" (Jim Tully, *Beggars of Life*, 1924, [2004], 80.)

Croaked, *p.p.*, hanged, executed, killed, murdered, died.
Crochta (*pron.* croċtə), *adj.*, *p.p.*, hanged; crucified; executed; destroyed; *fig.* murdered, died.

"**Croaked**, hanged. A flash term among keepers of prisons, who, speaking of a thief that was executed, observe, 'He was **croaked**.'" (Grose, *Dictionary of the Vulgar Tongue*, 1785, [1811].)

> CORA (*gaily*): Hello, bums. (*She looks around*) Jees, de Morgue on a rainy
> Sunday night! (*She waves to* Larry—*affectionately*) Hello, Old Wise Guy! Ain't
> you **croaked** yet?" (O'Neill, *The Iceman Cometh*, 1939, [1954], 615.)

In England, the penalty for stealing a swell's handkerchief was to be **croaked** (**crochta**, hanged). If you were an Irish patriot—like young Robert Emmett in 1803—the English **crochaire** (*pron.* croċïrə, hangman, executioner) would draw and quarter you after he **croaked** (**crochta**, *pron.* croċtə, hanged) you.

Croaker, *n.*, a doctor or surgeon. (Cant.)

Crochaire (*pron.* cročīrə), *n.*, a hangman, executioner, a gallows' bird, a wretch, a villain; *fig.* (*U.S. slang*), a doctor, a sawbones. Croker, crocus, *n.*, a doctor. (Irish Traveller Cant.)

The **croaker** (**crochaire**, *pron.* cročīrə), a hangman, an executioner was the name for the doctor that the poor could not afford to see until they were already croaking. A "croaker" brought death with him like the hangman.

> NORA: We've no money for doctors. They're bad luck, anyway. They bring death with them. (O'Neill, *A Touch of the Poet*, 1939, [1967], 147.)

"Beat it downstairs and tell the old ghost that a guy's dyin' up here. Tell her to send for a **croaker**." (Jim Tully, *Beggars of Life*, 1924, [2004],15.)

"Don't say '**croaker**'...say 'doctor.'" (Nelson Algren, *The Man With the Golden Arm*, 1951, 94.)

Crony, *n.*, a close intimate friend or associate; a pal, a chum. **Cronies,** *n. pl.*, fellow-friends, mutual pals.

Comh-roghna (*pron.* ko-ronə), *n. pl.*, fellow chosen-ones, mutual-sweethearts, fellow-favorites, close friends, mutual pals.

Comh- (*pron.* ko), *prefix*, mutual, joint, common, co-, fellow-, equal-, close-. **Roghna** (*pron.* ronə), *n.*, *pl.*, chosen ones, choice selections, ones selected, the choicest, favorites, sweethearts; *fig.* "pals." Is é mo rogha é thoghar dam féin, he is the chosen one I selected for myself; rogha grádha, a chosen lover. (Dineen, 908; Ó Dónaill, 1006.)

Crony is said to first appear in English during the Restoration Period, supposedly originating in the gobs of wise-cracking English college swells: "...vox academica...a term of university or college slang..." The most common etymology of "crony" is that it is "a borrowing from the Greek word *chronos*, meaning "time." (OED; *Oxford Dictionary of English Etymology*, 230; Barnhart, 236.)

However, **crony** appears in the 1811 edition of Grose's *Vulgar Tongue* with a decidedly *non-collegiate* definition, placing it firmly in the cant of the underworld. "**Crony**. An intimate companion, a comrade; also a confederate in a robbery." (Grose, *Classical Dictionary of the Vulgar Tongue*, 1785, [1811].)

Much like African-American gangsta' slang, the flash talk of the Irish slums of London's Seven Dials and St. Giles was all the rage with the youth of the English upper- and middle-classes in the 19th century.

Today, under the Bush administration, the word **"crony"** has made a spectacular comeback as a word of the zeitgeist. The "fellow-chosen-ones" of American crony-capitalism have put "confederate in a robbery" back into the definition of **crony**. "Safavian Guilty of Lying, Obstruction of Justice... Federal jury convicts former White House aide; case may embolden prosecutors to seek additional indictments against Abramoff **cronies**." (*Washington Post*, June 21, 2006, A01.)

"Usually, (my grandfather) would be wanting to go down to Carney's saloon... to have a beer or two with his **cronies**. I would sit at at the table behind them, sipping a soft drink, and sooner or later the talk would always get back to the troubles in Ireland." (Willie Sutton, Edward Linn, *Where the Money Was*, 1976, 25.)

Cross, *n*. Almost all Anglo-American dictionaries derive the English noun **cross** from the Old Irish **cros**.

Cros, *n*., a cross; a cross-road; a market place; the haft of a sword; the sign of the cross. **Cros** na Screaptra, the Cross of the Scriptures; an Cros Chéasta, the Crucifix. The Old Irish **cros** is probably derived from the Latin crux. (Dineen, 271; Ó Dónaill, 325; *MacBain's Gaelic Etymological Dictionary*.)

Cross, *v*., (*slang*), to double-cross; to cheat, betray, disobey. To put a **cross** on something or someone in Irish-American vernacular means to curse it. (*DAS*, 131.)

Cros, *v*., *vn*., to cross; the (*act of*) forbidding, affliction, prohibition, misfortune, mischief. (Dineen, 271; Ó Dónaill 325.)

"I was afraid mother would put a curse on my saloon—she called it putting the **cross**—so I gave it to a couple of my friends..." (Richard Butler, Joseph Driscoll, *Dock Whalloper*, 1934, 94.)

Cully, *n.*, a friend, a companion, a confederate.

Cuallaí, cuallaidhe (*pron.* kuəlí, kuəlíə), *n.*, a companion, an associate, a partner. (Dineen, 279; Ó Dónaill, 334.)

The English slang lexicographer Eric Partridge confirms that the word **cully** first appears in 17th century England as a low slang or cant word for "a man, a companion, a mate, a partner." However, he notes that **cully** slowly morphs into slang for "a fool or a dupe." Of course, in the 18th century criminal underworld—like the upper-reaches of 21st century crony-capitalism—one's crony or **cully** (mutual pal, confederate, mate, partner) can quickly become one's dupe or victim. When thieves fall out, a **cully** is a fool who trusts a crony.

Cute, *adj.*, clever, cunning, sly, shrewd, anything clever, a song, a girl, a boy, a trick, a deception, (*something or someone*) attractive in a clever way, with an artistic touch or clever flare. **Cutie,** *n.*, an attractive, clever-looking person; a person who is cunning and shrewd; a clever trick; an upstart; one who thinks himself clever; a smart prize-fighter; anything that is clever; a gimmick, a trick, a sly deception.

Ciúta (*pron.* k'útə), *n.*, a pregnant saying; a clever hit in conversation, a clever innuendo, a clever quip, a wisecrack, an ingenious trick, a "knack;" an artistic touch; know-how; *fig.* someone or something with an attractive, artistic, clever style. (Dineen, 197; Ó Dónaill, 235; An Seabhac, 1958, 21; Kevin P. Scannell, ed., *Corpas Comhthreomhar Gaeilge-Béarla*, 2005.)

Today's **cutie** or **cutey,** from the Irish **ciúta,** applies to anything or anyone that is attractive with a clever touch. "I'm no beauty but am counted a **cutie.**" (Chapman, *American Slang*, 93.)

You can even be a **cute** palooka. "Watching a **cutey** spar with an ordinary dull fighter." (A.J. Liebling, *Back Where*, 1938, 110.)

A real **cutie** always has "the knack" and a clever touch. "*The 'Scandals of '24'* started this **cutie** on the road to fame." (*DAS*, 1960, 136.)

Most Anglo-American dictionaries assert that the word "**cute**" is the apheitc of the English word "acute." (*New English Dictionary*, 1880; OED.) Of course, even a child knows there is nothing "acute" about **cute,** unless you are too cute. "He was going with a girl who had a brother who was very **cute**. Too **cute**, I would say, because he was always playing with a pistol..." (Louis Armstrong, *Satchmo*, 89.)

In 1924, a 19-year-old laundress from Brooklyn—dubbed the Bobbed-Haired Bandit—robbed a string of grocery stores with an automatic pistol, while sporting a **cute** bobbed-hairdo. Celia Cooney's crime spree made headlines across the nation. After the cops arrested her, she was the subject of a whole series of snazzed up stories for the King Features Syndicate. "Ain't I the **cute** little blonde?'" (Stephen Duncombe and Andrew Mattson, *The Bobbed-Haired Bandit: A True Story of Crime and Celebrity in 1920s*, 2006, 135.)

Celia Cooney was **cuter** than most people thought. She served her time, went straight, and raised two sons in Queens, New York as a single mother, without ever revealing to them that she was the **cutie** once known as the "Bobbed-Haired Bandit."

D

Dad, Daddy, *n.*, father; sugar daddy, a wealthy male lover who supports his mistress in return for sexual favors. Origin unknown. (*DAS*, 137, 138; *OED*.)

Daid, daidí, *n.*, father. "The Cladach fisherman in their own locality are called na **daidíní**; *al.* **daidí**." Ní hi gcómhnaidhe mharbhuigheann **daidín** fiadh, it is not every day daddy brings home a deer. (Dineen, 301.)

"My little **Daddy** lovin' all the time." ("Daddy," song, 1912; *DAS*, 137.)

The *OED* opts to reject the Welsh **Tad** and ignore the Irish **Daid**. "It has been assumed that our word (**Dad**) is taken from Welsh **tad**, mutated **dad**, but this is very doubtful; the Welsh is itself merely a word of the same class, which has displaced the original Celtic word for 'father' = Irish '*Athair*.'" (*OED*.)

In fact, the Irish **daid, daidí, daidíní**, and Gaelic **daidein**, Cornish **tat** and Welsh **tad**, are all "chips off the old block" of the Celtic language family.

Gaelic *Daidein*, daddy, Irish *daidín, daid*, Middle Irish *datán*, foster-father, *datnait*, foster-mother, Welsh *tad*, Cornish *tat*; Latin *tata*... Sanskrit *tatás*. "The

English **dad** is borrowed from the Welsh." (*MacBain's Gaelic Etymological Dictionary*, Sec. 12.)

Daddy-O, *n.*, an affectionate address for a man who is hip; *fig.* "Pops."
Daideo (*pron.* dad'əo), *n.*, grand-dad, grandfather. (Ó Dónaill, 362.)

"Big **Daddy-O**'s comin' home." (Tennessee Williams, *Cat on a Hot Tin Roof*, 1958; *DAS*, 138.)

"Hey, all you **Daddy-Os** and Mommy-Os out there! This is Jocko up here in the stratosphere!" (Jocko Henderson, R&B disc jockey, New York City, 1950s, from the author's memory.)

Darb, *n.*, any excellent person or remarkable thing. (*DAS*, 140.)
Daarp (*Irish Traveller Gammon/Shelta*), *adj.*, true, genuine, real.

"Thus little girl was a **darb**, and I was nuts about her." (Jim Tully, *Beggars of Life*, 1924, [2004], 34.)

Dander, *n.*, (*Orig.* U.S, 1830s) an angry temper, as in the phrase "to get your dander up." Barnhart echoes most Anglo-American dictionaries in deriving the mysterious word "dander" from an "...alteration of dandruff." (Barnhart, 251.)
Tintrí (*pron.* tint'ri), *adj.*, fiery, hot-tempered; *al.* **teintridhe**. **Teintidhe** (*pron.* t'ínt'ih), *indec. adj.*, furious. **Tinte** (*pron.* t'in'tə) *n.*, fire; flames; **teintreach** (*pron.* t'ent'r'ah), **tintreach**, *n.*, fire, a blaze or flash, lightning.

Dandruff is flaky, but not hot tempered. It is more likely **dander**'s angry roots are in words of Irish fire and fury like **teintidhe** (*pron.* t'ent'ih), furious, **tintrí** (*pron.* tint'rí), hot-tempered, **tinte** (*pron.* t'in'təh), fire, flames, and **teintreach** (*pron.* t'ent'r'ah), fire, blaze, flash, lightning. When you "get your **dander** up," you don't shed flakes of dandruff; you flash with fire and fury.

Darn, *excl.,* a word of disgust, disappointment, a cursed thing, a light version of damn!

Dothairne (*pron.* dohərnə), *n.,* damned, afflicted; evil, mischief, misfortune; affliction. Also used as exclamation: dith is **dothairne** ort! (*pron.* d'ih is dohərnə ort), bad scran (misfortune) to you!

> **Dothairne** (*pron.* dohərnə) as "**darn**" became a soft word for "damn," as in Gabby Hayes' famous exclamation: "Yer **darn** tootin!"

Dead Rabbit (gang), the alleged name of an Irish-American gang in New York City's Five Points slum in the 1850s. (See: "Gangs of New York Talk Back—in Irish.")

Dead Ráibéad, *n.,* a very big man, a big galoot.

Ráibéad, *n.,* a hulking person, a broad-shouldered, muscular man. **Dead** (*Eng.*), *adj.,* slang intensifier; *fig.* very. "He's a **dead** right kid." (Tully, *The Bruiser,* 1936, 31.)

> "**Rabbit.** A rowdy... **Dead Rabbit,** a very athletic fellow." (George Matsell, *Vocabulum,* 1859, [1997].)

> In Niall Ó Dónaill's *Foclóir Gaeilge-Béarla, Irish-English Dictionary,* published in Dublin in 1977, **ráibéad** (*pron.* rábæd) is defined as a "big hulking person." It is the Irish word **ráibéad** along with the English slang intensifier *dead,* meaning "very," that provide the simple solution to the 150-year-old mystery of the origin of this Irish gang moniker.

> A Dead Rabbit is a "dead **ráibéad**" is a "very big lug."

Dear, *adj.,* costly, expensive. Uncertain etymology.

Daor (*pron.* dær), *adj.,* costly, expensive; severe.

> When I think of the word **daor,** I think of my maternal grandmother, who we called "Nanny." Part Cherokee, mostly Irish, Nanny loved to shop in the kinds of stores she called "Cheap Johns," where nothing was too **daor** (costly, severe). Is **daor** an earra é (*pron.* iss dær en arə ay), it is a dear (expensive) article. (Dineen, 308.)

MacBain takes the Irish **daor**, costly, severe, **daoradh**, making dear, from Middle English *deere*, *deore*, dear, which the *OED* traces back to Old English word *déor*, "of uncertain etymology."

Dick, *n.*, a Pinkerton detective, a private eye, a spy, a plainclothes cop.
Dearc, *n.*, an eye. **Dearcaí**, *n.*, a watchman, a guard.

"Dick" as a slang word for a private "eye" or plainclothes detective became common with the rise of the Pinkerton Detective Agency in the U.S. after the Civil War. The Pinkerton's world-famous logo was the giant "All Seeing Eye." The Pinkerton private "eye" and labor union spy was christened a **dick** (**dearc**, an eye) by the Irish-speaking objects of its gaze: Molly Maguires, Fenians, Knights of Labor, and Wobblies.

> YANK: I know you got to watch your step wit a stranger. For all youse know, I might be a plain-clothes **dick**, or somep'n, dat's what yuh're tinkin', huh? (O'Neill, *The Hairy Ape*, 1922, [1954], 248.)

The Irish revolutionary James Connolly worked with the IWW in the United States and kept his eye on the Pinkerton **dicks** (**dearc**, **dearca**, eyes). Today's privatized security and surveillance companies make the old private **dick** look **cock**-eyed (**caoch**-eyed, half-blind).

> "It was brutal class warfare. Everywhere IWW men and their followers went down before the bullets of the state militias, federal troops and Pinkerton spies. Their leaders were jailed, hanged, and shot." (Shirley Quill, *"Mike Quill Himself: A Memoir*, 1985, 57, 58.)

> "He sure spliced us easy, didn't he Bill?" I said. "Yeah, but he was a mail order **dick** at that—'cause a good detective don't turn his back on a guy." (Jim Tully, *Beggars of Life*, 1928, [2004], 23.)

Soon the moniker **dick** got slapped on any plainclothes private "eye," whether he was a Pinkerton or not.

> LARRY: The papers say the cops got them all dead to rights, that the Burns **dicks** knew every move before it was made, and someone in the movement must have sold out and tipped them off. (O'Neill, *The Iceman Cometh*, 1939, [1954], 588.)

Dig, *v.*, to understand, comprehend, have a feeling for; realize; appreciate.

Tuig (*pron.* ttig, dig), *v.*, to understand, comprehend, have a feeling for; realize; discern, perceive. An **dtuigeann** tú (*pron.* an dig'an tu?), do you see (understand)? An **dtuigeann** tú leat mé? Do you understand my meaning? Are you diggin' me?

"'You **dig**?' is a short cut for 'You understand?'" (*New York World Telegram*, Oct. 6, 1936, 16.)

The musician Louis Armstrong popularized the New Orleans slang term "**dig**" in the 1930s. "The world really missed something by not **digging** Black Benny on that bass drum before he was killed by a prostitute." (Louis Armstrong, *Satchmo*, 1988, 90.)

The OED suggests that the **dig** of understanding and intellectual perception is from the English colloquial "dig" of a college student "digging" into homework. "Here the sunken eye and sallow countenance bespoke the man who dug sixteen hours per diem." (*Harvard Reg.* 1827, 1828, 303; *OED.*) The *Dictionary of American Slang* derives the hip **dig** from the "Celtic word...twig," meaning "to understand." There is no Celtic word spelled "twig" because there is no "Celtic" language. The vernacular "twig" and "dig" are both derived from from Irish "**tuig**."

"'**Twig** the old connoisseur,' said the squire to the knight." (Walter Scott, *St. Ronan's Well*, 1824; *OED.*)

It is probable that the Irish word **tuig** as "dig" was introduced into the African-American community by Irish- and Gaelic-speaking family members. The early history of the word **tuig** spelled "**dig**" is yet to be dug. An **dtuigeann** tú leat mé (*pron.* en digg'an tu l'at may), are you **diggin'** me?

Dingbat, n., a vagabond, a beggar, a hobo; a fool. (*DAS*, 148.)

Duine bocht (*pron.* din'ə boċt), a poor person, a miserable human being, a wretched pitiful person; *fig.* a beggar. **Daoine bochta**, poor people.

> The lingering sunset across the plain,
> Kissed the rear-end door of an east-bound train,
> And shone on a passing track close by,
> Where a **dingbat** sat on a rotten tie."

(L.F. Post and Glenn Norton, "Gila Monster Route," Lomax, *ABFS*, 1934, [1994], 24, 25.)

Dinger, *n.*, *adj.*, a remarkable person or thing; (*something*) very good.
Dian-mhaith (*pron.* diən'wah), *adj.*, very good, real good, tops, excellent; *adv.*, go dian-mhaith, very well. (Dineen, 333; Ó Dónaill, 402.)

"Well, I'll tell you—it'll be a **dinger** for a while—but Sully'll git him—Rory's fightin' things in there he can't hit—." (Jim Tully, *The Bruiser*, 1936, 118.)

Ditch, *v.*, to put off a train (*hobo slang*); abandon or discard a person or thing; displace someone or something.
De áit (*pron.* deh átch), (*removal*) off a place or spot; from a place or spot; *fig.* off-place or "displace." **De**, *prep.*, from, off; off of (*denoting removal or separation*). **Áit** (*pron.* atch), *n.*, a place, a position.

"We'll **ditch** this Greek and blow." (James M. Cain, *Postman Always Rings Twice*, 1934.)

"I had the young road kid's terrible aversion against walking the track for any man. My law was—to stay with the train, to allow no man to "**ditch**" me." (Jim Tully, *Circus Parade*, New York, 1927, 243.)

Dock, *v.*, to penalize a worker part of his pay, usually for being absent or late; to levy, assess, seize pay, levy against assets. Not recorded in English until the 1820s. (*Labor's Special Language*; *Dictionary of American Slang*, 152.)
Tobhach (*pron.* ttou'aċ), *vn.*, levying, exacting, assessing; demanding; seizure; a levy, an exaction, a seizure. **Tobhach** pá (*pron.* ttou'aċ pá), docking wages, docking pay.

"Hence arose numerous schemes for **docking** you in this quarter." (William Cobbett, *Weekly Reg.*, Apr.13, 1822, 81; *OED*.)

Doagin, do-gan (*Canada*), *n.*, a perjorative term for an Irish Catholic.
Do-dhuine (*pron.* do-ginə), *n.*, a wicked person. (Ó Dónaill, 427.)

Dogs, *n.*, feet; specifically a pair of human feet.
Do chos (*pron.* do'ċos), your feet.

> ERIE: She was a salesgirl in some punk department store, and she was sick of standing on her **dogs** all day, and all the way to Brooklyn, too. (O'Neill, *Hughie*, 1940, 278.)

Dogie, *n.*, a scrubby calf that has not wintered well and is anemic from the scant food of the cold weather, also a dogey. It is in the language of the cowboy "a calf who has lost his mammy and whose daddy has run off with another cow." (Ramon F. Adams, *Dictionary of the American West*, 1968, 96.)

Do-thóigthe (*pron.* dohóg'ə), *p.a.*, hard to rear, hard to fatten (as a calf); a sickly hard-to-feed calf; *fig.* an orphan calf or baby, without a mother to nurse them; *al.* **dothógtha**. (Dineen, 361; An Seabhac, 41.)

> "Whoopie-ti-yi-to, git along little **dogies**,
> It's your misfortune and none of my own."
> (*Anon.*, "Git Along Little Dogies," John Lomax, *CSFB*, 1910, [1986].)

Doggone, *excl.*, *adj.*, *adv.*, an exclamation of irritation, disappointment; someone or something nasty, crude, gross; darned. Not recorded in English till the 19th century. Origin unknown.

Dogairne, *n.*, a gross crude person or thing. **Dógan**, *n.*, a sort of oath or exclamation. (Ó Dónaill, 1977, 427; Dwelly, *Gaelic-English Dictionary*, 1901, 347.)

"Doney Gal," a traditional cowboy song.
Dona, *adj.*, poor; wretched; unfortunate, unlucky.

> We're alone **Doney** (**dona**, *pron.* doney, poor) Gal,
> In the rain and hail;
> Got to drive these **dogies** down the trail
>
> It's rain or shine, sleet or snow,
> Me and my **Doney** Gal are bound to go.
> Yes, rain or shine, sleet or snow,
> Me and my **Doney** Gal are bound to go.
> ... Get along, little **dogie**, on your way.

(John and Alan Lomax, *Cowboy Songs and Other Frontier Ballads*, 1910,
[1986], 8–11.)

Many of the songs in the Lomax's collection, *Cowboy Songs and Other Frontier
Ballads*, contain scores of Irish-American vernacular words and phrases in
their lyrics. See: "Git Along Little Dogies;" "Doney Gal;" "Good Bye, Old
Paint;" "The Skew-Ball Black;" "George Britton;" "The Lone Star Trail;" "The
Texas Cowboy;" "The Old Chishom Trail;" "The Railroad Corral;" and "The
Cowboy's Dream." (Lomax, *CSFB*, 1910, [1986].)

Doodle, *n.*, a silly fellow.
Dúdalaí, *n.*, a shy self-conscious person; a dunce; an awkward person; a stupid
person. (Ó Dónaill, 459; Dineen, 377.)

OED suggests the word **doodle** is from Low German *dudeltopf*, *figuratively* a
simpleton, literally meaning a "nightcap." An Irish **dúdalaí** is "a dumb dude"
with or without a nightcap.

"The Noodles and **Doodles** of the aristocracy." (William Cobden, *Speeches*,
1845; OED.)

Doozer, *n.*, a remarkable, excellent, outstanding person or thing, a humdinger.
(Partridge, *Dictionary of Slang*, 1961, [1984], 302.)
Duasóir (*pron.* duəsór), *n.*, a prizewinner; something outstanding or remark-
able; *al.* **duaiseoir**. (Ó Dónaill, 455, 456.)

"You know about our crosswinds, I've seen some **doozers** here, too." (*New
Yorker*, Aug. 26, 1985.)

Doozy, doosy, duzey, *adj.*, anything remarkable or excellent. (*DAS*, 156.)
Duasach (*pron.* duəsəċ, duəsəh), *n.*, *adj.*, a prize; generous, liberal, bountiful,
prize-winning, *al.* **duaiseach. Duas**, *n.*, a prize, a reward, *al.* **duais**. (Dineen,
373, 374; Ó Dónaill, 455, 456.)

Doozy does not enter *printed* American English until the first decade of the
20th century. It is said to be "of uncertain origin." The *OED* suggests **doozy**

may be related to "daisy." A **doozy** (**duasach**, *pron.* duŏsah, prize-winning) daisy is a **doozer** (**duasóir**, a prizewinner).

"I rung in the strippers (marked cards) and gave everyone a **duzey** of a duke (a hand) with the sucker blowing his top to hipe (up) the ante." (Goldin, O'Leary, *Dictionary of American Underworld Lingo*, 1950, 63.)

"The first orchestra I ever had was a real **doozy**." (Meredith Wilson, radio broadcast, Feb. 18, 1951; *DAS*, 156.)

Dork, *n.* a stupid person; an insignificant contemptible person.
Dorc, *n.*, a small, lumpish person; a midget, a dwarf.

The **Dork** of Cork is a novel by Chet Raymo. "Set in Cork, Ireland... (and) narrated by Frank Bois, a 43-year-old dwarf who has just completed a semi-autobiographical book. In a rambling internal dialogue he reminisces about... his early decision to sublimate his sexuality (after a prostitute told him, 'Be gone, ye little **dork**') by immersing himself in a passion for the moon and stars." (*Publishers Weekly*, 1993.)

In Raymo's magic tale, the "**Dork** of Cork" is not a **twerp** (**duirb**, **doirb**, a worm, an insect; a diminutive or pithless person), he is a poet of the night sky. (Dineen, 355, 356; Dwelly, 349.)

Dornick, *n.*, a stone handy for throwing. A small stone.
Dornóg, *n.*, a small casting stone; a handful. **Doirneog**, *n.*, a round stone.
Doirneag, (*Gaelic*), *n.*, a round stone of a size to fit a fist, or that can be thrown without inconvenience. (Dineen, 306; Ó Dónaill, 431; Dwelly, 349.)

"**Darnick** from the tomb of Abelard and Heloise." (Mark Twain, *Innocents Abroad*, 1869.)

Dornicks were known as "Irish confetti" in New York. "One day five coppers came into Matty's bar and arrested me for disorderly conduct, because some of the fellows had been tossing **dornicks** at the cops." (Richard Butler & Joseph Driscoll, *Dock Walloper*, 1934, 213.)

Drag race, *n.*, a short race between souped-up cars. **Drag**, *n.*, primary road in a city or town. Main **drag**.

De ráig (*pron.* de rág), suddenly, hurriedly, with a rush, sudden acceleration. **De**, *prep.*, from, off; of. **Ráig**, *n.*, hurried journey, rush; precipitate rush; *fig.* "pedal to the metal;" rapid acceleration. (Dineen, 873, 874; Ó Dónaill, 982.)

A **drag** (**de ráig**, sudden rush) race is usually over in seconds rather than minutes. To go "on the **drag**" (**de ráig**, rush) in the early-19th century London slums was to rush after wagons in the streets and snatch what you could. "**Drag**. To go on the drag; to follow a cart or waggon, in order to rob it. *Cant.*" (Grose, *Classical Dictionary of the Vulgar Tongue*, 1785, [1811].)

Dude, *n.*, a dapper dandy; a "swell," an affected, fastidious fop; a city slicker at a dude ranch. Origin unknown. (*Barnhart Dictionary of English Etymology*, 305.)

Dúd (*pron.* dood), **dúd(a)**, *al.* **dúid**, *n.*, a foolish-looking fellow; a dolt, a numb-skull; a clown; an idiot; a rubbernecker; a long-necked eavesdropper. **Dúdach**, *adj.*, rubber-necked; foolish-looking, queer. **Dúdaire**, *n.*, a clown, an idiot (County Kerry); a long-necked person; a dolt; an eavesdropper. **Dúdálaí**, *n.*, a stupid person; an idiot; a self-conscious person. (Dineen, 377, 378; Ó Dónaill, 459, 460; *Foclóir Póca*, 349, 350. See: "How the Irish Invented Dudes.")

Duds, dudde, *n.*, an article of clothing; clothes. The word **duds** first appears in English in the 15th and 16th centuries as the cant word "**dudde**." Origin unknown. (*OED.*)

Do éadach (*pron.* do'ædəċ, du'ædəh), *n.*, your clothing, your clothes.

"**Dudde**, clothes...*grossum vestimentum*, a dudde." (14th century; *OED.*) The cant word **dudde** soon acquired the English suffix "s" and became plural **duddis, duddes**, and finally **duds**. "We wyll fylche some **duddes**." (Harman, *Caveat*, 1566; Gotti, *Lexicographica*, 24.)

"**Dudes**, clothes." (Harmon, *Caveat*, 1566, in Gotti, *Lexicographica*, 24.)

"**Duds**, clothes." (Grose, *Classical Dictionary of the Vulgar Tongue*, 1785, [1811].)

A key strand of 16th century cant was the Irish language dressed up in ill-fitting English phonetic **duds**. The word **duds** remains popular today; though it is still classified as slang. Poor old **dudde**.

> MARTHY (*...in a low voice*): Listen! I'm goin' to beat it down to the barge—pack up me **duds** and blow. (O'Neill, *The Iceman Cometh*, 1939, [1954], 19.)

> HUCK FINN: "The king's **duds** was all black, and he did look real swell and starchy." (Mark Twain, *Huckleberry Finn*, 1885, [1994], 132.)

Duke, *v.*, to fight with the fists; to box; to hand someone something; to shake someone's hand. **Dukes**, a **duke**, "the **duke**," *n.*, a fist, a hand; clenched fists; a hand in a poker game; in boxing, to get "the **duke**," to have your fist raised over your head as winner. The verb and noun **"duke"** are abbreviated back formations from the Irish verb **tuargain** (*pron.* tuərgən, to beat, pound, batter, thump) and its verbal noun. (See: **duking**.)

"What you got to do is **duke** the guy five now and then and quit acting so goddamned high and mighty...Who the hell're you?" (George V. Higgins, *The Patriot Game*, 1982, 87.)

"I rung in the strippers (marked cards) and gave everyone a duzey of a **duke** (a hand) with the sucker blowing his top to hipe the ante." (Goldin, O'Leary, *Dictionary of American Underworld Lingo*, 1950, 63.)

"'Put up your **dooks**' is a kind invitation to fight." (Hotten, *Slang Dictionary*, 1874, 153.)

"Well, even if I lose the **duke** I got forty per cent of five hundred, ain't I?" (Jim Tully, *The Bruiser*, 1936, 22.)

Duking, dukin' it out, *vn.*, beating, punching, pounding, battering, thumping, hammering (it out).

Tuargain (*pron.* tuərgən) *v.*, to beat, pound, batter, thump, hammer. **Tuargain**(t) (*pron.* tuərgən) *vn.*, (*act of*) pounding, battering, thumping, hammering (with fists). Ag **tuargaint** a chéile lena ndoirne (*pron.* eg tuərgən a ċæl'ə lena nórn'ə), beating each other with their fists. (Dineen, 1226; Ó Dónaill, 1281.)

"To the sports editor: It seems ironic that while on the second page of your March 30 sports section there was an article entitled 'Violence in Athletics: an International Blight,' by Frederick Baron, you print on the first page a photograph of Gary Howatt **duking** it out with Jerry Butler." (*New York Times*, Apr. 13, 1975, 216.)

Dukie, *n.*, a nickname.

Tuarga (*pron.* tuarggə), *n.*, a solid block of a man. (Ó Dónaill, 1283.)

My Uncle **Dukie** (tuarga, *pron.* tuərggə, a solid block of a man) was built like a fire plug and made his living **dukin'** (**tuargain**[t], *pron.* tuərgən, hammering, pounding) it out as a small-time prizefighter during the Depression. **Dukie** kept his boxing career a secret, so he wouldn't get in **dutch** (**duais**, *pron.* dush, trouble) with my Aunt Tootsie.

Dutch, "in **dutch**," *adj. ph.*, in trouble, in disfavor. (*DAS*, 168.)

Duais (*pron.* dush), *n.*, trouble; misfortune. In **duais** (*pron.* dush), means "in trouble."

PARRITT (*bitterly*): To hell with them! I never want to see a whore again! I mean they always get you in **dutch**. (O'Neill, *The Iceman Cometh*, 1939, [1954], 594.)

HICKEY (*injuredly*): Hell, Larry, I'm no fool. Do you think I'd deliberately set out to get under everyone's skin and put myself in **dutch** with all my old pals..? (O'Neill, *The Iceman Cometh*, 1939, [1954], 642.)

BARTENDER: That's only her bull. (*Then with a sigh as he returns to the bar.*) Them lousy tramps is always getting this dump in **dutch**. (O'Neill, *Ah, Wilderness!*, 1934, [1967], 76.)

E

Eighty-six, *n.*, to be barred from a saloon (*or any place*); to be denied hospitality.
Éiteachas aíocht, Éiteachas aíochta (*pron.* et'əċəs íċtə, et'əhəs íċtə), *ph.*, denial of hospitality; refusal of lodging (for a night); refusal of service; *fig.*, to be barred or expelled. (Ó Dónaill, 25, 494.)

"I told him there's an organizer I **eighty-sixed** out of Dantes they should get rid of. McGreal told me it wouldn't matter." (Charles Brandt, *I Heard You Paint Houses: Frank the "Irishman" Sheeran and Closing the Case on Jimmy Hoffa*, 2004, 100.)

Jesus, Mary, and St. Joseph got the **86** (**éiteachas aíochta,** *pron.* et'əhəs íċtə, a refusal of lodging, a denial of hospitality) from every joint in Bethlehem.

F

Fan-tod, Fan-tods, *n.*, an excited, impulsive frame of mind; restlessness; a fidget; a fuss, a fit. "An unmeaning formation suggested by *fantastic* (&) *fantasy*." (*OED.*)
Fonn taodach (*pron.* fon ttædəċ, fon ttædə), an impulsive frame of mind, jittery excitation, a fierce humor, a quick temper, a fuss, a fit. **Fonn,** *n.*, temper, humor, frame of mind; inclination; excitation. **Taodach** (*pron.* ttædaċ, ttædə), *adj.*, spasmodic, impulsive, excited, fidgety; quick-tempered, fierce. *Al.* **taghdach.** Tá **fonn taodach** air (*pron.* tá fon ttædə ər), he is in a fuss. He's in a fit. (Ó Dónaill, 568, 1191, 1293; Dineen, 1172; Dwelly, 63, 450.)

Huck Finn got the **"fan-tods"** along the Mississippi River in the 1840s. "By-and-by I was close enough to have a look, and there lay a man on the ground. It most gave me the **fan-tods**...it was Miss Watson's Jim!" (Mark Twain, *Huckleberry Finn*, 1885, [1994], 36.)

"These was all nice pictures...but but I didn't somehow seem to take to them, because...they always gave me the **fan-tods**." (Twain, *Huckleberry Finn*, 1885, [1994], 86.)

Irish-born Harry Hope got the **fantods** in his saloon in New York City around 1910.

> HARRY HOPE: You and the other bums have begun to give me the grave-yard **fantods**. (O'Neill, *The Iceman Cometh*, 1939, [1954], 610.)

Faro, *n.*, a banking card game where the main move is called a "turn."
Fiaradh (*pron.* fiŏr-u, fiəroo), *vn.*, turning, (*act of*) turning, coiling, twisting. The **faro** game is the **fiaradh** (*pron.* fiəroo, turning) game.

"Another player... placed his last stack of checks on a card, saying to the (faro) dealer, 'Turn the cards, Sam, that's the last button on Gabe's coat.' The cards were turned and the player lost." (Jack Black, *You Can't Win*, 1926, [2000], 134.)

"I experimented and soon laid a solid foundation for the **faro**-bank habit which fastened on me later and kept me broke for years. (Jack Black, *You Can't Win*, 1926, [2000], 134.)

"Bedford followed Halsey... to an empty **faro** table and stood in front of the green cloth, its surface enameled with the representation of a full suit of spades." (Peter Quinn, *Banished Children of Eve*, 1995, 212.)

Fawney, *n.*, a ring. (Grose, *Classical Dictionary of the Vulgar Tongue*, 1785, [1811].)
Phoney, *al.* phony, *n.*, *adj.*, a fake, a sham; fake, bogus, false.
Fáinne (*pron.* fawn'ə, fá-nĭ), *n.*, a ring.

In the 18th century the Irish word **fáinne**, meaning a "ring," was transformed into a flash word "**fawney**," meaning a fake gold ring used in a trickster's scam, and then into the American slang word "**phoney**," meaning a fake or a sham. In the same way the Irish language was transformed from classical Celtic language of the Atlantic world into the **phoney** slang of an English-speaking empire.

"**Fawney**, a finger-ring." (J.H. Vaux, *Flash Dictionary*, 1812.)

"**Fawney** rig. A common fraud thus practiced: a fellow drops a brass ring, double gilt, which he picks up before the party meant to be cheated, and to whom he disposes of it for less than its supposed value, and ten times more than its real value." (Grose, *Classical Dictionary of the Vulgar Tongue*, 1785, [1811]; see: "The Gangs of New York Talk Back—in Irish.")

Feud, *n.*, a state of hatred and enmity: between individuals, families, clans, nation-states, etc. "Deadly **feood**." (Edmund Spenser, 1596.)

Fuath ard (*pron.* fuə ard), high hatred, great enmity. **Fuath** (*pron.* fuə), *n.*, hatred, hate, enmity. **Ard**, *adj.*, high, great, mighty, noble.

In 1877 the Gaelic scholar Charles MacKay proposed that the English word **feud** was derived from the Irish and Gaelic noun **fuath** (*pron.* fuə), meaning "hatred, hate; enmity, abhorrence, aversion; distaste; odium; a morbid aversion." Most Anglo-American dictionary editors derive the modern "**feud**" from the Old French *fede*, and Old High German *fihida*; which became a late medeival "northern dialect" word spelled variously "fede, fead, and feide." Then a puzzling new spelling, *feood*, *fuid*, and *fewd*, suddenly appeared in the early-16th century. The modern **feud** emerges from all the **feuding** orthography. (Charles MacKay, *Gaelic Etymology of Languages of Europe*, London, 1877, 170; Barnhart, 378; *OED*.)

Fuath ard (*pron.* fúə ard, high hatred, great enmity) is the origin of all **feuds**.

Finagle, *al.* phenagle, *v.*, to contrive and scheme, to achieve or ascertain something through artifice; to manipulate, to deceive skillfully, to wangle. The word finagle is not found *in print* in the English language until 1926. Origin unknown. (Barnhart, 383.)

Fionna aclaí, fionnadh aclaí (*pron.* finə aclí), agile contrivance, ingenious invention, adroit ascertainment. **Fionna, fionnadh** (*pron.* finah, finə), *vn.*, (*act of*) ascertaining, discovering; inventing, contriving; ascertainment, invention, contrivance. **Aclaí**, *adj.*, supple, limber, agile; smooth; adroit, ingenious, skillful. (Ó Dónaill, 546, 547.)

"Now you take a guy like me...trying to make an illegitimate dollar...which of course big business is trying to do the same. They're trying to **phenagle** us all out of a dollar." (David Maurer, *The Whiz Mob*, 1953, 165.)

Fil-i-me-oo-re-i-re-ay
Fillfidh mé uair éirithe (*pron.* fill'ih mæ úĕr í-ríhə).

> Time to get up, I'll go back,
> To work upon the railway.
> ("Paddy Works on the Erie," song, *ca.* 1850.)

The rousing refrain of "Paddy Works on the Erie"—**Fil-i-me-oo-re-i-re-ay**—has always been treated as "macaronic," or nonsense syllables. In fact, it is the Irish language concealed beneath English phonetic spelling.

Fink, *v.*, to act as a labor spy; to act as an informer; to spy, snoop; inform.
Fink, *n.*, a paid labor spy; a stool pigeon; an undercover detective; a strike-breaker. **Finking, finkin'**, *vn.*, acting as a spy; snooping; spying, inquiring, investigating, informing, snitching, contriving lies. Origin unknown.
Fionnachtain (*pron.* finnəċtən), *al.* **fionnaíocht, fionnacht** (*pron.* finnəċt), *n.*, *vn.*, (*act of*) discovering; making known; *fig.* snitching; finding out, investigating; inquiring, "snooping;" know by investigation; detecting, recognizing; inventing, contriving. **Fionnachtaí** (*pron.* finnəċtí), *n*, a finder, discoverer, investigator, "snoop." **Fionnachdainn** (*Gaelic*), *n.*, investigation. (Dineen, 456; Ó Dónaill, 546–47, 457; Dwelly, 437.)

A professional **fink** would *find out* as much as possible about a union by *investigating* suspected members, *detecting* plans, and *recognizing* leaders. Finks were also experts at *inventing* and *contriving* stories to frame union leaders in court.

"A few **finks**...stool pigeons, cranks, and crackpots," was how the Irish-speaking founder of the New York City Transit Worker's Union, Mike Quill, described **finkin'** (**fionnachtain**, *pron.* finnəċtən, contriving) finks who testified in front of the House Committee on Un-American Activities in 1938. Some Anglo-American dictionaries suggest **fink** and **finking** might be derived from the German *fink*, meaning a "finch;" or that **fink** might be rhyming slang for a Pinkerton, as in "Finkerton," but most agree that fink is of "unknown origin."

"Suppose you had to hire a private eye... Would you want one that **finked** on his friends? (Raymond Chandler, *The Long Goodbye*, 1953, 57.)

Not all private eyes were **finks**. Former Pinkerton private dick Dashiell Hammett went to jail in the 1950s because he would not **fink** to the House Un-American Activities Committee.

Flog ground sweat, *ph.*, to speak disrespectfully of the dead.

Fliuch grian-suite (*pron.* fl'uk gríŏn ssuet'), **fliúchadh grian-suite** (*pron.* fl'uċə gríŏn ssuet'), wet, dampen, or rain on a sunny-site; *fig.* piss on a grave. **Fliuch**, *vn.*, **fliuchadh** (*pron.* fl'uċə), wet, rain on, dampen; *fig.* piss on. **Grian-** (*pron.* gríŏn-), *prefix*, sunny-, sun-. **Suite** (*pron.* ssuet'), *n.*, site, place, spot.

"**Grownd-Sweat**, a Grave." (B.E.'s *Dictionary of the Canting Crew*, 1699.)

"Our guide spoke first: 'Now listen hear, I'm not out to **flog** old man Dunne's **ground sweat**, let him and all the faithfully departed, as they sez, rest in peace...'" (Peter Quinn, *Banished Children of Eve*, 1994, 7.)

Fluke, *n.*, a successful stroke in billiards made by accident or chance; a lucky stroke, an unexpected success; a piece of good luck; a rare reward. Uncertain origin. (Barnhart, 394.)

Fo-luach (*pron.* fo'luəċ), *n.*, a rare result, a rare reward, a rare payment, an occasional "payoff." **Fo-**, *prefix, in compounds*, occasional-, odd-, rare- .**Luach** (*pron.* luəċ), *n.*, value; result; reward, recompense, payment, "payoff."

Benny Binion, the Texas-Irish gambler, got rich on **flukes**. "In about 1928, I opened up what they call a 'policy'—it's kind of a numbers business—in Dallas, Texas. I started with fifty-six dollars that day. The first day I made eight hundred dollars. And, of course, it was kind of a **fluke** thing." (Mary Ellen Glass, *Lester Ben "Benny" Binion: Some Recollections of a Texas and Las Vegas Gaming Operator*, 1976, 3.)

The "Policy" game did not depend on a fluke (**fo-luach**, *pron.* fo'luəċ, rare result, occasional payoff) to make money. The profits were built in to the per centage. But a **fluke** can be bad, as well as good. "'It was only one shot, a **fluke**. What am I supposed to do about a guy with a tire iron?'" (William Kennedy, *Legs*, 1975, 141.)

"It was a prostitute who provided the last **flukish** twist to the scenario of my capture." (Willie Sutton & Edward Linn, *Where the Money Was: the Memoirs of a Bank Robber*, 1976, 306.)

Flunky, *n.*, a male servant in livery, *esp.* a footman, sideman, an attendant at your flank, a lackey; a term of contempt for anyone servile. Origin unknown.

Fulangaí (*pron.* fulangí), *n.*, a prop, a support (for a person), someone who props up and supports a champion (or a chief); *fig.* a footman or attendant; a patient, passive, long-suffering, enduring person. (Dineen, 500; Ó Dónaill, 594.)

In the early-20th century, "kinker" was a name for the star performers and aristocrats of the circus. The **flunky** was usually a bindle stiff or road kid like Jim Tully, who did all the work. "For the longer a circus plays in town, the easier it becomes for the kinkers and **flunkies.**" (Jim Tully, *Circus Parade*, 1927, 195.)

Flush, *adj.*, plentifully supplied (with money).

Flúirse (*pron.* flúrshə), *n.*, abundance, plenty. **Flúirseach** (*pron.* flúrshəċ, flúrshəh), *adj.*, abundant, plentiful.

Flúirse (*pron.* flúrshī), spelled *flush*, comes into the English language as 17th century cant. "Some dames are more **flush** in crownes then her good man." (Thomas Dekker, 1603.)

The phrase "**flúirse** de'n arán (*pron.* flúrshə dən arán) means "plenty of bread" and is taken fom an early text of the *Tales of Ossian*, dating to the 11th or 12th centuries. (Dineen, 464.)

The *OED* opines that the word **flush** in English is "perhaps onomatopoeic... suggested by fly, flutter, *etc.*, and an ending imitative of a swift sudden flight, *cf.* rush."

"Is glas gach gort arbhair agus gach má mhín anois. Beidh bainne **flúirseach** nó fairsing anois." Every corn field and level plain is now green. Milk is plentiful. (Humphrey O'Sullivan, ed., Tomás de Bhaldraithe, *Cin Lae Amhlaoibh, Diary of a Countryman*, 1827–1832, 1970, 98.)

JOE: In de days when I was **flush**... (O'Neill, *The Iceman Cometh*, 1939, [1954], 600.)

LARRY: Pat McGloin... was a police lieutenant back in the **flush** times of graft when everything went. (O'Neill, *The Iceman Cometh*, 1939, [1954], 594.)

Foot juice; *n.*, fortified wine.

Fuad juice, *n.*, wastrel juice, wretch juice, bum juice. **Fuad**, *n.*, a wretch, a wastrel, a vagrant, a bum; a thief.

"The wine dumps, where wine bums or "winos" hung out, interested me. Long, dark, barren rooms with rows of rickety tables and a long bar behind which were barrels of the deadly "**foot juice**" or "red ink," as the winos called it." (Jack Black, *You Can't Win*, 1926, [2000], 113.)

For fair, *adj.*, *adv.*, completely; complete.

Foirfe (*pron.* for'əf'ə), *adj.* complete; experienced; perfected, perfect.

Raised on "de Brooklyn docks," the character Yank speaks old New York Irish-American vernacular **for fair** in O'Neill's Pulitzer Prize-winning play, *The Hairy Ape*.

YANK: Choich, huh? I uster go to choich onct—sure—when I was a kid. Me old man and woman, dey made me. Dey never went demselves, dough... (*With a grin*) Dey was scrappers **for fair**, bot' of dem.On Satiday nights when dey bot' got a skinful dey could put up a bout oughter been staged in de Garden. (O'Neill, *The Hairy Ape*, 1921, [1954], 234.)

SID (*... suddenly he whistles*): Phew! This is a warm lulu **for fair**! (Eugene O'Neill, *Ah, Wilderness!*, 1933, [1967], 27.)

Frame, *v.*, *n.*, conviction and imprisonment on trumped-up charges based on lies and false evidence; to prosecute someone with fabricated evidence or lies.

Fíor a éimiú (*pron.* fírr ə æmú), denying truth, to reject truth. **Fíor** (*pron.* fírr), *n.*, truth. **Éimiú** (æmú), *vn.*, denying, rejecting, refusing. Duine a **éimiú**, to refuse or deny someone. Ná **héimigh** éisteacht linn, do not refuse to listen to us.

> MARGY: Just a minute. (*She faces Clara.*) You were almost dead when I found you in this room. I brought you back to life, and you try to **frame** me to save yourself... I'll get even with you... I'll get even. (Mae West, *Sex: A Comedy Drama*, 1926, [1997], 56.)

Freak, *n.*, *v.*, a freak of nature, a freak in a sideshow, a freak storm; sudden passion or fury; to become angry, furious, passionate, ferocious, wild, crazy.
Freaking, *n.* a fit of passion, fury, anger, madness.
Fraoch (*pron.* fræċ), *n.*, fury; fierceness, ferocity; passion; rage, anger; hunger.
Fraoch (*pron.* fræċ), *n.*, heath, ling, heather; *al.* a mane, a shaggy mane.
Fraochan (*pron.* fræċan), *n.* a fit of passion and fury.

The word **freak** suddenly begins to appear in the English language in the 16th century, through a fickle **freake** of fortune and the colonial conquest of Ireland. "I feare the fickle **freakes**... Of Fortune." (Edmund Spencer, 1590.)

The *OED* speculates that the word **freak** is "probably" from an obscure Old English word meaning to dance.

The fickle **freaks** of fortune, weather, sideshows, and madness are all descended from an Irish **fraoch** (*pron.* fræċ, fury) of nature. **Fraoch** na spéire (*pron.* fræċ nə spér'ə), a fury of heaven, agus **fraoch** na farraige (*pron.* agəs fræċ nə farəg'ə), and a fury of the sea are the primeval furies of Ireland who tossed their shaggy manes in the Atlantic blast and dwelled in the court of the queen of the fairies.

In the 1590s, an English poet and colonial bureaucrat in Ireland, Edmund Spencer, placed an English spell on the Gaelic **fraoch** (*pron.* fræċ, fury) of the tempest. "**Freakes** and furies soon seized the courtiers of the realm." (Cowley, 1661; *OED*.) Soon the **freak** of nature became the frightening **freak** (**fraoch**, *pron.* fræċ, fury, rage, passion) of the colony. "Ibrahim Pasha, in a **freak** of tyrannical fury, turned every Mahometan out of the city." (M.E. Herbert, 1867; *OED*.)

The "fickle **freakes** of fortune" saw the noble **fraoch** (*pron.* fræċ, fury) of the tempest ehumerized into the grotesque **freak** in a carnival sideshow.

"An association of... natural curiosities usually exhibited at booths... called the 'Freaks Union,' the word **freaks** being an abbreviation of the term 'freaks of nature' by which these monstrosities are described." (*Daily News*, Sept. 11, 1883; *OED*.)

In 1827, a Kilkenny schoolmaster, Amhlaoibh Ó Súilleabháin wrote in his diary of the **fraoch** (fury) of the howling Atlantic gale. "No fheadar an í banríon na bruíne do thóg an stoirm, agus chuir an **fraoch** feargach agus bolgán béicí a hiomaidh." "I wonder was it the Queen of the Fairies who caused the storm, and the angry **fury** of the sky, because I interefered with the moss of her bed and the pillows and puff balls of her couch." (Ó Súilleabháin, *Cinn Lae Amhlaoibh*, 1827.)

Professor MacBain provides the sanas (secret knowledge, etymology) of Irish **fraoch** (*pron.* fræċ, fury) and returns it to the heather of Ireland. "Fraoch: heather, Irish *fraoch*, Old Irish *froech*, Welsh *grug*, Cornish *grig*, Middle Breton *groegon*... Hence, Gaelic *fraoch*, wrath, Irish *fraoch*, Early Irish *fraech*, furor." (*MacBain's Gaelic Etymological Dictionary*, 1896, [1982].)

Freaky, *adj.*, strange, unusual; frightening, frenzied, manic, mad, rabid, raving, wild.

Fraochaidhe (*pron.* fræċí), *adj.*, fierce, furious; passionate; frenzied; angry; fretful; stormy. (Dineen, 486; Ó Dónaill, 579; Dwelly, 452.)

G

Gab, *v.*, to talk endlessly, to chatter. **Gab**, *n.*, gabbing, talking, (*act of*) talking too much; the gift of gab, fluency of speech, a gift for speaking; to reveal a confidence or secret, to snitch.

Gab, *n.*, a tattling mouth. **Gabair**, *n.*, a chattering talking fellow, prattler, chatterer (bird). **Gabach**, *n.*, a tattling female. **Gabach, gabaiche**, *adj.*, garrulous, scolding, talkative, querulous. **Geab** (*pron.* g'ab), *n.*, chat; **geabach**, *adj.*, talkative, "gabbing" (*Donegal*). (Dwelly, 466; Dineen, 522.)

Some Anglo-American dictionaries derive the English *gab* of chatter from the Old Icelandic *gabb*, *gabba*, meaning "mockery." The *OED* opts for an "apparently onomatopoeic" origin for **gab**. Professor MacBain associates Gaelic **gab** with Irish **gob**, a beak or mouth.

Gaff, *n.*, a hook; an iron hook, a fishing gaff; a ring to mark cards worn by a card mechanic. "Blow the **gaff**," to let out a secret; to reveal a plot, or give convicting evidence.

Gaf, *n.*, a hook, a crooked implement; *fig.* a trick, a scam.

Gage, **Gauge**, *n.*, marijuana.

Gaid (*pron.* gad, gadge, gaj), *n. pl.*, twisted twigs; withes, rope, hemp.

Gage or **gauge** is old slang for marijuana. A few twisted twigs of hemp and you had a stick of gage. **Gage** was also early cant for a pipeful of tobacco. "The first time that I smoked Marijuana (or) **Gage** as they so beautifully calls it some time, was a couple of years after I left Fletcher Henderson's Orchestra..." (Louis Armstrong, Thomas Brothers, eds., *Louis Armstrong, In His Own Words*, 1999, 112.)

"We tipped Frankie off on the routine and he burned up two sticks of **gauge** real fast..." (Mezz Mezzrow & Bernard Wolfe, *Really the Blues*, 1946, [1990], 94.)

Galla gaffa gassa, *ph.*, an old healing spell for toothache and pain.

Galar gafa gasta, *ph.*, disease seized fast; pain taken away fast.

Early in the 20th century, the American poet Carl Sandberg encountered a faith doctor, who chanted an old Irish spell of *fiosacht* (divination) to cure a toothache.

> For toothache the faith doctor wrote the words "**galla gaffa gassa**" on the wall. With a nail he pointed out each letter of the words, asking if the toothache was better. At the letter where the toothache was feeling easier he drove the nail in and the tooth stopped aching. **Galla gaffa gassa**.
> **Gassa galla gaffa**.

Goofer dust comes from the **goofer** tree. Sprinkle it in the shoes of the woman you love and she can never get away from you. **Galla gaffa gassa.** (Carl Sandburg, "The People, Yes," 1936.)

Galar *n.*, disease, distemper, affliction, distress, pain, trouble. **Galar** fiacal, toothache. **Gafa,** *adj., p.p.* of gabh, seized, grabbed, taken, caught, held; gripped; gafa ag slaghdán, in the grip of a cold, gafa san ucht, caught in the chest. **Gasta,** *adj.*, fast; quick, rapid. Siúl gasta, a fast walk. Rud a dhéanamh go gasta, to do something fast. (Ó Dónaill, 601, 615.)

Goofer dust, *n.*, a love powder. "Sprinkle it in the shoes of the woman you love and she can never get away from you." (Carl Sandburg, "The People, Yes," 1936.)

Comhbhá (*pron.* cofá, coufá) dust, *n.*, close alliance; affection, tenderness, sympathy, partiality; love (dust).

Galusses, *n.*, suspenders for trousers. "One-**gallus**" is a name for a one-suspender hick or poor country bumpkin

Gealas (*pron.* galas), *n.*, a suspender for trousers; (*plural*) a pair of suspenders. **Gealas,** *n.*, a beam of light, gleaming, beaming; brightness, gladness. (Ó Dónaill, 619; Dineen, 523.)

"An' I know by his clo'es an' his snuff-cullud face Da he comes from a scrubby an' *one-***gallus** race." (*Century Magazine*, Nov. 1881, 158; *OED.*)

> Cordelia Mulligan: I want to buy your father a pair of **galluses**.
> Tommy Mulligan: You're **gallus** enough now, eh Pop?
> (Edward Harrigan, *The Mulligan Guard*, 1878.)

Gealas in Irish means *both* a man's "suspenders" and "beaming." In Edward Harrigan's musical comedy, *The Mulligan Guard*, Tommy Mulligan puns the Irish word **gealas**. His father doesn't need any **galluses** (**gealas**, suspenders) because he is already "**gallus** (**gealas**, *pron.* g'alas, beaming, bright) enough," as in lit or tipsy.

"There's a big difference between a **gallus** story and a dirty deed." (J.M. Synge, *The Playboy of the Western World*, quoted in Peter Linebaugh, *London Hanged*, 1991, 288.)

Galore, *adv.,* in abundance, plenty.

Go leor, *adv.,* enough, in plenty, plentiful. **Leor,** *indec. adj.,* enough, plentiful, sufficient; **go leor,** enough, in plenty. Tá **go leor** airgid agam, I have plenty of money.

> **Go leor** comes into English as slang in the late-17th century "**Gallore** or **Golore**. Plenty." (Grose, *Classical Dictionary of the Vulgar Tongue,* 1785, [1811].)

Gam, Gams, *n.,* a leg, legs, long, shapely legs. Origin unknown.

Gamba (*pron.* gambə), *n.,* a leg. **Gambach** (*pron.* gambəċ), *adj.,* having long legs. (Dineen, 515.)

> "Regarding her superb **gams** with affection..." (V. Faulkner, Sept. 6, 1951, 35; *DAS.*)

Gammy, gammi, gamy, *adj.,* (*someone or something*) bad; crooked, or bent, as in a bandy leg.

Cama-legged; **cama**-chosach, bandy-legged; **cama**-, (*prefix in compounds*), **cama**-bóithrín, a crooked path (Dineen, 156.)

Gandy dancer, *n.,* a railroad track laborer whose work necessitates a *constant* jumping motion to gain leverage on a crowbar inserted under the railroad ties to straighten the tracks. Hence, the workers appear to be doing a constant never-ending dance down the railroad tracks. Origin uncertain.

Cinnte dancer (*pron.* kin'tə), **constant** dancer. **Cinnte** (*pron.* kin'tə), *adj.,* constant; ever; go **cinnte,** always, constantly. (Ó Dónaill, 229; Dineen, 191.)

> The **gandy** dancer is a rinnceoir **cinnte,** a "constant dancer," whether in fearthainn **cinnte** (*pron.* f'arhən kin-tə), constant rain, or withering heat, a **gandy** (**cinnte,** *pron.* kin-tə, constant) dancer jumps and twists, **cinnte** is i gcómhnaidhe, ever and always, down the railroad tracks. (Ó Dónaill, 229; Dineen.)

> "The term **gandy** dancer is applied specifically to a track laborer whose work, when prying on the end of a crowbar inserted under a railroad tie, necessitates a jumping up and down to gain a leverage. That peculiar movement

bears a faint resemblance to some imaginary style of dancing—hence gandy dancer..." (*Kansas City Star*, November 18, 1917.)

Garnish, *n.* money extorted from a new prisoner as a jailer's fee; money given in return for better treatment by jailers.

Garanna ar ais (*pron.* garanə er'ash), favors back, good turns returned, favors reciprocated; *fig.* favors in return for money (in jail). **Garanna**, *pl. n.*, favors, good turns, advantages, conveniences. **Ar ais** (*pron.* er' ash), *ph.*, back, in return.

"Any request was considered, provided it was backed up with 'rhino,' or ready cash. William Pitt, the keeper of Newgate (prison) in 1716, was estimated to have made three to four thousand pounds in **garnish**, the slang word for the bribe demanded by the keepers, over a period of three or four months when Newgate was full of rich, noble Jacobite prisoners for their part in the risings of 1715." (Lucy Moore, *The Thieve's Opera*, 1997, 23.).

Gash, *n.*, sexual activity; obscene term for a woman; a vagina.

Gairse (*pron.* garshə), *n.*, smut, lewdness, debauchery.

The Irish word **gairse** (*pron.* garshə, smut) means "debauchery and lewdness" without reference to gender or anatomy.

"You're young, and there's plenty of **gash** in the world, and the supply of moon goes on forever." (James T. Farrell, *Young Lonigan*, 1934, [2004], 300.)

Gash-hound, *n.*, one whose chief avocation is the pursuit of loose women, prostitutes, homosexuals and the like. (Goldin, O'Leary, *Dictionary of American Underworld Lingo*, 77, 1950.)

"I used to go to the Hotsy when I was in New York even before I knew Jack. It was quite a place before the big blowup. Plenty of action, plenty of **gash**. I met my wife there, Miss Miserable of 1929." (William Kennedy, *Legs*, 1975.)

Gawk, *n.*, a young awkward person, an immature, clumsy, person.

Géag (*pron.* g'æg, g'íŏg), *n.*, a youth; a young person; a young woman; *fig.* someone immature and awkward; a young scion; an offspring; a limb, a branch.

Mór **géag** den uaisle (*pron.* mór g'íŏg dən uəsh'lə), a young **gawk** (offspring) of the nobility.

Gawky, *adj.*, (*of young person*) awkward, ungainly.

Géagaí (*pron.* g'ægí, g'íŏgæ), *n.*, a tall, long-limbed, skinny boy or girl; *fig.* ungainly youth. **Géagach** (*pron.* g'ægaċ), *adj.*, long-limbed; having long skinny limbs or legs. **Geagán**, *n.*, a tall, slender boy or girl.

"**Gawkey**. A tall, thin, awkward young man or woman." (Grose, *Classical Dictionary of the Vulgar Tongue*, 1785, [1811].)

"Babe was an amazing contrast to the **gawky**-limbed, criminal-featured, dumb-minded companion at her side—Cokey Jenny." (Mae West, *The Constant Sinner*, 1930, 14.)

Gazoonie (*carnival, circus slang*), *n.*, a young boy, a road kid who works as a "flunky," the lowest level worker in a circus or carnival; a young hobo; an inexperienced or innocent youth; a punk. (*DAS*, 210; Goldin, O'Leary, 77.)

Garsún, *n.*, **garsuna**, *g.*, a young boy; a youth; a boy between eight and eighteen; *cf.* French *garçon*. Medieval Latin *garcio*, a groom. **Gasúr**, *n.*, young boy; a youngster. (Dineen, 521; Ó Dónaill, 614, 615.)

Gee! An exclamation of surprise or enthusiasm; also used for emphasis.

Dia (*pron.* d'iĕ, jíĕ), *n.*, God; a god.

In Ulster Irish the slender "d" of **dia** (god) is pronounced like an English "j" or the "g" in the exclamation **gee**! **Dia** linn! (*pron.* jíĕ linn), God help us! **Dia** leat! (*pron.* jíĕ l'at); *fig.* God help you! In O'Neill's plays, the exclamation **gee** is interchangeable with the word "god!"

TIM: Yuh sure are up against it, Kid. (*He appears deeply moved.*) **Gee**, I thought I was in bad, but yuh got me skinned to death. (Eugene O'Neill, *The Web*, 1913, [1988], 23.)

MARGIE (*eyes him jeeringly*): Why, hello, Tightwad Kid. Come to join de party? **Gee**, don't he act bashful, Poil?" (Eugene O'Neill, *The Iceman Cometh*, 1939, [1954], 650.)

In the late-19th and early-20th centuries, **Gee**, **Gee Whiz**, and **Holy Gee**, went from the vernacular of working-class Irish-America to the slang of newspaper cartoons and then into the mouths of American middle-class youth. Richard, the teenage protagonist of Eugene O'Neill's 1932 comedy, *Ah, Wilderness!*, recites a litany to **gee** (**dia**, *pron.* jíû, god), the old pagan deity of young love.

RICHARD (*thinking aloud*): Must be nearly nine... **Gee**, I'll bet Ma had a fit when she found out I'd sneaked out... (*He sighs and stares around him at the night*) **Gee**, it's beautiful tonight... for me an Muriel... **Gee**, I love tonight... God, it's so beautiful... (O'Neill, *Ah, Wilderness!*, 1933, [1967], 107, 108.)

But **gee** really took off in American slang as **gee whiz!**

Gee Whiz, an *exclamation* like **gee**, originating in the U.S., and said to be euphemism for the name of Jesus.
Dia Uas! (*pron.* jiû uəs), great god! Good God! Noble God! High God! Lofty God! **Dia** (*pron.* d'iû, jiû, jeea), *n.*, God, a god. **Uas** (*pron.* uəs), *adj.*, noble, good, great, distinguished, excellent, lofty, high; *al.* **uais**.

Gee Whiz came into style in the **gee whiz!** (**dia uas**, *pron.* jíû uas, great god) lingo of the Yellow Press in the 1890s.

"'What we're after,' said Arthur McEwen, the tall goateed Scot who gave brilliance to the *Examiner* editorial page, 'is the **gee-whiz** emotion.' Any issue that did not cause its reader to rise out of his chair and cry '**Great God!**' was counted a failure." (W.A. Swanberg, *Citizen Hearst: The Gee-Whiz Emotion*, 1961, 68.)

In 1894, the *Brooklyn Eagle* knew enough about the origin of "**Gee Whiz**" to put it in the Brooklyn-Irish gob of the fictional Gowanus canal dock-worker "Dusty" O'Dowd. "Den I explained how it wus dat I come to be out dere in de midway, wit me face done up in dat crazy fashion... See? **Gee whiz**, won I heard dat I almost dropped dead." (*Brooklyn Eagle*, Feb. 18, 1894, 4.)

In 1894 **Gee Whiz** shape-shifted into a **nag** (**n-each**, *pron.* n'aċ, a horse). "**Gee Whiz** and Ballot made an interesting race of the 2:45 close, the former well pushed by the stallion and winning each heat by a length or two." (*Brooklyn Eagle*, June 14, 1894, 5.)

Gee Whiz even got into vaudeville in the 1890s. "There is generally fun of the **gee-whiz** rattlety bang kind when Nellie McHenry is around." (*Brooklyn Eagle*, "The Theatre", May 25, 1895, 21.)

As the Yellow Kid usedta' say, "Hully Gee!"

Gee Whillikers, an exclamation like gee whiz.
Dia thoilleachas (*pron.* jíû hoill'ah'ċas), *excl.*, God's will!

Al., **dia thoilleachais**.

Geek, *n.*, (*carnival and circus slang*), a hairy, bushy, animalistic performer whose show consisted of grotesque acts like biting the head off a live chicken. Any hairy, unkempt, odd-looking person. Post-1990s, a brilliant, long-haired, disheveled computer **geek**.
Ciabhach (*pron.* kíahaċ), *adj.*, long-haired, hairy, bushy; disheveled, unkempt; *fig.* a long-haired, bushy-looking person. **Ciabhacht** (*pron.* kíŏaċt) *n.*, (*someone or something*) having long hair. (Dineen, 187; Ó Dónaill, 223.)

"Some historians distinguish between **geeks** who pretend to be wild men, and 'glomming **geeks**,' whose act includes eating disgusting things... In later years the geek show turned into a 'see the pitiful victim of drug abuse' show..." (*Carny Lingo website*, June 2006.)

In a cartoon in Willie Hearst's *San Francisco Examiner* in 1908, a **geek** was drawn as a hairy, bearded, disheveled, bomb-throwing Russian anarchist: "A **geek** who apends his spare time making Czar removers was slammed into the city cooler." (H.C. Fisher, comic strip, *San Francisco Examiner*, Apr. 13, 1908, 28.)

In Chicago hobos were **geeks**. "The jungle hiders come softly forth: **geeks** and gargoyles, old blown winos, sour stewbums and grinning ginsoaks." (N. Algren, *Chicago*, 1951, [2001], 59)

The studious **Geek**, unlike the freak, finally became respectable. "GIRL (*to Freud*): You **geek**." (C. Matheson & E. Solomon, *Bill & Ted's Excellent Adventure* (film script), 1986, 86.)

Geezer, *n.*, a fellow, a guy; an old eccentric man. (Goldin, O'Leary, *Dictionary of American Underworld Lingo*, 77; *DAS*, 211.)

Gaosmhar, gaosach (*pron.* ggæsar, gæsah), *n.*, a wise person, a "wiseguy," *al.* **gaoismhar, gaoiseach**.

Most Anglo-American dictionaries derive **geezer** from *guiser*: one who guises, a masquerader, a mummer.

"SOLDIER: Perhaps I'll meet that Belfast **geezer** on the other side." (Brendan Behan, *The Hostage*, 1958, [1991], 229.)

Geister, *n.*, a thief's confederate.

Gastaire, *n.*, a tricky person; a cunning, impudent fellow. (Dineen, 521; Ó Dónaill, 615.)

A **geister** was a wiseguy, or someone "in the know" in mid-19th century Irish-American gambling slang. (Jonathan Harrington Greene, *The Secret Band of Brothers*, 1841, 107–113.)

Gibberish, *n.*, jargon; the disguised speech of the underworld. "Unintelligible speech belonging to no known language; inarticulate chatter." (Grose, *Classical Dictionary of the Vulgar Tongue*, 1785, [1811]; *OED*.)

Geab ar ais (*pron.* g'ab er'ash), **gab ar ais** (*pron.* gab er'ash), back talk, backward chat; *fig.* back-slanged speech. **Gab**, (*Gaelic*), *n.*, to chat or talk a lot. **Geab** (*pron.* g'ab) *n.*, chat. (*Donegal.*) **Geabaire**, *n.*, a chatterer or blabberer. **Ar ais** (*pron.* er ash), back; backwards.

"Gibberish. The cant language of thieves and gypsies called Pedlar's French, and St. Gile's Greek... a sort of disguised language, formed by inserting any consonant between each syllable of an English word..." (Grose, *Classical Dictionary of the Vulgar Tongue*, 1785, [1811].)

The Irish language was transformed into English **gibberish.** "What (quoth the other) in a rage, thinkest thou that it standeth with Oneile his honor to writh his mouth in clattering English? and yet forsooth we must gag our iawes in **gibbrishing** Irish?" (Holinshed, *Chronicles of England*, 1577–86.)

"He repeated some **gibberish**, which by the sound seemed to be Irish." (Smollett, 1748; *OED.*)

Gigger, *n.*, a latch; a door. (Cant, 16th century.)
Gíogaire, *n.*, a squeaker; *fig.* a squeaky door.

Gigger is one of the earliest canting terms collected from the wandering vagabonds of 16th century England by early slang lexicographers.

"**Gigger**, a Door. (B.E.'s *Dictionary of the Canting Crew*, 1690, in Gotti, *Lexicographica: Language of Thieves and Vagabonds*, 87, 126.)

A **gíogaire** is a squeaky door; but a squeaky laugh is a **giggle**.

Giggle, *n.*, a merry squeaking laugh. A happy squeal. Imitative origin. (Barnhart, 432.)
Gíog gheal (*pron.* gíg h'al, gígyal), a happy squeak, a merry squeal, a slight, joyful squeak. **Gíog**, *n.*, a slight sound, a squeak, a squeal, a slender sound. **Geal** (*pron.* g'al), *adj.*, bright, happy, glad, merry, joyous. **Gealgháire**, *n.*, a light hearted laugh.

Giggle was considered "vulgar slang" well into the 19th century and is included in Francis Grose's *Classical Dictionary of the Vulgar Tongue* in 1811. Some Anglo-American dictionaries inexplicably derive the slang word **giggle** from *giglet*, an obscure English word for a "lewd woman." (*OED.*)

"I almost **giggled** out loud for I could see the guy looked scared stiff like a kid caught swipin' candy." (Jim Tully, *Beggars of Life*, 1926, [2004], 51.)

Gilpin, *al.* **gulpin,** *n.*, a lout, a jerk, an ill-mannered cur.

Guilpín, *n.*, a cur, a lout, an unmannerly person. (Dineen, 579; Ó Dónaill, 679.)

Jimmy Cagney played a bootlegger big shot in the film *The Roaring Twenties*, directed by Raoul Walsh. "For a wise guy it's fifteen miles, for a **gilpin** it's thirty." (Walsh, *The Roaring Twenties*, 1939.)

"What a **gilpin** I turned out to be!" (Walsh, *The Roaring Twenties*, 1939.)

Gimmick, *n.*, a gadget; a contrivance for dishonestly regulating a gambling game, an article used in a conjuring trick; a tricky or ingenious device, gadget, or idea. The word **gimmick** does not enter the printed English language until 1926. Origin unknown. (*OED*; Barnhart, 432.)

Camóg (*Irish*), **camag** (*Gaelic*), *n.*, a trick, a deceit, a scam; a hook; anything crooked; a stick with a crook; anything curved; a device, a gadget; a catch, a clasp, a comma; a camogie. (Dineen, 157; Ó Dónaill, 183; Dwelly, 157.)

The OED and others speculate that **gimmick** may be derived from a magic anagram. "It is an anagram of the word *magic*, and is used by magicians the same way as others use the word 'thing-a-ma-bob.'" (*Words*, Nov. 1936, 12/2; *OED*.)

Goldin and O'Leary's *Dictionary of American Underworld Lingo* gives the definitive definition. "**Gimmick,** *n.*, 1. (*Carnival*) Any of the various devices to control a gaming wheel. **Gimmicks** may be operated by means of a footboard, or "Ikey Heyman" axle, which controls the spin of the wheel (of chance)... The tripod, gaff, or gimmick is always rigged so it can be dismantled at a minute's notice if police investigate. 2. The trick; the catch; the deceptive element, whether concrete or abstract. 3. Any safety attachment on a lock; any gadget that complicates matters and confounds the tamperer. 4. Any device or means by which the element of chance is removed and an outcome prearranged: the fix. **Gimmick,** *v.*, To trick; to cheat; to use any kind of gimmick." (Goldin and O'Leary, *American Underworld Lingo*, 80–81)

"**Gimmick,** a device used for making a fair game crooked." (Maines & Grant, *Wise-Crack Dictionary*, 1926, 8.)

The Barnhart dictionary derives gimmick (camóg) from gimcrack. "Gimmick, slang, 1926, American English. A gadget or device for a trick or deception. Perhaps, alteration of 'gimcrack,' a useless trifle." (Barnhart, 432.)

A **gimmick** (**camóg**, **camag**, a trick, a hook, a device) is always useful.

Gin-i-ker, *n.*, pep, enthusiasm, jazz. A 1913 synonym for "jazz."
Tine caor (*pron.* chin'ə kær, jin'ə kær): a raging fire, lightning, a ball of flame. **Tine**, *al.* **teine** (*pron.* chin'ə, jin'ə), *n.*, fire; conflagration, incandescence; luminosity, flash. **Caor** (*pron.* kær), *n.*, a thunderbolt, a meteor, a round mass of flame, a glowing object.

Great balls of fire! It is the **gin-i-ker** (**tine caor**, *pron.* jin'ə kær, thunderbolt of fire) that produces "**jazz**" (**teas**, *pron.* ch'as, j'as, heat, passion, excitement).

On March 6, 1913, cub reporter Scoop Gleeson used the slang word "**gin-i-ker**" as a synonym for the hot new word "jazz."

"What is the 'jazz'? Why, it's a little of that 'old life,' the '**gin-i-ker**,' the 'pep,' otherwise known as the enthusiasalum..." (Edward Scoop Gleeson, *San Francisco Bulletin*, March 6, 1913.)

In 1938, on the twenty-fifth anniversary of the first appearance of the word "jazz" in San Francisco, Scoop Gleeson recalled the old **gin-i-ker**.

"Similarly, the very word 'jazz' itself came into general usage at the same time. We were all seated around the table at Boyes (Hot Springs) one evening and William ('Spike') Slattery then sports editor of *The Call* spoke about something being the 'jazz' or the old '**gin-i-ker** fizz.'" (E.T. Scoop Gleeson, *San Francisco Call Bulletin*, Sept. 3, 1938, 3.)

Gink, *n.*, a fellow, a man, a hobo (*frequently pejorative*). Origin obscure.
Geanc, geannc, geancaire, *n.*, a snub-nose; a short-faced surly person; a homely snub-nosed person; a crooked dumpy-looking person; one of the lower and more vicious kinds of fairies, a leprechaun. (Dineen, 526; Dwelly, 485; Ó Dónaill, 621; An Seabhac, 61.)

Gink was one of the last words of the Irish-American lawman, gunman, and gambler, Bat Masterson, who knew a surly, snub-nosed **gink** when he saw one.

> Bat Masterson was born Batholomew Masterson in Québec, Canada, in 1853...He was the son of Thomas Masterson and Catherine McGurk, both of Irish ancestry...On Oct. 25, 1921 the 68-year-old Masterson showed up for work (as a sportswriter in New York City), sat down at his typewriter and began tapping out a column. He died of a sudden heart attack before finishing, but he wrote enough to convey his hardscrabble view of life: "There are those who argue that everything breaks even in this dump of a world of ours. I suppose the **ginks** who argue that way hold that because the rich man gets ice in the summer and the poor man gets it in the winter things are breaking even for both. Maybe so, but I'll swear that I can't see it that way." (Edward T. O'Donnell, *Irish Echo*, August 9, 2006.)

"I went to the bar and called for a drink,
The bartender said I was a **gink**."
("The Old Chisholm Trail," Lomax, *CSFB*, 1910, [1986], 34.)

Gila Monster Route
"Nothing in sight but sand and space
No chance for a **gink** to feed his face;
Not even a shack to beg for a lump,
Or a hen-house to frisk for a single gump.
...He was ditched on the Gila Monster Route."
(L.F. Post, Glenn Norton, song, "Gila Monster Route," in Lomax, *AFSB*, 1934, [1994], 24–26.)

Rocky: And wait until the old **gink** finds out what she is. Watch him unload her." (Mae West, *Sex: A Comedy Drama*, 1926, [1997], 37.)

Rocky: I'd be a handy man to have around the house. That husband of yours is an old **gink**. (Mae West, *Sex: A Comedy Drama*, 1926, [1997], 87.)

Gism, *al.* gissom, jasm, jas'm, *n.*, passion, enthusiasm, energy; semen.
Teas ioma (*pron.* j'ass iomə, ch'ass iomə), an abundance of heat, passion, excitement. **Teas** (*pron.* t'as, j'as, ch'as), *n.*, heat, passion, excitement, fervor, highest temperature. **Ioma** (*pron.* iomə), *adj.*, abundance; excess.

Peter Tamony, the legendary San Francisco Irish-American folklore collector and etymologist, researched the published history of **gism** and **jasm**.

> The 1860 example of Jasm ("energy, enthusiasm") in *A Dictionary of Americanisms on Historical Principle*s... is from the work of Josiah Holland, a Massachusetts writer, while the 1848 example **Gism** ("strength, talent") cited in *Dialect Notes*, VI (X), 453, is a Rhode Island usage. John S. Farmer, *Americanisms, Old and New*, 1889, defines **Gism** as "a synonym for energy, spirit." M.M. Mathews in his *Dictionary of Americanisms*... defined **Jasm** as "...energy, enthusiasm... origin obscure. Possibly the same word as **gism**, semen." (Peter Tamony, *JEMF Quarterly*, Spring 1981, 11.)

"If you'll take thunder and lightning and a steamboat and a buzz-saw and mix 'em up and put 'em into a woman that's **Jasm**." (Josiah Holland, *Miss Gilbert*, 1860, 350.)

"Willin', but hain't no more **jas'm** than a dead cornstalk." (*Harper's*, Sept. 1886, 579/2.)

Glim, *n.*, a candle; a fire; a lamp; a light of any kind; a window, an eye.
Gealaim (*pron.* ga'lim), *v.*, I light or brighten. **Geal-laom** (*pron.* **g'al læm**): a bright blaze of fire, a bright flash, a bright white flame, a bright blaze, a bright shining, a gleam. Geal, *adj.*, geal-, (*in compounds*) bright, white (*of brilliant white color*). Geal, *n.*, white, brightness. **Laom**, *n.*, a blaze of fire; a shining brightly; a flash, a blaze. (Dineen, 631; Ó Dónaill, 619, 620.)

Glim first came to light in Irish-American vernacular in the 19th century and is "probably of Irish underworld origin" according to the *Dictionary of American Slang*. (*DAS*, 217.)

"'Bring me the **glim**,' commanded the tramp I had aroused." (Jim Tully, *Beggars of Life: A Hobo Autobiography*, 1924, [2004], 14, 15)

"Nix on that **glim**, we ain't got a license to clip (steal) around here. (Goldin, O'Leary, *Dictionary of the American Underworld*, 1950, 82.)

Glom, glaum, *v.*, to grab, snatch; to steal.
Glám, *n.*, grab, snatch. **Glám**, *v.*, to grab, to clutch, to grasp. (Ó Dónaill, 639; Dineen, 541.)

The Dictionary of American Slang derives **glom** from "hobo and underworld use." (*DAS*, 217.)

Glom, to grab, as in stealing. (Goldin, O'Leary, *Dictionary of the American Underworld*, 1950, 82, 83.)

"It may have been the Easter Season... but tis a fact, 'Chic' Hartley actually broke through his shell yesterday and **glommed** a couple of hits." (Scoop Gleeson, *San Francisco Bulletin*, April 15, 1912, 18.)

Glommer, *n.*, a grabber; a thief. (*DAS*, 217.)
Glámaire, *n.*, a grabber, a snatcher. (Ó Dónaill, 639.)

Gob, *n.*, mouth. (Slang.)
Gob, *n.*, beak, mouth.

"Of obscure origin; possibly ...Gael and Irish *gob* beak, mouth..." (*OED*.)

The American slang lexicographers Wentworth and Flexner put **gob** back into the **gob** of the Irish. "(**Gob**) came to the U.S. not from England, but directly from Ireland." (Wentworth and Flexner, *Dictionary of American Slang*, 1960, 218.)

Goo Goo, Goo Goos, *n.*, a derisive moniker given to upper-class "reformers" and "good government" types by Irish-Americans. The name **Goo Goo** is said to be derived from a contraction of the words "good government."
Guth (*pron.* guh), *n.*, a voice, a human voice; a sound, an utterance; a complaint, a reproach; blame, censure. **Guth guth** (*pron.* guh guh), complain, complain; reproach, reproach; blame blame; censure, censure; *fig.* blah, blah.

To Irish-American politicians, and their working-class supporters in Boston and New York, Protestant "reformers" were busybody swells, whose ideas of reform involved closing down saloons on Sundays, most workers' only day off in the early-20th century, and denying charity to those they deemed the unworthy and immoral. "Reform administrations suffer from a diarrhea of promises and a constipation of performance." (James Michael Curley, *I'd Do It Again: A Record of All My Uproarious Years*, 1957, 73.)

> The Good Government Association had been founded in Boston in
> 1903 by former Mayor Nathan Matthews Jr., and other bluebloods and
> social climbers. It was always open season for the **Goo-Goos** as far as I
> was concerned. (James Michael Curley, *I'd Do It Again: A Record of All My
> Uproarious Years*, 1957, 73.)

Five-time Boston Mayor James Michael Curley was born into an Irish-speaking family from Galway. Like many Boston ward heelers in the late-19th and
early-20th centuries, Curley gave speeches in English and Irish.

> (Martin) Lomasney, as I did later, also addressed certain voters in Gaelic if
> that was the only language they understood... (James Michael Curley, *I'd
> Do It Again: A Record of All My Uproarious Years*, 1957, 25.)

> Realizing the man (a voter) was a deaf mute, Joe immediately wigwagged
> his fingers in the deaf-and-dumb language, and the mute wigwagged back
> and nodded his head in agreement ... The Democratic leader... remarked:
> "How could you beat that combination? One of them talks in the deaf-
> and-dumb language and the other in Gaelic." (Curley, *I'd Do It Again: A
> Record of All My Uproarious Years*, 1957, 25.)

> [New York Mayor Jimmy] Walker himself memorialized this philosophy
> with one of his many critiques of the **"Goo Goos,"** or Good Government
> reformers, who were the bane of Tammany Hall. "A reformer," said
> Walker, "is a guy who rides through a sewer in a glass-bottom boat." (T.J.
> English, *Paddy Whacked*, 2005, 205.)

> Fitzgerald, their hated enemy, became mayor and the **"Goo Goos"** had a
> majority on the Council! Oh mother get a hammer, there's a fly on baby's
> head. (James Michael Curley, *I'd Do It Again: A Record of All My Uproarious
> Years*, 1957, 111.)

Goof, *n.*, a stupid person, a buffoon; a half-crazy person, a loudmouth, a
showoff; a goofball, a "nut case;" *al.* a stupid mistake. **Goofy,** *adj.*, stupid,
foolish, wild, crazy (as if on drugs), loud-mouthed, daft.

Gáifeach (*pron.* ga'fəċ, gá'fə), *adj.*, exaggerated, given to wild exaggeration,
flamboyant, ostentatious, loud, loud-mouthed; querulous. **Gáifeacht** (*pron.*
gá'fəċt), *n.*, exaggeration, loud-mouthedness; flamboyancy, ostentation.

Goofy, the cartoon dog, was known for his **goofy** (**gáifeacha**, *pron.* gá'fə,
exaggerated, loud) laugh.

Goofy, the cartoon character, made his first appearance ... in *Mickey's Revue* (1932). What distinguished the character... was not so much his appearance but his raucous laugh. That laugh, supplied by Disney storyman, musician, and former circus clown Pinto Colvig, made such an impression on Walt Disney and his staff that the character soon began to be featured in other cartoons. (*Disney Archives* online, June 2006.)

"You got a **goofy** look," Dick Buckford said... "Yeah, you're **goofy**! You're **goofy**." Dick sneered... "If you say I am, then you're a **goof** too!" (James T. Farrell, "Helen, I Love You," *Chicago Stories*, 1930, 1.)

When someone is **goofy**, they act like a wild and crazy guy, or a goofball. "A sodium pentobarbital capsule is a **goof**-pill." (H.L. Mencken, *American Language*, II, 1948, 682.)

Goon, *n.*, a fool. **Goony**, *adj.*, foolish, silly, humorous. Origin unknown.
Guan, *n.*, a fool. **Guanach** (*pron.* guənəh), *adj.*, foolish, silly. (Dineen, 578; Dwelly, 531.)

Goon does not appear in print in English until the late-1920s. Most dictionaries derive **goon** from the huge, hirsute, sub-human cartoon creature, "Alice the **Goon**," drawn by the American cartoonist, E.C. Segar, who also created "Popeye." (Chapman *American Slang*, 179.)

The word "**Goon**" was first popularized by college students who used it to mean any stupid person. Labor union lingo has given it a second meaning: a tough or thug. Rival unions and factions speak of another's "**Goon** Squads." (*Life*, Nov. 14, 1938, 6.)

The son of an Irish Captain in the British army in India, Terence Alan Patrick Sean "Spike" Milligan was the brilliant Irish **guan** (fool) on the BBC's *Goon Show* in the 1950s.

Gopher Gang, *n.*, Hell's Kitchen Irish gang in the early-20th century.
Comhbhá (*pron.* coufa, gofa), *n.*, alliance (gang), close alliance.

In the early-20th century, Owney Madden, "Tanner" Smith, and Tammany Hall big shot Jimmy Hines united the balkanized Irish gangs of New York's Hell's Kitchen into the **Gopher** (**Comhbhá**, *pron.* gofa, alliance) Gang.

Owney Madden! Why, Owney was my little pal. The papers called Owney the chief of the **Gopher** Gang on the West Side and he was waiting to be tried on the charge of having some of his men bump off an enemy in a saloon ... I knew Owney since he was a kid; he was an Irish cockney like myself... (Butler & Driscoll, *Dock Walloper: The Story of "Big Dick" Butler*, 1933, 189.)

Graft (1) (*orig. U.S.*), *n.*, profits from politics, called "contributions" today. Graft is whatever can be grubbed by politicians and government officials in exchange for votes, influence, and favors. **Grafter** (*orig. U.S.*), *n.*, a thief, a swindler; a corrupt politician on the take; a grubber, a mooch.

Grafa, grafadh (*pron.* grafǝ, grafah), *vn.*, grubbing, scrounging; hoeing.

Grafadóir (*pron.* grafǝdór), *n.*, a grubber; a scrounger a moocher; *fig.* a professional politician.

In Ring Lardner's *Baseball Stories*, written in 1914, a fictional Irish-American major league pitcher (and half-a-wise-guy), Jack Keefe, accuses his sister-in-law of being a **grafter** (**grafadóir**, grubber, scrounger).

She says I don't see why you can't take me if Allen takes Marie. And I says that stuff is all O.K. for Allen because him and Marie have been **grafting** off us all winter. And then she gets mad and tells me I should not ought to say her sister was no **grafter**. (Ring Lardner, in George W. Hilton, ed., *The Annotated Baseball Stories of Ring W. Lardner: 1914–1919*, Jan. 31, 1913, [1995], 110,111.)

Then he says I would not make no holler about your **grafting** off of me if that brat would shut up at nights and give somebody a chance to sleep. I said you should get all the sleep you need on the bench. Besides, I says, who done the **grafting** last winter and without no invitation? If he had said another word I was going to bust him but just then Marie come in and he shut up. (George W. Hilton, ed., *The Annotated Baseball Stories of Ring W. Lardner: 1914–1919*, Oct. 2, 1913, [1995], 154.)

In American slang, the word **grafter** is mainly applied to the professional political **grafter** (**grafadóir**, grubber, moocher), constantly scrounging for "donations" from corporations and lobbyists.

"Moiphy Voisus Hoist." The lyrics of a pro-Hearst, anti-Tammany Hall campaign song, from the 1905 New York mayoral race, explained how political **graft** worked:

> Everybody woiks for Moiphy;
> He only rakes in the dough.

"Moiphy" was Tammany Hall big shot Charles F. Murphy. At the end of the day, "Willie" Hearst lost the election when the Tammany machine raked in the ballot boxes along with the **graft**.

> There's honest **graft**, and I'm an example of how it works. I might sum up the whole thing by sayin': "I seen my opportunities and I took 'em." (George Washington Plunkitt in William Riordan, *Plunkitt of Tammany Hall*, 1905, [1963], 3.)

> **Graft** is an ugly word … graft may mean anything from greasing a cop's palm to shaking down a subway contractor for a million. (Butler & Driscoll, *Dock Walloper*, 1930, 129.)

> The man who makes money without doing anything for it is not only a **grafter**, he's a thief… Grafting will exist as long as there are favors to be done. (Butler & Driscoll, *Dock Walloper*, 1930, 129, 130.)

> Most of the **graft** nowadays (1920s) passes through the hands of lawyers, disguised as legal fees. (Butler & Driscoll, *Dock Walloper*, 1930, 130.)

> "Weeping Willie" Graham had a double **graft** (at the Haymarket). Aside from collecting two-bits off the girls as they passed in, he used to sponge on the suckers. (Butler & Driscoll, *Dock Walloper*, 1930, 115.)

Graft (2) (*Australian slang*), *n.*, work, especially hard work. American political **graft** is "nice work if you can get it."

Grifter, *n.*, a con man. A **grifter** is a specialized **grafadóir** (grubber), perpetually on the prowl for a mark: constantly searching saloons, hotels, train stations, and racetracks for a ripe **sucker** (**sách úr**, *pron.* sawċ úr, fresh fat cat).
Grafadóir, *n.*, a grubber, a scrounger.

> McGLOIN: I'd rather sleep in the gutter than pass another night under the same roof with that loon, Hickey, and a lying circus **grifter**! (Eugene O'Neill, *The Iceman Cometh*, 1939, [1954], 682.)

Grouch, *n.*, an irritable, cross, vexatious person. **Groucher,** *n.*, an irritable complainer. **Grouchy,** *adj.*, irritable; cross.

Cráite (*pron.* krá'chə), *adj.*, tormented, troubled, vexed, pained; annoyed.

Cráiteoir (*pron.* krá'chor), *n.*, a miserable, vexatious person. A miser.

Cráiteachán (*pron.* krá'chəċán), *n.*, tormented person; a grumbler, a wretch. A miser. (Ó Dónaill, 308; Dineen, 256.)

Grouch and **grouchy** do not appear in American "English" until 1900 and are classified as hobo and carny slang. Some dictionaries derive the **grouchy grouch** from an obscure English word *grutch*, which became obsolete in English in the 1680s.

> They began to get a **grouch** on against the gay-cats that kep' comin' to their camps. (J. Flynt, *Notes of an Itinerant Policeman*, 1900, 160.)

Grouch bag (*circus and carny slang*), *n.*, small bags made of chamois skin and tied about the neck. Circus workers as a rule did not like people who saved money. They called them **grouchy**. A grouch bag is a miser's bag. Also called a "plunge."

Ground-sweat, *n.*, a grave.

Grian suite (*pron.* griŏn sŭīt'), a sunny site, a sunny spot; *fig.* a gravesite.

The Night Before Larry was Stretched
(*ca.*1816)

The night before Larry was stretch'd,
  The boys they all paid him a visit...

Then in came the priest with his book
  He spoke him so smooth and so civil;
Larry tipp'd him a Kilmainham look,
  And pitch'd his big wig to the devil...

When he came to the nubbing-cheat,
  He was tack'd up so neat and so pretty;
The rambler jugg'd off from his feet,
  And he died with his face to the city.
He kick'd too, but that was all pride,
  For soon you might see 'twas all over;
And as soon as the nooze was untied,
  Then at darkey we waked him in clover,

And sent him to take a **ground-sweat**.

"Will Maher, a shoemaker of Waterford, wrote the song... Often quoted in song books and elsewhere." (www.fromoldbooks.org, accessed July 2006.)

Growler, *n.*, a small can used to carry fresh beer home from a saloon.
Gearr-ól úr (*pron.* g'ar-ól úr), *al.* **geárr-óil úr**, *n.*, a fresh quick-drink, a fresh short-drink, a fresh small-drink.

Gearr- (*pron.* g'ar), *prefix*, short-, brief-, small-, near-; quick-; **gear-shúilach**, fast-moving, rapid. **Gearr**, *adj.*, short, near (*distance or time*), soon, quick. **Ól**, **óil**, *g.*, drink; booze. **Úr**, *adj.*, fresh, new. **Úr**, *n.*, anything fresh or new. (Dineen, 528, 529; Ó Dónaill, 623.)

"The '**growler**' is the tin pail in which families are served the beer for their meals or for visiting friends, from neighboring saloons. When the beer is wanted, it is wanted fresh. It is therefore wanted quickly. Hence the 'rush' for it and back again." (*Brooklyn Eagle*, July 29, 1889, 2.)

My Little Side Door
I've a nate little bar for beer and cigar,
Fine whiskey and sweet lemonade;
About six o'clock there's no bar on the block
Can equal my family trade;
I've brandy and gin, there's no bar can begin
For to beat me in liquor galore;
They say: "how are you, Dan?" with **growler** in hand,
As they enter my little side door...
Oh it's "good evening, Dan," wid **growler** in hand,
They enter my little side door."
(Words by Edward Harrigan; music by Dave Braham, 1884.)

"TWO AMAZONS—Miss 'Plug' McCarthy and Miss Kitty Murray Pound Each Other in True Sullivan Style—...'**Rushing the growler**' is their favorite pastime, and if a stranger happens to pass, they have no hesitation grasping him by the arm and asking him to produce the 7 cents necessary for a can of beer." (*Brooklyn Eagle*, April 27, 1887, 6.)

The *Brooklyn Eagle* attempted an etymology of **growler** in 1889.

> RUSHING THE **GROWLER**—An interesting exchange of views is going
> on between the *Rochester Post-Express* and the *Buffalo Courier* about slang.
> *The Courier* wants to know about "rushing the **growler**." Why "**growler**?"...
> Selling beer in such quantities as tin pails will hold is much less profit-
> able than getting rid of it at 5 cents a glass, drank on the premises.
> Nevertheless the saloon keepers do not refuse this family custom ... Very
> often they complain of the size of the tin pails ... Hence the advent of
> these tin pails makes them complain or growl, as the homely vernacular
> of the tin pail brigade put it. This vessel which makes the bar keepers
> growl, itself comes to be called the "**growler**"... the beer it holds is wanted
> quickly so that it shall be fresh... (*Brooklyn Eagle*, July 29, 1889, 2.)

I asked my mother, who was born in Brooklyn in 1918, about the **growler**,
thinking I might get a funny story out of her. She did not think **growler** was
funny at all. It brought back memories. "They lived on the third floor and
used to pull 'the can' up on the end of a string so they could keep drinking."
(Author's notes, June 2005.)

> THEY WORKED THE **GROWLER**—And as a Result Mrs. Donnelly
> is Now in the Hospital—... Mrs. Donnolly ... refused to replenish the
> **growler** whereupon ... her husband struck her on the side of the head
> with the pitcher causing a horrible looking gash. (*Brooklyn Eagle*, Feb. 1,
> 1888, 4.)

The **growler** was rushed wherever Irish-American vernacular was spoken—
from New York to New Orleans. "Before she could say one word Mayann
threw her on the floor and began choking her to death ... she would have
killed her if it had not been for Black Benny and some of the boys who
gambled and rushed the **growler** around Liberty and Perdido." (Louis
Armstrong, *Satchmo: My Life in New Orleans*, 1954, 88, 112.)

Grumble, *n.*, complain, mutter in discontent. "Proximate source uncertain."
(*OED*, July 2006.)

Gruaim béil, *al.*, **gruaim béal**, gloomy speech, sullen speech, discontented,
surly speech, complaining talk. **Gruaim**, *n.*, gloom; sullenness; displeasure;
discontent; ill-humor, surliness, churlishness. **Béal**, *g.* (*pron.* bæl), *n.*, mouth,
talk, speech; **droich-béal**, an evil way of speech.

The Irish words **gruaim béil** (gloomy mouth or speech) emerge as the phonetically spelled *grumble* in the late-16th century. Grouchy **grumble** is considered vulgar slang well into the 19th century. No wonder grumble (**gruaim béal**, gloomy speech, sullen speech, complaining talk) is always groaning and moaning.

> **Grumble.** To grumble in the gizzard; to murmur or repine. He grumbled like a bear with a sore head. (Grose, *Classical Dictionary of the Vulgar Tongue*, 1785, [1811].)

Guffaw, *n.*, a burst of coarse laughter; a loud or boisterous laugh. "Etymology echoic." (*OED*, July 2006.)

Gáire foghar (*pron.* gá'rə faur), laughing sound or noise. **Gáire foghrach** (*pron.* gá'rə faurəċ, gá'rə faurəh), a resounding laugh, noisy laughter. **Gáire** (*pron.* gá-rə), *n.*, laughter, a laugh; act of laughing. **Foghar** (*pron.* faur), *n.*, sound, noise. **Foghrach** (*pron.* faurəċ faurəh), *adj.*, sounding, resounding.

> That silly fliskmahoy ... has ... done naething but laugh and greet, the skirl at the tail o' **guffa'**, for twa days successfully. (Scott, *Antiq.*, 1816; *OED*, July 2006.)

> Bill sat next to me at ringside and **guffawed** mountainously at Joe Gans' second trouncing of Jimmy Britt, a bout which introduced the famous 'ulna' bone alibi into pugilistic records. (Harry J. Coleman, *Give Us a Little Smile, Baby*, 1943, 171.)

Gump, *n.*, a chicken.

Colm (*pron.* kŭləm), *n.*, a dove, a pigeon; *fig.* a chicken, an edible "boid."

> "Nothing in sight but sand and space
> No chance for a gink to feed his face;
> Not even a shack to beg for a lump,
> Or a hen-house to frisk for a single **gump.**
> ...In a hostile burg on the Nickel Plate."
> (Post, Norton, "Gila Monster Route," song,
> in Lomax, *ABFS*, 1934, [1994], 24–26.)

Gunga Din, *n.*, a nickname given to an Indian water carrier by Irish "grunts" in the British colonial army in India in the 1890s. It appears in Kipling's poetic paean to imperialism "Gunga Din."

Gungaire Dian! Gungaire, dian! (*pron.* gungĭrə d'iən!), Quick Little Skinny-Rump! Little Skinny-Ass, (come) quick!

Gungaire, *n.*, a hunched-over, narrow-rumped, skinny-assed, shrunken little person. **Gunga**, *n.*, a shrunken, contorted posture, crouching, hunkered-down posture; *fig.* a small crouching person. **Gungach**, *adj.*, narrow-loined, narrow-rumped, skinny-assed; awkward; crouching, shrunken. **Dian** (*pron.* d'iən), *adj.*, swift, quick; eager, intense.

Gunga Din
By Rudyard Kipling

...Now in Injia's sunny clime,
Where I used to spend my time
A-servin' of 'Er Majesty the Queen,
Of all them blackfaced crew
The finest man I knew
Was our regimental *bhisti*, **Gunga Din**.
    It was **"Din! Din! Din!"**
    You limpin' lump o' brick-dust, **Gunga Din**!
    Hi! *slippery hitherao*!
    Water, get it! *Panee lao*!
    You squidgy-nosed old idol, **Gunga Din**.

The uniform 'e wore
Was nothin' much before,
An' rather less than 'arf o' that be'ind,
For a piece o' twisty rag
An' a goatskin water-bag
Was all the field-equipment 'e could find...
    It was **"Din! Din! Din!**
    You 'eathen, where the mischief 'ave you been?
    You put some juldee in it
    Or I'll marrow you this minute
    If you don't fill up my helmet, **Gunga Din**!"

(Rudyard Kipling, "Gunga Din," 1892.)

Guzzle, *n.*, *v.*, to drink with great vigor, to drink greedily.

Gus óil (*pron.* gus ól), *al.*, **gus** (a) **ól**, a vigorous drink; high-spirited vigorous drinking, (act of) gulping down drink. **Gus**, *pl.* -sa, *n.*, strong feeling, high spirit, vigor, force; motion. **Ól**, *g.*, **óil**, *n.*, drink; *vn.*, (*act of*) drinking, soaking, absorbing; **ag ól**, drinking, having a drink. (Dineen, 818, 819.)

Guzzle spelled *gusle*, and *guzle*, enters the printed English language in the 17th century. The *OED* derives **guzzle** from an Old French word meaning "to vomit or to chatter:" (*OED*, July 2006.) More than two hundred years later **guzzle** was still considered slang and set off by quotation marks in the *Brooklyn Eagle*.

> Whether Tilton took wine for his dinner was important to only the waiter who had to collect the lucre for the liquor. Whether Fulton **"guzzled"** beer was of just as much importance. (*Brooklyn Eagle*, Oct. 17, 1870, 2.)

> SAMPLING BROOKLYN WHISKEY—Three Poteen Dealers at Issue—Brandy at 75 Cents a Gallon—It is no wonder people die when one takes into consideration the fact that they drink such horrid stuff... Even old ladies ... have to **"guzzle"** these reptiles in a boiled condition. (*Brooklyn Eagle*, March 16, 1871, 2.)

> The visit of the legislature to Randall's Island on Tuesday and the **"guzzling"** of wine, rum, and brandy and the rowdy display which has been detailed in the morning papers was an edifying spectacle... Yet, these were the fellows who were elected to enact an act for suppression of temperance. (*Brooklyn Eagle*, March 15, 1855, 2.)

Hack, *n.*, a horse, or horse carriage, let out for hire; a hackney; (*deprecatively*) a sorry old horse, a drudge; later applied figuratively to any common hack, as in a political hack, or hack writer. A prison guard.

Each (*pron.* a'ċ, h-a'ċ), *n.*, a horse, a steed. **Each** Spáinneach (*pron.* a'ċ spán'aċ), Spanish horse, a variety of short horse; **each** uisce (*pron* h-a'ċ ishk'ə), a water horse; **each** ráis, a racehorse. (Dineen, 383.)

> "My horse, young man! He is but a **hack** hired from a roadside posting house." (Charles Dickens, *Barnaby Rudge*, 1840.)

BURNED ALIVE—Forty-Three Horses in New York This Morning—...It was learned that some of the horses that were burned were celebrated in racing circles, but for the most part were **hack** horses, bordered there by their owners. (*Brooklyn Eagle*, Feb. 27, 1879, 4.)

They recognize the ... apprehensive policy which lead(s) the **hack** politicians to decorate the city halls ... with bunting... (*Brooklyn Eagle*, Sept. 5, 1887, 2.)

Hackey, *al.* hackie, *n.*, a hack-driver; a horse-carriage driver, (*modern*) a cab driver. Origin uncertain. (*DAS*, 238.)

Eachaí (*pron.* a'čí, h-a'čí), *n.*, a horseman; *fig.* a horse-carriage or hack driver. It evolved in slang to mean a cab driver.

My Uncle Ranny worked as a **hackey** in New York from the 1920s until World War II. Jack Dempsey once rode in my Uncle Ranny's hack. When he got out, Dempsey tipped him a dime. Ranny threw it back and said, "Keep the change." (From author's memory.)

Hackney, *n.*, a horse let out for hire; a draught horse; a horse and small carriage for hire; (*20th century*) a motor driven cab.

Each ceannaich (*Gaelic; pron.* h-ač k'anič, h-ač k'anǐh), *n.*, a post-horse, horse kept at an inn or post-house for use by mail carriers, or for rent to travelers; a purchase-horse, a hire horse. **Each** (*pron.* h-ač), *n.*, a horse. **Ceannaich,** *n.*, hire; purchase. **Ceannach** (*pron.* k'annəh), *n.*, ceannaigh, *g.*, purchase horse; (Dwelly,376; Dineen,176–178; An Seabhac, 20, 21.)

Each ceannaich (*pron.* h-ač k'anič, h-ač k'anǐh), meaning "a post horse or hire-horse," is the simple Gaelic solution to the origin of the word **hackney**; which is later applied to any horse or horse-carriage for hire. In the 20th century it becomes a name for a motor-driven (horseless) carriage or cab. (Dwelly, 376; Dineen, 176.)

Hanker, *n.*, a craving or yearning; *v.*, to crave or yearn.

An-ghá (*pron.* anghá, h-anghá), *n.*, a great need, a very great want. **An-** (*hyphenated intensive prefix*), great; very. **Gá,** *al.* **gábhadh** (*pron.* gáwŭ), *n.*, want, need, requirement, necessity; distress; *al.* **gádh.** Tá **an-ghá** agam leis (*pron.* tá h-ángha agəm l'esh), I want it very badly.

Hanker: Not known before 1600; history obscure... (*OED*, July 2006.)

Hanker (an-ghá, *pron.* h-anghá, a great need or want) is another Irish phonetic word that appears in English at the beginning of the 17th century, along with thousands of **hankering** Irish immigrants, fleeing the wars of the Tudor conquest. Three centuries later, *hanker* was still a word of the vulgar tongue.

"**Hanker.** To **hanker** after any thing; to have a longing after or for it." (Francis Grose, *Classical Dictionary of the Vulgar Tongue*, 1785, [1811].)

Heckle, *v.*, to verbally harass, to rant. In 19th century Scotland the public questioning of candidates to Parliament was called heckling.
Éamh call (*pron.* h-æw call), screaming out complaints; ranting, scolding. **Éamh** (*pron.* h-æw), *vn.*, (*act of*) crying out, screaming, complaining. **Call,** *n.*, need, want, necessity, loss.

> Many Anglo-American dictionaries derive the **heckle** of loud verbal complaint and harassment from the English verb *heckle*, meaning "to dress flax." (*OED*.)

> "By this time, Fitz was in real difficulty. The peanut gallery had begun to **heckle** by yoo-hooing and tossing unshucked peanuts stageward, shouting the while..." (Harry J. Coleman, *Give Us a Little Smile, Baby*, 1943, 65.)

Heckler, *n.*, a verbal harasser; a person who shouts loud abuse (at a baseball umpire, politician, or speaker). (Barnhart, 472.)
Éamh callaire (*pron.* h-æw callĭrə), a shouting ranter; a screaming loudmouth; a loud shouting scold. **Éamh** (*pron.* h-æw), *vn.*, (*act of*) crying out, screaming, complaining. (Ó Dónaill, 478; Dineen, 393.) **Callaire,** *n.*, a crier; a loud talker, a ranter, a loud speaker, a loud-mouthed person. (de Bhaldraithe, 425; Ó Dónaill, 181; Dineen, 155.)

The loud **heckler** (**éamh callaire,** *pron.* h-æw callĭrə, a screaming loudmouth) does not enter the English language until the late-1880s, where it spent most of its time screaming and complaining at political rallies.

Hecklers, Windjammers, and Orators.

"Mr. Shepherd is not afraid to have questions addressed to him ... and he replied to this particular **heckler** by saying that while it weas true that he was now counsel for the glue company, his client in the event of his election would be the City of Brooklyn and the City of Brooklyn alone." (*Brooklyn Eagle*, Oct. 25, 1895, 6.)

Heeler, ward heeler, *n.*, a ward-level political representative; the foot soldier of the old Irish-American urban political machine.

Éilitheoir (*pron.* éló′r, h-ælór), one who demands or charges; a petitioner; a claimer; a friendly petitioner, a claimsman, an advocate; one who makes friendly inquires about; one who visits in a friendly manner. (Dineen, 402; Ó Dónaill, 487.)

In New York City and Brooklyn you went to your ward **heeler** (**éilitheoir**, *pron.* éló′r, h-ælór, claimsman, advocate) "with your personal problems, and all he asked in exchange for his help was your vote. He was the man to see for a job, a liquor or pushcart license, a bucket of coal when there was no money to buy one, help in making out citizenship papers, or in bailing a husband out of jail." (William L. Riordan, *Plunkitt of Tammany Hall: A Series of Very Plain Talks on Very Practical Politics*, 1905, [1963], xvi.)

> The noun **éilitheoir** (*pron.* éló′r, h-ælór, a friendly petitioner or advocate) is related to the Irish verb **éilighim** (*pron.* élím) and means: "I look for, demand, call to account, sue for; I make a friendly quest for; I visit; I pursue." This is a job description of a ward **heeler**.

The well-heeled editors of most Anglo-American dictionaries derive the word *heeler* from the *heel* of a shoe: "One who follows at the heels of a leader or 'boss'; an unscrupulous or disreputable follower of a professional politician. U.S." (*OED*.)

In the old immigrant, working-class neighborhoods of New York City, a ward **heeler** was often a do-gooder. "Everyone in the neighborhood knew (Al Smith) by then, even a local fellow named Eddie Cantor. In his memoirs, Cantor wrote that Smith 'was a **ward heeler** and a do-gooder, the first I'd ever known, the nearest thing to a knight in shining armor that ever showed up around Catherine, Oliver, Madison, Monroe, or Henry streets.'" (Robert A. Slayton, *Empire Statesman: The Rise and Redemption of Al Smith*, 2001, 63.)

Al Smith went from ward **heeler** to Governor of New York State. Of course, the other party's ward **heeler** (**éilitheoir**, *pron.* h-éló'r, claimsman, petitioner) was always a **grafter** (**grafadóir**, grubber, scrounger; *fig.* a thief).

> There is a good deal of dirty work going on among the Republican ward **heelers** and workers in the way of intimidating voters. In the Seventeenth Ward (*ed.* Greenpoint, Brooklyn) some of these men called at the houses of voters of the poorer class and threatened them with arrest upon a charge of illegal registration... (*Brooklyn Eagle*, Nov. 2, 1876, 4.)

Helter skelter, *adv.*, "In disordered haste; confusedly, tumultuously, pell-mell. (1593)... while *helter* has no explanation other than its suggestive sound and rhyme with *skelter*, the final element is probably based on *skelte*, to hasten, scatter hurriedly... The adjective meaning of disorderly or confused is first recorded in 1785; the noun about 1713." (Barnhart, 475.)

Áilteoir scaoilte (*pron.* ál-t'or' skílt'ə, h-ál-t'or' skílt'ə), a run amuck clown; an unconstrained wild prankster; a loose-limbed trickster; a joker running loose. The Joker is wild! **Áilteoir**, -ora (*pron.* h-ál-t'or'), *n.*, a trickster, a practical joker, one who plays pranks, an "arch" fellow, a frivolous person, the clown in a circus; an acrobat. (Dineen,16; Ó Dónaill, 19.) **Scaoilte** (*pron.* skílt'ə), *p.p. of* **scaoil**, *adj.*, scattered; broken loose, broken free, unconstrained, run-amuck; released, let go; loose-limbed. Madraidhe scaoilte, dogs a-loose, hounds run-amuck.

Áilteoir scaoilte spelled **helter skelter** is often used in English as a metaphorical adverb and adjective, meaning "disordered haste; a-loose, amuck, confusedly, tumultuously, pell-mell;" like a joker run wild or a run-amuck clown." **Helter skelter** is a wild and crazy guy.

> **Helter Skelter**. To run helter skelter, hand over head, in defiance of order. (Grose, *Classical Dictionary of the Vulgar Tongue*, 1785, [1811].)

> **Helter-skelter** have I rode to thee, and tydings do I bring. (Shakespeare, *Henry IV*, 1597, Act V, Scene III.)

Henry Colton, the king of the faro gamblers in New York City in the 1840s.

An Rí Ghealltain (*pron.* ənrí gh'al'tĭn), the King of Bets, the King of wagering. In New York City in the 1840s, the Big Easy faro dealer Pat Herne teamed up with top faro banker Henry Colton, who "was regarded as a sort of supreme tribunal of gaming ... and in gambling circles throughout the United States his decisions were binding." (Herbert Asbury, *Sucker's Progress*, 1938, [2003], 170, 235; T. J. English, *Paddy Whacked*, 2005, 47-55.)

Hep, hip, *adj.*, well-informed, knowledgeable, wise, in-the-know; smart, stret-smart; stylish. Unknown origin. (*OED.*)

Aibí (*pron.* h-abí; *contraction* h-ab'), *adj.*, mature, quick, clever, quick-witted; *fig.* wise.

Hep (and hip) are derived from the simple contraction of the Irish word **aibí** (*pron.* h-abí; *contraction* h-ab', mature, quick, clever) since to be **hep** or **hip** is to be **duine aibí** (*pron.* dinǝ h'abí), a quick-witted person, or **páiste aibí**, a clever, mature baby with a **súil abaí**, a keen eye.

> By running with the older boys I soon began to get **hep**. (Louis Armstrong, quoted in Chapman, *American Slang*, 1987, 211.)

> Hep, to be hep, experienced in the underworld; sophisticated; having underworld wisdom; alert. Having inside information; aware of; "wise to." "Nix! The sucker is hep." (Goldin, O'Leary, *Dictionary of American Underworld Lingo*, 1950, 94.)

Hick, *n.*, a peasant, a rural person, a country fool.

Aitheach, *al.* **athach** (*pron.* ahǝċ, h-ahǝċ), *n.*, a churl, a peasant, a rent-payer; *fig.* a hayseed.

Hick was classified as low cant and vulgar slang well into the 20th century. Most Anglo-American dictionaries derive the word *hick* from an obscure nickname for Richard.

Hick (**aitheach,** *pron.* h-ahǝċ, a churl, a peasant) dates back in its literate form to early medieval manuscripts of the Cattle-Raid of Cooley (Táin Bó Cúalnge). Cuchulain's charioteer Fergus refers to one of the Great Hound of Ulster's vanquished opponents as "**aithech**-matud" (*pron.* h-ahǝċ matud), a dog of a churl. (Strachan, *Táin*, Glossary, 42.)

> Ni tochrad dam dano in t-**aithech matud** ol Fergus glieid frisin coin móir nád n-árgarad.—It is of no annoyance to me, said Fergus, that the dog of a

churl should have waged battle with the great hound for whom he was no match. (John Strachan, *Stories from the Táin*, 1903, 33.)

Hick, any Person of whom any Prey can be made...; also a silly Country Fellow. (B.E.'s *Dictionary of the Canting Crew*, 1700.)

Hick. A country hick. An ignorant clown. (Grose, *Classical Dictionary of the Vulgar Tongue*, 1785, [1811].)

JAMIE: You let **hick** town boobs flatter you with bunk about your future. (O'Neill, *Long Day's Journey Into Night*, 1955, 164.)

STICKS NIX **HICK** PIX (*Variety*, July 17, 1935.)

Hinky, *adj.*, (*someone or something*) bad, wicked; suspicious; wrong; odd; insecure, jumpy; untrustworthy.

Ainigí (*pron.* anĭgí, hanĭgí), *adj.*, wicked, bad; fretful, nervous; peevish.

"Driver of the pimpmobile looks **hinky**." (Joseph Wambaugh, Chapman, *American Slang*, 1987, 214.)

"**Hinky Dink**" Kenna was the diminutive leader of Chicago's wide-open "Levee District," from the late-1880s to the early-1920s, along with his hulking, dapper partner, "Bathhouse" John Coughlin.

Ainigíocht tanaidh(e) (*pron.* h-anĭgíĉt taníg), slim wickedness. "Slim Wicked" (Kenna).

Kenna's response to the cheers of the organization was characteristic. "If I am elected," he told his supporters, "I will try to show the people I am not as bad as I am painted on account of the name **Hinky Dink**." (Lloyd Wendt & Herman Kogan, *Lords of the Levee: The Story of Bathouse John and Hinky Dink*, 1943, 117.)

...I nibbled at the faro games but was careful and never got hurt. Every night I looked into **Hinky Dink**'s and Bathouse John's bars and heard the same old alarm, "here comes the wagon." (Jack Black, *You Can't Win*, 1926, [2000], 153.)

For all his hard-lipped demeanor, Kenna, like Coughlin was a benevolent man. In the dire depression that swept the entire country that winter (1893)... **Hinky Dink** fed more than any other. In one week at the height of the misery, he cared for 8,000 destitute men... Kenna's activities that winter were those of a Good Samaritan, but they also gave him an idea.

Every one of those men could vote. (Lloyd Wendt & Herman Kogan,
Lords of the Levee: The Story of Bathouse John and Hinky Dink, 1943, 91.)

And then—louder—like a college yell. "What's his name? Well what
do you think—He's ouh frien' is **Hinky Dink**!" Then the Grand March
began... (Jim Tully, *Beggars of Life*, 1924, [2004], 89.)

Hoax, *n.*, deliberate trickery; something intended to deceive; *v.*, to gain an
advantage, fraud, deception, dupery; to joke or deceive. "Etymology: probably contraction of **hocus**: to trick into believing or accepting as genuine
something false and often preposterous." (*Merriam-Webster Online*, July,
2006.)

Olcas (*pron.* olkəs, h-olkəs), *adj.*, mischief, naughtiness, spite, wickedness, evil.

Probably contraction from hocus, in hocus-pocus. (Macaulay quoted in
Webster's Revised Unabridged Dictionary, 1913.)

Hocus, *n.*, a deceiver, a hoaxer; mischief; (*underworld slang*) opium; *v.*, to curse or
jinx; to deceive, to hoax; to drug someone.

Olcas (*pron.* olkəs, h-olkəs), *adj.*, mischief, naughtiness, spite; wickedness, evil,
misfortune.

"Well, I reckon you have lived in the country. I thought maybe you
was trying to **hocus** me again. What's your real name, now?" (Twain,
Huckleberry Finn, 1885, [1994], 46.)

Hocus, hokus, *n.*, opium. (Vincent Joseph Monteleone, *Criminal Slang:
The Vernacular of the Underground Lingo*, 2003, 120.)

Hokum, *n.*, bunk or bunkum; (*theater and vaudeville slang*) any stage device, gag,
or routine, designed solely to please an audience; "any proved song, joke,
or line that is sure to elicit laughter, tears, or applause from an audience;
proved but hackneyed or trite material." Origin unknown. (Wentworth &
Flexner, *Dictionary of American Slang*, 262.)

Oll-chumadh (*pron.* oul-ċuməh, h-oll-ċumah), a huge made-up story, a vast
invention; *fig.* a lengthy ad-lib or improvisation. **Oll-**, *prefix*, great-, huge-,
etc. **Cumadh** (*pron.* cuməh), *vn.*, (*act of*) contriving, composing, inventing,
making-up; a made-up story.

"Is iontach an scéal so ... nó mura **cumadóireacht** di féin é.—It is a wonderful story ... or unless it was pretence and invention on her part." (Humphrey O'Sullivan, *Cin Lae Amhlaoibh*, 1827, [1970], 16.)

Hokum is first cousin to **bunkum** (**buanchumadh**, *pron.* buənċuməh, an endless-invention, a long made-up story).

> The big laughs for jasbo, **hokum**, and gravy, as we call broad humor, frequently come from the women in the house... (Walter Kingsley, *New York Times*, July 4, 1915, X2.)

> "Nut acts" are popular, but the artists of this genre are proverbially unreliable. They deal in the brands of humor known as "jazz," "hokum," "jasbo," and "gravy." (*New York Times*, Dec. 23, 1917, 38.)

> **Hokum** ... they lap it up. (Carl Sandburg, *Slabs of Sunburnt West*, 1922.)

Holler, *n.*, a loud yell, a loud complaint; *fig.* an African-American work-song; *v.*, to shout; to complain to the cops.

Oll-bhúir (*pron.* h-oll-oor), *n.*, a terrific yell, a great roar. (Dineen, 820.) **Oll-**, *prefix*, great-, huge-, vast-, *etc.* **Búir**, *n.*, bellow, roar, yell. **Búir**, *v.*, to bellow, to roar, to yell.

According to most Anglo-American dictionaries, the word *holler* is an American dialect word, derived from the English *hollo*.

Holler did not become popular until the 19th century and was considered underworld slang for a victim's loud cry. "*Holler*, plaint of a victim." (J.M. Sullivan, *Criminal Slang*, 1908, 13.)

> When a mark discovers he has been robbed ... (and) notifies the police, he is said to cry copper or **holler** copper... (David Maurer, *Whiz Mob: A Correlation of the Technical Argot of Pickpockets with Their Behavor Pattern*, 1955, 108.)

Holy Cow, *excl.*, an oath and exclamation of surprise, regret, consternation, relief, etc. (*DAS*, 264.)

Holy Cathú (*pron.* cahú), *bilingual excl.*, holy sorrow! Holy grief! Holy trial! **Cathú** (*pron.* cahú), *vn.*, sorrowing; sorrow, contrition; temptation, trial. Mo **cathú** é! (*pron.* mə cahú ay) Alas! My sorrow! My grief!

Holy Cathú (*pron.* cahú, sorrow, grief, trial) as **Holy Cow** is a bilingual exclamation of *unhappy* surprise and consternation. But over time it became just another unexplained exclamation like **Holy Moly** and **Holy Gee**! The Chicago Cubs' baseball announcer Harry Caray was known for his exclamations of **Holy Cow**! which he had trained himself to say to avoid cursing on the air. **Holy Gee**!

Holy Gee, *excl.*, an oath and exclamation of surprise, consternation, relief.
Holy Dia (*pron. pron.* jíě), Holy God!

> When the young man learned who it was that he had tried to prevent from taking a seat, he [Democratic boss Hugh McLaughlin, *ed*] exclaimed "**Holy Gee**, I feel like the man who had found out he was fighting Sullivan without knowing it and then fainted away." Mr. McLaughlin smiled good naturedly on the discomfited usher. (*Brooklyn Eagle*, Feb. 22, 1892, 4.)

> The boy delivered the message and Green said "**Holy Gee**." He went out and met the policeman ... he did not see the shooting. (*Brooklyn Eagle*, Nov. 10, 1893, 7.)

Holy Mackerel, *excl.*, an oath and exclamation of surprise, consternation, amazement, relief, etc.
Holy Mac ríúil (*pron.* mac reeúl), Holy Royal Son! Holy Noble Son! Holy Princely Son!

In New York City you can find **Holy Mackerel** on a tugboat. But it is not a pious fish. It is an Irish-English phrase of amazement and surprise.

> Excerpt No. 1
> A typical day for McAllister Towing
>
> DISPATCHER: McAllister...
> BM: Well, you got any ship work going?
> DISPATCHER: Oh sir, yes sir, always. It's been very busy.
> BM: Very busy.
> DISPATCHER: Very busy, outstandingly busy.
> BM: Well, how many ships have we handled today?
> DISPATCHER: Uh, today, we had 2, 4, 6, 8, 10, 12, 14, 16, 17—17 ships today.
> BM: **Holy mackerel!**
> DISPATCHER: Yeah, we're doing good Cap', we're really going at it.

(*NYU Glucksman Ireland House Oral History Project*—Interviewers: Kerri Farrell, Linda Dowling Almeida, Marion R. Casey.)

Holy Moly, *excl.*, an exclamation of surprise, amazement, awe.

Holy Moladh (*pron.* mol'ə), *n.*, (holy) praise, (holy) praising. **Moladh** (*pron.* mol' ə), *n.*, (*act of*) praising, praise; a song of praise, a panegyric, a eulogy. Moladh le Dia! (*pron.* mol'ə le jíě), praise be to God!

"This dull acamedician (whose most intelligent comment is 'Why, **holy moly!** You're afloat in dialectics!') is led on a dizzying tour of Paris, overwhelmed by a crazed author..." (Nancy Ramsey, *New York Times*, Aug. 31, 1986, BR13.)

Honky, *n.*, an African-American racial epithet for white people; perhaps derived from *hunky*.

Aingí, *al.* **aingidhe** (*pron.* aŋ'gí, h-aŋ'gí), *adj.*, wicked, bad, evil; fretful; furious. Seanduine **aingí** (*pron.* sh'andinə aŋ'gí), a peevish, wicked old man.

Honky tonk, honky tonky, *n.*, a cheap saloon, featuring gambling, dancing, prostitution, drugs, and wild, wicked behavior. (*DAS*, 265,266.)

Aingíocht tarraingeach (*pron.* angiċt tarrangəċ, angiċt tarrangah), alluring wickedness; seductive evil. **Aingíocht** (*pron.* angiċt, h-angiċt), *n.*, wickedness, evil; fury; malignancy; *al.* **aingidheacht**. **Tarraingeach** (*pron.* tarrangəċ), *adj.*, drawing, pulling; alluring; attractive; seductive.

> The (Brooklyn) Navy Yard had its impact on me too. Sands Street, the sailor's **honky-tonk**, ran just parallel to High Street and directly into the Navy Yard three blocks away. A three-block carnival. Three blocks of whorehouses and street hookers, free-flowing liquor and noisy revelry ... The music pouring from the dance halls, the sea-chanteys arching over the swining doors of the saloons, the ricky-ticky piano... (Willie Sutton & Edward Linn, *Where the Money Was: The Memoirs of a Bank Robber*, 29, 30.)

Hoodoo, *n.*, a cause of bad luck, a jinx; a person or thing whose presence brings bad luck; a magician or necromancer; an evil spirit; an eerie-looking rock pinnacle, or earth pillar, formed by erosion and nature; a mountain in Canada.

Uath Dubh (*pron.* uəh doo, h-úŏ doo), dark specter, evil phantom, a malevolent thing; horror, dread; a dark, spiky, evil-looking thing. **Uath** (*pron.* uəh, h-uəh), *n.*, a form or shape; a spectre or phantom; dread, terror, hate. Old Gaelic name for the hawthorn. **Dubh** (*pron.* doo, duv), *adj.*, dark; black; malevolent, evil; wicked; angry, sinister; gloomy, melancholy; strange, unknown. (O'Donaill, 457, 1294; Dineen, 374, 1287; de Bhaldraithe, *English-Irish Dictionary*, 755; Dwelly, 988.)

Hoodoo only enters the American language in the early-1880s. Most dictionaries derive **hoodoo** from *voodoo*, a syncretic religion of the African diaspora. But there is only a minor semantic connection. **Hoodoo** rocks are a name for "grotesque eroded landforms" in deserts all across America. There are **hoodoos** in Alberta's Dinosaur Provincial Park and in the Okanagan Valley in British Columbia. In the 1880s, the "**hoodoo** man" was in Brooklyn.

"I'M NO GYPSY, I'M IRISH," SAYS EDWARD O'ROURKE
...His Arrest as **Hoodoo** Man
Miss Myers Says That O'Rourke
Was Introduced by a Woman as a Gypsy King

Edward O'Rourke, the young man arrested in Flatbush Saturday, accused of posing as a **hoodoo** man and of collecting $50 from Margaret Meyer, a servant... (*Brooklyn Eagle*, July 8, 1901, 20.)

The **Hoodoo** was also a gallows bird.

"HARD LUCK AND A **HOODOO**—"
The Tale of a Hangman's Cap and Noose
It is a tale of the **hoodoo** the writer is about to tell—a hoodoo which began active business in Brooklyn... (*Brooklyn Eagle*, March 25, 1894, 20.)

The **hoodoo** haunted a Brooklyn baseball park in 1887.

"A **HOODOO** SHOT—Why the Brooklyn Base Ball Team Is Winning—"
...A shadowy figure with wings that spread out at least twelve feet flew in the window ... It was the **hoodoo** beginning his deadly work ... The red haired girl ... and the white horse ... are the mascots purchased two weeks ago by Manager Byrne immediately after the terrible series of disasters... Everything has now prospered and the terrible **hoodoo** has fled. (*Brooklyn Eagle*, Aug. 11, 1887, 4.)

In 1883, in Scranton, Pennsylvania, the Irish **Hoodoo** was a necromancer.

A young man named Hogan charged Foster Rankin, Edward Horan, Dennis Sullivan, and Albert Hodge with necromancy and conspiracy before Alderman Fuller today... (T)he other night ... after having some wine, they introduced him to a magician, or "**Hoodoo**," who was supposed to work supernatural wonders. The "Hoodoo" passed his hands over Hogan's head, and made him think he was President Judge of Lackawanna County. (*New York Times*, Aug. 26, 1883, 1.)

In the 19th century, English colonialism was a **hoodoo**. "In Ireland ... he fled from him on sight, for fear he would 'hoodoo' them in some way." (Thomas Addis Emmet, *Incidents of My Life*, 1911, 75.)

Brooklyn poet Walt Whitman visited **hoodoo** land in Yellowstone Park. "I had wanted to go to the Yellowstone river region—wanted specially to see ... the 'hoodoo' or goblin land of that country." (Walt Whitman, *Specimen Days*, 1883, [1887], 229.)

But the **hoodoo** has always been Irish. Today the great dark phantom of the hoodoo in Ireland has been demoted to a jinx in sports.

Leinster break Munster **hoodoo** with late show—CELTIC LEAGUE FINAL—Leinster 24 Munster 20. (*The News Letter*, Belfast, Ireland; December 17, 2001.)

Hot diggity, *excl.*, an exclamation of excitement, delight, enthusiasm.
Árd-iachtach, *al.* **ard-iachtadh** (*pron.* árd íéċ'taċ, h-árd íéċ'tə), crying out loud; loud crying.
Ard, *al.* **árd**, *adj.*, *prefix*, loud, mighty; **árd-iachtach**, loud crying, crying out loud. **Iachtadh**, *vn.*, yelling, shouting, shrieking, groaning. Ag éigheamh agus iachtadh ortha de múraibh na cathrach, yelling and shouting to them from the city walls. (Dineen, 584.)

Hot diggity dog, *excl.*, exclamation of excitement and delight.
Árd-iachtach-tach! (*pron.* h-árd-íéċ'tə-taċ), a loud oath; a loud declaration; crying out loud! Árd-iachtach, *n.*, loud crying. **-Tach**, -teach, *suffix in compounds*, declaring, declaration. (Dineen, 584, 1152.)

Oh, **hot diggity**, dog ziggity
Boom what you do to me

It's so new to me
What you do to me.
(Al Hoffman & Dick Manning, "Hot Diggity," 1956.)

Hot dog! *excl.*, Exclamation of excitement and happiness.
Árd-tach! (*pron.* h-árd-taċ), loud oath! Loud declaration, as in "I declare!" *Fig.* Curses! **Ard**, *adj.*, **ard-**, *prefix*, loud; loud-. **-Tach** (*pron.* taċ), *n.*, *suffix in compounds*, declaring; declaration; an oath. (Dineen, 1152.)

Hot Sketch, *n.*, a lively, funny, colorful character; a card, someone who is a laugh or a scream.
Ard scairt (*pron.* h-árd skartch), loud laugh, loud scream; great guffaw.

> "He's a **hot sketch**, that guy..." ("Tad" Dorgan, "Indoor Sports," cartoon,
> *San Francisco Call*, April 3, 1915, 10.)

The cartoonist, Tad Dorgan, was a **hot sketch** (**árd scairt**, *pron.* h-árd scartch, loud laugh, total scream) himself. Thomas Aloysius Dorgan ("Tad") was born in San Francisco in 1877. He worked for the *San Francisco Bulletin* and *The Call*, before he achieved national fame as a syndicated cartoonist, and prolific coiner of slang, on William Randolph Hearst's *New York Journal*. Tad's nickname would become synonymous—and eponymous—with Irish-American vernacular or slang, as spelled out in this 1917 review of the play, *Putting on Airs*, in *Variety*.

> Middle Aged Irish widow of a wealthy contractor, who made his money in "Dish Alley" (the slums), still resides there with her son, whom she sent to college to study for the medical profession. She still retains her old fashioned method of living and "Tad" vocabulary. The boy is engaged to a society girl, but is ashamed of his mother... (*Variety*, April 20, 1917, 12.)

> "He's a **hot sketch**!" ("Tad" Dorgan, "Indoor Sports," a cartoon, *San Francisco Call*, Dec. 9, 1914, 10.)

Hudson **Duster** gang, n., an early-20th century New York Irish gang.
Dusta, *n.*, dust; *fig.* cocaine.

The moniker **Duster** is said to have derived from the Hudson Duster's prodigious use of "dust" or cocaine. The **Duster** turf was along the Hudson River docks, where they sometimes battled with Owney Madden's Gopher gang from Hell's Kitchen. Eugene O'Neill hung out with the Hudson **Dusters** in a Sixth Avenue joint called "the Hell Hole."

> ...the Hudson **Dusters** accepted Eugene. His polite manner with everyone, his familiarity with the sea and water-front life... his being an O'Neill—all the **Dusters** were Irish—all served to give him special status... The **Dusters** called him "the Kid." (Louis Sheaffer, *O'Neill: Son and Playwright*, Vol. I, 1968, [2002], 334.)

Humdinger, *n.*, (*something or someone*) very good, or outstanding; *adj.*, remarkable. (*DAS*, 276; Chapman, 228.)

Iomar-dian-mhaith (*pron.* h-imŭr-diən-wa), (*something or someone*) very good, very outstanding. **Iomar-**, *in compds. intensive prefix.*, very-. **Dian-mhaith** (*pron.* díən-wa), *adj.*, very good, tops, excellent; *adv.*, go dian-mhaith, very well. (Dineen, 333, 603.)

"Arnold Moss gave us a **humdinger** of a talk." (Chapman, 1987, 228.)

Hunch, *n.*, an intuitive premonition; a sense of knowing or perceving something.

Aithint (*pron.* ahənch, h-ahənch), *n.*, knowledge, recognition, perception, discernment, intuition; *v.*, to know, recognize; intuit, discern, intuit; *vn.*, (*act of*) knowing, recognizing, perceiving, inferring, discerning. Aitghnim, **aithin**, and **aithint**, *v.*, know, recognize, see, infer, understand, distinguish, perveive. D'**aithint** sé go raibh fearg orm, he perceived (had a hunch) that I was angry with him. (**aithint** = aithin, aithne) (Ó Dónaill, 32, 33; Dineen, 31, 32, 33.)

Tim Moran, an Irish-American yegg "on the lam" from the law in O'Neill's first play, *The Web*, written in 1913, and Larry Slade, a disillusioned old "Wobbly," who recognized no law, in one of O'Neill's final plays, *The Iceman Cometh*, both had an Irish-American vernacular **hunch** (**aithint**, *pron.* ahənch, h-ahənch, perception) in their vocabulary.

Tɪᴍ: Gee, Kid, I got a feelin' in my bones they're after me. It's only a **hunch**, but it's never wrong yet. (Eugene O'Neill, *The Web*, 1913, [1988], 25.)

Lᴀʀʀʏ: I have a strong **hunch** you've come here expecting something of me. (Eugene O'Neill, *The Iceman Cometh*, 1939, [1954], 591.)

The old **faro** game was based on **hunches**. "One fatal evening, as I stood watching a **faro** game making mental bets and winning every one, the devilish **hunch** came to me that I was lucky and ought to make a play... I made a bet, lost it, got stuck, and feverishly played in my last dollar... The gambling bait is the curse of a thief's life." (Jack Black, *You Can't Win*, 1926, [2000], 178.)

Hunky, *n.*, a racist epithet for Polish and other Slavic peoples.
Aingí (*pron.* angí, h-angí), *adj.*, wicked, bad. (See: **honky**)

I

Ice, *n.*, the graft a carnival owner has to pay to local authorities to set up and operate in a locale. If the carnival uses "flat joints," crooked games, or rigged prize wheels, or if it carries a contingent of grifters and three-card-monte games, the **ice** (**íos-**, minimum) goes up. Carnivals with "Cooch" shows also paid more.
Íos- (*pron.* íss-), *prefix*, minimum; **íosta** (*pron.* ísstə, *cont.* íss-), *n.*, a minimum.

"One of my jobs ... was taking care of (Tex) Rickard's **ice**. I assume you are familiar with the term? ...Payoff money," he said. "The big New York City boxing writers came to Rickard's office once a week, usually on Friday, and I gave them their **ice**—seventy five dollars... They took the money and wrote what we told them." (Roger Kahn, *A Flame of Pure Fire: Jack Dempsey and the Roaring Twenties*, 1999, 37, 38.)

Ikey Heyman axle, (*carny and circus slang*), *n.*, a hidden foot pedal, or foot break that controls a wheel of fortune or prize wheel. The gimmick.

Ag Céimnigh (axle) (*pron.* eg cé'imanïh), stepping, treading (axle), a hidden axle or foot-break. **Céimnigheach**, *n.*, a footman.

> The **Ikey Heyman** Axle is the hidden "gaff" or foot-pedal on a wheel of fortune, or jackpot wheel: a secret friction device on the axle stops the wheel wherever the wheel-operator wants. Up until the 1960s, the person who controlled the gaffs on the gambling wheels and games of chance was called a "Conducer." (*Carny Lingo Online*, June 2006.)

J

Jack, *n.*, money.

Tiach, *al.* tiag (*pron.* j'aċ, *Ulster*), a small purse, a wallet, a budget; *fig.* money. (See: **jag**.)

"**Jack**" was playwright Eugene O'Neill's favorite term for money. In his Pulitzer Prize-winning drama, *The Iceman Cometh*, set in a Raines Law hotel dive around 1910, Rocky, the bartender, discusses the benefits of **jack**.

> ROCKY: ... Not dat I blame yuh for not woikin'. On'y suckers woik. But dere's no per centage in bein' broke when yuh can grab good **jack** for yourself and make someone else woik for yuh, is dere? (O'Neill, *The Iceman Cometh*, 1939, [1954], 702.)

In O'Neill's final play *Hughie*, a penny-ante gambler named "Erie" Smith recalls the ups and downs of **jack**.

> ERIE: Some nights I'd come back here without a buck, feeling lower than a snake's belly, and the first thing you know I'd be lousy with **jack**, bettin' a grand a race. (O'Neill, *Hughie*, 1941, 284.)

But the real ruler of the underworld—and America—has always been named **Jack** (**tiach**, *al.* **tiag**, *pron.* j'aċ, a purse, a wallet; a budget; *fig.* Money).

Jackpot, *n.*, the pot of **jack** at the end of every gambler's rainbow.

Tiach-pot (*Irish-English compound; pron.* j'aċ pot), *n.*, the pot with the "jack;" the purse-pot, or money-pot.

Jack-roll, *v.*, to "roll" or rob a drunk of his "jack," meaning his wallet or money.

Jackroller, *n.*, a "low-class" thief who rolls drunks for their wallets.

Tiach roll (*Irish-English compound; pron.* j'aċ-roll), *v.*, "rolling" or robbing a drunk, from the act of rolling over a passed out lush and glomming his **jack** (wallet, small purse; *fig.* money). A lush-roller.

Jag (1), *n.*, a load for the back; a pedlar's wallet. A leather bag or wallet; a pocket; a saddle-bag, a satchel.

Tiach (*pron.* j'aċ, ch'aċ), **tiag** (*pron.* j'ag, ch'ag), *n.*, a satchel, a knapsack; a vessel; a small bag, a wallet, a small purse; *al.*, **tiachóg** (*pron.* j'aċóg), tiachán, a knapsack, a bag, a satchel. (*Irish and Scots-Gaelic*) **Tiachag** (*pron.* j'aċag, ch'aċag), *n.*, a purse, a small bag. (Dwelly, 949; Ó Dónaill, 1233; Dineen, 1203.)

> **Jag,** a parcel or load of any thing, whether on a man's back, or in a carriage. (Francis Grose, *A Provincial Glossary*, 1787; OED.)

> There's nae room for bags or **jaugs** here. (Walter Scott, *St. Ronan's Well*, 1824.)

Jag (2), *n.* to be drunk, "on the drink;" a prolonged drinking spree or "bender." Later applied to any period of obsessive indulgence in a thing, emotion, or interest, etc., a crying jag.

Deoch (*pron.* jĭ~ûċ j'oċ), *n.*, a drink; ar **deoch** (*pron.* er j'oċ), in one's cups, on a drunk; an **deoch**, the drink; **deoch** an dorais (*pron.* jĭ~ûċ ən dor'ash), a parting drink; **deocadh**, act of quaffing, drinking.

> CORA: My dogs was givin' out when I seen dis guy holdin' up a lamppost ... Jees, he was paralyzed! One of dem polite **jags**. He tries to bow to me, imagine...? (O'Neill, *The Iceman Cometh*, 1939, [1954], 616.)

Jake, *adj.*, good, satisfactory, okay, the best; *al.*, approved of, fixed, as in: "Everything was 'jake' with the police..." (*DAS*, 284.)

Deach (*pron.* j'aċ), *comp. adj.*, best, the best; *fig.* okay. An rud is **deach** agus is measa (*pron.* ən rud iss j'aċ agus iss m'asə), the best and worst thing. (Ó Dónaill, 374.)

> "What are you dummying up for? You can crack. These ghees (fellows) are **jake**." (Goldin, O'Leary, *Dictionary of American Underworld Lingo*, 1950, 109.)

> Jakeloo, jakerloo (*Australia & New Zealand*), *adj.*, "jake," the best, good, okay.

Jasm, gism, *n.* an abundance of energy, enthusiasm, passion; semen.

Teas ioma (*pron.* j'as iomə, ch'as iomə), an abundance of heat and passion; *fig.* semen.

> The 1860 example of **jasm** ("energy, enthusiasm") in *A Dictionary of Americanisms on Historical Principles* is from the work of Josiah Holland, a Massachusetts writer... M.M. Mathews in his *Dictionary of Americanisms*, published in 1951, defined **jasm** as "...energy, enthusiasm... origin obscure. Possibly the same word as *gism*, semen." (Peter Tamony, *JEMF Quarterly*, Spring 1981, 11.)

> If you'll take thunder and lightning and a steamboat and a buzz-saw and mix 'em up and put 'em into a woman that's **jasm**. (Josiah Holland, *Miss Gilbert*, 1860, 350.)

> Willin', but hain't no more **jas'm** than a dead cornstalk. (*Harper's*, Sept. 1886, 579.)

Jass, *n.*, an early spelling for jazz.

Teas (*pron.* j'ass, chass), *n.*, heat, passion, excitement, highest temperature. (Ó Dónaill, 611; Dineen, 517–518.)

In a special March 1917 issue of *Victor Record Revue* published to promote the Original Dixieland **Jass** Band's first **Jass** record, the Victor Company was still trying to decide how to spell the hot new word **Jass**.

> Spell it **Jass**, Jas, Jaz, or Jazz—nothing can spoil a Jazz band. Some say the **Jass** band originated in Chicago. Chicago says it came from San Francisco—San Francisco being away across the continent... Anyway a

Jass band is the newest thing in cabarets. (*Victor Record Review*, March 7, 1917; Peter Tamony, *Jazz: The Word, And Its Extension To Music*, JEMF *Quarterly*, Spring, 1981, 10.)

Jazz, *n.*, a name given to African-American music; excitement, passion, enthusiasm; heat; "hot air," excessive verbal passion; something or someone hot or exciting; sexual intercourse, to have sex with someone.

Teas (*pron.* j'ass, chass), *n.*, heat, passion, excitement, ardor, enthusiasm, anger, highest temperature. (Ó Dónaill, 611; Dineen, 517–518; Dwelly, 942.)

Not a single musician in New Orleans—black, white, or Creole—used the word **Jass** or **Jazz** for hot music until the Original Dixieland Jass Band (ODJB), a motley crew of Irish, Sicilian, and working-class white boys from the back streets of the Big Easy, hit the music-biz jackpot in March 1917, when they recorded the first **Jass** record in history in New York City: *Dixieland Jass One Step* and *Livery Stable Blues*. (*Louis Armstrong, In His Own Words*, 1999, 83, 218, 175; Tamony, *Jazz: A Quarterly of Music*, 37–39; David Meltzer, *Reading Jazz*, 1992, 42; Peter Tamony, *JEMF Quarterly*, Spring 1981.)

The Secret of "Jazz"

In the red-light districts of San Francisco's Barbary Coast, Chicago's First Ward, New York's Tenderloin, and New Orleans' Storyville, where the hot new music had been born, that old Irish word **teas** (*pron.* ch'as, j'as, heat, passion, excitement) also meant **sexual** "heat, passion, excitement."

The word **Jazz** was ... a sex word in California and was a common localism in San Francisco when I arrived there in 1899 and until I left there (for Chicago and *Kelly's Stables* fame after September 1914). I shall be glad to swear on oath before a notary public that **Jazz** as a sex word was not only used in San Francisco before the (1906) earthquake and fire, but that it was of such common use that it was a localism. During those days I played at Luna's Mexican restaurant on Geary Street with Miguel Luna and Harry Warren. They played nights at a (whore) house on Stockton Street and I heard the word **Jazz** repeatedly. (Richard Holbrooke, *Storyville* magazine, 1974, 48, 55; Tamony, *JEMF Quarterly*, Spring 1981, 12–16.)

Thirty-five years ago (*ca.* 1890) I played the trombone... I made tours of the big mining centers when the West was really wild ... I was piloted to dance resorts—honky tonks. The vulgar word **jazz** was in general currency in those dance halls thirty years or more ago. (Clay Smith, *Etude* magazine, Sept., 1924, quoted in Holbrooke, "Our Word Jazz," *Storyville*, 1974, 48, 49.)

Jazz was so full of **jasm** and **gism** (**teas ioma**, *pron.* j'ass iomə, an abundance of heat and passion; *fig.* semen) no one could, or would, write it down. In 1913, it was a word you learned by ear—like jazz music.

In James T. Farrell's novel, *Gas House McGinty*, written during the **Jazz** Age and set in Chicago in 1914, Farrell's **Jazz** had absolutely nothing to do with hot music. It is the **jazz** (**teas**, *pron.* j'as, ch'as, heat, passion, and excitement) of sex.

> He thought of the girls he had had in the past. There was the time he was fourteen and Nellie O'Brien had copped his cherry...The bird who invented **jazzing** was a bum inventor to throw in all those complications and grief. (James T. Farrell, *Gas-House McGinty*, 1932, [1950], 130.)

> "Hell, if you guys can't buy your way in, I don't know how in hell you'll ever get by St. Peter. With all the women you claim to be **jazzin'**, it ought to take a hell of a lot more than the back pay to slip you by," said Heinie. (Farrell, *Gas-House McGinty*, 1932, [1950], 140.)

Sidney Bechet set the tone for succeeding generations of African-American musicians with his hatred of the word **jazz**. "Jazz, that's a name the white people have given to the music... **Jazz** could mean any damn' thing: high times, screwing... It used to be spelled **Jass**..." (Sidney Bechet, *Treat It Gentle: An Autobiography*, 1960, [1978], 3.)

Jazzbo, Jasbo, Jazz-bo, *n.*, (*someone or something*) infused with great heat, passion, enthusiasm, high spirits, and excitement. Vaudeville slang for wild physical comedy, exuberant slapstick, hokum.

Teasbach, teaspach (*pron.* j'asbah, ch'asbah, t'aspə), *n.*, (*of person*) animal spirits, exuberance; heat, liveliness, ardor, passion, sultriness; heat of the blood; wantonness; (*of horse*) spiritedness, tendency to cavort; (*of cattle*) tendency to gad about. *Al.* **teasbhach, teasmhach**, doublet with **teasach**, great heat. (Dineen, 1194, 1195; Ó Dónaill, 1222.)

Tá **teasbach** air (*pron.* tá j'asbah er), he has an excess of animal spirits; *fig.* he is a **jazzbo**. Bainim an **teasbach** de, I cool his ardor. Le barr **teaspaigh** a rinne sé é, he did it through an excess of animal spirits. Nach air atá an **teasbach**, isn't he rather exuberant, isn't he the **jazzbo?**

In New York, **Jazzbo** was the name for a spirited, jumping horse:

> Hunters and Jumpers ... Harry J. Graham's... **Jazzbo**... (*New York Times*, Sept. 21, 1917.)

In Chicago, **jazbo** was a hot foxtrot.

> *Jazbo Foxtrot*, by Arthur S. Shaw, Jan. 3, 1916. (Forster Music Publishers, Chicago, E375282; cited in Geoffrey C. Ward, Ken Burns, *Jazz—An Illustrated History*, 2000; ADS.)

In show biz, the old **jasbo** was wild, exuberant slapstick comedy.

> I gave them gravy, and hokum
> And when they ate it up I came through
> With the old **jasbo**.
> (Walter Kingsley, *New York Times*, July 2, 1916, x4.)

In vaudeville the **jasbo** (or "jazzbo") was the high-spirited finale of the show. "[John Philip] Sousa ... says [the word] jazz slid into our vocabulary by way of the vaudeville stage, where at the end of a performance, all the acts came back on the stage to give a rousing, boisterous *finale* called a '**jazzbo**.'" (Whiteman, McBride, *Jazz*, 1926, v, 122.)

In Los Angeles, the **jasbo** was in a hot race across the desert.

> Mucho Peppo...
> Road Race Special Promises Plenty Live Stuff...
> The Howdy Special which annually makes the run across the desert to Phoenix at the time of the Phoenix road race, promises to be a record-breaking **Jasbo** party this year... John Weise has a great record for the **Jasbo** stuff, but A. T. Smith is out to break all records on the trip to Phoenix. (*L.A. Times*, August 17, 1914, 2.)

In Michigan, **jazzbo** was a moniker for a passionate army officer.

> TESTIFIES MRS SCOTT
> TOLD OF INDISCRETIONS
> Michigan Congressman's Secretary
> Relates Hotel Clerk Story
> at Divorce Trial

Alpena, Michigan, Jan. 2 (1925)... On another occasion, Miss Kennedy
testified, Mrs. Scott told her the hotel clerk was becoming jealous of an
army officer referred to as "**Jazzbo**." (*New York Times*, Jan 3, 1925, 2.)

Fittingly, during the Jazz Age, "**Jasbo**" became a poem.

In the same number of the *American Mercury* ... features are..."**Jasbo**
Brown" (a poem) by Dubose Heyward. (*New York Times*, Sept. 6, 1925, 21.)

Jazzy, *adj.*, spirited, lively, exciting, hot.

Teasaí (*pron.* j'así, chassí), *adj.*, hot, warm, ardent, passionate, exciting, fervent,
enthusiastic, spirited, fiery. Fonn **teasaí**, vehement desire; duine **teasaí** (*pron.*
din'ə j'así), a hot-headed person, a passionate person.. (Dineen, 1194; Ó
Dónaill, 1221.)

Jerk, *n.*, someone of little or no account; a fool, a stupid person; a loser; "a boob;
chump; a sucker." (A.J. Pollock, *Underworld Speaks*, 1935, 63.)

Déirceach (*pron.* jércəċ, jércəh), *n.*, a beggar, a mendicant, someone who takes
charity; *fig.* a bum; also, an alms-giver; someone who provides charity, a
charitable person. (Dineen, 326.)

It is not surprising that the Irish looked on both the recipient and dispenser
of charity as a **jerk**. Most organized charity in Ireland and the United States
in the 19th century came with a requirement that the charity seeker convert
to Protestantism. The Quakers were the one exception to this rule.

Beggars and **jerks** who "took the soup" (*fig.* alms and charity), were
looked upon as reprehensible as the swells and **jerks** who ladled out
"the soup" with (religious) strings attached. Only a poor hopeless **jerk**
(**déirceach**, *pron.* jércah, a beggar, a bum) took charity from a rich **jerk**
(**déirceach**, *pron.* jércah, alms-giver).

Jiffy, *al.* **jeffy**, *n.*, a very short space of time; only in phrases as "in a jiffy," in a
hurry.

Deifir (*pron.* j'ef'ər), *n.*, hurry, haste; speed, hustle. (Dineen, 323; Ó Dónaill,
390.)

In a **jiffy** is always "in a **deifir**" (*pron.* j'ef'ər), in a hurry or haste, with the final "r" of **deifir** (*pron.* j'ef'ə), clipped off in a jiffy (haste, hurry). Déan deifir, to make haste. Tá deifir (an tsaoghail) orm, I am in a (great) hurry. **Deifir** (*pron.* j'ef'ər) came into English as "jeffy" in Grose's *Dictionary of the Vulgar Tongue*.

> It will be done in a **jeffy**: it will be done in a short space of time, in an instant. (Grose, *Dictionary of the Vulgar Tongue*, 1785, [1811].)

Jeffy came to America "in a jiffy" in the 19th century, but still needed quotation marks around it to set it off from Standard English. "Ex-Mayor Stryker's new store ... will now be made ready for occupation 'in a **jiffy**,' or perhaps less time." (*Brooklyn Eagle*, April 15, 1851, 3.)

> Long hit a fly to left center. Both Kelly and Anderson were after it in a **jiffy**... (*Brooklyn Eagle*, April 16, 1899, 10.)

> London, July 22—At the first days racing of the Royal July Windsor meeting to-day the Lorillard-Beresford stable's 3 year old bay filly **Jiffy** II won the Eton handicap... (*Brooklyn Eagle*, July 22, 1898, 2.)

Jizz, *n.*, excitement, heat passion. Jizz is mainly used in Ireland in the phrase, "put some **jizz** (passion, excitement, heat) into it!" (See: **jazz, jass**.)

John, *n.*, a sugar daddy who is keeping a girlfriend, i.e., paying her expenses in return for sexual favors; (*obsolete*) a girl's steady boyfriend; the client of a prostitute. (*DAS*, 295; *OED*.)

Teann (*pron.* t'ann, ch'ann, j'ann, joun), *n.*, a champion; a firm man; *fig.* a well-to-do man; a support; a resource; *adj.*, wealthy, well-to-do, strong, well-established, steadfast. Cara **teann**, a steadfast, constant friend; feirmeoir **teann**, a well-to-do farmer. Teannaim sparán, I fill a purse well. **Teanntóir**, *n.*, a backer, a helper, a support. (Dineen, 1191.)

Dictionary of American Slang also defines "**John**" as a "girl's steady boy friend." The word originally implied sexual intimacy but does not now always have a sexual connotation." (*DAS*, 295.)

> Mary was describing the techniques she used to get money from the "**Johns**" who formed her principal source of revenue. (William Burroughs, *Junkie*, 1953, [1972], 27.)

Joint, *n.* "Almost any building, apartment, room, or sheltered area ...A joint may mean any kind of saloon, speakeasy, nightclub, café, eating place, soda fountain, hotel, house, apartment, room, store, or any other place. It may be a carnival concession, a jail, a dance hall, an opium or marijuana den, a hangout, a poolroom, a garage, etc." (*Carnival slang*), *n.*, a stall or tent in a carnival or fair; a concession stand. (*DAS*, 296, 297.)

Díon (*pron.* jínn), **díonta** (*pron.* jínntə), *n.*, a shelter, a roof, state of being wind and watertight; *fig.* a shelter of any kind, a house, shack, shanty, lean-to, "roof over your head," tent. **Díonta** (*pron.* jínnta), *p.p.*, sheltered (from elements), protected. **Díonta** = **díon**, *n.* (Ó Dónaill, 413.)

The earliest quote in the *OED* using the slang word **joint** for a shelter or house is from the pen of the inimitable Pierce Egan (1772–1849), the best-selling London Irish writer and prolific coiner of flash talk and slang. "I had my education at the boarding-school of Phelim Firebrass; and when I slipt the **joint**, and fang'd the arm, he strengthened the sinews." (Pierce Egan, *Real Life in Ireland*, 1821; *OED*.)

> Dock workers used to hang out at liquor **joints** where a stiff shot of rye or gin could be had for a nickel. (Butler & Driscoll, *Dock Walloper*, 1933, 26.)

> ROCKY: Don't call this **joint** a dump. (Mae West, *Sex: A Comedy Drama*, 1926, [1997], 35.)

At the end of the day, a joint can be a mansion or a tent.

> "You can build up yonder... Where's your **joint**?"... It took some time to discover that by a "joint" he meant my tent. (P. Allingham, *Cheapjack*, 1934, 16.)

> PARRITT: ...I've been in some dumps on the coast, but this is the limit. What kind of **joint** is it, anyway? (O'Neill, *The Iceman Cometh*, 1939, [1954], 587.)

Juke, juke joint, *n.*, a roadhouse with booze and music for dancing.

Diúg (joint) (*pron.* júg or joog), *v.*, drink, tipple, drink to the dregs; drain; suck. **Diúgadh** (*pron.* joog'ah), *vn.*, (act of) drinking, tippling, drinking to the dregs. **Diúgaire** (*pron.* júgar), *n.*, a drinker, a tippler. **Diúgaireacht** (*pron.* júgaraċt), *n.*, drinking, tippling. (Ó Dónaill, 413.)

Most Anglo-American dictionaries derive **juke** from the Gullah word *juke* or *joog*, meaning "disorderly and wicked," of West African origin; *"cf.* Wolof *dzug* to live wickedly." (*OED*; Barnhart, 558.)

Whether "juke" is Gullah or Irish, or Gaelic-Gullah, you always **diúg** (*pron.* joog, drink to the dregs, tipple) in **juke** joints, whether they are *joog* (*dzug,* disorderly, wicked) joints or not. Juke joints are wicked fun.

K

Kabosh, *al.*, **kibosh, kybosh,** *n.*, in phrase "to put the kabosh on" to kill, dispose of, finish off. Origin obscure. (Dolan, *Dictionary of Hiberno-English*, 1999, 153; *OED.*)
Caidhp bháis, death cap. **Caipín**, *n.*, a cap, a hood. **Bás**, *n.*, **báis** (*pron.* básh), *g.* death. **Caidhp** (*pron.* caĭp), *n.*, cap; bonnet. (*Botany.*) The **caidhp bháis** (*pron.* caĭp-aash, death cap) is also the Irish name for *Amanita phalloides*, the death cap mushroom. Death usually happens within a week after consumption.

> In Irish-America and in Ireland, to put the **kabosh** or **kibosh** (**caidhp** [an] **bháis,** *pron.* caĭp-aash, cap of death) on something means metaphorically to kill it. (*Cork Slang Online.*)

> The *Oxford Dictionary of Etymology* claims the word **kibosh** is "apparently associated with 'bosh' [Turkish *boş*, empty, worthless], nonsense." (Dolan, *Dictionary of Hiberno-English*, 1999, 153.)

Caidhp (an) bháis (*pron.* caĭp-aash) was the black cap a judge placed on his head before sentencing someone to be **croaked** (**crochta,** hanged.)

Keen, *v.*, wail, lament; *n.*, the chants and elegies of Irish women at funerals and wakes.
Caoin (*pron.* keen), *v.*, **caoineadh** (*pron.* keen'ə, keen'ah), *vn.*, keen, lament, wail; *n.*, act of mourning, lamenting, wailing, deploring; a lament, an elegy; a keen. Bean chaointe, a keening woman. (Dineen, 161; Ó Dónaill, 187.)

Keening was heard in Irish-American neighborhoods all across the United States, until the Catholic Church "put the kabosh" on the **keen**. Jim Tully's family settled in rural Ohio in the 19th century, where professional **keeners** **keened** the dead in both Irish and English.

> Three old women soon entered. They were the **keeners**, or professional mourners for the dead—for a fee. (Jim Tully, *Shanty Irish*, 1928, 149.)

> The voices of the **keeners** rose in a terrifying wail. (Tully, *Shanty Irish*, 1928, 153.)

Keister, *n.*, a safe, a strongbox; a suitcase; a salesman's display-case; a pocket; *fig.* buttocks; Etymology unknown. (*OED.*)
Ciste (*pron.* kisht'e), *n.*, a chest, a coffer; a store; a treasure; a treasure-chest.

In the last half of the 19th century, well-endowed "cans" were symbols of wealth and power, as well as feminine pulchritude and desirability: Today among the rich, bone-skinny keisters are all the rage. Irish immigrants came to America with all of their treasure in their asses and backs. They worked their **keisters** off to save their family's ass.

> *Keister*, a satchel; also what one sits on. (*American Speech* VI, 1939, 439.)

> You know how to pull a bit (serve sentence easily), always on your **keister**. (Goldin, O'Leary, *Dictionary of American Underworld Lingo*, 1950, 114.)

> An open sample case of liberal dimensions ... the typical "**keister**" of the street hawker. (Collier & Westrate, *The Reign of Soapy Smith*, 1935, 1; *DAS*, 301.)

Kid, *n.*, a young goat; a child; a term of affection; a moniker.
Cuid (*pron.* kid, cuid, kidj), *n.*, share, part, portion; a term of endearment, love, affection. A **chuid** (*pron.* a khid), my dear; mo **chuid** de'n tsaoghal (*pron.* mo khid den tæl), all I have, my darling; a **chuid** inghean (*pron.* a khid inyían), his daughters; a **chuidín** (*pron.* a khidín, a khijín), my little dear. (Dineen, 281, 282; *Foclóir Póca*, 326.)

Anglo-American dictionaries derive the word **kid** from an 11th century English word *kide*, meaning a young goat. Kid meaning "a child" enters the printed English language in the 16th century as a so-called low slang or cant word. (Barnhart, 564; *OED*.)

> **Kid**, a little dapper fellow, a child. (Grose, *Classical Dictionary of the Vulgar Tongue*, 1785, [1811].)

In Irish-American vernacular a **kid** is anyone you love, like, admire, or care about, as well as a generic term for children. The **kid** in question could be 8 or 80, but **a kid** (**a chuid**, my dear, my loved one) is always someone you care about. The English *kid* is a young goat you skin for a pair of *kid* gloves. In the 17th and 18th centuries, poor Irish "kids" were hunted down to sell.

> The Ships ... often call at Ireland to victual, and bring over frequently white Servants... Such as come bound by Indenture commonly call'd **Kids**, who are usually to serve four or five Years. (H. Jones, *Virginia*, 1724, 53.)

> In 1673, a "kidnapper" was defined in Richard Head's *The Canting Academy* as "a fellow that walketh the streets, and takes all advantages to pick up the younger sort of people, whom with lies and many fair promises he inticeth on board a ship and transports them into foreign plantations." (Maurizio Gotti, *The Language of Thieves and Vagabonds, Lexicographica*, 36.)

Stealing **a kid** (**a chuid**, my darling) from an Irish mother was robbing the **cuid** (portion, part) that she loved more than any other.

In O'Neill's play, *The Web*, set in the New York slums in the first years of the 20th century, Tim Moran is a "yegg" (armed robber) on the "lam" from the law, who tries to save a young woman and her baby from a "cadet" (pimp).

> TIM (*to Steve*): D'yuh think I'm goin' to stand by and let yuh beat her up cause she wants to keep her **kid**? ...Git outa here before I croak yuh.
> (...*Steve goes out and can be heard descending the stairs... Rose looks up at him from the bed... Then she breaks into convulsive sobbing.*)
> TIM (*making an attempt at consolation*): There, there, **Kid**, cut out the cryin'. He won't bother yuh no more...
> TIM (*kindly*): That's a bad cough yuh got, **Kid**.
> ROSE: ...I went to a doc about a month ago. He told me I had the "con" and had it bad... he said I'd have to be careful or the **kid** 'ud catch it from me... (*She sobs.*) I don't even kiss her on the mouth.
> TIM: Yuh sure are up against it, **Kid**. (*He appears deeply moved.*) Gee, I thought I was in bad...
> (Eugene O'Neill, *The Web*, 1913, [1988], 20–23.)

Jack Black became a road **kid** in the 1880s.

"You're welcome to travel with me, **kid**, if you want to jungle up for a month or two," my companion said. "The fruit will be getting' ripe south, and there'll be green corn and new spuds and the gumps are fat already. I promise myself some famous mulligans around these parts..." (Black, *You Can't Win*, 1926, [2000].)

In the 19th century, **Kid** became an Irish-American moniker of affection and admiration for boxers, ball players, and "sports."

"**KID**" KENNARD

Defeats Billy Murray in a Prize Fight
A Thirteen Round Contest at Rockaway
Beach Last Night—

The much talked of and three times postponed fight between Jim Kennard, the St. Paul **Kid**, and Billy Murray was fought on Rockaway beach last night. (*Brooklyn Eagle*, Nov. 3, 1896, 5.)

In the underworld a **kid** was a cully and a pal.

Kid Duff (Dubh, *pron.* doo, duv, dark) was the **Dark Kid**; the **Clinic** (**Claonach**, *pron.* clænać, crooked, deceitful) **Kid** could not be trusted; the **Postal** (**Postúil**, Conceited) **Kid** had a big head.

But at the end of the day the Irish **Kid** (**Cuid**) as an English "young goat" is a Brooklyn-Irish joke.

IRISH **KID**

Pat—Oi want to get a pair av shoes foor th' bye.
Clerk—Certainly, sir. French **kid**?
Pat—No soor, he's an **Irish kid**.
(*Brooklyn Eagle*, March 22, 1897, 12.)

A **kiddo** (**a chuid ó**, my darling, oh; my dear) is a "dear kid."

Kike, *n.*, a vulgar offensive name for a Jew.

Ciabhóg (*pron.* k'i'óg), a person adorned with a forelock or sidelock; *al.* a forelock, a sidelock. **Ciabhóg** (*pron.* k'i'og, a forelock, a sidelock curl) is the Irish word for the long sidelocks of the Orthodox Jews called *peyos*, as well as a person that wears forelocks or sidelocks.

It is revealing that the hate and violence in a racist epithet is most often provided by the speaker—and not the word itself. In Irish **ciabhóg** (*pron.* k'i'og, sidelock) is just a side curl.

There are scores of theories on the origin of the word **kike** (ciabhóg, *pron.* k'i'og, a person adorned with a forelock or *peyos*). It is said to be derived from an alteration of -*ki* (or -*ky*), a common ending of the personal names of Eastern European Jews; or from the Yiddish *kikel*, circle, because Jews who could not sign their names would make a circle; or from the alteration of the names Issac or Ike. (Chapman, *American Slang*, 263; *OED*.)

Leopold Bloom, the central character of James Joyce's *Ulysses*, was not a **ciabhóg** (*pron.* k'i'óg; a person adorned with a forelock), though he was both Irish and Jewish.

> It took just a whispered "**kike**" or "Jew bastard" ... and fists were flying... (Mezz Mezzrow and Bernard Wolfe, *Really the Blues*, 1946, [1990], 6.)

> Election Day in Chicago was always a boon to the boys in the Home. As soon as the polls opened, I went with Bill to see a ward heeler...
> "Let's see, your name's Abe Goldstein. You live at 422 Halstead Street. Go in an' vote."
> "Listen, Mister, what the devil," Bill yelled. "Do you want to get him pinched? How kin he vote with a name like that and the map of Ireland on his face?"
> "Well, it's the last name I have on the list. Take it or leave it... A cabbage by any other name 'ud take just as long to cook."
> "Listen, Red, I look more like a kike than you do. Trade names with me," suggested Bill. This weighty matter settled, neglected future citizens of America, we walked in and voted. (Jim Tully, *Beggars of Life*, 1924, [2004].)

Kinker, *n.*, a circus performer, a circus act.
Geanncach (*pron.* g'ank'ah), *adj.*, snubby, surly, rude, snooty; *fig.* a "stuck-up," snooty person. **Geannc a** chur ort féin, to turn up one's nose. (Ó Dónaill, 623; Dineen, 526.)
Kinkers, *adj.*, surly, rude; fig. snooty person) were the stuck-up stars of the circus.

The performers were more snobbish than any class of people I have ever known. They did not talk to the lesser gentry of the circus save only to give commands. They were known as the **"kinkers"** to us. We looked upon them with mingled disdain and awe. (Jim Tully, *Circus Parade*, 1927, 22.)

For the longer a circus plays in a town the easier it becomes for **kinkers** and flunkies. The work became a mere matter of detail, like in a penitentiary or any other institution. (Tully, *Circus Parade*, 1927, 195.)

Kitty, *n.*, a pot or pool of money, made up of contributions from several people; a pool into which each player in a card-game puts a certain amount of their winnings, to be used in meeting expenses, room rent, refreshments, food, etc.; the money taken by the winner of a game. Also, "earnings, liquid capital, a reserve fund; a sum of money made up of contributions by people involved in a common activity." (Barnhart, 567; *DAS*, 307; *OED*.)

Cuid oíche (*pron.* cuidíhi), a night's entertainment or lodging; a share, part, or portion of the night; a supper; a "cuiddihy." (Dineen, 281; Dwelly, 288.) The **kitty** also became a name for the money and swag that a **faro** banker cut up at the end of the night with his crew: the mechanic (dealer), case keeper, cappers, ropers, and shills.

Knack, *n.*, a special skill or aptitude; an acquired faculty of doing something skillfully; a personal habit of acting or speaking in a particular way; (*obsolete*) a trick, a deception. The meaning of a skill or talent is first recorded in English in the 16th century. Uncertain origin. (Barnhart, 567; *Oxford American Dictionary*, 366; *OED*.)

Gnách (*pron* gnác), *al.* **gnáth,** *n.*, custom; manner; practice; usage, habit, experience; a common, familiar, usual practice; *adj.*, customary, common, usual, habitual, constant. "**Gnách = gnáth**." (Ó Dónaill, 650, 651.)

Nack, to have a nack; to be ready at any thing; to have a turn for it. Nacky, ingenious. (Grose, *Classical Dictionary of the Vulgar Tongue*, 1785, [1811].)

By the 14th century, Anglo-Norman ruling families in Ireland like the Fitzgeralds had acquired the **knack** (**gnáth, gnách,** *pron.* gnác, custom, usage, habit) of speaking and writing in Irish, rather than the King's English. The Statutes of Kilkenny of Edward III were enacted in Ireland

in 1367 to stop the spread of this treasonous practice. "...many English
of the said land, forsaking the English language... live and govern
themselves according to the manners, fashion, and language of the Irish
enemies... (It) is forbidden that any Irish... pipers, story-tellers, bablers,
rimers, mowers, nor any other Irish agent shall come amongst the
English, and that no English shall receive or make gift to such; and that
shall do so...shall be taken, and imprisoned..." (*Statutes of Kilkenny*, 1367.)

She ne used no suche **knakkes** smale. (Chaucer, *Book of the Duchess*, ca.
1369.)

Eugene O'Neill had a **knack** for vernacular.

HICKEY: My old man used to whale salvation into my heinie with a birch
rod. He was a preacher in the sticks of Indiana, like I've told you. I got
the **knack** of sales gab from him, too. (O'Neill, *The Iceman Cometh*, 1939,
[1954], 622.)

Knicknack, *al.* **nicknack,** *n.*, a curiosity; a small, unusual article, more for orna-
ment or sentiment than use.

Neamhghnách (*pron.* n'ah ċnáċ, n'ah ɣnáċ), *adj.*, unusual, uncommon,
uncustomary, (*something*) extraordinary, unusual, uncommon; *fig.* a curiosity. **Neamh-** (*pron.* n'ah), *neg. prefix*, in-, un-; non-. **Gnách** (*pron.* gnaċ), *adj.*,
common, usual, customary. (Dineen, 1927, 786; Ó Dónaill, 898.)

A **knicknack** is an uncommon thing or curiosity. It was also considered a
vulgar slang word well into the 19th century. "Nicknacks. Toys, baubles,
or curiosities." (Frances Grose, *Classical Dictionary of the Vulgar Tongue*, 1785,
[1811].)

DAN MULLIGAN: Mac, it would try the patience of a saint to see all my
little **knickknacks** that I've treasured for years, carried off by specula-
tors. Tisn't the money valuation of them, Mac, that grieves me, they're
ould true and tried friends like yourself. (Edward Harrigan, *Cordelia's
Aspirations*, 1883, typescript.)

Kook, *n.*, a crazy, eccentric person; someone who is cuckoo.

Cuach (*pron.* cuəċ), *n.*, a cuckoo; a squeaky voice (*like a cuckoo*); a fool. (Dineen,
277.)

Most dictionaries derive **kook** from the abbreviation of the English *cuckoo*. But the Irish **cuach** (*pron.* cuəċ, cuckoo bird, fool) is naturally abbreviated. The actor Edd Byrnes played a character named **Kooky** on the hit TV show *77 Sunset Strip*. **Kooky** was a hip Hollywood **kook** (**cuach**, *pron.* cuaċ, cuckoo) with a duck's ass haircut.

L

Lag, *n.*, a weak person or thing, a feeble person; a weak creature; *v.*, to **slacken** one's pace, as from **weakness** or sloth; to fail to keep pace with others; to hang back, fall behind, remain in the rear. Origin obscure. (*OED.*)

Lag, *n.*, a weak person or thing, a feeble person; a weak creature; weakness; *adj.*, weak, faint, feeble, sick; unenthusiastic. An **lag** is an **láidir**, the weak and the strong. **Lagaigh** (*pron.* lagí), *v.*, weaken; slacken. Lagaigh mo neart (lagí mə n'art), my strength weakened; luas a **lagú**, to slacken speed. **Lagú**, *vn.*, weakening; slackening; abatement. **Lagar**, *n.*, weakness, slackening. (Ó Dónaill, 738, 739; Dineen, 623; Dwelly, 562, 563.)

The Irish **lag** (weak, feeble; a weak person or thing) and its verb **lagaigh** (*pron.* lagí, to weaken; slacken), first **lag** into English slang and cant in the 16th century "To **Lag**. To drop behind to keep back. **Lag** last; the last of a company." (Grose, *Classical Dictionary of the Vulgar Tongue*, 1785, [1811].)

The *OED* derives **lag** from a distortion of the English word *last*. "In some parts of England *fog, seg, lag*, or *foggie, seggie, laggie* are used in children's games as substitutes for 'first, second, last.' This suggests the possibility that lag may have originated in the language of sports as an arbitrary distortion of *last*... The current hypothesis that the adjective (**lag**) is (derived from) Welsh *llag* (earlier *llac*), Irish and Gaelic *lag*, (meaning) slack, weak, is highly improbable." (*OED.*)

Gaelic *lag*, weak, Irish *lag*, Early Irish *lac*, Middle Irish *luice* (pl.), Welsh *llag*, sluggish... Latin *langueo*, English *languid... slack*, also lag, from Celtic. (*MacBain's Dictionary of Gaelic Etymology, Sec.* 23.)

Lam, (on the) **lam,** *n.,* on the run, a hurried escape; *v.,* to be in flight from the law; to jump bail, or escape custody; to beat, to strike; to attack. Unknown origin. (Barnhart, 573, 574; *Dictionary of American Slang,* 312.)

Léim *(pron.* læm), *v.,* jump, leap, bound; fly up or out; start suddenly; attack; rush at. **Léim** *(pron.* læm); **leum** *(Gaelic),* *n.,* a sudden start, a bound; fight, quarrel; sudden rage, impulsive anger; *vn.,* (*act of*) jumping, leaping, bounding; flying up or out; (*act of*) attacking; rushing at. (Dineen, 654; Dwelly, 586; Ó Dónaill, 775, 776.)

When you "jump" bail you are on the **lam** (**léim,** *pron.* læm, jump) from the law. Anglo-American lexicographers derive the word **lam** from the English verb *to lame,* as in cripple. The Irish word encompasses the **lam** (**léim,** *pron.* læm, to jump, to fly up or out) of precipitate flight, and the **lam** (**léim,** *pron.* læm, to rush at, to attack) of beating and attack. Both meanings of **lam** survive in Irish-American vernacular.

> Weary met Studs and **lammed** away with both fists. (James T. Farrell, *Young Lonigan,* 1932, [2004], 84.)

> After he (the pickpocket) has secured the wallet he will... utter the word "**lam!**" This means to let the man go, and to get out of the way as soon as possible. (A. Pinkerton, *Thirty Years a Detective,* 1884.)

Lick, *v.,* to beat; to overcome, to defeat, to surpass.

Leag, *v.,* to knock down; to throw down; to put down (as a wrestler); to demolish; to destroy; to fell; to lay low, to bring down, to lay down.

> **Lick,** to beat. (Grose, *Classical Dictionary of the Vulgar Tongue,* 1785, [1811].)

In Irish-American vernacular you never merely beat someone, you **lick** (**leag,** *pron.* l'ag, demolish) them. John Morrissey learned the art of the **lick** (**leag,** knock down) in the 1840s and 1850s, on his journey from the slums of Troy, New York, to the heavyweight championship of the world. "I'm here to say I can **lick** any man in this place." (John Morrissey quoted in T.J. English, *Paddy Whacked,* 2005, 14.)

In Edward Harrigan's wildly popular *Mulligan Guard* musical comedies of the 1870s and 1880s, Dan Mulligan and his neighbors are constantly threatening to **lick** (**leag,** knock down, throw down, demolish, destroy) one another, and then proceeding to do it. Men **lick** (**leag,** knock down) political rivals;

women **lick** (**leag**, demolish) husbands, and kids **lick** (**leag**, throw down) one another.

> DAN MULLIGAN: ...Tommy, I'm not too ould but I can **lick** any Dutchman. (Edward Harrigan, *The Mulligan Guard*, typescript, 1878.)

> LOCHMULLER (*eats sausage*): I'm not afraid—you talk mit me—I can **lick** der whole Mulligan Guard. (Harrigan, *The Mulligan Guard*, typescript, 1878.)

> Danny asked if Davy could **lick** Studs, and Davy said he wasn't afraid of anybody... (James T. Farrell, *Young Lonigan*, 1932, [2004], 192.)

Lollygag, lallygag, *v.*, to idle; to dawdle; to loll about; to kiss, fondle, to neck. **Lollygagger, lallygagger**, *n.*, a youthful lay-about; a young dawdler, idler. Origin uncertain.

Leath-luighe géag (*pron.* l'a-liɣ g'æg), a reclining, leaning, lolling youth. **Leath-luighe géagdha** (*pron.* l'a-liɣ g'æggə), youthful reclining; *fig.* a youthful laya-bout. **Leath-luighe** (*pron.* l'a-liɣ), *n.*, (*act of*) leaning, lolling, laying about, reclining. **Géag** (*pron.* g'æg, g'íōg), *n.*, a youth, a young person. An ghéag gheal, the beautiful youth. **Géagdha** (*pron.* g'æggə), *adj.*, youthful. (Dineen, 522, 649; Ó Dónaill, 616, 617, 771.)

> That left most of the summer free for play, swimming, berry picking, and general **lollygagging**. (F. Sullivan, *New Yorker*, Aug. 4, 1952; *DAS*, 323.)

> "**Lally-gaggin**" was Grandmother's word for love-making. (*Journal of American Folk-Lore*, 1949.)

A **lolly** (leath-luighe, *pron.* l'a-liɣ, leaning, lolling, reclining) pop **lollygags** in one's mouth.

Longshore, *n.*, existing on or frequenting the docks; found or employed along the docks, (*someone or something*) close to docks or ships. **Longshoreman**, *n.* a dockworker who unloads cargo from ships. Longshore is said to be an aphetic word derived from English words *along shore*. (*OED*; Barnhart, 609.)

Loingseoir (*pron.* loŋ'shór, longshor), *n.*, a shipman, boatman, mariner, sailor; anyone who works with ships. **Long**, *n.*, a vessel, a ship; **long** guail, a collier, or ship's coal loader.

Most revolutions start along the waterfront. There must be something in the air that makes radicals out of seaman and dockworkers... A real **longshoreman** is never so happy as when he is using his fists or his steel bail hook on an enemy. (Butler, Driscoll, *Dock Walloper*, 1933, 205.)

Loogin, *al.* loogan, *n.*, a fool, an idiot.

Leath-dhuine (*pron.* l'ah-ginə), *n.*, a half-wit, a fool, an idiot. Ná dein **leath-dhuine** diot, don't play the fool. (Dineen, 649; Ó Dónaill, 771.)

"That **loogin** is all loose, his bean is all screwy," said Johnny O'Brien. (James T. Farrell, *Young Lonigan*, 1932, [2004], 41.)

"Good morning, Simon ... Say, listen to this **loogin'** here," Mac said to Simon Murray who had entered, smoking a cigar and wearing a panama. (Farrell, *Gas-House McGinty*, 1932, [1950], 103.)

Loogan, an idiot. Even though the dude is hot, he's a real **loogan**. (*Urban Slang Dictionary*.)

Lucre, *n.*, gain, profit, advantage (now only with unfavorable implication); gain for a low devious reason; filthy lucre, foul lucre. (*Dictionary of American Slang*, 133.)

Luach óir (*pron.* lúŏċ ór, luəċ ór), reward of gold, wages of gold, price of gold, payment of money. **Luach** (*pron.* luəċ), *n.*, price, value, cost, wages, fee; reward, recompense, payment. **Ór,** *g.*, **óir,** *n.* gold; money. (Dineen, 822.)

Most Anglo-American dictionaries derive **lucre** directly from the Latin *lucrum*, meaning "gain, profit, advantage," which is a cognate with Irish **luach** (*pron.* luəċ) and Old Irish *lóg*. (*Barnhart Dictionary of Etymology*, 613; Dineen, 678; Ó Dónaill, 803; *MacBain's Gaelic Etymological Dictionary*, Sec. 25.)

Lulu, a lulu, *n.*, *adj.*, an amazing person or thing; (*something or someone*) remarkable or amazing; often used ironically or sarcastically. (Chapman, *American Slang*, 274.)

Liú lúith (*pron.* lú lúh), a howl, a scream, a vigorous yell of joy; a loud wail or cry; *fig.* a "complete scream," a howler. **Liú,** *n.*, a scream, a howl, shout, yell, wail, call out; *vn.*, crying. Screaming. **Lúth** (*pron.* lúh), *g.*, **lúith,** *n.*, strength, vigor, power.

A lulu can be spectacular or awful, but it's always "a scream."

> Farrell's two baser was a **lu-lu**. (*New Orleans Lantern*, Nov. 10, 1886, 6.)

> Sheffield then hit a **screamer** to 3rd ... and the bases were loaded for Rodriguez. (Brian McMillan, *Off the Facade*, July 30, 2004.)

> "I tought you was goin' to do him so dat his friends wouldn' reckonize him; you ought to go in for sluggin' as a steady business, you'd be a reglar **lulu**, yer kin fight so much better wit yer mout' dan yer kin wit yer hans," and Maud laughed so heartily she came very near swallowing the chewing gum in her excitement. (*Brooklyn Eagle*, "The Gowanusians," May 15, 1892, 6.)

> "I don't know how guys get to be as dumb as Noonan. He's a real **Lulu**." (James T. Farrell, *Gas-House McGinty*, 1933, [1950], 32.)

Lunch, *n.*, a meal most often taken at midday. Origin uncertain. "Perhaps evolved from *lump*, on the analogy of the apparent relation between hump and hunch, bump and bunch..." Lunch does not begin to appear in English until the end of the 16th century. (*OED; ODEE*, 1978, 540.)

Lóinte (*pron.* lónchə), *pl. n.*, food, rations, provisions. **Lóin-fheis** (*pron.* lón-əsh), *n.*, a feast of meat. (Dineen, 675; Ó Dónaill, 797.)

A saloon in New York City in the 1850s was called a "lunch" because it served free **lunch** (**lóinte**, *pron.* lónchə, food, provisions, grub) with the booze.

> UNION SALOON—No.149 Pearl Street... Linneman Brothers have just opened a saloon, or **lunch**, at the above place.... The best quality of liquors always on hand. Free lunch every day from 10 to 12 AM, when they will be happy to see their friends. (*New York Times*, July 1, 1852, 3.)

> Mac moved to the free-**lunch** counter at the left of the entrance... "How come you're wide open, Mike? Didn't you know there's a Volstead law?" Mac heard, as he helped himself to a ham sandwich and a hard boiled egg. (James T. Farrell, *Gas-House McGinty*, 1933, [1950], 7.)

Lón, lóinte (*pron.* lónchə), *pl.*, from Middle Irish *lón*, Old Irish *lóon*; cognate with Old Breton *lon*. (*MacBain's Gaelic Etymological Dictionary*.)

Luncheon, *n*., a (formal) lunch. Origin uncertain.

Lóintean (*Gaelic, pron.* lónch'an), *n. pl.*, food, fare, provisions; an abundance of food. **Lóinte án** (*pron.* lóncha án), elegant food, splendid fare. **Lóin-fheis án** (*pron.* lón-ash án), an elegant, splendid feast of meat. **Án**, *adj.*, elegant, splendid. (Dwelly, 596; Dineen, 675; Ó Dónaill, 797.)

Barnhart's dictionary believes "luncheon" may have developed from the Middle English word *nonechenche*. (*Barnhart Dictionary of Etymology*, 615.)

> No little scraps of bounty … but large **Lunchions** of Munificence. (H. More, 1685; *OED*.)

> On returning to the train they found sumptuous **luncheons** spread out in the van… the travelers sat down to the ample hoard. (*Brooklyn Eagle*, May 13, 1843, 2.)

M

Ma, *n*. mother.

Máthair (*pron.* ma'hĭr), *n*., mother; source.

In Michael Patrick MacDonald's memoir *All Souls: A Family Story from Southie*, **Ma** is the source of the family's survival.

Mac, or **Mack**, *n*., a man; a fellow; a term of direct address.

Mac, *n*., son; boy; young person; fellow; descendant.

Mac is often used in direct address, as in "Hey, **Mack**!" Although today "buddy" and **dude**, are used more frequently.

Machree, *n*., term of affection.

Mo chroí (*pron.* ma krí), my heart. Grá **mo chroí** tú, you are my love. The song "Mother **Machree**" was written by J.R. Young, Chauncey Olcott, and Ernie Ball in 1910.

Macushla, *n.*, a term of affection; my darling, my loved one.

Mo chuisle (*pron.* mə kishl'ə, mŭ cush-lĭ), my (heart's) pulse. (See: **acushla**.)

> SID: (*raptly*): Ah, Sight for Sore Eyes, my beautiful **Macushla**, my star-eyed **Mavourneen**... (Eugene O'Neill, *Ah, Wilderness!*, 1933, [1967], 50.)

Mammy, *n.*, mother.

Mamaí, *n.*, mammy; a childish name for mother. (Dineen, 705.)

> In Ireland **Mammy** is a common name for mother. In the U.S.A., when used in reference to African-American women it "is considered an ethnic slur." (*Wikipedia*.)

Mark, *n.*, the target of a scam, or crooked gambling game, a sucker.

Marc, *n.*, a target; a goal; (*of person*) a mark. Marc a chur suas, to set up a mark. (Ó Dónaill, 834.)

> In the 19th and early-20th centuries, a **mark** (**marc**, target) out on a **spree** (**spraoi**, fun, sport, frolic) was lured by a **roper** (**rábaire**, a dashing fellow) into a crooked **faro** (**fiaradh**, *pron.* fiəroo, turning) game; where a **capper** (**ciapaire**, a goader) goaded the **sucker** (**sách úr**, a fresh new "fat cat") to **slug** (**slog**, swallow, gulp) the high-class **whiskey** (**uisce**) and wager his **jack** (**tiach**, *pron.* jiak, small purse; *fig.* money) with abandon.

> HOPE (*more drowsily*): I'll fire both of you. Bejees, if you think you can play me like an easy **mark**, you've come to the wrong house. No one ever played Harry Hope for a sucker. (Eugene O'Neill, *The Iceman Cometh*, 1939, [1954], 582.)

> MOSHER (*dejectedly*): Yes, Harry has always been weak and easily influenced, and now that he's getting old he'll be an easy **mark** for those grafters. (O'Neill, *The Iceman Cometh*, 1939, [1954], 652.)

> It is not intelligence but integrity which determines whether or not a man is a good **mark**. (David Maurer, *The Big Con: the Story of the Confidence Man*, 1940, [1999], 103, 104.)

Mark Anthony, *al.* **Mark Antony** (*gambling slang*), *n.*, a super sucker.

Marc andána, a rash and reckless mark, a foolish mark. **Marc**, *n.*, a target; (*of person*), a mark. **Andána** (*pron.* andánə), *adj.*, rash, reckless, foolhardy, foolish; given to taking unnecessary risks. "That fellow is only **andána**, only a fool. (Ó Dónaill, 834; Dolan, *Dictionary of Hiberno-English*, 1998, 9.)

> We played and he lost twenty-eight bucks to me. What I didn't know was that there was a **Mark Anthony**—that's a super sucker—on the sidelines. The game was being staged for his benefit. At closing time my opponent said in a loud voice, "I'll be back tomorrow night with more money." He was, too, but not to play me. He played **Mark Anthony** and took him for eight hundred dollars. He was just using me the day before to make himself look like a loser. (Robert Byrne, *McGoorty: A Pool Room Hustler*, 1972, [2004], 19.)

Masher, *n.*, a dandy; a fashionable young man of the late Victorian era; a man fond of the company of women; (*in the U.S.*) a handsome male flirt; (*pejorative*) a womanizer; a lout who makes indecent advances towards women.

Maise (*pron.* mash'ə), *n.*, adornment, beauty, comeliness, attractiveness. **Maiseach** (*pron.* mash'aċ, mash'ah), *adj.*, beauteous, handsome, graceful, clever; well-dressed. (Dineen, 701; Ó Dónaill, 821.)

In Brooklyn in the 1870s, **masher** was a word for a handsome flirt.

> THE TEMPTATIONS THAT BESET A GOOD LOOKING POLICE-MAN.

> On one of the Brooklyn ferries is detailed a policeman who by some is termed handsome. The fellow only misses being good looking by one degree; that is, he is always scowling... The "peeler" soon gained the reputation for being what is termed a "**masher**," and many are the ladies whose hearts palpitate as Joe takes them by the arm as they trip across the street, going over from the ferry gates. (*Brooklyn Eagle*, May 25, 1877, 1.)

But **masher** was more commonly an epithet for a womanizing cad.

> PUNISHING A MASHER

> The burly form of a young man in a pea jacket and with a Bowery dude expression of impudence in his face and carriage blocked the way so the lady could not enter the door..."Will you please let me enter?" and the man's reply delivered with the impudence of a professional **masher**, "Why certainly, my dear." (*Brooklyn Eagle*, Dec. 13, 1887, 4.)

...one whose dress or manners are calculated to elicit the admiration of susceptible young women—a "**masher**." (Theodore Dreiser, *Sister Carrie*, 1900, [2004], 3.)

Mash, *n.*, love; to attract amorous attention; a crush.

Maise (*pron.* mash'ə), *n.*, attractiveness. **Maiseach** (*pron.* mash'aċ, mash'ah), *adj.*, attractive, beauteous, handsome.

> A Great **Masher** ... when she returned home she very unwittingly made a remark that she had made a big "**mash** on Hank Davis." (*Brooklyn Eagle*, Aug. 5, 1882, 4.)

Mavourneen, *n.*, a term of affection like *macushla*.

Mo mhuirnín (*pron.* mŭ vúrnín), my dear one, my love. **Muirnín**, *n.*, darling, sweetheart.

The actor Gene Lockhart played Uncle Sid in the 1933 Theatre Guild production of Eugene O'Neill's comedy *Ah, Wilderness!*, also starring George M. Cohan.

> Sɪᴅ (*raptly*): Ah, Sight for Sore Eyes, my beautiful **Macushla**, my star-eyed **Mavourneen**... (O'Neill, *Ah, Wilderness!*, 1933, [1967], 50.)

> Sɪᴅ (*with drunken gravity*): Careful, **Mavourneen**, careful! You might have hit some place beside the head. (O'Neill, *Ah, Wilderness!*, 1933, [1967], 51.)

Mawley, *n.*, a hand; boxing gloves. (Pierce Egan, *Boxiana*, 1824.)

Malye (*Irish Traveller Gammon* or *Cant*), *n.*, a hand; from Irish *maille*, a tool.

Mawley as slang for *hand* was popularized by the 19th century London Irish boxing writer and slang lexicographer, Pierce Egan. **Mawley** is derived from Irish Traveller Cant or Gammon word *malye*, hand, from the Irish word *maille* (*pron.* mal'ə), a tool.

> **Mawley**. A hand. Tip us your mawley; shake hands with me. Fam the mawley; shake hands. (Grose, *The Classical Dictionary of the Vulgar Tongue*, 1785, [1811].)

Mayhem, *n.*, violent behavior; assault; severe injury; wild chaos, confusion, disorder. Uncertain origin.

Mayhem, *v.*, to inflict physical injury on someone, to cause chaos, disorder; also used figuratively. (*OED*; Barnhart, 643.)

Maidhm, maoim (*pron.* maim, mï-im), *n.*, a cataclysm; a violent eruption; a burst, a rupture; an explosion; a crash; a battle; a complete defeat, a rout; an overwhelming blow; a severe injury.

Maidhm (*pron.* maim, mï-im), *v.*, burst, erupt, defeat, destroy; rout; detonate.

Maidhm (*pron.* maim, mï-im), *n.*, a severe injury. Do-gníomh **maidhm** ar, I inflict **severe injury** on. (Dineen, 696, 697; Ó Dónaill, 816, 817.)

Most Anglo-American dictionaries derive mayhem from the verb *maim*, to wound, mutilate; or render powerless; said to be from Old Middle French and Norman *mahaignier*—of "uncertain origin." (Barnhart, 643; *OED*.) In the 12th century, the Norman conquerors inflicted **mayhem** on Ireland that was compared by the poets to "**maidhm** na Traoi" (*pron.* mï-im nə Trí), the cataclysm of Troy.

Maoim (*Gaelic*), *n.*, terror, onset, eruption, surprise, Irish *maidhm*, a sally, eruption, defeat, Early Irish *maidm*, a breach or breaking, defeat "Some give the root as allied to Sanskrit *math*, stir, twirl. (Dineen, 697; Ó Dónaill, 816, 817; An Seabhac, *Foclóir Gaeilge-Béarla*, 1958, 82; *MacBain's Gaelic Etymological Dictionary*.)

Mick, *n.*, a derogatory slang term for an Irish person. (*Australia*) A Roman Catholic. **Micks**, *pl.*, people of Irish origin living in North America.

Mic, *n.*, *pl.*, sons, boys, children, descendants; a term of affection.

A slang word of derision in English is a word of family connection and affection in the Irish language, **a mhic** (*pron.* a vic), my lad.

> SARA (*frightened now*): But you'll never be let see him! His servants will keep you out! He'll have the police arrest you, and it'll be in the papers about another drunken **Mick** raising a crazy row! (Eugene O'Neill, *A Touch of the Poet*, 1946, [1967], 22.)

> "What are you?" ... "American," I said. "Irish-American..." "I shoulda figured dat," he said. "A fuckin' **Mick**." (Pete Hamill, *The Drinking Life*, 1994, 76.)

He thought of himself, so much cleverer than the Irish. The **micks** were lousy, all right. (James T. Farrell, *Young Lonigan*, 1932, [2004], 185.)

Mihall, *n.*, a "code" name for a Transit Workers Union (TWU) meeting in New York City in the 1930s and 1940s. The Irish language was used by TWU organizers as a secret language to confound *finks* (informers) and *beakies* (supervisors).

Meitheal (*pron.* m'əhəl, mi-hŭl), *n.*, working party; a gang or a party, especially of reapers, a number of men employed at any special work, as hay-making, turf-cutting. The **meitheal** (*pron.* m'əhəl, mi-hŭl) embodied **cómhar** (*pron.* kó'r, cooperation, mutually borrowed labor; alliance, reciprocity) in rural Ireland much like a trade union in the subways of New York City.

> Mike [Quill] devised a uniquely Irish system for calling a meeting of the secret union... On the small farms in Ireland, neighbors band together to help each other cut the turf and stack the hay for the winter. In Gaelic this gathering of farmers is called **mihall**... and every farmer's son working for the IRT knew the word. Mike would phone a ticket agent on the company intercom and talk about having a **mihall** Tuesday or Wednesday... The conversation was *half-Gaelic half-English* [*ed.* italics], and the beakies gave up in disgust. They may have suspected the men were talking in code, but it was a code they didn't bother to crack. There wasn't a Gaelic speaker among them. (Shirley Quinn, *Mike Quill Himself: A Memoir*, 1985, 67.)

Mill (*obsolete*; *cant*), v., to rob; to break, to kill; to box; *n.*, a boxing match. (Grose, *Classical Dictionary of the Vulgar Tongue*, 1785, [1811]; Egan, *Boxiana*, 1824.)

Mill, *v.*, to break, to injure; to damage, to destroy. **Milleadh** (*pron.* milĭ, mil'ah), *n.*, injury *vn.*, (*act of*) injuring, destroying, damaging; spoiling. **Millteoir**, *n.*, a destroyer. (Dineen, 742, 743; Ó Dónaill, 859, 860.)

> "I'll **mill** your glaze; I'll beat out your eye." (Grose, *Classical Dictionary of the Vulgar Tongue*, 1785, [1811].)

> To **mill** a bleating cheat; to kill a sheep. (Grose, *Classical Dictionary of the Vulgar Tongue*, 1785, [1811].)

> In my study I have a print by Thomas Rowlandson of a **milling** match between Tom Cribb, the champion of England, and Tom Molineaux, an

American Negro ... on September 28, 1811. This was a return match ... and Pierce Egan, the Froissart of the London prize ring, wrote concerning the second match: "It is supposed that near 20,000 persons witnessed this tremendous **mill.**" (A.J. Liebling, *The Sweet Science*, 1951, [2004], 107.)

Miller, *n.*, a boxer; a murderer. "**Miller,** a Killer..." (B.E.'s *Dictionary of the Canting Crew*, 1699.)

Míle (*pron.* m'íl'ə), *n.*, a warrior; a soldier; a champion, a hero. **Mill,** *v.*, to break, to injure; to damage, to destroy. (Dineen, 742; Ó Dónaill, 859, 860.)

One person's killer is another person's **miller** (**míle,** *pron.* m'íl'ə, hero, warrior, soldier; champion; destroyer.)

> Next rings the fame of gallant Crib
> A cool and steady **miller.**
> (*Sporting Magazine*, 1812; OED.)

> A day or two later, the **milling** coves and the flash coves (fighters and knowing boys) would set out in wagons or hackneys, with plenty of Cyprians and blue ruin (sporting girls and gin) to keep them happy and on their way. (A.J. Liebling, *The Sweet Science*, 1951, [2004], 50.)

Moniker, *n.*, an (assumed) name, a nickname, an underworld name.

Munik (*Irish Traveller Cant*), *n.*, a name. Derived from metathesis of Irish *ainm*, name: m-ain + ak = munak, munik, name.

> "The van is alright; I have had the '**monnick**' (slang word for name) taken off it." (*New York Times*, Nov. 11, 1895; OED.)

> Most of the names and "monickers" for confidence men in this book are genuine... The **Clinic Kid** has made a fortune swindling wealthy patients who visited a famous mid-western clinic. (David Maurer, *The Big Con*, 1940, [1999], xix.)

In fact, the **Clinic** (**claonach,** *pron.* clænəċ, crooked) Kid's monicker was crooked in Irish.

Moolah, *al.* moola, mullah, mola, *n.*, money. Origin unknown. (*OED.*)

Moll óir, *al.* **mol óir** (*pron.* mol ór, mul óir), a heap of gold or money. **Mol, moll,** *n.*, a heap; a large amount; a large number. **Ór,** *n.*, **óir,** *g.*, gold; money; an t-ór, the gold, money. Moll airgid, a heap of money. (Dineen, 822; Ó Dónaill, 876.)

> "I never saw the day wherein no matter how much **moola** I had I could not use some more." (John O'Hara, *Pal Joey*, 1940.)

Jack Abramoff enthused in an email to his partner, "Scammer" Scanlon, about the heap of gold to be made from Native American gambling casinos.

> "I'd love us to get our mitts on that **moolah**." (Jack Abramoff quoted on NBC's *Today Show*, Jan 4, 2006.)

> **Moolah**: money. (*Australian Slang Online.*)

Mow (*obsolete*), *v.*, to have sexual intercourse.
Moth (*Gaelic*; *pron.* moh), *n.*, sex. **Moth** (*Irish*; *pron.* moh), *n.*, a penis, the male organ of generation. (Dwelly, *Faclair Gaidhlig Gu Beurla*, 1901, [1994], 673; Dineen, 763.)

> **Mow**. A Scotch word for the act of copulation. (Grose, Egan, *Classical Dictionary of the Vulgar Tongue*, 1785, [1811].)

> Why should na poor people **mow**. (Robert Burns, *Poems & Songs*, 1792.)

Muck (*poker slang*), *v.*, to fold cards, to turn your cards over face down in center of the table; to "kill" your cards; to "bury" your hand; *n.*, the pile of dead cards covered over facedown in the center of the (poker) table.
Múch *pron.* múċ), *v.*, to smother; to cover over, to deaden, to suppress, to bury. **Muchadh** (*pron.* múċah, múċə), *n.*, obliteration, obscurement; *vn.*, (*act of*) smothering; covering over, suppressing. Tá sé **muchta** (*pron.* tá shay muċtə), it is buried, it is "mucked."

> **Muck**: To fold. To discard one's hand without revealing the cards... ("Poker Jargon," *Wikipedia*.)

> He didn't have the outs so he **mucked** his hand. (*Poker Glossary*.)

Mucker, *n.*, a person who does dirty work; an unrefined person; a troublesome person; a contemptible individual; a laborer; a common word for a "fellow" in Ireland.

Mucaire, *n.*, a swineherd, a boor; a hick, a rustic, a countryman; a slovenly worker; (*of person*) a pig. (Dineen, 766; Ó Dónaill, 882.)

> [The] Company ... paid $3 for miners and $2.50 for "**muckers**," or underground laborers. (*Harper's Weekly*, May 20, 1899.)

In Boston, **mucker** became a nickname for an Irishman, said to derive from fact that Irish immigrants often worked the dirtiest jobs. In Ireland, it's slang for a pal.

> "Hey **mucker** give us some wackey." Hey, pal, give us some marijuana.
> (*Derry Slang Online; Urban Dictionary Online.*)

Mug (1), *n.*, a face, an ugly face; a scowling face; a rude, rough person; a boxer; a gangster, a criminal; (*criminal slang*) a policeman. (Chapman, 292.)

Muc, *n.*, a pig; anything resembling a pig or a hog; (*of person*) a piggish, hoggish individual, a swine; a scowl; a beetled brow, a scowling face; a piggish face. **Múchna**, *n.*, surly appearance; piggish scowl. Muc ar mala, a scowl, a beetling of brows, a piggish **mug**.

Most Anglo-American dictionaries derive the slang word *mug* from an English drinking mug with an ugly face painted on it. In Irish-American vernacular, a **mug** (**muc**, a scowling, beetle-browed face) is a pig-faced *mucker*.

"The Gowanusians" was a series of fictional tales in the *Brooklyn Eagle* of the 1890s that featured a middle-class reporter's version of the slang and vernacular of working-class Irish-Americans who lived and worked near the Gowanus Canal in the 1890s.

> "Youse kin bet yer socks dat dere is one pig faced **mug** dat I'm partic'ler about seein', in a pea green hurry, see?" (*Brooklyn Eagle*, "The Gowanusians—Slob Gets Out of Jail," Dec. 20, 1891, 14.)

> His **mug** was often disfigured with the claret (blood) trickling down.
> (Pierce Egan, *Boxiana*, 1824.)

> De **mug** what plays de flute has de music all t'himself when de odder **mugs** in de orchestra don't do nottin. (E.W. Townsend, *Chimmie Fadden*, 1895, 17.)

He'd be ... making **mugs** at his own self in the bit of a glass we had hung on the wall. (J.M. Synge, *Playboy of Western World*, 1907.)

Mug (2), *v.*, the act of strangling, choking a person. **Mugged**, *p.p.*, strangled, choked; assaulted from behind with a chokehold.

Múch (*pron.* múċ), *v.*, to smother; suffocate, choke; press upon, squeeze together; stifle, throttle; destroy; quell, pacify. **Muchadh** (*pron.* múċah, múċə), *n.*, obliteration, obscurement; *vn.*, (*act of*) smothering; covering over, suppressing. **Múchta** (*pron.* múċtə), *p.p.*, choked; throttled; smothered, suffocated. Ghabhadar araon **múchadh** na gríosaighe ar a chéile, they choked one another savagely. (Dineen, 765, 766; Dwelly, 674, 675; Ó Dónaill, 882.)

> "I've been **mugged** three times, but never beaten up." (Chapman, *American Slang*, 292.)

> The verb "to mug" is derived by most Anglo-American dictionaries from "drinking mugs made to resemble grotesque human faces." (Chapman, *American Slang*, 292; OED.)

Muggy, *adj.*, humid, warm sultry weather, having a stuffy, stifling, smothering atmosphere.

Múchadh (*pron.* múcah, múc'ə), *vn.*, smothering, suffocating, choking; stifling, stuffy. **Múchta** (*pron.* múctə), *p.a.*, choked, smothered, suffocated. Bhíomar **múchta** ag an teas, we were suffocated by the heat. Aimsir **mhúchta**, muggy weather. (Ó Dónaill, 882.)

Most Anglo-American dictionaries derive the word **muggy** from Old Norse *mugga*, drizzle. (*American Heritage Dictionary*; *Merriam-Webster Dictionary*.)

Mugsy, *al.* Muggsy, *n.*, a moniker for a mug. The most famous "Mugsy" was the film character "Mugsy" McGinnis, played by actor Leo Gorcy in more than seventy Hollywood films, made between the 1930s and 1950s, about a group of NYC slum kids called the "Bowery Boys" or the "Dead End Kids." "Mugsy" was the Irish-American gang leader.

Muc saobh (*pron.* muc sӕh), a twisted, scowling face; *fig.* a mug with a crooked scowl. **Muc**, *n.*, (*of person*) a piggish individual, a swine; a scowl; a beetled brow, a scowling mug; a piggish visage. **Saobh** (*pron.* sӕh, síh, sӕv), *adj.*, slanted, twisted; wayward, capricious; foolish, mad, paradoxical; crooked, perverse

In the movies, "**Mugsy**" McGinnis had a perpetual twisted scowl on his puss. **Mugsy** is also a common name for a mutt.

Mullarkey, malarkey, malachy, malaky, *n.* exaggerated, foolish talk, usually intended to deceive, seduce, or charm; beguiling baloney.
Meallacach (*pron.* m'aləkəċ, m'aləkəh), *adj.*, alluring, charming, beguiling, deceitful. Glór **meallacach**, beguiling speech. **Meallaireacht**, *g.*, **meallaireachta** (*pron.* m'alərakta), *n.*, deception, beguilement, coaxing, seduction; amusement. Cainte **mellaireachta** (*pron.* ka'nt' m'alərakta), deceptive, beguiling speech; coaxing, amusing speech.

> "**Malachy**—you said it." (Tad Dorgan, *Malarkey: Tad, and Its San Francisco Roots*, 1924; Peter Tamony, *Western Folklore, Vol. 33, No. 2*, Apr., 1974, 158–162.)
>
> "It's a wonder you notice me," I told him. "That's a lot of **malaky**," says he. (J.P. McEvoy, *Hollywood Girl*, 1929.)
>
> "Hollywood is in the business of manufacturing **malarkey**." (Bob Thomas quoted in Chapman, *American Slang*, 279.)

Mutt (*slang; orig. U.S.*), *n.*, a dog, *esp.* a mongrel; an inferior, lowbred animal or person. A lowbred person; a person of hybrid ancestry; often used affectionately. Uncertain origin.
Mada (*pron.* madə, mŏdə), *n.*, a dog, *esp.* inferior breed, a cur, a mutt; *al.* **madadh, madra**.

The word **mutt** is not recorded in American printed English until 1900. **Mutt** is also of uncertain origin. Like most **mutts**. Some Anglo-American lexicographers derive **mutt** from *muttonhead*, as in a sheep's head. But a muttonhead is a dunderhead or a dolt. Most **mutts** are (street) smart. *New York Times* columnist and writer Dan Barry is a self-described Irish-American **mutt** from Long Island, New York.

> I knew that we were among the many **mutts** of America, barking from fenced-in, third-of-an-acre yards that were chockablock across the island.

I also knew that a few other children in our neighborhood had distinctive backgrounds, ones that stood out among the squirming progeny of former Bronx and Brooklyn tenement dwellers. (Dan Barry, *Pull Me Up*, 2004, 21.)

N

Nag (*slang*), *n.*, a horse; a worn out horse; a racehorse. Uncertain origin. (Barnhart, 692.)

N-each (*pron.* n-a'ċ), (*form of*) **each** (*pron.* a'ċ), *n.*, horse. Cóiste sé **n-each** (*pron.* cóshtə shæ n-a'ċ), a coach and six horse. Fir nə **n-each** (*pron.* f'ir nə n-a'ċ), the horsemen.

> **Nag** ... of unknown origin ... first recorded 1598. (*Online Etymology Dictionary.*)

Nan, Nanny, Nana, *n.* grandmother.
Nain, *al.* **naing**, *n.*, grandmother.

> In my family we called my maternal grandmother **Nan** or Nanny. My great grandmother was **Nana** Number 2.

Natty, *adj.*, neat, sharp-looking. "Origin uncertain... Perhaps neat + y." (*OED.*)
Néata (*pron.* nætə), *adj.*, neat, nice; affable. (Dineen, 793.)

> Francis Grose, the 18th century English slang lexicographer, called **natty** a cant word. "**Natty** Lads. Young thieves or pickpockets. Cant." (Grose, *Dictionary of the Vulgar Tongue*, 1785, [1811].)

Natty (**néata**, *pron.* næta, neat, sharp-looking) is a very neat Irish word.

Nincumpoop, *al.***nikumpoop,** *n.*, a ninny; a fool; a blubbering dolt. Uncertain origin. (Barnhart, 705.)

Naioidhean (ar) chuma búb (*pron.* níyean (ər) ćumə boob), an infantile idiot, a baby in the shape of a blubbering boob. Naoidhe (ar) chuma búb (*pron.* níye [ər] ćumə boob), a baby in the form of a howling boob.

> In doing it, or after he had done, had he looked like a fool... like a ninny... like a **nincompoop**... (L. Sterne, *Life of Tristram Shandy*, 1760.)

Ninny, *n.*, a simpleton, a childlike fool.

Naoidheanach (*pron.* ní-yanəć, ní-yánəh), *al.* **naoidheanta,** *adj.*, childish, childlike, infantile. **Naoidheán** (*pron.* ní'yán), *n.*, an infant, a baby. **Naoínda,** *al.* **naoínta,** *adj.*, infantlike, childlike; *fig.* someone infantile. Cómh lag le **naoidheanán** (*pron.* kó lag l'ə ní-yanán), as weak as a baby. (Dineen, 781; Dwelly, 685.)

> Not long since I discovered a nest of **Ninnies** in this great wombe the Worlde. (Robert Armin, 1609; *OED.*)

Nugy, a nugy, a noog, *n.*, a rub, rap, or whack on the head with the knuckles.

Aonóg (ænóg), *n.*, a nip, a pinch; *fig.* a little whack. **Aonóg** + y = a noogy, a little nip, a little pinch, a playful smack. (Dineen, 53.)

Nut, nuts, *n.*, the **nut** hand is the most powerful hand in a poker game, also called the **nuts**; anything or anyone excellent; basic fixed expenses, overhead; (*underworld*) the minimum payoff to police to stay in business; a devoted enthusiast, an avid fan; someone with an acquired talent, skill, or knowledge; a testicle; a head; a crazy person; *al.* to be very fond of someone or something.

Neart (*pron.* n'art), *n.*, strength, power, force, energy, vigor; might; ability, skill; abundance, a sufficiency, enough. (Dineen, 792, 793; Ó Dónaill, 908, 909; Dwelly, 687.)

(1) A **nut** or the nuts can be anyone or anything that is excellent, powerful, vigorous, and energetic. (2) **Nut,** the nuts, (*poker slang*), *n.*, to have the *nut* or *nut hand* is to hold the strongest possible cards in a poker game, also called

the *nuts*. Any gender can have the **nuts** (neart, *pron.* n'art, power) in poker, le **neart** lámha (*pron.* l'ə n'art láwə), by strength of a hand of cards. (3) **Nut** (*U.S. slang*), *n.*, the amount of money required; overhead costs, basic expenses, whether legitimate, or graft to politicians. Tá mo **neart** agam, I have enough, I have my **nut**. **Neart** (*pron.* n'art), *n.*, enough, plenty; *fig.* a sufficiency.

Today, the old Irish **neart** (*pron.* n'art, power, strength) has been transformed into the wacky American *nut*. Though crazy people are often powerful, as in the expression, "He fought like a **nut**." That's the Irish **neart** (*pron.* n'art, power, strength, force, energy) in an English phonetic nutshell.

O

Oliver, *n.*, the moon.
Oll ubh óir, oll uibh óir (*Munster Irish*; *pron.* oll uv ór, oll iv ór), a great golden egg; *fig.* the moon.

> Oliver. The moon. (Matsell, *Vocabulum*, 1859; Asbury, *Gangs of New* York, 1928, [1998], 352; Grose, *Dictionary of the Vulgar Tongue*, 1785, [1811].)

P

Pash, *n.* a long and enthusiastic kiss; passion. "Australian and New Zealand term for French or tongue kissing. Used mainly by teenagers and preteens. Used also in a situation so that adults won't know what they are talking about..." (*Urban Dictionary Online*.)
Páis (*pron.* pásh), *n.*, passion.

Pet, *n.*, a favorite animal or child; a spoiled child; a favorite of any kind (*person, project, or peeve*).
Peata (*pron.* p'atə), *n.*, a pet, a favorite, a tamed animal; the youngest of a family; a pet child, pet lamb, pet bird. **Peata** cuaiche, a pet cuckoo. **Peataireacht**, *vn.*, (*act of*) petting. (*Proverb*) "Peata duine agus peata muice, an dá pheata is

measa amuigh, a human pet and a porcine pet are the two worst possible."
(Dineen, 836.)

> "A prisoner's *got* to have some kind of a dumb **pet**, and if a rattlesnake
> hain't ever been tried, why, there's more glory to be gained in your being
> the first to ever try it." (Twain, *Huckleberry Finn*, 1885, [1994].)
>
> For years my **pet** aversion had been the cuckoo clock. (Twain, *Tramp
> Abroad*, 1880.)

Pharaon, *n.*, an early name for the gambling game of faro.
Fiar araon (*pron.* fiər aræn), to turn both, to turn two together.

Pharaon and **faro** are said to be derived from the word *Pharaoh* for an
Egyptian monarch, supposedly a common image on the backs of 16th and
17th century French card decks, which were later imported to England. No
evidence of Pharaoh face cards in France or England in 17th, 18th, or 19th
centuries has ever been documented.

In **pharaon** and **faro** the main move is called "the turn" and occurs when the
faro dealer turns out *two* cards together from the card shoe and places them
face up on the faro layout. The first card is a loser, and all wagers on it are collected by the bank; the second card is a winner for the gambler who has bet
on it and pays two to one. The Irish and Gaelic verbal phrase **fiar araon** (*pron.*
fiər aræn, to turn both, to turn two together) is the source of the mysterious
word **pharaon**. (See: "Sanas of Faro and Poker.")

Phoney, *al.* **fawney**, *n.*, a false thing; a person who is a poseur; a ring; not real or
genuine; *adj.*, false, insincere, fake, counterfeit. (Chapman, *American Slang*,
327.)
Fáinne (*pron.* fán'ə), *n.* a ring.

Phoney is derived "from late-18th century British underworld slang *fawney*
from Irish **fáinne**, 'a ring,'" referring to a swindle called the Fawney Rig.
(Chapman, *American Slang*, 327; OED; Barnhart.)

> Fawney Rig. A common fraud thus practiced: A fellow drops a brass ring,
> double-gilt, which he picks up before the party meant to be cheated, and

to whom he disposes of it for less than it is supposed, and ten times more than its real value. (Grose, *Dictionary of the Vulgar Tongue*, 1785, [1811].)

The Irish word **fáinne** was transformed into the flash word **fawney**, meaning a fake gold ring used in a grifter's scam, and then into the 19th century American slang word **phoney**, meaning a fake, counterfeit, or sham. In the same way, the Irish language was transformed from the first literate vernacular of Europe in the 5th century into the 18th century cant of the crossroad. The despised tongue of the London Irish slum became the hip slang of the **swell** (sóúil, comfortable, wealthy) set. That's **phoney**.

Pigeon, *n.*, (*underworld*) an informer; a stool pigeon. (Asbury, *Gangs of New York*, 1927, [1998], 352; Chapman, 329.)

Béideán (*pron.* beed'án, beeján), *al.* **biaideán**, *n.*, a false accuser, a calumniator. Ag **béideán** (*pron.* ag beeján), making a false accusation or a malicious misrepresentation; slandering. (Ó Dónaill, 93, 102; Dineen, 85, 92; Dwelly, 80.)

> **Pigeon**, a thief that joins in with other thieves to commit a crime, and then informs the officer, who he pigeons for, and for this service the officer is supposed to be *occasionally* both deaf and blind. (George Matsell, *Vocabulum: The Rogue's Lexicon*, 1859, [1997], 66.)
>
> "Don't come here again... I don't like **pigeons**." (Raymond Chandler, "Finger Man", 1934; Chapman, 329.)

Piker, *n.*, a timid gambler who makes only small bets; a stingy person; a vagrant; a coward.

Picear (*Gaelic*), *n.*, a rogue, a mean fellow; an avaricious person; a pilferer; a niggardly, stingy person; a churl. (Dwelly, 721.)

Most Anglo-American dictionaries derive **piker** from an epithet for someone from Pike County, Missouri, the historic region which gave us the key dialects of Mark Twain's greatest novels. Huck Finn was poor but he was no **picear**. Many lexicographers derive the word **piker** from the *pike* in turnpike. What this has to do with a two-bit gambler is only a **piker**'s guess.

Piker is a man who plays very small amounts. Plays a quarter, wins, pockets the winnings, and keeps at quarters. (Matsell, *Vocabulum The Rogue's Lexicon*, 1859, [1997].)

"They called us **pikers** because we didn't bet high enough." (David Maurer, *The Big Con*, 1940, [1999], 41.)

Pill, *n.*, a baseball or golf ball. (Chapman, *American Slang*, 330.)

Peil (*pron.* p'el), *n.*, a ball, a football; Irish football; a large potato.

"Well, you go get the **pill** then," Paulie said. "Come on and give me my bats," Coady said.... "Go and get the ball, and we'll give you your bats," said Studs. (James T. Farrell, *Young Lonigan*, 1932, [2004], 132.)

Plunge (*hobo slang*), *n.*, a hobo's stash of money. To make a **plunge** meant to make a pittance through begging.

Bail ainnis (*pron.* bal'anish), miserable wretched prosperity, a pittance; *fig.* a tiny stash of money. **Bail**, *n.*, prosperity, condition. **Ainnis** (*pron.* anish), *adj.*, miserable, wretched, afflicted, poor. Srathair na hainnise, the yoke of poverty.

Crippled wounded thieves, fugitives, and escaping prisoners ... are sheltered in the beggar's humble "flop," his small "**plunge**" (the money he begs) is divided with them, and he carries messages any distance to their friends and relatives. (Jack Black, *You Can't Win*, 1926, [2000], 98.)

Gold Tooth and his tribe prepared to go into the town to make a "**plunge**." He detailed a couple of men to take the main "drag," another to make the railroad men's boarding houses, another to the saloons. (Jack Black, *You Can't Win*, 1926, [2000], 142.)

Pogue ma hone, *al.* pug mahone, pugga mahone, *ph.*, kiss my ass.

Póg mo thóin (*pron.* póg mə hón), kiss my rump; kiss my bottom; kiss my ass. **Póg** (*pron.* póg), *v.*, to kiss. The Irish word *póg* (kiss) is derived from the Latin word *pax* (peace). **Mo** (*pron.* mə), *poss. adj.*, my. **Tóin** (*pron.* tón), *n.*, bottom, rump; *fig.* ass.

In Cleveland, **Pug Mahone**'s is the name of an Irish pub. Some people even name their pugs **Pug Mahone**.

"Hello! We have a one-year-old male pug named **Pug Mahone**. He loves running in the park with all his doggy friends..." (http://pug.meetup.com/.)

The Pogues were founded in King's Cross, north London, in 1982 as **Pogue Mahone**—"pogue mahone" being the Anglicization of the Irish **póg mo thóin**, meaning "kiss my arse." (*Wikipedia*.)

In NYC, in the 1950s, we pronounced **póg mo thóin** "pugga mahone."

Poke (*hobo, carnival underworld slang*), *n.*, a wallet, pocket or purse; money. (Matsell, *Vocabulum: The Rogue's Lexicon*, 1859; Chapman, *American Slang*, 339.)
Poc, *n.*, a bag, a pack. **Poca**, *n.*, bag, little sack, satchel. **Póca**, *n.*, a pocket, a pouch, a bag; a purse. (Dineen, 850, 851; Dwelly, 729.)

"There I was with only about $85 in my **poke**..." (John O'Hara, *Pal Joey*, 1939; *DAS*, 399.)

Poker (game), *n.*, an American card game. Origin unknown.
Póca, *n.*, pocket (game)

Poker is a short card game that is played out of your **póca** (pocket) and against the other gambler's **póca** (pocket or purse). There is no bank or "house" in poker. A faro (**fiaradh**, *pron.* fiŏr-u, fiəro, turning) game needed a skilled dealer ("mechanic"), an assistant dealer, and a case keeper, as well as cappers, ropers, and shills, to seed the game with the house's "jack," work the marks, and feed a constant supply of fresh suckers to the faro "Tiger." Faro also required a large investment of cash for the house bank. In a **poker** game the gambler carried all his paraphernalia, a deck of cards and a bankroll, in his back **póca** (pocket).

The word *pocket* is a key term in the vocabulary of the **poker** (**póca**, pocket) game. The two "hole" cards in No Limit Texas Hold 'em poker are called *pocket* cards; two pair is a *pocket* pair, and two aces are *pocket* rockets. Poker (póca, pocket) is the ideal name for the democratic card game of the American crossroad. There is no house bank. It is one pocket against another in the poker (póca, pocket) game.

Poker (2), *n.*, any frightful object, especially in the dark; a bugbear. A word in common use in 19th century America. (Bartlett, *Dictionary of Americanisms*, 1859, 330.)

Púca, *n.*, a hobgoblin, a bogey, a sprite or ghost. Old Norse *puki*, an imp. (Dineen, 864.) Púca an duibh-ré, Jack O'Lantern, the spirit of darkness. Welsh *pwca*, a hobgoblin.

Poultice Route (*hobo slang*), *n.*, the land of milk and honey; the southern route.
Ball deas (*pron.* bal d'as), a nice place, a pretty spot, a southern place. **Ball**, *n.*, spot, place. **Deas**, *adj.*, nice, pretty; southern.

> "So long, kid. May see you out West next fall when I make the **poultice** route." (Jack Black, *You Can't Win*, 1926, [2000], 41.)

Policy, the policy game, *n.*, the "Numbers Game" or policy racket in New York, New Orleans, and Texas.
Pá lae sámh (*pron.* pá lae sáw), easy payday (game).

The "Easy Payday" game was easy to play; not so easy to win. The smallest odds were 600-1. There was no insurance involved, unless you owned the policy wheel.

> [Jimmy Hines] had a stranglehold on the **policy** racket on the Bronx, and he was moving in on Harlem, where the real **policy** money was. When he did get control, he wasn't satisfied with the outsized odds. He hired Abbadabba Berman, a human calculator to rig it further. (Sutton & Linn, *Where the Money Was*, 1976, 135,136.)

> The game of **policy** is a kind of unlawful penny lottery. (Jacob Riis, *How the Other Half Lives*, 1890.)

> In about 1928, I opened up what they call a "**policy**"—it's kind of a numbers business—in Dallas, Texas. I started with fifty-six dollars that day. The first day I made eight hundred dollars. And, of course, it was kind of a fluke thing. (Mary Ellen Glass, *Lester Ben "Benny" Binion: Some Recollections of a Texas and Las Vegas Gambling Operator*, 1973, 3.)

Puck, pook, pooka, poker, *n.*, an evil demon, a mischievous sprite or spirit; a hobgoblin.

Púca, *n.*, a pooka, a hobgoblin, a bogey, a sprite. (Dineen, 864.)

Pud, *n.*, penis.

Bod (*pron.* bod, bud), *n.*, penis.

All Anglo-American dictionaries derive **pud** from the word *pudding* and the phrase *pull pudding*, hence *pull your pud*. This is silly **pudding** from dictionary editors who have never owned an Irish pocket dictionary. If they had, they might have pulled out an Irish **bod** (*pron.* bud, penis) from *Foclóir Póca*, a pocket dictionary, on page 279.

> ...for the man who lifts his **pud** to a woman is saving the way for kindness. (James Joyce, *Finnegan's Wake*, 1939.)

Punk, *n.*, a contemptuous term for a young boy or man; a young hood; (*circus, carnival, show business*) a youth or novice, a young animal; a hobo's young companion; a young gay male.

Ponach (*Gaelic; pron.* pûnəċ), *n.*, boy, lad. (Dwelly, 731.)

James T. Farrell's first novel, *Young Lonigan*, is about a **punk** (**ponach,** *pron.* pûnəċ, boy, lad) becoming a young man on the streets of Chicago in the years before World War One.

> He remembered it better than the day he was just a **punk** and he had bashed the living moses out of that smoke who pulled a razor on him. (James T. Farrell, *Young Lonigan*, 1932, [2004], 5.)

> "Oh, you're tough! I see! Thanks for the tip! You're a tough **punk**, not afraid of nuthin', Huh! You want your snotty puss bashed in a little more." (Farrell, *Young Lonigan*, 1932, [2004], 86.)

> "Gee, he's a real bull," Danny O'Neill whispered too loudly. "Yeh, he's a real bull, **punk**; and you better clamp that trap shut." (Farrell, *Young Lonigan*, 1932, [2004], 86.)

Puncher, *n.,* a cowboy.

Paintéar (*Irish & Gaelic; pron.* pant'ær, panchær), *n.,* a tying cord or rope, a noose, a lasso, a snare for catching animals, which is formed by rope or cord made fast at one end, while the other end terminates in a running noose through which the animal is caught. (Dineen, 829; Dwelly, 715.)

> Curiously ... the word **"puncher"** was created but a comparatively few decades since [1936], its derivation is now unknown unless it relates to the metal-pointed goad occasionally used for stimulating cattle when they were being urged to board railway cars. (P.A. Rollins, *The Cowboy,* 39, 40; *DAS,* 411.)

The cowpuncher took his moniker from the lasso or **paintéar** (*pron.* panchær, tying cord or rope, noose, lasso), which was his primary tool when he was "punchin'" (roping, snaring) the little "dogies."

> I jumped in the saddle and grabbed holt the horn,
> Best blamed cow-**puncher** ever was born.
>
> I'll sell my outfit just as soon as I can,
> I won't **punch** cattle for no damned man.
>
> I'll sell my saddle, buy me a plow,
> And I'll swear, begod, I'll never rope another cow.
> ("The Old Chisholm Trail," Lomax, *CSFB,* 1910, [1986], 28–33.)

Puss, *n.,* a mouth, a face, a sour, pouting face; an ugly puss.

Pus, *n.,* a lip, the mouth (*generally only in contempt*), a sulky expression, a pouty mouth. (Dineen, 867; Ó Dónaill, 976.)

> Studs felt pretty good ... A sun was busting the sky open, like Studs busted guys in the **puss.** It was a good day. (Farrell, *Young Lonigan,* 1932, [2004], 134.)

> "I see! I GOTTA SLAP YOUR **PUSS,** and then run the gang of you in, give you a nice little ride in the wagon and let your old ladies come down to the station bawlin' to get you out." (Farrell, *Young Lonigan,* 1932, [2004], 86.)

A few Anglo-American dictionaries derive **puss** from the Irish word **pus** (a lip; a mouth; a pouty mouth); but they are clueless about **pussy.**

Pussy (1), *n.*, (*slang*) vagina.
Pusa, *n.*, *pl.*, lips; (*Latin*) labia.

Most dictionaries derive the slang term **pussy** (**pusa**, lips) from the English word *puss* for a cat, which is of unknown origin. (*OED*; *Merriam-Webster*; Barnhart, 867.)

Pussy (pusa, lips) is a wicked word because it is from the "bad language" of the colony and slum.

> "I liked the Irish worst of all; it sounded so horrid, especially as I did not understand it. It's a bad language." (George Borrow, *Lavengro*, 1851, Everyman *edn.* [1961], in Peter Linebaugh, *London Hanged*, 1991, 292.)

> She crossed over to the opposite wall and wrote a very bad word—***pussy***. (Carson McCullers, *The Heart is a Lonely Hunter*, 1940, 37.)

Pussy (**pusa**, lips) and labia are synonymous.

> As quickly as possible we change places, and I begged her first to bring herself forward over my mouth that I might kiss her **pussey**... (*The Pearl: A Journal of Facetiæ and Voluptuous Reading*, No. 6, Dec. 6, 1879.)

Pussy (2), *n. adj.*, an effeminate male; a wimp; a whiner; a crybaby.
Pusaire (*pron.* pusərə), *n.*, a whimperer, a blubberer, a whiner, a whinger, a crybaby. **Pusach** (*pron.* pusəċ, pusə), *adj.*, pouting, whimpering, sulking; ready to cry. **Pusachán,** *n.*, a pouter, a sulky person; a blubberer, whimperer.

Perhaps, the **puss** (**pus**, pouty mouth) of the **pussy**-cat also explains its name?

Q

Quare (*Hiberno-English*), *adj.*, odd, eccentric, strange, unusual; (*intensive*) great.
Corr (*Irish; pron.* cor), *adj.*, odd, occasional; queer, peculiar, strange; dismal, unusual; uneven, rounded, curved; peaked, projecting; *al.* **corra, córr. Córr**

(*Gaelic*), *adj.*, excellent, great, eminent; odd, not even; singular. (Ó Dónaill, 299; Dineen, 250; Dwelly, 254.)

A "**quare**-fellow" is a queer-fellow is an odd-fellow or peculiar person. But a **quare** fellow can also be a *great fellow* or *singular person* in Hiberno-English. Interestingly, the definition of **córr** in Gaelic is "excellent, great; singular" as well as "odd." **Queer** (**corr**, odd), isn't it? (Dwelly, 254; Dolan, *Dictionary of Hiberno-English*, 211.)

> **Quare**, queer, *adj.*, very "*quare* an' nice" = very nice. (W. Patterson, *Glossary of Words of Antrim & Down*, 1880.)

> "What was the commotion last night round in D Wing? Did the **quare** fellow get a reprieve? ...Now which **quare** fellow do you mean?" (Brendan Behan, play, *Quare Fellow*, 1954.)

Queer, *adj.*, *n.*, odd, strange, peculiar, eccentric, in appearance or character; of questionable character, suspicious, dubious, queer fellow, an eccentric person; a homosexual; to look queer or odd; (*thieve's cant*) bad; worthless; *also*, counterfeit money. **Queer**-, *prefix*, odd-, eccentric-, peculiar-. **Queer**, *v.*, to spoil, or put out of order; to tamper with, to spoil, to disturb, to queer the deal, queer the pitch, queer the game. Of doubtful origin. (*OED*, July 2006.)

Corr (*pron.* cor), *adj.*, odd, occasional; peculiar, eccentric, strange; dismal, unusual; uneven; (*Scots-Gaelic*), excellent, great, eminent; *al.* corra, córr. **Corr** (*pron.* cor), *pl.* -a, *n.*, heron, crane, stork; an unusual looking bird; *fig.* a long-necked, odd-looking person. **Corr**-, *prefix*, odd-. **Corraigh** (*pron.* courí), *v.*, to move, stir; to tamper with, to queer; to disturb; to move a person (*to anger*); to rouse; agitate. (Ó Dónaill, 299; Dineen, 250; Dwelly, 254.)

Queer, quire, queyr, and *quer* begins to appear as a **queer** new word in English canting dictionaries in the 16th and 17th centuries. Bhí sé riamh **corr**, he was always odd, eccentric, an outsider; agus is **corr** an fear é, and he is a peculiar fellow, a strange man, agus aimsear **corr** is eadh í seo, and these are strange times.

> **Queere**, base, roguish, naught. (B.E.'s *Dictionary of the Canting Crew*, 1699.)

> **Quire-bird**: such as haue sung in such cages as Newgate, or a Countrie Gaole, and hauing their belles giuen them to fly, they presently seek to

build their nests under some honest man's roofe… (Awdeley, *Fraternitye of Vacabondes*, 1561, in Gotti, *Language of Thieves & Vagabonds*, 20.)

The queer-bird was amadán **corra**-ghlic, an evasive cunning fool, or a fox in fool's clothing. (Dineen, 250; Dwelly, 254.) Queer also became underworld slang for "airgead **corr**," odd money; queer jack; *fig.* counterfeit coins or bogus bills.

"Bogus" is base coin, "**queer**" is counterfeit paper. (*Police Gazette*, 1847.)

"We're here because we're **queer**…" (Brendan Behan, *The Hostage*, 1958.)

Quirk, *n.*, peculiarity of manner; an abrupt turn or twist, a sudden shift; a facial or physical tic. Of unknown origin. (*Oxford Dictionary of English Etymology*, 1978, 733.)

Corrach (*pron.* cŏr'aċ, cor-ŭċ), *adj.*, unstable, uneven, unsteady, shifty, uneasy, unsettled. (*Of persons*) shifty, unreliable. Corrach (*Gaelic*), *adj.*, abrupt, passionate; inconsistent; wavering; unsteady, unstable. Súile corrach (súlə coraċ), shifty eyes. (Dineen, 250; Dwelly, 254.)

Quirky, *adj.*, tricky, shifty, odd; full of quirks or shifts

Corraiceach (*pron.* corəcah, coricəċ), *adj.*, unsteady; odd; shifty; an ceann corraiceach, the quirky one, the odd one; Bheith corraiceach, to be the odd man out. **Corr-chaoi** (*pron.* cor-ċí), *n.*, odd-way, eccentric-manner, unusual-mode, odd-condition.

R

Rabbit, *n.* "A rowdy. 'Dead **Rabbit**,' a very athletic fellow." (George Matsell, *Vocabulum*, 1859, [1997], 113.)

Ráibéad, *n.*, a hulking person; a big man. **Ráibéardaí**, *al.* **rábaire**, *n.*, a loose-limbed, active person; an athletic person; a dashing fellow; *al.*, **ráibach**. **Ráib**, *n.*, a hero, a valiant man. (Ó Dónaill, *Foclóir Gaeilge-Béarla, Irish-English Dictionary*, 1992, 977, 981; An Seabhac, *Foclóir Gaeilge-Béarla*, 1958, 108.) (See: "Gangs of New York Talk Back—in Irish.")

It was a copper named Van Orden who gave birth to the baloney about the dead bunny.

VAN ORDEN: "About five years ago… one night while they were holding a meeting, a dead rabbit was thrown into the room, and the circumstance gave the seceders the title of 'Dead Rabbits.'" (*New York Times*, July 7, 1857, 1.)

Rabbit sucker. Young spendthrifts. Fast men. (Grose, *Classical Dictionary of the Vulgar Tongue*, 1785, [1811]; Matsell, *Vocabulum*, 1859, [1997].)

A DEAD RABBIT OFFER.

To the Editor of the *New York Times*, Tuesday, July 7, 1857. Your paper of yesterday speaks of one of the parties concerned in the riot in the Sixth Ward… "the Dead Rabbit Club"—as a gang of Thieves, Five-Pointers, Pickpockets, &c. Now if your reporter wishes to earn $25, I hereby offer to give him, or any other one, that sum of money who will prove, satisfactorily, that a single member of that Guard (by the way, there is no such club as the Dead Rabbits) is a Five-Pointer, a thief or pickpocket. I am willing to submit the question to the decision of any Police Justice in this city… Marcus Horbart, No. 25 Mulberry Street. (*New York Times*, July 8, 1857, 5.)

"Dead Rabbits" are thieves; there is another set called "Black Birds," which consist principally of Irish; they are hand in glove with the "Dead Rabbits." (*New York Times*, July 7, 1857, 1.)

Racket, *n.*, disturbance, loud noise, uproar, din; a loud quarrel; noisy disorderly conduct; a police social function in NYC; a party at Manhattan College in the 1960s; a "beer racket." The word racket does not enter the English language until the mid-16th century. Origin uncertain.

Raic ard (*pron.* rak'árd), loud uproar, noisy quarrel, loud disturbance; *al.*, noisy fun and sport; a shindig. Raic, *n.*, uproar, ruction, disturbance, riot; fun, high-spirits, sport. Ard, *adj.*, loud. Raic ard a thógáil, to cause a loud uproar, to create a noisy rumpus. D'éirigh an racán ar fud an halla, pandemonium broke loose in the hall. Lucht racán, brawlers, rowdies. Racaid (*Gaelic*) *n.*, a loud noise. Beidh sé ina raic, there will be ructions, a riot, an uproar. Dearg-raic, a violent melee. (Ó Dónaill, 978, 981; Dineen, 873; Dwelly, 743.)

Skeat takes the English (racket) from the Gaelic. (*MacBain's Gaelic Etymological Dictionary*.)

Racket (**raic ard**, loud uproar) is two Irish words as the last "woid" in *The Iceman Cometh*.

> They pound their glasses on the table, roaring with laughter, and Hugo giggles with them. In his chair by the window, Larry stares in front of him, oblivious to the **racket**. (O'Neill, *Iceman Cometh*, 1939, [1954], 728.)

Racket (2), *n.*, organized crime as business; any occupation (legitimate or not); a carnival or circus concession; a scam.

Ragaireachd (*pron.* rager∂ċd), *n.*, (*Gaelic*) violence; extortion, oppression, roguery **Racaireacht** (*pron.* raker∂ċt), *n.*, dealing, selling. **Ragair**, *n.*, an extortioner, a violent man, villain, rogue, deceiver; *cf.* **reacaire**, **reacadóir**, *n.*, a seller, a dealer; an extortioner (Ó Dónaill, 988; Dineen, 872, 882; Dwelly, 744.)

A **racket** is illegal *selling* and *dealing*, whether drugs, guns, protection, or murder-for-hire. Someone involved in a racket is a **racketeer** (**racadóir**, **reacadóir**, a seller, a dealer; a sportive character), though often there is nothing "sporting" about them.

The origin of the term **racket** is said by most dictionaries to be related to the loud slang word *racket*. But a criminal *racket* is an underworld business deal sealed in silence or *omerta*. **Racket** as a slang word for criminal activity and the business of crime only enters the English language in the 19th century.

> **Racket**, some particular kinds of fraud and robbery are so termed. (J.H. Vaux, *Flash Dictionary*, 1812.)

> "Big Tim" Murphy, who is seldom long without a **racket**, is trying to muscle his way into the retail Cleaners and Dryer's Union. All places are being rapidly filled—none but the surest gunmen need apply. (*New York Times*, May 28, 1929, 1.)

Racketeer, *n.*, a gangster-businessman; someone in the business of organized crime. **Racketeer** (like racket) is a very recent addition to the American language, only emerging in 1927 in Chicago, where crime and business merged with the ascension of Brooklyn's own Alphonse Capone.

Racadóir, reacadóir, *n.*, a dealer, a seller; a sportive character, a dashing fellow; an extortionist; *cf.* **racaire**, **reacaire**, **ragaire**. **Ragair** (*Gaelic*), *n.*, an extortioner, a violent man, villain, rogue. **Ragaireachd,** *n.,* violence, practice of violence; extortion; roguery, villainy. (Ó Dónaill, 988; Dineen, 872, 882; Dwelly, 744.)

A racketeer can be a drug **racadóir** (dealer), an arms **racadóir** (dealer), or a **racadóir** (seller) dealing in extortion. A **ragaire** (extortionist) is a **racadóir** (seller) of deals you can't refuse.

CHICAGO FIRM MAKES GUNMAN A PARTNER
Old Business Concern Take In Scarface Al Capone as A Protector

Chicago, May 27... Alphonse Capone, the same "Scarface Al" who not long ago was the "king" of the city's bootleggers and vice lords ... is the invited partner of a leading business man who for years fought the threats, violence, and extortions of **racketeers**. (*New York Times*, May 28, 1928, 1.)

Organized labor has more **racketeers** than Job had boils. The American Federation of Labor knows this, as well as I do, but seems powerless to do anything to clean its house. (Richard Butler, Joseph Driscoll, *Dock Walloper*, 1933, 98.)

The cause of organized labor has been terribly damaged in the public mind by the **racketeer** type of leader, who works for his own pocket, without regard for the welfare of the laboring man, the employer or the general public. (Butler, Driscoll, *Dock Walloper*, 1933, 98.)

"We got to get a strong man in the White House ... to kick out the bankers and grafting politicians and **racketeers**." (James T. Farrell, *Judgment Day*, 1935, 76.)

Rag, ragtime, *n.,* a highly syncopated music originating among African-Americans, said to be derived from the "ragged" music of the cakewalk. By the mid-1890s ragtime became wildly popular throughout North America.

Ráig, *n.,* a rush, gadding about, an impulse, impulsiveness, a fit of madness, frivolity, happiness, lightheartedness, acting the fool, revelry; noise;. **Ráig**-time (rush-time) is joyous music, characterized by its impulsive, driving syncopation and rapid shifts of tempo and melody.

Ragged (music), *n.*, an early name for ragtime; music played during the cake-walk.

Ráigíocht (*pron.* rágiċt) *n.*, strolling about; acting the tramp, vagabonding; slumming about; gadding; acting outrageously; frivolity, noise. **Ráigí**, *n.*, a vagabond; a gadabout, a stroller; a slummer, a tramp.

Ragged music was an early name given to the syncopated string music played by African-Americans during the cakewalk dance, when slaves would "turn the world upside down" for a night, gadding about and promenading in costumes parodying their masters' fancy duds and manners. The best cakewalkers would win the cake. The term "ragged music" is derived by Anglo-American dictionaries from the English word *ragged*, because the music was said to be as *ragged* as the costumes of the slaves during the cakewalk. But there is nothing *ragged* about **ráig**-time (rush-time; happy-time) music. It is joyous music, full of high-spirits and frivolity; a propulsive syncopated musical form, characterized by sudden shifts in tempo and melody, frequent breaks, and fast musical runs.

Raspberry, razzberry, *n.*, a Bronx cheer. Sharp, harsh criticism or rebuke; "specifically, a vulgar derisive noise made by sticking the tongue between the lips and then blowing vigorously; the bird..." Said to be from Cockney slang, *raspberry tart*, for a fart. (*DAS*, 419.)

Raiseadh búirthí (*pron.* rash'ə boorí), a bellowing flood; a roaring spout, a bellowing blast. **Raiseadh** (*pron.* rash'ə, rash'ah), *n.* emitting profusely, spouting; a burst; a great blast; flooding; *al.* **roiseadh**, *n.*, ripping; bursting, spouting. **Búir**, *n.*, a bellow, a blast. **Búireach**, *n.*, bellowing, roaring. Tairbh **búirthí**, a bellowing bull. Raiseadh cainnte, a burst of talk; ag raiseadh bréag, eascainí, spouting lies, curses. (Dineen, 874; Ó Dónaill, 1009; An Seabhac, 1958, 16.)

> The tongue is inserted in the left cheek and forced through the lips, producing a peculiarly squashy noise that is extremely irritating. It is termed, I believe, a **raspberry**. (Barrere & Leland, *Dictionary of Slang*, 1890, 171.)

Razz, *v.*, to verbally blast someone, to verbally harass and deride; to rip into someone with words; to tear into a person with shouts and curses; to give someone the "raspberry" or the "bird."

Rais (*pron.* rash), *al.*, **rois** (*pron.* roïsh, rosh), *n.*, a blast, a burst; a volley; a rush; a flood. **Rais** chainte (*pron.* rash ċant'ə), a burst of speech; **rois** mhallachtaí (*pron.* rash wallaċtí), a hail of curses, a flood of imprecations; **rais** mór cainnte, a great flood of talk. **Roiseadh** (*pron.* roïshah), *n.*, (*act of*) ripping, tearing; a spate; a blast; a rip; a burst.

Razzamatazz, *n.*, showing off, high spirits, excitement, boastful baloney, publicity, hype.

Roiseadh mórtas (*pron.* roïshah mórtəs), a blast of high spirits and exultation; a burst of boastfulness and bragging. **Roiseadh** (*pron.* roïshah), *n.*, (*act of*) ripping, tearing; a spate; a blast; a rip; a burst. **Mórtas**, *n.*, boastfulness; high spirits.

> **Razz·ma·tazz** [ràzmə táz]... 1. Exciting showiness: showiness that is designed to be impressive and exciting, especially in the context of a stage show or other spectacle 2. double-talk: language that is intended to confuse and conceal (slang) [Late-19th century. Origin ?] (MSN Encarta Dictionary)

Rhino, *n.*, a cant term for money; ready rhino, ready cash; "scratch."

Rianú (*pron.* riənú), *vn.*, engraving, cutting, etching, scratching; **rionnaiocht** (*pron.* riəníċt), *n.*, an engraving; *fig.* "scratch."

> Coins were the only form of money up until 1633, when the first "banknote," actually a goldsmith's note, was issued... In Britain paper money did not effectively supersede metal coins until the early-1900s. ("Money Slang," www.businessballs.com.)

The prized *engraving* of the realm was a gold coin engraved with royal heads, also called **rhino** (**rianú**, engraving.) The term *rhino* appears in cant dictionaries at about the same time that paper money and bank notes go into circulation in England. People instinctively preferred *ready rhino* ("scratch," coins, cash) to paper money. Today the agency responsible for producing U.S.

money is called the Bureau of Engraving and Printing. The first published quotation in the *OED* for the term **rhino** is from Ireland in 1699.

> It was pretty to see the Squire choused out of so fair an estate with so little ready **rhino**. (Dunton, *Conversations in Ireland* in *Life & Errors*, 1699, [1818]; *OED*.)

> **Rhino.** Money (*Cant*). (Grose, *Classical Dictionary of the Vulgar Tongue*, 1785, [1811].)

> "Well you see, I'm first mate of the Flying Dragon from Queenstown... I want to get a room ashore here for a week or two, till the ship's loaded. Here's my **rhino**." (Edward Harrigan, *Mulligan's Silver Wedding*, 1883, typescript.)

Ring, "**ring** in," *v.*, to surreptitiously deal in a marked deck of cards, or a pair of loaded dice. To "ring in a cold deck" means to deal in a marked deck for a "square" (honest) one. In Ireland and Britain **ring** or **ringing** is old slang for dealing, exchanging, trading, or distributing, something *illegal*.

Roinn (*pron.* rínn), *v.*, to deal; to distribute, to trade; *vn.*, dealing (cards).

> **Ring in** a cold deck (*v. phrase*), bring in a crooked deck. Ring in a deck (*v. phrase*), bring in a deck. Sometimes spelled *wring* in. (Wiesenberg, *Official Dictionary of Poker*.)

Honest Irish words became illegal English slang words.

> **Ringing** the changes, is a fraud practised by smashers, who when they receive good money in change of a guinea, &c., **ring in** one or more pieces of base with great dexterity and then request the party to change them. (J.H. Vaux, *Flash Dictionary*, 1812.)

Rip, *n.*, a worthless, dissolute fellow. A *little rip* is a mischievous child.

Rop, rob, rap, rab, *n.*, a brute; an animal, a pig; *al.*, a nuzzler, a pet, a little animal.

My mother called me a little **rip**.

River Card, *n.*, also known as "Fifth Street." The **river** card is the final card in Texas Hold 'em poker. It is the card of final calculations and bets.

Ríomhaire (*pron.* rívər'ə, *Munster*), *al.*, **ríofa** (*pron.* ríf'ə), *n.*, calculator (card), reckoner (card), counter (card), computer (card). **Ríomhadh** (*pron.* rívəh, *Munster*), *vn.*, reckoning, (*act of*) reckoning, arranging, setting in order; calculating; reckoner, calculator; *al.* **rímhe** (*pron.* rív'ə).

The **river** card is the card of final calculation, reckoning, and computation. In a poker game, everyone knows when the **river** (**ríofa**, *pron.* ríf'ə, calculator) card flows.

Rollick, *n.*, a rave; a wild good time, *v.*, to frolic, to rave, to go on a rave or a spree; to be carefree; to go on a ramble or escapade. **Rollicking**, *vn.*, *adj.*, raving, wild, joyful; having a good time; going on a spree. **Rollick** is said to be "of obscure origin" and only appears in English in the 1820s.

Ramhallach (*pron.* rawəlaċ), *n.*, a rave; *vn.*, (*act of*) raving, rambling, ranting, delirious (from drink), dreaming, talking foolishly; rambling, fanciful, fooling around.

> The group of children claims particular attention. The description we have given of Padyheen, the beggarwoman's son, may do for the boys …Nothing can be more spirited—"**rollicking**" the Irish call it—more free from embarrassment or more graceful. (*The Illustrated London News*, "Ireland and the Irish," Aug. 12, 1843.)
>
> THE SINGERS OF ERIN… Much of it is anonymous, but it is very much a part of the Irish poetry. It deals with the life of the peasant, and the street gamin, its talk is of the common things … It ranges in sentiment from the **rollicking** *Cruiskeen Lawn* to the grim *The Night Before Larry Was Stretched* … (*Brooklyn Eagle*, Feb. 23, 1901, 7.)
>
> All jump wid joy, I'm a **rollicking** Irish boy. ("The Rollicking Irish Boy," song, *The Maid of Arran*, L. Frank Baum, 1882.)

Rookie, *n.*, a recruit, a raw inexperienced person, a novice; (*N. America*) a first-year player on a team. "Origin uncertain, perhaps a corruption of recruit." (Barnhart, 936; *OED*.)

Rúca, *al.* **rúcach**, *n.*, a raw, inexperienced person, a novice; a rough rawboned person; a clown, a rustic, a rural person, a hick, a boor. (Ó Dónaill, 1014; Dineen, 921.)

From Ireland to India, colonials have always been used to oppress other colonials. The Irish **rúca** (raw, inexperienced person, rural person) made up more than one-quarter of the British army in the 19th century. In *Barracks Room Ballads*, published in 1892, Rudyard Kipling recorded the hybrid vernacular of the rank-and-file grunts and **rookies** in British colonial forces in India and Afghanistan.

> For 'e saw the set o' my shoulders, an' I couldn't 'elp 'oldin' straight
> When me an' the other **rookies** come under the barrick-gate. (Kipling, *Barrack Room Ballads*, 1892.)
> The men that fought at Minden, they was **rookies** in their time –
> So was them that fought at Waterloo! (Kipling, *Barracks Room Ballads*, 1892.)

Some **rookies** were Irish and Indian.

> Father Victor stepped forward quickly and opened the front of Kim's upper garment.
> "You see Bennett he's not very black. What's your name?"...
> "They call me Kim Rishti Ke. That is Kim of the Rishti."
> "What is that—'Rishti'?"
> "Eye-rishti—that was the regiment—my father's."
> "Irish—oh, I see."
> (Kipling, *Kim*, 1901.)

In the United States the army **rúca** (raw inexperienced person) became an athletic **rookie**.

> At Syracuse, where the sport is new, an enthusiastic squad of "**rookies**" is hard at work... (*New York Times*, March 11, 1900, 10.)

> Cal tried out Lefty Delano, a New Brunswick southpaw **rookie**. (*Chicago Record-Herald*, March 1, 1913, 12.)

Root, *v.*, to cheer wildly, to yell, to harangue, to rant and rave; to give support and encouragement for someone or something (like a team or a political candidate); to cheer enthusiastically for a team. **Rooter** (*orig.* U.S.), *n.*, a person who loudly and vociferously cheers and **roots** for a sports team; (*baseball*) a loud, passionate fan.

Rad (*pron.* rod); *al.*, **radadh** (*pron.*, rodə), *v.*, rant, rave, harangue, yell, bellow; *vn.*, ranting, raving, yelling, talking at random, reveling. **Rabhd** (*Gaelic*; *pron.* raud), *n.*, a rant; a boast; coarse, unbecoming language; a harangue. **Radaire** (*pron.* rod-ïrə), *n.*, ranter, yeller, coarse bellower, comical shouter, prattler. **Rabhdair** (*Gaelic*; *pron.* roudər), *n.*, a boaster; verbose talker, prater, coarse jester; someone who uses coarse or unbecoming language. **Rabhdalach**, *adj.*, coarsely or vulgarly sportive. (Dineen, 868, 870–871; Dwelly, 135; Ó Dónaill, 978–980.)

The earliest example of the slang word "**root**" in the *OED* is an Irish-American **rooter.**

> Murphy has done little but "**root**" for the Giants this year. (*New York Semi-Weekly Tribune*, Nov. 5, 1889; *OED*, 2006.)

The words **root** and **rooter** only come into *print* in the American English language late in the 1890s. But both words have old roots in Irish and Scots-Gaelic, which were spoken by many New Yorkers and Brooklynites in the late-19th century. In neighborhoods like Greenpoint, Brooklyn in the 1920s, the U.S. Federal Census recorded a number of families with both Irish and Scots-Gaelic speaking **rooters** in them. They all **rooted** for the Brooklyn Dodgers! (Ward 17, ED 910-912, Precinct 48–50; Precinct 52; Precinct 150–161, Kings County, New York, 14th U.S. Federal Census, 1920.)

> **Take Me Out to the Ball Game**
> Let me **root**, **root**, **root** for the home team,
> If they don't win it's a shame.
> For it's one, two, three strikes, you're out,
> At the old ball game.
> (Jack Norworth and Albert Von Tilzer, "Take Me Out to the Ball Game," 1908; *Baseball Almanac*.)

All Anglo-American dictionaries derive the loud Irish-American **root** of the ballpark from the English *root* of a pig rooting in the muck with its nose. "Root, *v.*, cheer or support a contestant, 1889, American English, probably derived from sense of root (2): 'to dig with the snout.'" (*Barnhart Dictionary of English Etymology*, 937.)

Rub, *v.*, run; to run away. *Cant.* Of obscure origin. (*OED.*)

Rop, *al.*, **ropadh** (*pron.* ropə), *v.*, dart, dash, rush, run; thrust; *vn.*, (*act of*) rushing, dashing, darting. **Ropadh** amach (*pron.* ropə əmaċ), to dash out.

> In early cant, **rub** meant to *rush* or *run*. To **rub**. To run away. Don't rub us to the whit; don't send us to Newgate. (Grose, *Classical Dictionary of the Vulgar Tongue*, 1785, [1811].)

Ruffler, *al.* rufler, *n.*, a braggart, a swaggering vagabond, an arrogant fellow, "one who makes much stir or display... a douty braggard." **Ruffler** is one of the earliest recorded cant words in the English language. (J. Awdelay, "The Fraternitye of Vacabondes," 1561, in Maurizio Gotti, *Language of Thieves and Vagabonds*, 17; *OED.*)

Ráflálaí, *n.*, a rumormonger, a noisy chatterer, a gossip, a spreader of canards. **Ráfla**, *n.*, excessive chattering; a gossiping party, a rumor-mongerer; a chatterbox. **Ráflach**, *adj.*, noisy; fond of spreading rumors, given to raillery, mockery, jeering, vituperation, and canard. (Dineen, 872; Ó Dónaill, 980.)

Tá **ráfla** ort, you have too much jeering talk. Tá **ráfla** ar a teanga, she is a chatterbox. Chomh gréisceach le **ráflálaí**, as greasy as a rumormonger.

> The various members of this underworld also included **rufflers** and masterless men—that is, unemployed people who lead an idle life and sleepeth by day, and walketh in the dark, leading a disorderly life... (J. Awdelay, "The Fraternitye of Vacabondes," 1561, in Gotti, *The Language of Thieves and Vagabonds*, 17.)

> In the whole, a notable **ruffler**, and in euery part a dowty braggard. (Gabriel Harvey, *Pierce's Super*, 1593; *OED*.)

> **Rufflers**, the first rank of canters; also notorious rogues pretending to be maimed soldiers or sailors. (Grose, *Dictionary of the Vulgar Tongue*, 1785, [1811].)

Irish was carried to the 16th century crossroads of rural England by Irish refugees, fleeing the wars and famines of the Tudor era.

There is about an hundredth of Irish men and women that wander about to begge for their lyuing, that hath come ouer within these two yeares. They say they have been burned and spyled by the Earle of Desmond... (Harman, 1566, [1869], 82, in Gotti, *The Language of Thieves and Vagabonds*, 12.)

Below are a few words from the 16th century cant dictionaries of John Awdeley and Thomas Harmon with their Irish derivations.

Prygman, "[He] goeth with a stycke (stick) in his hand like an idle person. His propertye is to steale cloathes of (off) the hedge..."

Prioca (man), a short stick (man). **Priocaire** (man), *n.*, one who pinches, or stings with a stick.

Priggar, of Palfreys, stealer of horses.

Priocaire, *n.*, a pincher, a stinger; *fig.* a thief.

Jackeman, "He that can write and reade, and sometime speake Latin."

Diaga-man (*pron.* diəgə, jiəgə), holy-man; godly-man.

Tinkard, "(He) ... in the mean season goeth abroad a begging." **Tincéir,** *n.*, a tinker.

Patrico, Patriarke, "He (who) doth make marriages." **Paidreacha, paid-reachán,** prayers; one who prays, a prayer; *fig.* a priest.

Autum (*cant*), a church.

Ard urraim (*pron.* árd urəm), high veneration, high holiness.

Autum Bawler, a parson of the Church of England.

Ard urramach bailitheoir (*pron.* árd urəməċ bal'ihór), Reverend Collector (*of tithes and rent*).

Ken, a house, a room, any type of shelter.

Ceann, *n.*, a head; a roof; *fig.* a house or shelter. (*Synecdoche*)

Lybbeg, beds.

Leapacha, *n. pl.*, beds. **Leaba,** *n.*, a bed.

S

Simollion, simollions, *al.* **simoleon, simoleans,** *n.*, one dollar; often used in plural.

Suim oll amháin (*pron.* sim oll ə'wán): one big sum; *fig.* one dollar, a "buck."

Some Anglo-American dictionaries derive the word **simollion** from Napoleon, who issued money called napoleons (a twenty franc coin). The word **simollion** does not appear in the American language until the late-19th century. When I was a kid, **simollion** was only used in the plural, echoing effects of postwar inflation on both the dollar and slang. (Chapman, *American Slang*, 399.)

> For all his southern origins and shanty Irish upbringing, (Jimmie) Rodgers was very much a product of the American mainstream, with his eyes on the main chance...
>
> Rodgers... proceeded to explain "how I happen to be making fifteen hundred **simoleans** per week ... while two years earlier I walked on Canal Street with holes in my shoes and my stomach empty." (Nolan Porterfield, *The Life and Times of America's Blue Yodeler*, 1979, 112, 170.)
>
> "580 **simollions**!" (Raoul Walsh, *They Drive By Night*, 1940.)

Sap, *n.*, a fool, a weak ineffectual person, an easy mark, a pushover.

Sop, *n.*, a wisp of straw; a useless lout, a cowardly weak fellow; a silly person.
Sopaire, *n.*, an unkempt or lazy fellow; a lout. **Sopach** (*pron.* sopəċ), *adj.*, useless, silly (*person or thing*). **Sopachán,** a wispy person, a "strawman," an unkempt person; a feckless person, a lout. **Sop** de dhuine (*pron.* sop də ginə), a wispy person, a useless person. (Dineen, 1089; Dwelly, 874; Ó Dónaill, 1135.)

Sor **Sop** (Sir **Sap**) is a character in the Irish Wren plays, dressed in a straw suit, masked, and armed with a sword or a bladder tied to a rod, representing an Englishman nobleman, who is always defeated by an Irish knight called Seán Scot. (Dineen, 1089.)

> Rocky: ...But den what kind of a **sap** is he to hang on to his right name? (O'Neill, *The Iceman Cometh*, 1939, [1954], 584.)

Scally, *n.*, "...a slang term, originally used in the north-west of England to describe the unemployed working class, who have little or no education, and are stereotypically involved in antisocial behavior, and sports fans." (*Wikipedia.*)

Scolla (*pron.* scollə), *n.*, a term of contempt, a contemptible, churlish person; *also*, sickly looking animal or person. **Scollaire**, *n.*, a clown, a churl. **Scollóir**, *n.*, a scold; a brawler.

Scallawag, scallywag (*orig. U.S slang*), *n.*, a rogue, a contemptible fellow; a good-for-nothing; a mean, rude fellow; (*U.S. Reconstruction Era*) a corrupt, political rogue, a carpetbagger, a blackguard; (*also used affectionately and humorously*) a mischievous male of any age, as in "you old scallywag;" *al.*, undersized, sickly looking cattle.

Scolla-wag, **scollaire**-wag, **scallaire**-wag (*Irish-English compound*), *n.*, a churlish-wag; a sickly looking animal. **Scolla** (*pron.* scullə), *n.*, a term of contempt, a churlish person; *al.*, sickly looking animal or person. **Scollaire**, *n.*, a clown, a churl. **Scollóir**, *n.*, a scold; a brawler. **Scallaire**, *n.*, an insulter, an abuser, an abusive, insulting person. (Dineen, 954, 980.) **Wag** (*English, of uncertain origin*), *n.*, a mischievous boy, a scamp, a truant; a clown, a churl, (*in wider use*) a young man, a rogue.

> **Scalawag**, a favorite epithet in western New York for a mean fellow; a scape-grace. (Bartlett, *Dictionary of Americanisms*, 1848.)

Scallawag was also 19th century American cattle-drovers' term for sickly cattle.

> The number of miserable "**scallawags**" is so great that ... they tend to drag down all above themselves to their own level. (*New York Tribune*, "Cattle Report," 1854.)

Scam, *n.*, a crooked trick, a deceit, a swindle; a con, a racket; *v.*, to scam, to trick, to swindle, to defraud. Origin obscure. (*OED.*)

'S cam é (*pron.* s'cam æ), it is a trick, it is a deception. **'S cam** é (*pron.* s'cam æ), it is a fraud. **'S** (*contraction, copula, is, pron.* iss), is. **Cam**, *n.*, crookedness, a deceit, a trick. **'S cam** é (*pron.*'s cam æ), it is crookedness, it is dishonesty.

Scam doesn't **scam** its way into American slang until the early 1960s. It is the antonym of the slang term *square* as in fair play.

'**S cóir** é (it is honesty, it is fair play) is square.

'**S cam** é (it is a trick) is a **scam**.

In 1963, *Time Magazine* was one of the first publications to pick up on the crooked new slang word **scam**. "He ... worked ... as a carny huckster... 'It was a full **scam**.'" (*Time Magazine*, June 1963.)

A carny **scam** is also called a **gimmick** (**camóg, camag**; a crooked stick, a device, a trick, a deception). (See: **Ikey Heyman** axle.)

Scoot, *v.*, to go suddenly, to rush, to dart; to go away hurriedly; to move or convey suddenly or swiftly; *al.*, to squirt. (See: **skidoo**.)

Sciurd (*pron.* shkúrd. shkoord), *v*, to rush, to dash, to fly quickly, to hurry, to run quickly; to squirt. **Sciuird** (*pron.* shk'úrd'), *al.* **sciúrd**, *n.*, a rush, run, or race; a violent burst of water. **Sciuird** reatha, a rapid run. (See: **sciúrdadh**.) (Ó Dónaill, 1056; Dineen, 974, 975.)

Sciurd leat (*pron.* shkúrd l'at), hurry on, scoot along.

Sciurd sé isteach (*pron.* shkúrd shæ ĭsht'aċ), he dashed, he scooted in.

Sciurd anall chugainn uair éigin (*pron.* shkúrd ə'nal ċugin uər ægin), scoot (run) over to see us some time. (Ó Dónaill, 1056; Dineen, 974, 975.)

Scoot scoots into the English language as a slang word in the early-19th century.

Scrag, *n.*, a lean person; a thin neck of mutton, an animal neck, a human neck; (*derisive*) a mean person. **Scrag** (*slang*), *v.*, to hang on the gallows, to get your neck stretched; *fig.* to kill or execute (*someone*).

Scrog, *al.* **scroig**, *n.*, a neck; especially a small thin neck; a long stretched neck; *fig.* a neck that has been stretched on the gallows; *al.*, a mean person. (Dineen, 901.)

In Ireland in the late-18th century, the Irish noun **scrog**, meaning "a long, thin neck, or a rubberneck," was transformed into a slang word *scrag*, meaning "to stretch a neck on the gallows." To be scragged was to be hanged.

"**Scrag**-boy" (**scrog**-boy, neck-boy) was a name for the hangman in the West of Ireland in the late-18th century. The gallows stretched even the thickest Irish rebel's neck into a *scrog* (a long thin neck).

> "De **scrag**-boy may yet be outwitted." (John Edward Walsh, *Ireland 60 Years Ago*, 1847, [2005].)

> **Scragged.** Hanged.—Scraggy. Lean, bony. (Grose, *Dictionary of the Vulgar Tongue*, 1785, [1811].)

> "When he is **scragged** in Detroit…" (Damon Runyon, *Guys and Dolls*, 1931; *DAS*, 449.)

Scram, *v.*, to depart hastily; to get away, to "split." Origin unknown.

Scaraim (*pron.* scarəm), *v.*, I get away, I escape, I depart; I separate. **Scaraim** ó, I depart from, I escape from; I bid adieu to, I separate (*fig.* "split") from. **Scaraim** le, I leave.

In the 1930s, the first person Irish verb **scaraim** splits to America and takes on a new identity as a transitive slang verb spelled *scram*. Soon even the *New York Times* was **scramming**.

> "I had it all planned to **scram** out of here after that sleep." (*New York Times*, Jan. 8, 1932, 5.)

Screw, *v.*, to scram; to leave or depart hastily. (*DAS*, 452.)

Scaradh (*pron.* scar'ŭ), *vn.*, getting away, escaping, departing; separating; *fig.* splitting.

Screw is an old Irish-American vernacular word for *scramming*.

> "**Screw**! This fellow's on to us." Duffy whispered to Thaw. At the same time Duffy tried to bluff the rube. (Butler, Driscoll, *Dock Walloper*, 1933, 170.)

> And when I finish up my last number I **screw** and go around the corner to have a cup of coffee. (John O'Hara, *Pal Joey*, 1939, 13; *DAS*, 452.)

Today, the old **screw** (**scaradh**, *pron.* scar'ŭ; escaping, departing) of quick departure has been rendered obsolete by the English slang word *screw*, meaning to have sexual intercourse.

Scoop (*newspaper vernacular*), *v.*, to sweep the competition; to snatch away an exclusive from a rival; to beat someone to a story.

Scuab, *v.*, to sweep, to snatch away; sweeping; snatching.

Scoriocting (*New York City*), *n.*, a phonetic word for all-night parties.

Scoraíocht, *al.* **scoraidheacht** (*pron.* scoríċt) *n.*, a festive gathering, an assembly; a gossiping visit to a neighbor's house; evening pastime; social evening. (Dineen, 982; Ó Dónaill, 1061.)

Transit Workers' Union founder Michael Quill was born in Gortloughera, Kerry; but he **scoriocted** all over New York as a young man.

> Gortloughera was a popular gathering place for the neighbors. They
> played cards, sang songs of olden times and discussed the news. Stories
> were told round the fire, particularly during the long winter nights. It was
> called **Scoriocting** (scor-EEK-ting), and it was an unbreakable rule that
> the children must not speak or interrupt the grownups. (Shirley Quill,
> *Mike Quill Himself: A Memoir*, 1985, 13.)

Scrounger, *al.* **scrunger**, *n.*, a mooch, a borrower, a grubber; *al.*, a rummager; one who asks for small items that others are about to throw away or sell. **Scrounge**, *al.* **scrunge**, *v.* to mooch, to borrow; to rummage, to grub, to seek out. Unknown origin. (*DAS*, 453; *OED*.)

Scrabhadh an tír (*pron.* scraw'ŭ ən chír), scraping, scratching the land; *fig.* grubbing everything and everyone. **Scrabh** (*pron.* scrau), *v.*, to scratch, scrape, claw; ag **scrabhadh** airgid (*pron.* əg scraw'ŭ ar'əg'əd), scraping money together; *fig.* grubbing. **Scrabhadh** (*pron.* scrawoo), *vn.*, (*act of*) scraping, scratching; swiping; a quantity, especially that cut in the sweep of a scythe; eagerness. **Tír** (*pron.* jeer, chír, tear), *n.*, land, country, region, nation, the people of a country, everyone, the public. (Dineen, 1214.)

Scrounger, scrounge, scrunge, and scrunger scrape their way into English slang during World War One.

> **Scrunger**. Scrunge. (*Webster's American Dictionary*, 1909.)

Even as late as the 1940s, **scrounge** and **scrounger** were considered new words.

The instructor managed to "**scrounge**"—a new and useful word offered us by the G.I.—two additional blackboards... (Thomas H. Glenn, *Word Study*, October 1946; *DAS*, 453.)

Scut, scutt, skut, *also* skout, a general term of contempt; said to be derived from an obscure English word for a rabbit's tail.

Scódaí, *n.*, a term of contempt for a person; a reckless, careless person. **Scuadar, scuadán**, *n.*, a slob; a sloppy, slovenly person.

In O'Neill's play *Anna Christie*, written in 1921, Burke is an Irish seaman who falls in love with Anna.

BURKE: Let you not be thinking I'm the like of them three weak **scuts** come in the boat with me. I could lick the three of them sitting down... (O'Neill, *Anna Christy*, 1922, [1954], 32.)

Scootch (*Brooklyn slang*), *n.*, a jerk.

Scuaid (*pron.* scuəd', scuəj), *n.*, a slob; an unkempt, sloppy person.

Scootch (or scutch): a real pain in the ass. (Jim Lampos and Michaelle Pearson, *Brooklynisms*.)

Shirt Tail (*gang*), *n.*, a 19th century New York City street gang.

Siortálaí (shírtálí), *n.*, rummager, forager, ransacker. **Siortáil** (shírtál), *v.*, to rummage, forage; *vn.*, searching, ransacking; knocking about. Síortuigh mé an teach (*pron.* shírti mæ en ch'aċ), I ransacked the house. (Ó Dónaill, 1101; Dineen, 1040.)

The name **Shirt Tail** was said to be derived from the gang's habit of wearing their shirts outside their pants. This is akin to claiming that a "Dead **Rabbit**" (**ráibéad**, a big hulking person) was a dead bunny and the Hell's Kitchen "**Gopher**" (**cómhbhá**, *pron.* coufa, cova, alliance) gang was named after an eight-toothed rat. The **Shirt Tail** (**siortálaí**, *pron.* shírtálí, ransacker) gang were Irish famine immigrant kids who foraged and ransacked lower Manhattan in the 1850s for anything that wasn't nailed down.

Paradise Square (in the Five Points) was claimed by the earliest of the gangs, mostly Irish, including ... **Shirt Tails**, Chichesters, Patsy Conroys,

Plug Uglies, Roach Guard, and Dead Rabbits. (T.J. English, *Paddy Whacked: The Untold Story of the Irish-American Gangster*, 2005, 17.)

Slew, *al.* slue, sloos, *adj.*, *n.*, a very large number; a great amount.

Slua (*pron.* sluə), *n.*, a host, a legion, an army; a crowd, a multitude, a throng, a fairy host, a flock of over 500; *al.* **sluagh.** (Dineen, 1062.)

The Irish word **slua** does not enter the English language until the 1840s and 1850s, when millions of Irish immigrants poured into North America in a vast hungry **slua** (a host, an army, a multitude, a throng). **Slua** was mispronounced, misspelled, and reclassified as a slang word spelled *slue, sloo,* and finally, **slew.**

In fact **slua** is derived from the Old Irish *sluag, slóg,* and cognate with the Welsh *llu,* Cornish *lu,* Gaulish *slôgi.* Yet, in Wentworth & Flexner's *Dictionary of American Slang*, published in 1960, the ancient **slua** (*al.* **sluagh**, *pron.* sluə) as *slew* was still classified as slang, thoughts the editors had traced the new slews etymology back to the Irish language, the first literate vernacular in Europe. (*MacBain's Gaelic Etymological Dictionary*, Sec. 34.)

Eugene O'Neill's father and grandparents were among the Irish **sloos** who fled the mass starvation of Ireland in the mid-19th century. In O'Neill's play *Anna Christie*, written in 1921, Burke is an Irish seaman who falls in love with Anna.

> BURKE (*his anger rushing back on him*): I'll be going surely! And I'll be drinking **sloos** of whiskey will wash that black kiss of yours off my lips...
> (Eugene O'Neill, *Anna Christie*, 1922, [1954], 61.)

Shack (1), *n.*, a roughly built house; a shanty, a hut, a cabin of wood or mud; *v.*, to "shack up," to live with an unmarried lover.

Teach (*pron.* t'aċ, ch'aċ), *n.*, a house, a dwelling, a habitation, a building.

The word **shack** for a roughly built house does not appear in American English until 1878 and is said by many dictionaries to be derived from the "Mexican *jacal,* Aztec *xacalli,* wooden hut." Shack is also thought to be derived from the English word *shake,* since houses called shacks are often rickety shanties that presumably "shake" easily. (Barnhart, 990; *OED*.)

How a Mexican-Aztec word made its way into Brooklyn vernacular in the 1880s is never explained.

> Three men went to sleep in a **shack**, leaving a big fire in the stove. The house caught fire from the logs... (*Brooklyn Eagle*, Jan. 2, 1887.)

Shack (**teach,** *pron.* ch'aċ, a dwelling) soon became a synonym for a shanty.

> One day the editor of this strange sheet was standing in front of a sod **shanty** when he saw a horse and a buggy appear...The proceeding was repeated as he approached the **shack** and finally Adams made out the man to be an elderly gentleman with iron gray whiskers ... He took a stool and looked around the **shack**... (*Brooklyn Eagle*, Mar. 18, 1888, 12.)

A **shack** could even be a mansion. The "Sanctimonious Kid" was a Civil War veteran and "yegg," who schooled young Jack Black in the dubious skills of a house burglar in the late-1890s. One of Jack Black's first assignments was to "case" fifty wealthy homes in Oakland.

> "I want you to look over some of those **shacks**," said the Sanctimonious Kid. (Jack Black, *You Can't Win*, 1926, [2000], 105.)

Shack (2), (*hobo slang*), *n.*, a brakeman on railroad train, occupant of the caboose or shack. The *shack* (a brakeman) took his name from his living quarters. A *shack master* is railroad slang for a conductor.

Teach (*pron.* t'aċ, chaċ), *n.*, a house, a dwelling, a habitation of any kind (including the caboose on a train).

The early-20th century writer and novelist, Jim Tully, was the son and grandson of Irish famine immigrants—like Eugene O'Neill. But, unlike the upper-middle-class O'Neill, Jim Tully became a road kid and hobo before he was sixteen.

> The freight train moved slowly off the side track. "We can't keep out of sight, as the train's too short and the country's too flat. All we kin do is take a chance on the **shacks** and con bein' regular guys," said Bill. (Jim Tully, *Beggars of Life*, 1924, [2004], 55, 56.)

> Once safely inside, we peaked out of the door in the direction of the caboose. A man's head was seen to pop back from the window. "It's dollars to doughnuts the **shack** saw us," I wagered. (Jim Tully, *Beggars of Life*, 1924, [2004], 57.)

He was ditched by a **shack** and a cruel fate
The con high-balled and the manifest freight
Pulled out on the stem behind the mail
And she hit the ball on a sanded rail.
("Gila Monster Route," Alan & John Lomax, *American Ballads & Folk Songs*,
1934, [1994], 24–26.)

Shack (3), *v.*, to move along, to amble. Obsolete slang; origin unknown.
Teacht (*pron.* ch'aċt), *vn.*, approach, arrive; coming, coming along. Is fada an
teacht aige é, it is a long time coming.

> "I **shacked** down some of the hills, (partly run)." (B. F. Hallett, 1833;
> *OED.*)

Shag, *n.*, a police chase; sexual intercourse; *v.*, to chase or hunt something; to
"shag" (chase) fly balls in baseball; to leave quickly, to speed off; (*teenage slang*)
to harass, to prey upon. Origin unknown. (Chapman, *American Slang*, 388;
Vincent Monteleone, *Criminal Slang*, 1949, 204; *DAS*, 461; *OED.*)
Seilg (*pron.* shələg), *v.*, to hunt, to chase; to prey on. **Seilg** (*pron.* shələg), *n.*,
hunt, chase, prey, "catch" or "bag;" quest, search, catch; *vn.*, hunting,
chasing, prowling, preying on; seeking out. Ag **seilg** liathróid (*pron.* eg'
shələg liəród'), catching (*shagging*) a ball. **Seilg** an mhadra rua (*pron.* shələg en
wadrə ruə), hunting (*shagging*) the fox. (Dineen, 1002; Ó Dónaill, 1073, 1084;
Dwelly, 797.)

Shag in Irish-American vernacular means to chase or hunt something,
whether baseballs in an outfield or a woman in a pub. Shag is English male
slang for both the sexual chase and the object of the shag (hunt), sexual
intercourse. Although in North America shagging means chasing anything.
In Chicago in 1913, Studs Lonigan and his gang were *shagged* through the
streets, after tossing eggs at some German janitors.

> They legged it, yelling like a band of movie Indians... They laughed, and
> Weary said they could have licked the lousy foreigners anyway, only
> it was more fun getting **shagged**. (James T. Farrell, *Young Lonigan* 1932,
> [2004], 173.)

> Demons would come and lean over his bed ... until his old man came and
> **shagged** them away. (James T. Farrell, *Young Lonigan*, 1932, [2004], 66.)

Dogs can hunt and chase, as well as humans.

> "He watched familiar looking airedale dog **shag** about." (James T. Farrell, *Young Lonigan*, 1932, [2004], 192.)

Shamrock, *n.*, a clover, used as a symbol for Ireland. It is said St. Patrick used the shamrock to explain the Christian concept of the Trinity to the Irish. Fr. Patrick S. Dineen believed the shamrock was "possibly a survival of the *trignetra*, a Christianized wheel or sun symbol." The red shamrock is associated with the pre-Christian sacred site of Tara.

Seamróg (*pron.* sh'amróg), *n.*, a shamrock, a clover. The four-leaved shamrock is believed to bring good luck. (Dineen, 1004.)

Shan Van Vocht, *n.*, "Poor Old Woman," a literary name for Ireland in the 18th and 19th centuries.

Seanbhean Bhocht (*pron.* shænvæn voċt), a poor old woman.

Today the "Poor Old Woman" of Ireland is one of the richest nations in the EU; though the shadow of the Shan Van Vocht is still there beneath the Irish **snazz** (**snas**, gloss, polish, wealth).

Shanty, *n.*, a shack, an old cabin, a ramshackle house; *adj.*, poor, common, unrefined, rude, uneducated, not common any more, except in the term "shanty Irish." The word **shanty** first appears in American English in the early-19th century. (*DAS*, 463.)

Seantigh, *al.* **sean tí** (*pron.* shæntí), *n.*, an old house. **Tí** is the genitive singular of **teach** (*pron.* ch'aċ), a house. **Tigh** is the dative singular form, used in certain phrases like tigh Bhriain, in Brian's house. **Sean** (*pron* shan), *adj., prefix*, old.

Terence Dolan's *Dictionary of Hiberno-English* derives the word **shanty** from the Irish *seantigh* (*pron.* shæntí), an old house. Chapman's *American Slang* also derives **shanty** "probably" from Irish. (Dolan, *A Dictionary of Hiberno-English*, 1999, 236; Chapman, *American Slang*, 389.)

The *OED* derives shanty from the French *chantier*, "an establishment regularly organized in the forests in winter for the felling of trees; the head-quarters at which the woodcutters assemble after their day's work." But a **shanty** (**seantigh**, *pron.* shæntí, an old house) is never a "regularly organized establishment." It's just a little old **shack** (**teach**, *pron.* ch'aċ, house, dwelling). (Clapin, *Dictionary of Canadian-French, OED*.)

> A wooden **shanty** in Second Avenue near the corner of Twenty Second Street was nearly destroyed by fire yesterday at 1 o'clock. (*New York Times*, Jan. 29, 1852, 1.)

Even an English dictionary **dude** (**dúd, dúid**, *pron.* dood, numbskull) should know that the "**Shanty** Irish" were not French. They were poor Irish immigrants like Jim Tully's grandfather Hugh.

> Outspoken and diplomatic, there was in him a quality which often pierced to the heart of things. He had at least one great quality—detachment. He did not live to please others... "I'm just plain **Shanty Irish** an' I'll go to hell when I die—so thire's no use to worry." (Jim Tully, *Shanty Irish*, 1928, 117.)

Shape, shape up, *n.*, the old longshoreman hiring system, which forced dock workers to dash from pier to pier to "snap up" a day's work. The hated **shape up** pitted worker against worker and encouraged violence, favoritism, and kickbacks.

Séap, séap (up) (*pron.* shæp), *n.*, dash, a mad rush; snap; a mad dash or furious lunge; *al.* **seáp. Seápáil**, *vn.*, (*act of*) shaping, posturing, shaping up.

To Brooklyn longshoreman and their families in the 1880s—from Red Hook to Greenpoint—"making a **shape**" (**séap**, *pron.* shæp, mad rush) for a ship was the only way to work.

> Pat knows a Calcutta ship that is for unloading, and expresses his intention of "making a **shape**" for her. (*Brooklyn Eagle*, Nov. 8, 1885, 6.)

Every morning the longshoremen would beat it from ship to ship, running for a job.

> "What does Hanson think we are—stooges? There's no ship in here tonight," Snapper muttered. "Come on; let's beat it over to Smith ... before everybody else does!" (*ILWU Education Project Online*.)

> In 1934 men died in the struggle to abolish the abuses of the old "**shape-up**" system... a union-controlled hiring hall was the demand without

which the other demands would be almost impossible to enforce and protect. ("The Dispatcher," *ILWU Education Project Online*.)

It took the San Francisco General Strike of 1934 to kill the hated **shape** (**séap**, *pron.* shæp, rush) up system, so longshoremen could finally walk to work.

Sheeny, *n.*, an ethnic slur word for a Jew.

Sianaí (*pron.* shiəní), *n.*, a whiner, a whinger, a bawler, a wretch. (Ó Dónaill, 1090; Dineen, 1025.)

> "In de foyst place I kin speak twelve languages. Of course I can't read dem nor write dem, but I kin hold up my end of de conversation wid any mug, no matter what part o' de woild he comes from, except de place where de Polocker **sheenies** come from in Russia. Oh, gee whiz! I come near to losin' tree or four o' me front teet' tryin' to loin how to pronounce dem ... woids." ("The Gowanusians," *Brooklyn Eagle*, Jan. 14, 1894, 17.)

> Leo "Bow" Gistenson, our leader, didn't like the way a cop down by the lake called him **"sheeny."** The next thing you know Bow had him in a bear-hug, swinging him off the ground. (Mezz Mezzrow and Bernard Wolfe, *Really the Blues*, 1946, [1990], 6.)

Shebeen, *n.*, an underground bar, an unlicensed pub or after-hours joint.

Síbín (*pron.* shíbín), *n.*, an illicit public house.

A **shebeen** (**síbín**, *pron.* shíbín, an illicit public house or bar) is the concert hall of the colony. In Ireland in the late-1870s, the shebeens never closed.

> It's a bit of a **shebeen** that place: it stays open all hours. (Charles Kickham, *Knocknagow*, 1879; Dolan, *Dictionary Of Hiberno-English*, 1999, 237.)

The **shebeen** spread to Africa and the Caribbean. *Sound of the Shebeen, Volume I* is a collection of various reggae and ska artists from Jamaica, released in April 2005. In apartheid South Africa, the illegal **shebeen** was at the center of an underground culture of resistance and rebellion.

> For one to stay informed one had to frequent the **shebeens**, says Doc Bikitsha, one of South Africa's veteran journalists. No wonder the legendary tales about black South African journalists who could only produce

good stories for their editors after they had visited a **shebeen**. (Popular South African Culture—"**Shebeens**," by Vusi Mona.)

Shindig (*Irish-American*), *n.*, a house party, a celebration; (*New York City*) a party in an apartment or flat; *fig.* a row, a racket, a commotion. Today, a shindig is any kind of celebration. Some Anglo-American dictionaries derive an Irish shindig from the English words *dig* and *shin*. Uncertain origin.

Seinnt-theach (*pron.* shent-aċ), *n.*, a party-house, a house party, a musical celebration. **Seinnt** (*pron.* shent), *vn.*, playing music, singing, celebrating; *fig.* partying. **Seinnteoir** (*pron.* shent'ór), *n.* a player, a performer of music. **Seinm**, *v.*, I play music, I sing, I celebrate. **Teach** (*pron.* -t'aċ), *suffix*, -house. Bó-theach (*pron.* bo-aċ), a cow-house; cloig-theach (*pron.* clog-aċ), a bell-house; rígh-theach (*pron.* rí-aċ), a palace. (Dineen, 1017, 1185.)

The word **shindig** (**seinnt-theach**, *pron.* shent'aċ, house party) first appears in print in the United States in the 1850s and becomes associated with Irish rowdiness and violence, as well as music, dancing, and drinking. English slang lexicographer Eric Partridge was so unnerved by an Irish **shindig**; he couldn't hear the music.

> Shindig. An altercation, a violent quarrel, a tremendous fuss... (Eric Partridge, *Dictionary of Slang and Unconventional English*, 1984, 1050.)

A Brooklyn-Irish **shindig** in 1858 could get wild.

> Patrick Fox and his brother John went to a "**shindig**" on Saturday night; danced considerably, and liquered [*sic*] himself into a fighting humor... (*Brooklyn Eagle*, June 7, 1858, 3.)

> Went through all the New York suppers, balls, **shindigs**. (*Brooklyn Eagle*, March 19, 1870, 2.)

In my family's old neighborhood of Irishtown, Brooklyn, a **shindig** was "a ball" if Biddy Hoolahan was there.

Biddy Hoolahan, the Belle of Irishtown

There's a charming buxom damsel who resides in Irishtown,
Her name is Biddy Hoolahan, she weights two hundred pounds,
She came from dear old Gran-u-ail, and well it's understood
She's the boss of all the **shindigs** in that famous neighborhood.

She has no use for fol de role; she dresses plain and neat;

> She wears her skirts just long enough, but not to sweep the street.
> When going to church on Sundays she wears an old plaid shawl,
> A relic from her native spot—the County Donegal...
> (Michael J. Shay, *Brooklyn Eagle*, Dec. 15, 1901, 42.)

My father would sometimes pour a little salt on the kitchen floor, sing a medley of Cohan songs, and dance the "old soft shoe." The origin of the **shindig** was a **céilí** (*pron.* cay'lí, a friendly visit, a social evening; an Irish dancing session) in the kitchen.

Shindy, *n.*, a shindig, a music party, a dance; a loud celebration; *fig.* a racket, uproar; a fight. Unknown origin. (Barnhart, 997.)

Seinnte (*pron.* shentə), *p.a.*, played, sang, celebrated. **Seinnt** (shent + y), *vn.*, playing music, singing, celebrating.

> **Shindy**. A dance. Sea phrase. (Grose, *Classical Dictionary of the Vulgar Tongue*, 1785, [1811].)

When an Irish colleen (**cailín**, a girl, a maid) danced and sang the night away, the *Brooklyn Eagle* of 1853 did not approve.

> City News and Gossip...When you see a girl so weak that she can't sweep her own seven by nine chamber, and then goes to a **shindy** and dances all night with the power of a locomotive, make up your mind that she is got up on bad principles. (*Brooklyn Eagle*, October 28, 1853, 3.)

The music of the colony—jigs, reels, blues, **jazz**, reggae, hip-hop, zydeco, and salsa—has always associated with violence by upper class swells.

> SLIGO'S **SHINDY**—Serious Disturbance feared at Pending Contest—A Strong Military and Police Force Called in to Preserve Order. (*Brooklyn Eagle*, March 27, 1891, 1.)

In 1860, Ann O'Neal of Brooklyn got in trouble for wild **shindies** in her house on Warren Street.

> DISORDERLY HOUSE—Ann O'Neal was arrested by officer Wilson of the 3rd for keeping a disorderly house in Warren Street. Her counsel ... put in a plea of not guilty, and intends to prove that ... midnight **shindies** that disturbed her neighbors were but the harmless sports of overjoyed spirits... (*Brooklyn Eagle*, June 28, 1860, 3.)

The Irish-American vaudeville star, Maggie Cline threw a **shindy** every night she sang her theme song, "Throw Him Down, McCluskey."

> Maggie Cline ... is one of the primal women, like Brunnhilde or Boadicea, of astounding force and not devoid of charm. She had the luck to find a song which embodied the inborn love of a **shindy** which pulsed in her own veins and that of most of her race. (*Brooklyn Eagle*, Sept. 22, 1896, 5.)

Shonicker, *n.*, a racist term for a Jew.

Sionnach (*pron.* shi~ûn-oċ, shinəċ), *n.*, a fox. **Sionnach** ó thor (*pron.* shinəċ ó hor), fox from a bush.

> Andy and Johnny O'Brien, the two youngest in the gang, stopped the **shonickers**. (James T. Farrell, *Young Lonigan*, 1932, [2004], 173.)

> Kenny said Andy was playing a trick on them, because his old man was the sheeny fox-in-the-bush they always saw on fifty-eighth street. (Farrell, *Young Lonigan*, 1932, [2004], 176.)

Shoo, *v.*, *excl.*, an exclamation used to **shoo** someone or something away, to force impetuously, or **shoo** a fly, a bird, a nuisance; to rush, to dash, to hasten away.

Sitheadh (*pron.* shi-ŭ), *n.*, act of rushing, a thrust, a lunge, rush, swoop, onrush; forcing impetuously. Violent attack or onset. **Sitheadh** iolair (*pron.* shi-ŭ iolar), a bird's swoop. Thug siad **sitheadh** síos chun na trá (*pron* hug shiəd shi-ŭ shís ċun nə trá), they rushed (shooed) down the strand. (Dineen, 1044; Ó Dónaill, 1103; Dwelly, 846.)

A **shoo-in** is a horse sure to **shoo** (**sitheadh**, *pron.* shi-ŭ, dash) past the competition and **shoo** (**sitheadh**, *pron.* shi-ŭ, rush) in to an easy win.

> "I will put against him the buzzing fly that was **shooed** out of reputation and fame by the late member from Massachusetts (laughter and loud raps by the Chairman)." (*New York Times*, Jan. 29, 1876, 2.)

> Ireland, to their credit, struck first ... and Horgan and O'Gara combined to **shoo** Foley over in the corner but France replied with two quick tries to keep out of range. (*The Telegraph*, London, Feb. 16, 2004.)

Shoo Fly, *n.*, a "shoo-fly" is a member of the NYPD's Internal Security Division, whose job is to **shoo** crooked cops off the street and into jail.

Shill, *n.*, a gambler's accomplice, a circus barker, a spieler, an auctioneer; a confederate of a con man, a carny pitch man; a decoy or plant, who gambles with house money. A **shill** is also a hack journalist or broadcaster, who disseminates propaganda for vested political or corporate interests. Unknown origin. (Barnhart, 997; *DAS*, 466; Goldin, O'Leary, 1959, 191.)

Síol (*pron.* shíl), *v.*, to sow, to seed, to propagate; to broadcast, to publish, to disseminate (propaganda); *n.*, seed; *fig.* cause. **Síolaire** (*pron.* shílirǝ), *n.*, a seeder, a disseminator, a broadcaster. **Síolaim** (*pron.* shílam), *v.*, I sow; I propagate; I publish, I broadcast. **Síolaim** an creideamh (*pron.* shílam en cred'ŭw), I propagate the faith. **Síolchur** (*pron.* shílċur), *n.*, propaganda. (Dineen, 1035–1037; de Bhaldraithe, *English-Irish Dictionary*, 558; Ó Dónaill, 1098.)

> **Shill**... A carnival swindler's aide who mingles with the crowd, luring victims to be swindled by guile and by ostentatious prearranged winnings; any swindler's apprentice. (Goldin, O'Leary, *Dictionary of American Underworld Lingo*, 1950, 191.)

> And so a fake horse-poolroom which took bets was set-up, **shills** were used in place of real betters, fake races were called with convincing fervor, and the results were all that could be desired. (David Maurer, *The Big Con*, 1940, [1999], 33.)

> The GOP faithful ate up Cheney's barroom riff on Kerry's alleged "sensitive" side just as they did earlier when Bush's **shill**, TV talk-show host Dennis Miller, made the crack that Kerry and running mate John Edwards should "get a room." (Robert Scheer, "GOP Convention Looney Tunes," *The Nation*, Sept. 7, 2004.)

The writer Eddie Stack provided me with his memories of a **sheeler** in County Clare in the 1950s.

> I used to hear hustlers referred to as "right **sheelers**"... often they were out of towners who docked in for a market or fair day ... they'd be with the guy selling the day-old chickens or dubious hawkers of second-hand clothes or shoes. I remember a guy used to be with Bowsie Casey, a sort of barker, and one time he was extolling the virtues of a liquid that restored hair on bald men. I was maybe 5 or 6 and asked the **sheeler** how

the liquid stayed on a bald head? He dismissed me saying—"Go back to school, sonny." (Eddie Stack, Sept. 30, 2006, e-mail to author.)

Shot, *n.*, an important or influential person; a big "shot." (Wentworth & Flexner, *Dictionary of American Slang*, 1960, 472.)

Seód (*pron.* shód; *Gaelic*), *n.*, jewel; *often fig.* a chief, a hero, a valiant man, a warrior; *al.* **seád, séad** (*Irish*). (Dwelly, 808.)

> "Known? Hell, he's a **shot**." (James M. Cain, *Mildred Pierce*, 1941.)

Skedaddle, *n.*, a quick flight, a rush, a dash, a scurry; *v.*, to flee quickly, to go away, leave, or depart hurriedly; to run away, or "clear out." Origin unknown.

Sciord ar dólámh (*pron.* shkírd er dóláw), *ph.*, to flee or fly quickly, rush all-out; flee vigorously (with both hands and feet). **Sciord** (*pron.* shkírd), *v*, to flee, fly quickly, rush, burst forward; hurry, dash, rush. **Sciuird** (*pron.* shkúrd'), *al.* **sciord, scíord, sciúrd**, *n.*, a rush, run, or race. **Sciuird** reatha, a rapid run. **Dólámh** (*pron.* dóláw), *n.* (*In phrases*) **ar dólámh** (*pron.* er dóláw), all-out, strenuously. Tá siad ag imeacht dólamh, they are fleeing as fast as they can, they are going all-out.

Skedaddle scoots into American vernacular during the Civil War. The sheet music of "A Welcome to James Stephens" was first published in New York City in 1865, not long after the Fenian leader **skedaddled** out of an English jail. It is written in imitation of a thick Irish brogue.

> All hail to Jimmy Stephens,
>   The hero and the man,
> Who will lead us on to victhory
>   If anybody can!
> He has shnapped his Irish fingers
>   In the dastard Saxon's face
> And **skedaddled** to this counthry
>   Like a trav'ler at his aise...
> (Michael O'Donnell, in Robert Wright, ed., *Irish Emigrant Ballads and Songs*, 1865, [1975], 215.)

This Civil War song from 1862 bemoans a **skedaddling** Union Army.

Skedaddle

...At Donelson how fierce our men
A fort did build—a Secesh pen,
From whence old Floyd did there and then
    Skedaddle.

Fort Henry saw our ditches deep
And batteries on the sandy steep,
There we again (it makes one weep)
    Skedaddled.
(*Brooklyn Eagle*, "**Skedaddle**," Aug. 6, 1862, 1.)

Skedaddle: run away. (*A Gaelic Glossary*, http://www.tlucretius.net/Sophie/
Castle/gaelic.html.)

Skedaddle, *scoot*, and *skidoo* are three Irish-American vernacular cousins, who
are always in a hurry.

Skidoo, the present day equivalent of the older skedaddle. (Krapp, *Modern
English*, 1909, 209; *DAS*, 480).

Sketch (*slang*), *n*., a very funny person; a card, a character, a hot sketch; someone
who is a laugh or a scream. Also used ironically.

Scairt (*pron*. scartch), *n*. a loud laugh; a convulsive laugh; a guffaw; a scream.
Scairt ag gáiridhe (*pron*. scartch eg gári'ǝ), I burst out laughing. **Scairtire**
(*pron*. scartchirǝ), *n*., someone who laughs convulsively; *al*. scairteoir.
(Dineen, 953; Séamus Ó Duirinne, Pádraig Dálaigh, *Educational Pronouncing
Dictionary of the Irish Language*, 140.)

The slang terms **sketch** and **hot sketch** were first popularized in the early-
20th century by the Irish-American cartoonist Thomas Aloysius Dorgan,
known as TAD.

"He's a hot **sketch**, that guy." (TAD Dorgan, "Indoor Sports," *San Francisco
Call*, April 3, 1915, 10.)

TAD Dorgan was a **hot sketch** himself.

Lipton's Cafe was only a hop, skip and spit diagonally from the (Hearst)
Tribune Building. It was the lolling ground and snack bar for two-fisted
guzzlers among early-century newspapermen, including Tom Dorgan,

a cartoonist who had no peer as a wit. (Harry J. Coleman, *Give Us a Little Smile, Baby*, 1943, 34.)

"He's a **sketch**, he's comical." (Maines & Grant, *Wise-Crack Dictionary*, 1926.)

The terms **sketch** and hot **sketch** are often used ironically.

This Roberts is a hot **sketch** for a fighter, anyway! (Witwer, *Leather*, 1921, 176; *DAS*, 274.)

'Ski, *n.*, whiskey, cheap booze.

Uisce (*pron.* ish'kə), *n.*, water; **uisce beatha** (*pron.* ish'kə b'ahə), water of life, whiskey.

'Ski is merely a contraction of the Irish word **uisce** (*cont.* -**sce**), meaning water, which gives us the word *whiskey*, which gives us a cheap contraction for cheap whiskey—**'ski**.

ANNA CHRISTIE: Guess I do look rotten—yust out of the hospital two weeks. I'm going to have another **'ski**. What d'you say? Have something on me? (Eugene O'Neill, *Anna Christie*, 1920, [1954], 14.)

Skidoo, *v.*, to go away, flee, fly quickly, leave, or rush hurriedly. Origin unknown. (*OED*.)

Sciordadh (*pron.* shkird-ŭ), *vn.*, fleeing, absconding, flying quickly, rushing, dashing, bursting forward, hurrying. **Sciord** (*pron.* shkird), *v.*, to flee, abscond, fly quickly, rush, burst forward; hurry, dash, rush. (Ó Dónaill, 1054, 1056; Dineen, 974, 975.)

Chapman's *American Slang* derives **skidoo** from skedaddle.

Often a command or a bit of advice: "**Skidoo**, skidoo and quit me—H. McHugh." [Coined in 1906 by Billy Van, a musical comedy star, from skedaddle.] (Chapman, *American Slang*, 401.)

But, **skidoo** wasn't "coined" by Bobby Van in 1906. It's what O'Day said to McGann at the Polo Grounds in October 1905.

When McGann had been called out on strikes in the first he yelled a loud and emphatic "No!"

O'Day looked at the big player critically for a moment and then con-
temptuously remarked: "Be good, Daniel. Take a seat and think it over.
Now **skidoo**." (*New York Times*, Oct. 14, 1905, 10.)

Skidoo is also the name of an Irish rock band.

Skidoo play their last gig ... in the Wacky Apple on Friday, 7th April...
Their strongest support was always in the south east [of Ireland].
(*Munster Express*, April 7, 2006.)

James Joyce knew that the ancient Irish **skidoo** hadn't *skedaddled* since the
Ice Age.

"We have done ours gohellt with you, Heer Herewhippit, overgiven it,
skidoo! ...house the once queen of Bristol and Balrothery..." (James Joyce,
Finnegan's Wake, 1939.)

Skinny, *n*., inside information; revelation; rumor.
Sceitheanna (*pron*. shki'an'ə), *al*., **sceith** (*pron*. shkih), *n*., (*act of*) spewing; giving
away, divulging (a secret). **Sceith**, *v*., spew; give away, divulge, disseminate.
Rún a **sceitheadh** (*pron*. shkih'ə a roon), to divulge a secret; **sceithadh** ar
dhuine, to inform on someone, to betray someone. **Sceitheann** meisce mí-
rún (*pron*. shkih'an mesh'kə mí-roon), drunkenness gives away ill-secrets.

The **skinny** does not reveal itself in printed American English until the
1950s.

"What's the **skinny**" means "What's up?" (*American Speech*, 1959.)

Skip, *v*., to absent oneself; to abscond; to depart; to leave hastily. **Skip**, *n*., (*bail
bondsmen*) a bail jumper; to do a "skip-trace" means to track down a bail
jumper on the **lam** (**léim**, *pron*. læm, jump) from the law.
Scaip, *v*., to scatter, disperse, flee. **Scaipeadh** (*pron*. scap'ə), *vn*., scattering,
spreading, dispersing, fleeing. Tá scaipeadh clainne an mhadaidh ortha
(*pron*. tá skap'ə an clannə wadai orhə), they are scattered far and wide like
the dog's family. Scaip siad ar fud an bhaile (*pron*. scap shiəd ar fud an wal'ə),
they scattered all over the town. (Ó Dónaill, 1038; Dineen, 952.)

In Edward Harrigan's 1870s musical, *The Mulligan Guard*, young Tommy lives
in the Mulligan's Alley near the Five Points. In the opening scenes, Tommy

makes it clear he doesn't want any of his father's "casino" (grumbling) about his "Dutch" (Deutsch, German) girlfriend, Katy Lochmuller.

> TOMMY MULLIGAN (*to Katy*): My old man told me the Dutch was no good, but it don't make no difference, I'm twenty-one, and he can't give me any of his casino. I'm going to marry you just the same, if we have to **skip** to another country. (Edward Harrigan, *The Mulligan Guard*, 1878, typescript.)

> "The **skip** took off...with a girlfriend." (John D. McDonald quoted in *American Slang*, 402.)

Slab Town, *n.*, an early moniker for Chicago.
Slab, *al.* **slaba**, *n.*, mud, mire, ooze, slob. (Dineen, 1047.)

The Irish word **slab** is a borrowing from the Scandinavian *slab* and probably dates back to the Viking invasions of Ireland and Britain in the 8th and 9th centuries. In the 1850s, Chicago was a crossroads **slab** (mud) town of bogs, shacks, and shanties, inhabited by nationalities galore.

> Chapter One—The Evolution of **Slab** Town: ...The country on both sides of the main stream of the Chicago River was very low and wet; a depressing expanse of bogs and sloughs ... under water for several months of the year. (Asbury, *Gangs of Chicago*, "**Slab** Town," 1940, 3.)

> It was because of this unique system of building that Chicago received the name of **Slab** Town, by which it was generally known throughout the country except when it was being referred to as the Mud Hole of the Prairies. (Asbury, *Gangs of Chicago*, 1940, 16.)

Slack, *v.*, to droop, incline; fade; flag, become limp; to weaken.
Sleabhach (*pron.* shl'auċ), *v.*, to droop, incline; fade, flag, become limp; *fig.* weaken. **Sleabhach** (*pron.* shlauċ), *n.*, droop, slouch; inclination, slant; a worthless, lazy, person; a careless attitude. **Sleabhcadh**,(*pron.* shlauċ'ə), *vn.*, drooping, slouching; inclining; limpness. (Dineen, 1052, 1053; Ó Dónaill, 1109.)

Tá na prataí ag **sleachcadh** (*pron.* tá na pratí eg shlauċ'ə), the potatoes are wilting. Chuir sé **sleabhach** air féin (*pron.* ċur shay shlauċ ar fain), he walked with a slouch. Bhí **sleabhach** ar a bhéal (*pron.* vi shlauċ er a væl), his mouth was slack. Ag **sleabhcadh** leis an ocras (*pron.* eg shlauċə lesh ən ocrəs), becoming slack from hunger.

Slacker, *n.*, a slouching, lazy, spiritless person.
Slabhcar (*Gaelic; pron.* slaukər), *n.*, a slouching fellow; a spiritless person (*Sutherland*). **Sleabhacán** (*Ulster; pron.* shlauċán, shlauċár), *n.*, a worthless, careless, lazy person; *al.* **sleabhach**. (Dwelly, 848; Dineen, 1052, 1053.)

The *Oxford English Dictionary* derives **slack** and **slacker** from the Old English *slacian* and *aslacian*, comparing them to cognates in Dutch, Icelandic, and Norwegian. According to MacBain, the Gaelic **slabhcar** (*pron.* slaucar, an apathetic person) is derived from the Norse *slókr*. "**Slabhcar**, a slouching fellow (*Sutherland*), a taunter; from Norse *slókr*, slouching fellow, whence English *slouch*." (*MacBain's Gaelic Etymological Dictionary*.)

Slacker is not in Chapman's *American Slang*, or Wentworth and Flexner's *Dictionary of American Slang*; though **slacker** first slouches into American vernacular as a military *shirker* in the late-19th century. One hundred years later, Richard Linklater's 1991 film *Slacker* (**slabhcar**, *pron.* slaukər, a spiritless person) captured an American zeitgeist of spiritless youth.

Slat, *pl.*, **slats**, *n.*, a rib or ribs, especially those of a person.
Slat, *pl.*, **slata**, *n.*, a rib, ribs (*of the body*). (Dineen, 1052.)

"Wouldn't that split your **slats**?" (*DAS*, 1903, 485.)

"...Pokes (him) in the **slats**." (Ben Hecht, *New Yorker*, 1928; *DAS*, 485.)

Slob (*slang*), *n.* a slovenly person, a dirty person; a loser, an ineffectual person; a fat clumsy person. Some Anglo-American dictionaries derive **slob** from *sloppy*. (Wentworth & Flexner, *Dictionary of American Slang*, 488.)
Slab, *al.* **slaba**, *n.*, mud, ooze; a slob, a dirty, slovenly person, a mucker; a softfleshed person. **Slabaire, slabálaí**, *n.*, a sloppy worker; a slacker. **Sláibair** (*Gaelic*), *n.*, slovenly person. The Irish and Gaelic word **slab** is derived from the Scandinavian word *slab*. (*MacBain's Gaelic Etymological Dictionary*; Ó Dónaill, 1105; Dineen, 1047; Dwelly, 848.)

"**Slob**" (**Slab**, "Dirty") McTerrigan was a fictional **slob** who appeared in a series of comical stories in the *Brooklyn Eagle*, later turned into a book about the lives of the Irish-American woikin' stiffs who lived along the Gowanus Canal in the 1890s.

> THE GOWANUSIANS
> **Slob**, **Slob**'s Slang, and the Stupefied Stranger
>
> **Slob** has acquired during his life a vocabulary of slang which is so large he can scarcely keep track of it himself. Some of his speeches sound like riddles to those who are unfamiliar with the peculiar method of speaking common in Gowanus... (*Brooklyn Eagle*, Jan. 22, 1893, 3.)
>
> THE GOWANUSIANS
> **Slob** Gets Out of Jail and Goes on a Hunt for Dusty O'Dowd
>
> "Phwhere did yez get the raise, **Shlob**?" said the saloon keeper, with a sly wink at a half dozen of "de gang," who were seated near the red hot stove in the back room. "Shure ye haven't disgraced yer family by goin' to work, have ye?" (*Brooklyn Eagle*, The Gowanusians, April 3, 1892, 6.)
>
> "[Harry] Hope is one of those men whom everyone likes on sight, a soft-hearted **slob**, without malice, feeling superior to no one, a sinner among sinners, a born easy mark for every appeal." (O'Neill, *The Iceman Cometh*, 1939, [1954], 576.)

Slogan, *n.*, an Irish and Scottish war cry or battle cry; the distinctive phrase, cry, motto of any person or group.

Slua ghairm, *al.* **sluagh ghairm** (*pron.* sluə ghar'əm) *n.*, host shout, army cry; a battle cry. (Dolan, *Dictionary of Hiberno-English*, 1998, 246; Barnhart, 1019; *OED.*)

From the early-16th to mid-19th centuries the Irish word-phrase **slua ghairm** (*pron.* sluə ghar'əm), a battle cry or war cry, was variously spelled **slogorne**, **sloghorne**, **slogurn**, and **slogan**, demonstrating how Irish words morph in English-speaking gobs.

Slop, *n.*, mud, ooze. **Sloppy**, *adj.*, slovenly, untidy.

Slab, *n.*, mud, ooze, slop; slob. **Slapach** (*pron.* slapəċ, slapəh), *adj.*, slovenly, untidy. **Slapaire** (*pron.* slap'ĭrĭ), *n.*, a slovenly, untidy person.

Anglo-American dictionaries derive the words **slop** and **sloppy** from Old English *cūsloppe* for cow dung. The word **sloppy** does not appear in English vernacular until the 19th century. (Barnhart, 1019.)

Slug (1), (*slang*), *n.*, a gulp, a sudden swallow, the amount of liquid taken in a single swallow; a swig; *v.*, to swallow, gulp, drink quickly.

Slog, *v.*, to swallow, gulp, drink quickly. **Slog**, *n.*, a gulp, a sudden swallow, the amount of liquid taken in a single swallow; a swig.

Slug is derived from the Irish **slog**, gulp, Old Irish *slucim, slocim*; root *slug, lug*, swallow. (Dineen, 1061; Ó Dónaill, 1114; MacBain, Sec. 23.)

> "I think this is little better than the last drink we had," ruminated the man from Tennessee, as he poured down an awful **slug** the barkeeper had poured him. (*Brooklyn Eagle*, Jan. 13, 1884, 6.)

Slog (to swallow) spelled *slug* is not slang; it is an Irish gulp.

Slug (2), (*slang*), *v.*, to strike a hard blow, to beat, to punch; to hit a baseball with a bat. Uncertain origin. (Barnhart, 1021; *OED*.)

Slac (*Irish, Gaelic*), *v.*, to bat; to thrash, batter, drub, bruise. **Slacaire** (*Irish*), **slacair** (*Gaelic*), *n.*, a batter; a beater, a bruiser, a thrasher. **Slacadh** (*pron.* slak'ə), *vn.*, (*act of*) batting, beating with a bat, thrashing, bruising. **Slacainn**, *n.*, beating, thrashing, mauling, bruising. **Slacairt**, *n.*, beating, battering. (*Jurisprudence*) battery. **Slacaí**, *n.*, a batsman. (Ó Dónaill, 1106.)

> SULLIVAN TO **SLUG** SMITH—The American and English Champions to Fight for $10,000 (*Brooklyn Eagle*, Jan. 21, 1886, headline, 4.)

> Help the Brooklyns to Beat the Athletics ... it is to get runs in that men should go to the bat, and not to **slug** for three baggers and home runs to make a record for averages. (*Brooklyn Eagle*, May 3, 1889, 1.)

Slugger, *n.*, a batter; a mauler a bruiser; *al.* **slogger** (*early-19th century*).

Slacaire (*Irish*), **slacair** (*Gaelic*), *n.*, a batter; a beater, a bruiser, a thrasher, one that beats with a mallet or bat; a mauler. (Dineen, 1047; Ó Dónaill, 1106; Dwelly, 848.) "... Irish *slacairim*; root *slag*... Early Irish *sligim*, beat, strike, *slacc*, sword..." (*MacBain's Gaelic Etymological Dictionary*, Sec. 23.)

He got away from a **slogger**, but immediately commenced an exchange of blows. (Pierce Egan, *Boxiana*, 1829.)

The demoralized condition of the public taste in sports, occasioned by the era of slugging matches, which set in with the advent of that king of the **sluggers**, Sullivan, seems to have culminated in the brutal exhibition at the Polo Grounds on Thanksgiving Day... (*Brooklyn Eagle*, Dec. 7, 1884, 4.)

In New York City and Brooklyn in the 1880s there were political **sluggers** *go leor*.

THE POLITICAL **SLUGGERS** IN COURT (*New York Times*, Aug. 7, 1883, 8.)

Mr. Flichie said he had been knocked out by the political **slugger** of the Fourth ward and he had remained out. (Laughter.) (*Brooklyn Eagle*, Sept. 11, 1883.)

A **slugger** (**slacaire**, a batter) was a powerful hitter on a baseball diamond, too.

BASEBALL GAMES... Welch, too, was in splendid form, and retired the "**sluggers**" from Buffalo with three safe hits. (*New York Times*, Aug. 30, 1884, 5.)

Slum (1), *n.*, a "section in a city where the poorest people live... (1825) originally a cant or slang word meaning a room..." Unknown origin. (Barnhart, 1021.)
'S lom é (*pron.* s'lum æ), *ph.*, it is an exposed vulnerable place; it is poverty.

A slum is not just poor; it is bare-naked poverty and distress, stripped and laid open to the elements. **'S** (*contraction*), **is**, (*copula; pron.* iss), is. **Lom** (*pron.* lum), *n.*, a bare place or thing; an unprotected or vulnerable place; poverty, distress. (See: "Sanas of Slum.")

Slum (2), *n.*, a package of bank bills. Cheap carnival prizes bought in large quantities. (Matsell, *Vocabulum*, 1859, [1997]; *DAS*, 490.)
Slam (*Irish*), **Slaim** (*Gaelic*), *n.*, a heap, a quantity, handful; a cargo; booty, plunder. **Slaim**, *n.*, great booty, a heap. Scottish *slam*, a share or possession acquired not rightly, *slammach*, to seize anything not entirely by fair means.

Swedish *slama*, heap together. (Dineen, 1049; *MacBain's Gaelic Etymological Dictionary*.)

Smack, *n.*, a blow; a blow with the palm of the hand; a kiss.
Smag, *n.*, a blow, a pounding. **Smág,** *n.*, a paw. **Smac,** *n.*, the palm of the hand.
Smeach (*pron.* sm'aċ), *n.*, a smack; a blow; a snap; a smack (of lips); a kiss.
Smeachaire (*pron.* sm'aċərə), a kisser. (Dineen, 1063, 1065; Ó Dónaill, 1115, 1116, 1117; Dwelly, 858.)

Most English dictionaries derive **smack** and **smacker** (a kiss, a blow) from Low Dutch *smakken*, Low German *smacke*, German dialectical *schmacke*, Danish *smæk*, and Swedish *smäck*. The Irish **smeach** (*pron.* sm'aċ, a blow; a kiss) is found in early Irish dictionaries, where a *kiss* could also mean **smeach** (*pron.* sm'aċ, a blow, a smack). (Dineen, 1063, 1065.)

> She let free ... her nipped elastic garter **smackwarm** against her **smackable** woman's warmhosed thigh. (James Joyce, *Ulysses*, 1922.)

Smacker, *n.*, a kiss. Also a "kisser," meaning the lips or mouth.
Smeachaire (*pron.*smaċərə), *n.*, a kisser; a kiss. **Smeachadh** (*pron.* smaċ'ə), *vn.*, smacking with the lips; (*act of*) kissing. (Dineen, 1065.)

Every night during the Roaring 20s, "Texas" Guinan, queen of the New York speakeasies, would throw an Irish **smacker** (**smeachaire**, *pron.*smaċərə, kiss) to the crowd and holler, "Hello Suckers!"

> "Slip me a **smacker**, sister." (Jimmy Durante, Chapman, *American Slang*, 406.)

Smashing, *adj.*, something wonderful or excellent.
'S maith sin (*pron.*'s mah shin), that is good.

Smithereens, *n.*, small fragments, atoms; in phrase "blow to smithereens."
Smidirín (*pron.* smid'ərín), *n.*, a small fragment. (Dineen, 1066.)

A body would tink it hardly safe to stand here under 'em, in dread dey'd come tumblin' down, may be, an' make **smiddereens** of him, bless de mark! (Gerald Griffin, *Collegians*, 1829, [2000].)

Smudge, *al.* smutch, *n.*, a dark stain, a dirty smear; thick suffocating smoke; a smudge pot **Smudge**, *al.* smutch, *v.*, to soil, stain; smirch; to mark with dirty smears. Obscure origin. (*OED.*)

Smúid (*pron.* smúd', smúj), **smúit** (*pron.* smútch, smút'), *n.*, dirt, grime; stain; smoke; dust, soot. Smúidigh, smúitigh (*pron.* smúj'ih, smút'ih), *v.*, to darken, to smoke. Tá **smúid** ar na ballaí (*pron.* tá smúj ar na ballí), the walls are grimy. (Dineen, 1069, 1070; Ó Dónaill, 1120, 1121.)

Snakin' the deck (*poker and faro slang*), to mark or meddle with a deck of cards for the purposes of cheating.

Snoíochán (*pron.* sníóċán), marking, clipping, cutting, meddling with (a deck of cards); *al.* snoíodóireacht. (Dineen, 1076.) (see: **snoidhe**)

If a **poker** (**póca**, pocket) game is **square** ('**s cóir** é, it is fair play) any smart lucky gambler can be a winner. But if a dealer is **snakin'** (**snoíochan**, *pron.* sníóċán, marking, clipping, cutting, meddling with) the deck, putting in the **gaff** (**gaf**, a crooked device), or **ringing** (**roinn**, *pron.* rínn, to deal) in a cold deck (marked cards), every gambler is a loser.

Snap, *n.*, a sudden snatch or catch at something; a quick movement or effort. A slight or hasty meal or mouthful; a snack. A sudden closing of the jaws or teeth in biting.

Snap, **snab** (*Irish*), *n.*, a snatching, a sudden assault or seizure; a bite; a snap saying; power to grasp or hold. Snap codlata, a *snap* of sleep; thug sé **snap** orm, he broke in suddenly on me, he *snapped* at me in conversation. **Snapaim**, *v.*, I snap, snatch violently; I growl, I *snap* (verbally); do shnap sé uaim é, he snatched it from me. Bhain sé **snap** as an úll, he took a snap (bite) out of the apple. (Ó Dónaill, 1124; Dineen, 1074.)

German *schnapp*, *schnappe*, is the most common etymology for **snap** provided in Anglo-American dictionaries.

Snap (*U.S. origin*), *n.*, a brief and sudden spell of cold, winter, sharp and sudden frost; a short spell of cold weather; a cold snap.

Snab, *n.*, a short spell, brief time, or quick turn; **snab** oibre, a short spell of work; níor thugas acht **snab** beag ann, I only spent a short while there.

> The late cold **snap** was pretty keen and far south as Cincinnati. (*Brooklyn Eagle*, Nov. 5, 1841.)

> "A cold **snap**," a period of sudden cold weather. A common expression. (Bartlett, *Dictionary of Americanisms*, 1848.)

A faro **snap** (**snab**, a short spell or quick turn) is a fast **faro** (**fiaradh**, *pron.* fiŏroo, turning) game played quickly or on the run.

> A few of the river gamesters ran Faro **snaps** when ashore in St. Louis, but most of them concentrated on Poker. (Herbert Asbury, *Sucker's Progress*, 1938, 280.)

Snazz, *al.* **snaz**, *n.*, polish, gloss, elegance, style, class; *v.*, to polish, gloss, make elegant; as in the phrase, "**snazz** up." Origin unknown. (*OED*.)

Snas, *n.*, polish, gloss, elegance, style, wealth, class. **Snasaigh**, *v.*, to polish, gloss; *fig.* to make elegant, stylish, classy. (Dineen, 1074; Ó Dónaill, 1124.)

> Anyway, even if it wasn't top of the range, there was no accusing my Ghia version of a lack of **snazz**. It was Ford **snazz**, obviously, but it was still **snazz**. The steering wheel had mock aluminum spokes—elitist, quietly racy and, above all, screamingly Essex. (*The Guardian*, June 21, 2005.)

Snazzy, *adj.* stylish, flashy, glossy; attractive, elegant, classy. Origin unknown.

Snasach (*pron.* snasəċ, snasəh), *adj.*, glossy, polished, neat, elegant, wealthy, swanky, classy. (Dineen, 1074; Ó Dónaill, 1124.)

Snazz and its glossy adjective **snazzy** do not appear in the printed American language until the early-1930s. **Snazzy** brought **snazz** (**snas**, polish, gloss, elegance, style, wealth, class) to American English in the early-1930s, when it was needed.

> **Snazzy**, *adj.*, fancy, flashy. **Snazz**, *n.*, 1932, American English, of uncertain origin; sometimes thought of as a blend of snappy (in the sense of stylish, elegant) and jazzy. (*Barnhart Dictionary of English Etymology*, 1026.)

Snazzy colors that boys like. (Sears Roebuck catalog, 1942; *DAS*, 495.)

My father, Daniel Patrick Cassidy, was a very **snazzy** guy. (Author's memory, April 2007.)

Sneak, *v*., to move or walk in a stealthy or slinking manner; to creep or crawl furtively; to slink, or skulk. **Sneak**, *n*., a sneaking, shifty, underhanded person. One who steals in a sneaking manner; a sneaking, shifty, underhanded person. Doubtful origin. (*OED*.)

Snighim (shniɣəm), *v*., I creep, I crawl. **Snigheach** (*pron*. shniɣaċ), *adj*., creeping, crawling. **Snagaim**, *v*., I creep, crawl, or move slowly. **Snag**, *n*., a small creeping thing or person; a "crawler;" (*ornithology*) a tree-creeper. **Snagadh** (*pron*. snag'ə), *vn*., creeping. **Snagaire**, *al*. **snagóir**, *n*., a sneak, a creeper. (Dineen, 1071, 1078; Ó Dónaill, 1121, 1122.)

The *Barnhart Dictionary of English Etymology* traces the word **sneak** to the Irish **snighim** (shniɣəm), *v*., I creep, I crawl. (Barnhart, 1026.)

Sneak was considered vulgar cant well into the 19th century, though the **sneaky sneak sneaked** into Shakespeare.

"A poore unminded Outlaw, **sneaking** home." (Shakespeare, *Henry IV*, Act 4, Scene 3, 1596.)

Sneak, a pilferer. Morning **sneak**; one who pilfers early in the morning... To go upon the sneak; to steal into houses whose doors are carelessly left open. *Cant*. (Grose, *Dictionary of the Vulgar Tongue*, 1785, [1811].)

Sneaker, *n*., someone who sneaks, or acts surreptitiously; an athletic shoe.
Snagaire, *n*., a sneak, a creeper, a crawler. (Dineen, 1071.)

Sneaky, *adj*., creeping, crawling, shifty, underhanded.
Snagach, *adj*., creeping, crawling. **Snagaí**, *n*., creeper, crawler. **Snigheach** (*pron*. shniɣaċ), *adj*., creeping, crawling. **Snagaire**, *n*., a sneak, a creeper, a crawler. (Dineen, 1071, 1078.)

Jesus at the Movies: Some prominent proselytizers hope to save America—and the world—by doing some "**sneaky** preaching" through a new movie they're calling "one of the greatest outreach tools of the church in this century." (Sarah Posner, *Alternet*, Oct. 13, 2006.)

Sneeze, *n.*, a sudden spasmodic flow of breath and mucous pouring out of the nose and mouth; *v.*, to sneeze, to spasmodically expel breath and mucous from the nose and mouth.

Sní as (*pron.* sní'as), flowing out of, pouring out of. **Sní,** *n.*, pour down, flowing, coursing, (*act of*) dripping, dropping, shedding, flowing as a stream; leaking. **Snigh,** *v.*, pour (down), flow, course. **As,** *prep.* & *adv.*, out of, from.

> According to the OED the change in form from *fn-* to *sn-* is attributed to a possible misreading or misspelling of *fnesen, fnesan,* as *nesen* after the initial combination *fn-* became unfamiliar, but it seems more likely that the initial sound of *f* was gradually lost, producing *nesen* in the early 1300s, and that, influenced by such words as *snort* and *snore, s* began to appear. (Barnhart, 1026.)

Sní as (*pron.* snee'as, flowing, dripping, leaking, coursing out of) is not to be sneezed at. It is the Irish origin of the English *sneeze.*

Snigger, snicker, *n.*, a half-suppressed laugh; a gasp of laughter; *v.*, to laugh in a half-suppressed, stammering manner.

Snag gáire (snag gár'ə), *n.*, gasp of laughter, snort of laughter; a hiccough of a laugh. **Snag,** *n.*, gasp, fit, catch (*in breath*), snort, stammer, hiccough. **Gáire** (*pron.* gár'ə), *n.*, laugh, laughter. Snag anála, a catch in breath. Tháinig snag ina ghlóir, his voice faltered. Tá snag caointe sa leanbh, the child has taken a fit of sobbing. (Ó Dónaill, 1121, 1122; Dineen, 1071.)

The OED derives **snigger** from an obscure Scottish or "Irish-English" word *nicker,* meaning the *neigh* of a horse. There is no satisfactory explanation of how *nicker* became *snicker.* **Snicker** and **snigger** are still considered slang in the 19th century.

> *Snickering,* Laughing in his Sleeve or privately. (B.E.'s *Dictionary of the Canting Crew,* 1690.)

> To **Snicker,** or **Snigger.** To laugh privately, or in one's sleeve. (Grose, *Dictionary of the Vulgar Tongue,* 1785, [1811].)

Snide (*U.S.*), *n.*, a thin emaciated horse or mule; anything thin, worn, worn out; *adj.*, inferior, shoddy, of poor quality.

Snoite (snŭ~itĕ, snot'ə), *n.*, *p.p.*, thin, emaciated, worn-out, wasted away; *fig.* of poor quality. Snoite ó obair, worn out (or emaciated) from hard work; **snoite** anuas de sna cnámhaibh, having the flesh worn from the bones. (Ó Dónaill, 1126.)

Benny Binion traded in horses and mules. In his Texas-Irish vernacular a thin emaciated horse was called a **snide** (**snoite**, thin, emaciated) or a *dink*. Irish speakers settled in south Texas and Louisiana in the late-18th century, when it was still ruled by Spain. (Dineen, 1169; Ó Dónaill, 1200, 1201.)

> "Well, in them days, everybody mostly traded somethin' if there's somethin' wrong with them. [The horses] had heaves in those days, they were wind-broke horses and balkies ... so they had to go on out of the country to where they weren't known. Like I said before they called them **snides** and dinks." (Mary Ellen Glass, *Benny Binion In His Own Words*, 1976, typescript, 5.)

In Irish-American vernacular anything **snide** is thin, worn out, or inferior. A **snide** jungle is a hobo camp stripped of any resources such as cans, food, or wood. **Snide** silver is silver of a thin, inferior, or poor quality. **Snide** is also a slang word for counterfeit money that is so poorly made that it was worthless.

> "This is a pretty **snide** jungle," he said, "no cans." (Jack Black, *You Can't Win*, 1926, [2000], 57.)

> *Snide stuff*, bad money. (George Matsell, *Vocabulum*, 1859, [1997].)

> The observant and experienced E.R. says "The utterers of *Snide* pewter (base silver) are almost all Irish." (J. Clay, *Prison Chaplain*, 1861.)

Snoot, *n.*, the human nose; a snob, a snooty person; to snub, to treat with disdain. **Snooty**, *adj.*, haughty, high and mighty, conceited; snobbish; stuck-up. (*DAS*, 497.)

Snua ard (*pron.* snuə ard): a high profile, a lofty visage, a noble visage, a high and mighty appearance, a high, lofty countenance; a stuck-up face. **Snua**, *n.*, appearance, aspect, face, form, complection. **Snua-**, in *compds.*, -visaged, countenance. **Ard**, *adj.*, *n.*, high, lofty, noble, mighty; great, tall, noble, proud. An airde, people in high places; the nobility. **Snooty** = **snua ard** + y. (Dineen, 57, 58; Dwelly, 44; Ó Dónaill, 58, 59, 26.)

Snoot is most often derived by Anglo-American lexicographers from the English word *snout*. But a *snout* is a pig's nose that roots down in the muck. A **snoot** (**snua ard**, a high lofty visage) has its nose in the air and is stuck-up, not down. **Snoot** enters the English language as slang in the 1860s, which is ironic considering **snoot**'s high and mighty appearance. Snobby **snooty** does not appear in slang until the 1920s.

> Pokin' him one in the **snoot**. (A. Kober, *The New Yorker*, 1949; *DAS*.)

> "Astronomers, a generally vain and **snooty** class of men." (H.L. Mencken, 1948, in Chapman, *American Slang*, 411.)

Sock, *v*., to hit hard, to strike; to drive in or thrust into something. Obscure and uncertain origin. (*OED*; Barnhart, 1030.)

Sac, *v*., to thrust, cram, stuff, shove, poke, clap, whack.

> About one hundred yards from home, Spicer pulled Beppo out, and "**socked** in" his spurs. (*Spirit of the Times*, July 15, 1843, 234; *OED*.)

In the 19th century American West, when you **socked** (**sac**, thrust) something into someone's back, you stabbed them.

> The corporal "**socked**" [an awl] in the thick of his back. (T.J. Greene, *Texian Expedition*, 1845; *OED*.)

To **sock** (**sac**, thrust) someone into jail was to throw them into the clink.

> The very next day they put me in jail—**socked** me right in with them two Hodges. (J.H. Beadle, *Western Wilds*, 1878; *OED*.)

To **sock** someone, means to give them a **sac** (poke) in the nose.

> "I'll **Sock** ye, I'll drub ye tightly." (B.E.'s *Dictionary of the Canting Crew*, 1690.)

> There was a lot of damn mashers like that and they all needed a **sock** in the puss. (James T. Farrell, *Young Lonigan*, 1938, [2004], 79.)

But when you **sock** it to someone, it can also have a sexual connotation, as in the chorus to Aretha Franklin's song, "Respect."

Sock (sac, thrust) it to me; **sock** (sac, poke) it to me, **sock** (sac, shove) it to me! (Aretha Franklin, "Respect," 1967.)

That sisterly gospel energy contributes to "Respect:" [Aretha Franklin's] sisters, Carolyn and Erma, sing the unforgettable "**sock**-it-to-me, **sock**-it-to-me, **sock**-it-to-me" chorus. Franklin notes in her book that soon after they invented that phrase as a song lyric, the television show *Laugh-In* picked up the slogan. (John Valentine, *The Independent Weekly*, "Reading the Juke Box," Feb. 16, 2000.)

"The pace never let up. If it wasn't a short clip of a raincoated adult falling off a tricycle, it was a shot of Richard Nixon solemnly declaring '**Sock** it to me!'" (Tim Von Pein on Rowan & Martin's *Laugh-In*, http://www.timvp. com.)

So long, *ph.*, good-bye, farewell.

Slán (*pron.* slawn), *n.*, farewell; safety, security; *adj.*, healthy, safe. **Slán** agat, **slán** leat, goodbye. Cúig céad **slán** chum dúthaigh m'athair, farewell five hundred times to my father's country. (Song lyric, Dineen, 1050.)

The phrase *so long* enters the American language in the 1860s in the poems of Walt Whitman. It has been derived by English dictionary editors from the German *so lange*, Arabic *salam* (peace), Hebrew *shalom*, and Norwegian *sa lenge*.

I whisper **so long**! And take the young woman's hand ... for the last time. (Walt Whitman, "Songs of Parting," *Leaves of Grass*, 1865.)

The slang lexicographer Robert Chapman derives **so long** "perhaps from Irish **slán**, farewell." (Chapman, *American Slang*, 414.)

So Long, It's Been Good To Know Yuh (Dusty Old Dust)

I've sung this song, but I'll sing it again,
Of the place that I lived on the wild windy plains,
In the month called April, county called Gray,
And here's what all of the people there say:
So long, it's been good to know yuh;
So long, it's been good to know yuh;
So long, it's been good to know yuh.

This dusty old dust is a-gettin' my home,
And I got to be driftin' along."
(Woody Guthrie, "So Long, It's Been Good To Know Yuh (Dusty Old
Dust)," 1942.)

Soogan, sugan, *n.*, a blanket, a bedroll, a sleeping mat carried by a hobo or itinerant worker. (*DAS*, 528.)

Súgan, *n.*, a straw mat; a pad stuffed with straw. **Súgan** saic, a pad or sack stuffed
with straw. (Ó Dónaill, 1180.)

> She pushed aside the **soogan**, the heavy square comforter, and laid him
> on top of the blankets... and pulled out two wool sacks stuffed with straw,
> two blankets, and another **soogan**. She made up a bed quickly on the
> bench... (Pleasant T. Rowland, *A Magazine Reader for 6th Grade*, February 2,
> 1993.)

Sore, *adj.*, annoyed, bitter, irritated; outraged, offended, violated, angry. (*DAS*,
503; Chapman, *American Slang*, 415.)

Sár, *n.*, outrage, bitterness, humiliation. **Sáraitheach**, *adj.*, transgressing, frus-
trating; injurious, offensive.

> ANNA CHRISTIE (... *forcing a smile*): I'm not **sore** at you, honest. (O'Neill,
> *Anna Christie*, 1921, [1954], 37.)

> PEARL: Don't get **sore**. Jees, can't yuh take a little kiddin'? (O'Neill, *Iceman
> Cometh*, 1939, [1954], 612.)

Spalpeen, *n.*, a common workman, a farm-worker, a harvester; (*used contemptu-
ously*) a low or mean fellow; a scamp, a rascal; a lad, a boy.

Spailpín, *n.*, a seasonal hired laborer, a migratory farm worker; a person of low
degree; a rude person; a scamp; a tramp. Gan fios agam féin nach **spailpín**
ó'n Midhe thú; without knowing that you are not a tramp from Meath. (Ó
Dónaill, 1138.)

The word **spalpeen** is still used in my wife Clare's Scottish and Irish-Canadian
family. (Author's memory, March 2007.)

Sparring, *vn.*, *(act of)* fighting; boxing; contention, struggle. Obscure origin. (*OED.*)

Spairn (*pron.* spar'n), *al.* **sparainn** (sparənn), *n.*, fight, contention, contest, struggle, rivalry; *vn.*, *(act of)* fighting, contending, struggling, wrestling. **Spairn,** *v.*, to fight, wrestle, contend, struggle. **Sparainneach** (*pron.* sparənnah, sparənnaċ), *adj.*, contentious, quarrelsome, combatative. **Spairní,** *n.*, a fighter, sparrer, wrestler. Sparainn-phupa, a prizefighter. (Dineen, 1093; Ó Dónaill, 1138.)

Sparring (**sparainn,** fighting, contending) only fights its way into the English language in the late-17th century. A sparring match is more like wrestling than a prizefight. Sparring partners are paid to pull their punches. Though there are exceptions to every rule.

> Shane always remembered the ten days with Jack Gill. A murderous puncher... He did not play to the gallery. Neither did he ask his **sparring** partners to pull their punches. "If they're man enough to whip me, I've got no business being among the top-notchers." (Jim Tully, *The Bruiser*, 1936, 21.)

> "Now listen, Kid—throw punches till you die—you got a hundred bucks on yourself—three to one... now don't **spar** a second. Throw punches..." (Jim Tully, *The Bruiser*, 1936, 22.)

Spic, *n.*, a racist term for a Spanish-speaking person.

Spioc (*pron.* spic), *n.*, a spark; a "firebrand," a person of irate, impulsive, hot-tempered ways. **Spioc** fir, a man subject to sudden fits of temper. **Spioc** mná, an excitable woman. (Dineen, 1099.)

Spic and **span,** *adj.*, super-clean; bright and white, shiny and white.

Spiaca 's bán (*pron.* spiəcə 's bán), *ph.*, bright and white; brilliant and white, shiny and beautiful. **Spiaca, spiagí,** *adj.*, bright, glossy, shiny, brilliant. **'S,** *cont.*, agus, and. **Bán,** *adj.*, white, fair; *fig.* beautiful.

> My Lady Batten walking through the dirty lane with new **spicke** and **span** white shoes. (Samuel Pepys, *Diary*, Nov. 15, 1665.)

Spiel, spieling (1), *vn.*, *(act of)* gambling; *v.*, to gamble; to play music.
Spieler (1), *n.*, a gambler; a card-sharp, a swindler. (*Obsolete in U.S.*)

The **spiel** of gambling and playing music is derived from the German *spiel*, play, game, play; *fig.* gamble; to play (cards, dice); to play (music).

> **Speiler**, a gambler... **Spieling**, gambling. (George Matsell, *Vocabulum*, 1859, [1997].)

Spiel (2), *n.*, a carnival or circus barker's speech; the ballyhoo; a sharp, persuasive talk, used to entice a listener; a hyped-up sales pitch; a speech used to advertise an attraction. The carny barker's **spiel** of the ballyhoo is derived directly from the Gaelic word **speal**.

Speal (*Gaelic*), *present participle*, mow, cut down; using cutting words; using words like a scythe; mowing down (with words). **Spealach**, *adj.*, like a hook or scythe; using cutting words. **Spealadh**, *vn.*, using sharp, ready-spoken, satirical, spoofing words. **Spealanta**, *adj.*, quick, ready; sharp, satirical, using cutting words; clever, active; fast-talking, ready spoken. (Dwelly, 879, 880; Dineen, 1095.)

The German *spiel* of "play" is often given incorrectly as the source for the spiel of the ballyhoo and sales pitch.

> **Spiel**—The selling phase of a bally, made on a show front by the talker to the gathering tip, convincing the onlookers that they absolutely must see the show. (*Carny Lingo online.*)

> Your capable beggar on the street does not say "please." He rips off his **spiel** in such exact and precise language that he gets your dime without it. You so admire his "art" that you do not miss the "please." (Jack Black, *You Can't Win*, 1926, [2000], 8.)

Spieler (2), *n.*, a carnival or circus barker; a pitchman; a person who delivers a persuasive eloquent speech. (Chapman, *American Slang*, 418.)
Spealair (*Gaelic*), *n.*, mower; one that cuts fast; a satirist; one who uses sharp, cutting, vivid, clever language; a sharp-spoken person. (Dwelly, 879, 880; Dineen, 1095.)

Slug Finnerty was the chief **spieler**. He had lost an eye in a brawl many years before. (Jim Tully, *Circus Parade*, 1927, 45.)

The **spielers** worked in league with the "dips" or pickpockets. (Jim Tully, *Circus Parade*, 1927, 44.)

Spon, *n.*, money (from sponduliks). (*DAS*, 510.)

Sparán, *n.*, a purse, a money bag, a money pouch. **Sparán** na scillinge, the shilling purse, and, **sparán** na pinginne, the penny purse, are the two purses carried by the leprechaun in Irish folktales. (Dineen, 1094.)

Sponduliks, spondulics, spondulix, *al.* **spondoolies**, *n.*, money; small coins; ready cash. Of fanciful formation. (*OED*.)

Sparán tuilteach, sparáin tuillteach (*pron.* sparán tilt'aċ, spur'án tŭ'iltəċ), *pl.*, overflowing purse, overflowing money bags. **Sparán**, *n.*, a purse, a bag of money. **Sparán** na scillinge, inexhaustible purse; **sparán** na pinginne, the penny purse, the two purses of the leprechaun (*folk*). **Sparánaí**, *n.*, a treasurer, purseholder. **Tuilteach** (*pron.* tilt'aċ, tŭ'iltəċ), *adj.*, overflowing. **Tuilleadh**, *vn.*, (*act of*) adding or increasing; tá **tuilleadh** airgid uaim, I want more money. (Dineen, 1094, 1271, 1272; Ó Dónaill, 1139.)

> "I ain't as rich as old Jim Hornback ... but I've told him a many a time... I wouldn't trade places with him... not for all his **spondulicks** and as much more on top of it. Says I—" (Twain, *Huckleberry Finn*, 1885, [1994].)

> "...Urania shall have scoop in much **spondulics** and rocks. Hoop-ha!" (Bret Harte, *Novels and Stories of Bret Harte*, 1900, 255.)

James Joyce found the **spondulics** in Dublin at the turn of the 20th century.

> "—By God! perhaps you're right, Joe," said Mr. O'Connor. "Anyway, I wish he'd turn up with the **spondulics**." (James Joyce, "Ivy Day in the Committee Room," *Dubliners*, 1914, [1993], 119.)

W.C. Fields as Cuthbert Twilly was on a never-ending quest for **spondulicks**.

> "Have you any of the elusive **spondulicks** on you?" (W.C. Fields, *My Little Chickadee*, 1940.)

Spree, *n.*, fun, sport; a drinking bout. "Slang word of obscure origin, *cf.* spray." (*OED.*)

Spraoi, *n.*, fun, sport, a drinking bout. Ag déanamh **spraoi**, playing, sporting, having fun. Ba mhór an **spraoi** é, it was a great spree. Dul ar an **spraoi**, to go on a drinking bout. (Ó Dónaill, 1147.)

Seomra **Spraoi** (*pron.* shómrə spree, fun room) is a collective in Dublin.

> Today in Ireland there is virtually nowhere indoors for people to congregate that isn't a pub or overpriced café. Many people will be aware of the success of autonomous social centres in other European cities, independent of local authority, church, business or other controlling body. These spaces have provided a focal point for many of the social movements in the West, where public spaces have been eaten away by consumerism, property speculation and the culture of the car. Seomra Spraoi is a loose collective working to set up such a space in Dublin and has just acquired a premesis on the Quays right in the centre of the city. (www.**seomraspraoi**.org/)

Spunk, *n.*, spirit, courage, energy; *fig.* semen. (*OED.*)

Sponc, sponnc, *n.*, spirit, courage, energy, passion; tinder, coltsfoot used as tinder; touchwood; a spark, a spark of life. **Sponcán**, *n.*, a spark; a flare up of passion. *Cf.* French *éponge*. Cuir **sponc** éigin ionnat féin, be more energetic, look alive. (Dineen, 1102; Ó Dónaill, 1146.)

> Of obscure history; probably related to funk... *Cf.* also punk... (*OED.*)

Spunk (**sponc**, energy, passion) brings an Irish spark to English in the 16th century.

> **Spunk**. Rotten touchwood, or a kind of fungus prepared for tinder; figuratively, spirit, courage. (Grose, Egan, *Dictionary of Vulgar Tongue*, 1785, 1811.)

> Tᴏᴍᴍʏ Mᴜʟʟɪɢᴀɴ: ... Katy ain't got **spunk** enough to tell you. (Edward Harrigan, *The Mulligan Guard*, 1878.)

> "I didn't answer up prompt. I tried to, but the words wouldn't come. I tried for a second or two to brace up and out with it, but I warn't man enough—hadn't the **spunk** of a rabbit. I see I was weakening; so I just give up trying..." (Twain, *Huckleberry Finn*, 1885, [1994].)

Spunky, *adj.,* spirited, courageous, energetic, lively.

Sponcach (*pron.,* spuncɔh, spuncɔċ), *adj.,* spirited, energetic, courageous, lively.

> Huck Finn was a **spunky** Irish-American kid. Finn or O'Finn is a common Irish surname and is an Anglicized version of the Irish word *fionn,* meaning "white."

Square, *adj.,* honest, fair; fair play; just or equitable; fair, honest, honorable, straightforward. **Square**-deal, square-dealer, square play, square-player, square-shake, square thing.

'S cóir é (*pron.* s'cór æ), it is fair play, it is honesty. **'S,** contraction of Irish copula *is.* **Cóir,** *n.,* justice, equity, propriety, fair play, honesty, proper condition. Déanfad **cóir** duit, I will see you get fair play. (Dineen, 227.)

> "..if report be **square** to her." (Shakespeare, *Anthony and Cleopatra,* Act 2, Scene 2, 1606.)

Square (**'s cóir** é, it is fair play) is the opposite of **scam** (**'s cam** é, is a trick, it is a fraud). In the 1850s, a **square** game was an honest game.

> In New Orleans it was customary for such houses as gave entertainment, to set ordinary claret wine before their guests, but no other kind was given by any of the "**square**" gambling houses in that city. (John Morris, *pseudonym* John O'Connor, *Wanderings of a Vagabond,* 1873, 66.)

If a faro game was a **scam** (**'s cam** é, it is a trick), the food and wine served was **swell** (**sóúil,** sumptuous, luxurious, delicious). A crooked gambling house could always afford to stuff a sucker before skinning him.

> Our country has been prolific of inventors, from railroads and telegraphs to matches and patent medicines, but as yet none have invented a game played with cards that is a fair, **square,** honest game, acknowledged as such. (O'Connor, *Wanderings of a Vagabond,* 1873, 158.)
>
> "So these two frauds said they'd go and fetch it up, and have everything **square** and above-board; and told me to come with a candle. We shut the cellar door behind us, and when they found the bag they spilt it out on the floor, and it was a lovely sight, all them yaller-boys." (Twain, *Huckleberry Finn,* 1885, [1994].)

Squeal, *v.*, to divulge or reveal information to the police; to inform, to snitch on someone; to act as an informer. (Matsell, *Vocabulum*, 1859, [1997]; *OED*.)

Scaoil (*pron.* skŭ~íl, scíl), *v.*, to divulge, reveal, make known; *fig.* to snitch; to publish, to broadcast. **Scaoil** an scéil sin, the broadcasting of that news. **Scaoilteach**, *n.*, apt to divulge, snitch, spread abroad. **Scaoilteacht**, *n.*, a divulger; *fig.* an informer. A scéal a **scaoileadh**, to reveal their story. Rún a **scaoileadh**, to divulge a secret. (Ó Dónaill, 1041; Dineen, 957, 958.)

The word **squeal** (**scaoil**, to divulge, to reveal) does not reveal itself in the American language until the 1850s.

> A thief is said to squeak and **"squeal"** when, after his arrest, he gives information against his accomplices, or where the stolen property may be found. (George Matsell, *Vocabulum: Or, The Rogue's Lexicon*, 1859, [1997], 131.)

> Rose (*calmly*): ...D'yuh think Steve knew yuh? He'd **squeal** sure if he did—to get the reward. (O'Neill, *The Web*, 1913, [1988], 24.)

> Another witness testified that just before I left the pool hall he had heard me say to Gleason: "I am going to take care of you for **squealing** on me." (Willie Sutton, *Where the Money Was*, 1976, 31, 32.)

Squealer (*Slang*), *n.*, a snitch, an informer.

Scaoileadh (*pron.* skŭ~íl'ə), *vn.*, (*act of*) divulging, revealing, publishing, broadcasting. **Scaoilteoir**, *n.*, a releaser, a divulger; *fig.* an informer. **Scaoileadh** rún, revelation of a secret; scaoileadh scéil, spreading of a story.

Stiff, *n.*, a worker, a common working man or woman, especially a manual laborer or factory worker, a fellow, a regular "Joe" or "Jane;" a migratory worker; a hobo, a bindle-stiff; also, a dead person.

Staf, *n.*, a burly person, a strong, husky, muscular person; *fig.* a worker. Staf an bais (*pron.* staf ən bash), the stiffness caused by death. (Dineen, 1117, 1118.)

In the 1880s, Irish migrant laborers, railroad workers, ditch diggers, and working **stiffs** were often called hobos and tramps. "Indeed ... the equation of Irishness and tramping became even more pronounced during the Gilded Age." (Todd DePastino, *Citizen Hobo*, 2003, 114.) But by the early-20th century, the working **stiff** had been transformed into a Wobbly.

I ran across a bunch of **stiffs**
　Who were known as Industrial Workers
They taught me how to be a man —
　And how to fight the shirkers.
("Songs of the Workers: On the Road, in the Jungles, and in the Shops,"
Cleveland I.W.W. Publishing Bureau, 1916; in Todd DePastino, *Citizen
Hobo*, 2003, 114.)

"The Blanket Stiff," an illustration of a working **stiff** with a blanket roll slung across his shoulder, first appeared in the *Workingman's Paper* and was subsequently adopted as a symbol by the I.W.W. newspaper *Industrial Worker* in 1910.

The "Blanket **Stiff**"—He built the road—
With others of his class, he built the road,
Now o'er it, many a weary mile, he packs his load.
(*Industrial Worker*, April 23, 1910; De Pastino, *Citizen Hobo*, 2003, 109.)

Stink, *n.*, huffiness, pique, spite, fuss.

Stainc, *n.*, huffiness, huff, pique, spite, peeve. **Stainceach**, *adj.*, huffy, piqued, petulant, peevish.

Most dictionaries derive **stink** of huffiness and pique with a stinky smell.

He decided to make a **stink** about it. (Chapman, *American Slang*, 428.)

Stitches (*phrase*) "in **stitches**," *n.*, in a state of laughter, in a condition of joy, fun, hilarity, comicality. "Often derived from the notion of laughing so hard that it gives one the stitches, or sudden sharp pains." (Chapman, *American Slang*, 428.)

Staid aiteas (*pron.* stad'atchəs), a state of joy and fun, a comical state, a condition of delight, (in) a state of hilarity. **Staid**, *n.*, a state, a condition. **Aiteas** (*pron.* atchəs), *n.*, joy, fun, comicality, hilarity.

When you are "in **stitches**" (**staid aiteas**, *pron.* stad'atchəs, a state of joy) you are not in pain, you are in a state of delight.

Stock, *n*, in phrase "stock of a man," a husky, muscular man.

Staic. *n.*, a husky, thick-set person. **Staic** fir, a well-set, husky man.

> A narrow-minded man also, without sympathy or imagination, capable
> of cruelty; a tough, stiff-necked **stock** of a man, fit to deal with Bobadilla
> perhaps, but hardly fit to deal with the colony. (Filson Young, *Christopher*
> *Columbus*, 1906, 143.)

Stool pigeon, *n.*, a shill, a decoy, a plant; a police informer; a labor spy; a professional snitch, a stoolie.

Steall béideán (*pron.* shta'l bæd'án, shta'l bæj'án), to spout rumors, to spill out
lies and calumny. **Steallaire béideánach** (*pron.* sht'allïrə beejánəć), a gossipy,
slanderous tattler, a falsely accusing informer. **Steallaire** (*pron.* sht'alïrə), *n.*, a
spouter; a tattler, a snitch, an informer; a gossip, a taleteller, a rumormonger.
Steall (*pron.* sht'al), *v.*, to spout, to spurt; to tattle, to snitch. **Stealladóir**, *n.*, a
tattler, an informer. **Stealladh** (*pron.* shta'lə), *vn.*, tattling. **Stealladóireacht**,
n., (*act of*) tattling, spouting. **Béideán** (*pron.* bæj'án), *al.* **biaideán**, *n.*, a false
accuser, a calumniator; gossip, slander, calumny. Ag **béideán** (*pron.* eg
bæj'án), making a false accusation of an offense or a malicious misrepresentation of someone's words or actions; prating, gossiping, spreading rumors,
calumniating, slandering. **Béideánach, béidaránach**, *adj.*, given to gossiping, calumny, falsely accusing. (Ó Dónaill, 93, 102, 103, 1164; Dineen, 85,
92, 1124; Dwelly, 80.)

Almost all dictionaries derive the slang term *stool pigeon* from the alleged
English practice of tying a pigeon to a stool with a string for use as a decoy;
though a decoy for what is never made clear. Only a **kook** (**cuach**, a cuckoo,
a fool) would tie a pigeon to a stool. A *pigeon* in underworld slang isn't a bird
or a duck, it's a **stoolie**.

> **Pigeon**, a thief that joins in with other thieves to commit a crime, and
> then informs the officer, who he pigeons for, and for this service the
> officer is supposed to be *occasionally* both deaf and blind. (George Matsell,
> *Vocabulum: The Rogue's Lexicon*, 1859, [1997], 66.)

> They are always drinking and smoking, though never known to spend
> a cent, and serve as **stool pigeons**, informers, and decoy ducks. (Mike
> Walsh, *The Subterranean*, May 31, 1845, 2.)

Stool-pigeon, a decoy robber, in the pay of the police, who brings his associates into a trap laid for them. (Bartlett, *Dictionary of Americanisms*, 1859.)

Hugo (*raises his head and peers at Rocky blearily*): Capitalist swine! Bourgeois **stool pigeons**! Have the slaves no right to sleep even? (Eugene O'Neill, *The Iceman Cometh*, 1939, [1954], 579.)

Stud (poker), *n.*, a new form of poker, where the house controls the deal.
Stad, *n.*, stop; halt; *v.*, to stop, to stay, to halt.

In **stud** (stad, stop) poker the deal does not rotate from player to player but stops (**stad**, to stay, to stop) with the house dealer.

Of all the varieties of Poker which have appeared since the game was first played in New Orleans, only **Stud** has achieved importance as a gambling house attraction... (A) **Stud** table, with a house man dealing and taking a kitty from every pot, has been part of the equipment of almost every gaming resort in America. (Herbert Asbury, *Sucker's Progress*, 1938, 34.)

Stutter, *n.*, a stammer; to stammer; act or habit of stammering; stutterer; a stammerer; *v.*, to falter, to stop and go. **Stutterer**, *n.*, a person who stammers and stutters.
Stadadh (*pron.* stad'ə), *vn.*, (*act of*) stopping, pausing, hindering, faltering, stammering. **Stadaire** (*pron.* stadĭrə), *n.*, stammerer, stutterer. (Dineen, 1117; Ó Dónaill, 1158, 1159.)

And though you hear him **stut-tut-tut-ter**, He barks as fast as he can utter. (Jonathan Swift, *Traulus*, 1730.)

A **stutter** (**stadadh**, *pron* stad'ə, stopping, pausing, faltering) step is a stop and go step.

Sucker, *n.*, a person easily deceived or cheated; an easy mark; a greenhorn, a dupe. (*DAS*, 527; *American Slang*, 433; *OED*.)
Sách úr (*pron.* sáċ úr, sawċ úr), a fresh "fat cat," a new well-fed fellow; a new prosperous person. **Sách** (*pron.* sawċ), *n.*, a well-fed person; a "fat cat;" a prosperous person; *al.* **sáthach**. **Úr**, *adj.*, new, fresh, green, recent, moist, tender,

raw; noble. Ní thuigeann ní mhothaíonn an sách an seang, the well-fed person does not understand, nor feel for, the lean (hungry one).

> **Sucker**. A term applied by gamblers to a person that can be cheated at any game of cards. (George Matsell, *Vocabulum: The Rogue's Lexicon*, 1859, [1997].)

> As a gambler, (Mike) McDonald was the most powerful ever to operate in Chicago, and one of the three or four most important that have yet appeared to harass the American **sucker**. But a niche in the gambling hall of fame would have been reserved for him if he had been the most insignificant of tinhorns, for it was Mike McDonald, according to Chicago legend, who coined the sagest and truest of aphorisms, "There's a **sucker** born every minute." (Herbert Asbury, *Sucker's Progress*, 1937, 288.)

> Sure thing players began to work on a large scale in Chicago during the early 1850s... and were so successful at roping **fat suckers** that sharpers of this class flocked into Chicago from all parts of the country. (Asbury, *Sucker's Progress*, 1937, 280.)

> Mosher: I miss Doc. He was a gentleman of the old school. I'll bet he's standing on a street corner in hell right now, making **suckers** out of the damned, telling them there's nothing like snake oil for a bad burn." (Eugene O'Neill, *The Iceman Cometh*, 1939, [1954], 628.)

> Erie: You shoulda seen the doll I made the night before last. And did she take me to the cleaners! I'm a **sucker** for blondes. (O'Neill, *Hughie*, 1940, 266.)

The last word in *Hughie*, the last play written by Eugene O'Neill, is **sucker**.

> He chuckles, giving the Night Clerk the slyly amused, contemptuous, affectionate wink with which a Wise Guy regales a **Sucker**. (O'Neill, *Hughie*, 1940, 293.)

Sunday punch (*U.S. slang*), *n.*, a hard effective blow with the fists; any powerful attack; a powerful knock-out blow (of the fist). (*DAS*, 528, 529; *OED*.)

Sonnda, *al.* **sonnta**, *adj.*, powerful, strong, courageous, bold (punch). (Ó Dónaill, 1134; Dineen, 1088.)

> *Sunday Punch* was the title of a 1942 film, starring William Lundigan as Irish-American boxer Ken Burke, directed by David Miller and written by Fay and

Michael Kanin. It was also the title of a boxing novel published in 1979 by Edwin Newman.

> The jab I learned wreaked havoc on the nose of Buckley the home bully.... About the same time, I learned the value of the **Sunday** punch, which was simply to strike first. In reform school I would study experts on the **Sunday** punch and hone my own ability. (Edward Bunker, *Education of a Felon*, 2000, 6.)

> "And lay a **Sunday** punch on your snoot..." (Damon Runyon, 1932, in *DAS*, 529.)

Swank, swanky, *adj.*, stylish, classy, ritzy; rich, wealthy, swell, luxurious; often applied to shops, hotels, or apartments. Origin unknown. (Chapman, *American Slang*, 435; *OED*.)

Somhaoineach (*pron.* sowĭnaċ, sowĭnaċ + y), *adj.*, wealthy, rich, ritzy, swell; valuable, costly, precious. (Dineen, 1086; Ó Dónaill, 1133; An Seabhac, *Learner's Irish-English Pronouncing Dictionary*, 1958, 133.)

Some English dictionaries suggest that **swank** is derived from Middle English *swanken*, to sway, from German *schwanken*, to sway, to totter.

It is not surprising that **swank** makes its debut in early-20th century Irish-American vernacular. By then a few Irish-Americans - like the Kennedy and Ford families - had become **swank**. Today Ireland has become somewhat swank (**somhaoineach**, *pron.* sowĭnaċ, wealthy) itself.

> **Somhaoineach**, (sowĭnaċ), *adj.* wealthy. (An Seabhac, *Learner's Irish-English Pronouncing Dictionary*, 1958, 133.)

Swell, *adj.*, enjoyable, joyful, cheerful, pleasing; excellent; grand, fine, stylish, elegant, luxurious; hospitable; delicious, sumptuous. **Swell**, *n.*, an upper-class dude, a stylish sport; a wealthy, socially prominent person. (*DAS*, 532; *OED*, Chapman, *American Slang*, 436.)

Sóúil, *adj.*, cheerful, joyful, enjoyable, happy, glad; prosperous, wealthy, (*someone or something*) comfortable, luxurious, grand, elegant; *fig.* a wealthy person or gentleman; (*of food*) satisfying, delicious, appetizing, delectable, delightful, scrumptious, tasty, exquisite. *Al.* **sóghmháil**; (*Scots-Gaelic*) **sòghail**. (Dineen, 1081; Ó Dónaill, 1137; Dwelly, 869.)

Most Anglo-American dictionaries derive the cheerful, prosperous, delicious slang word **swell** from the painful, protuberant, swollen Standard English *swell*, from Old English *swellen*. (Barnhart, 1101.)

But the slang **swell** is not swollen or *swellen*; it is **sóúil**, cheerful, joyful; prosperous, comfortable, luxurious, wealthy, splendid, classy; satisfying, delicious, appetizing, delectable, scrumptious, and exquisite.

Swells are not swollen; they are **sóúil** (prosperous, wealthy, elegant). A **swell** desert is not a protuberance; it is **sóúil** (delicious). And a **swell** gal isn't bloated, she's cheerful and grand. Ain't dat **sóúil**?

> **Swell**. A gentleman. A well dressed man. The flashman bounced the
> **swell** of all his blunt; the girl's bully frightened the gentleman out of all
> his money. (Francis Grose, *Classical Dictionary of the Vulgar Tongue*, 1785,
> [1811].)
>
> Any thing remarkable for its beauty or elegance, is called a **swell** article;
> so, a **swell** crib, is a genteel house. (J.H. Vaux, *Flash Dictionary*, 1812.)
>
> "...the king's dud was all black, and he did look real **swell** and starchy."
> (Twain, *Huckleberry Finn*, 1885, [1994].)
>
>
> Toby: I come down with the **swells**.
> Reilly: It's **swell** for you, you're a **swell** of the ocean.
> Toby: Yes, and **swells** of the ocean are high rollers.
> (Edward Harrigan, *Reilly & The 400*, typescript, 1890, 61.)

Swoon, *n., v.*, sleep, slumber; a fainting fit; to faint. Uncertain etymology.

Suan (*Irish*) (*pron.* súŏn), **suain** (*Gaelic*), *n.*, sleep, slumber; lethargy, repose. **Suanaim**, *v.*, I sleep, slumber, repose. **Suanán**, *n.*, slumber, a doze. **Suanmhaire**, *n.*, sleepiness, drowsiness, lethargy. Duine **suan**, a slumberer. **Suan**-bhrocht, a sleep-charm, a narcotic; **suan**-codladh, slumber; **suan**-ghalar, lethargy, sleeping sickness. Tá **suan** ag teacht orm, I feel drowsy, lethargic, sleepy. (An Seabhac, *Learner's Irish-English Pronouncing Dictionary*, 1958, 138; Dineen, 1139; Ó Dónaill, 1178.)

Many Anglo-American dictionaries derive **swoon** "from Old English *geswōgen* in a faint ... past participle of *swōgan*, as in *āswōgan* to choke, of uncertain origin." (*Barnhart Dictionary of English Etymology*, 1103.)

Suain (*Gaelic*), sleep, from "Irish *suan*, Early Irish, Old Irish *súan*, Welsh *hun*, Breton *hun* ... Latin *sopor*, sleep; Sanskrit *svápnas*." (*MacBain's Gaelic Etymological Dictionary*, Sec. 37, online.)

T

Tally, *n.*, a score in baseball made by a runner touching all four bases safely; a bill for an amount due; reckoning; the act of counting.
Táille, *n.*, score, charge; reckoning, number; fee; rate; fare; wages.

> The first game of the Philly series has ended, and here's the official **tally**: No hits for Barry Bonds, 22 for everyone else. (Bruce Jenkins, *San Francisco Chronicle*, May 5, 2006.)

> Barry Bonds is now actually within touching distance of Babe Ruth ... the league would not hold any event to mark the overtaking of Babe Ruth's **tally**. (*Girls Talk Sports*, Nov. 10, 2006.)

Tantrum, *n.*, "a fit of bad temper or ill-humor; 1748, in Samuel Foote's *The Knights*; of unknown origin." (Barnhart, 1115.)
Teintrighim, *v.*, I flash-forth; *fig.* I have a tantrum or fiery fit. **Tintríocht**, *n.* fierceness, hot temper. **Tintrí**, *adj.*, fiery, hot-tempered (*Donegal*); **Teintidhe**, *adj.*, fiery, fierce, wild. Rámhaill **theintidhe**, furious raving; Sasanach **teintidhe**, a fierce Englishman. (Dineen, 1201; Ó Dónaill, 1236.)

Taunt, *n.*, gibe, insult, jeer; *v.*, to gibe, to vex, to gibe, to needle, to provoke, to incite. Origin obscure. (*OED*.)
Tathant (*pron.* tahənt), *vn.*, (*act of*) urging, inciting; pressing; vexing. **Tathantuighim**, *v.*, I urge, incite; press something) on a person. Cuirim **taithint** innte, I taunt (vex, press) her. (Dineen, 1183; Ó Dónaill, 1213.)

Teem, *v.*, to overflow; to overflow with water, to torrent, to pour, to gush; to deluge; to fill up, throng, abound, assemble. **Teeming**, *vn.*, (*act of*) overflowing, pouring water; *adj.*, full, plentiful, gushing, pouring.

Taom (*pron.* tæm), *al.* **taomanna** (*pron.* tæmanə), *n.*, an overflow, a torrent, a flow of water; a fit. **Taomadh** (*pron.* tæm'ə), *vn.*, (*act of*) pouring, overflowing, raining heavily. Ag **taomadh** fearthanna (*pron.* eg tæmah farhənə), pouring rain. (Dineen, 1173, 1174.)

Tiger, *n.*, a name for faro.

Diaga, *adj.*, holy, divine, godly. **Diagaireacht**, *n.*, divinity.

The **Tiger** (**diaga**, divine, holy; diagaireacht, a divinity) was the god of the odds.

Throng, *n.*, a crowd, a mass of people; *vn.*, (*act of*) crowding.

Drong (*pron.* droŋ), *n.*, a multitude, a body of people; group; party, troop, faction, tribe, folk; a great assemblage of people. An **drong** dhaonna, the human race; *al.*, an **drong**, the common herd, the rabble, the throng. (Dineen, 570; Ó Dónaill, 452.)

Twerp, *n.*, "a stupid or inferior person; 1925, of unknown origin." (Barnhart, 1178.)

Duirb, *al.* **doirb**, *n.*, an insect, a worm, a dwarf, a small insignificant person, a diminutive insignificant creature; a small fish, a small fry. (Dineen, 355, 356; Dwelly, 349.)

NYC's Transit Worker's Union founder, Mike Quill, was born in Kerry in 1905. Irish was his first language. In the early-1950s, Quill journeyed to San Francisco to help bus and streetcar drivers win a 40-hour workweek.

> An obnoxiously zealous reporter hovered around the union office for hours... and then tailed us as we drove to the St. Francis Hotel. "I'll get rid of the **twerp**," Mike announced as he jumped out of the car at a red light. (Shirley Quill, *Mike Quill Himself*, 1985, 237.)

Twig, *v.*, to understand, comprehend, discern; to observe.

Tuig, *v.*, to understand; comprehend, discern, realize; *fig.* observe, see.

The Irish **tuig** of understanding produces the **twig** of discernment and observation.

> As Europe is now **twigging**, the best breeding ground for innovators who know how to do business is often big, competitive companies. (*The Economist.*)

Twig, to observe.

> "**Twig** the copper, he is peery," (observe the officer), "he is watching us." (Matsell, *Vocabulum*, 1859, [1997], 142.)

U

Uncle, (*in phrases*) "say uncle," "cry uncle," *n.*, to surrender; to cry for mercy or quarter.

Anacal, *n.*, mercy, quarter; *fig.* surrender.

The phrases "cry **uncle**" and "say **uncle**" first appeared in print in the American language after World War One, at a time when the whole world was hollering **uncle** (**anacal**, mercy).

W

Wallop, *n.*, a blow; a whack; (*in baseball*) a hit; *v.*, to hit; to strike. Uncertain origin. (Barnhart, 1217.)

Bhuail leadhb (*pron.* wual lĭbb), strike a blow, hit a whack. **Buail, bhuail** (*pron.* wuəl), *v.*, to beat, to strike, to hit. **Leadhb** (*pron.* lĭbb), *n.*, a stroke, a blow. **Leadhbadh** (*pron.* llibah), *vn.*, (*act of*) beating, thrashing whacking. Bhuail sé leadhb air (*pron.* wuəl shay lĭbb ar), he gave him a wallop. (An Seabhac, 1958, 75.)

Wanker, *n.*, a masturbator; a jerk-off; a creep; a loser. Origin uncertain. (Maven's *Word of the Day*, www.randomhouse.com.)

Uath-anchor (*pron.* uəh-anċor), self-abuse; masturbation; *fig.* a masturbator. **Uath-** (*pron.* uəh), prefix, auto-, self-. **Anchor** (*pron.* anċor), *n.*, abuse, ill-treatment, ill-usage. Níor thugador aon anchor dó, they gave him no abuse. (Dineen, 44.)

> A fan of self-abuse (also "**Wanker**"). (*Irish Slang in Under 20 Seconds.*)

> "I suppose it all originates from our repressed Victorian sexuality, from back when everybody thought they were the only ones to suffer the secret shame of being an actual **wanker**." (*Urban Dictionary* online.)

> A gentleman identified as "Mr. F.," a rugby player in his university days who works as a sports trainer, is convinced that **self-abuse** is the way to a robust physique ... Thanks to the **wanker's** diet, he pants, he's now well on his way to a slimmer, healthier physique. ("Pudgy porkers pare pounds with new **wanker**'s diet," *Mainichi Daily News*, April 29, 2003.)

Welt (*slang*), *v.*, to beat, to strike, to thrash.

Bhuailte (*pron.* wueltə), *p.p.*, beaten, struck. Tá an fear sin **bhuailte**, that man is beaten.

> "I **welt** the door with me foot." (Edward Harrigan, *The Mulligan Guard*, 1878.)

Wisht (*imperative*), be quiet! Shut up!

Éist (*pron.* h-éisht), (*imperative*), listen! Hush! **Éist** do bhéal (*pron.* h-éisht do væl), shut up! Hush your mouth.

Whale, *v.*, to beat, strike, hit. "Of obscure origin." (*OED.*)

Buail, bhuail (*pron.* wuəl), *v.*, to beat, to strike, to hit. **Bhuail** sé dorn orm (*pron.* wuəl shay dorn orm), he hit me with his fist. **Bhuail** sé buille de bhata orm (*pron.* wuəl shay billĭ de wata orm), he whaled me with a stick. **Bhuail** sin a bhfaca mé riamh, that beats anything I have ever seen, that beats everything. (Ó Dónaill, 152.)

> "He used to always **whale** me when he was sober and could get his hands on me." (Twain, *Huckleberry Finn*, 1885, [1994].)

Whiz, *adj.*, *(someone or something)* outstanding, superior, excellent; *n.*, a person who is exceptionally skilful or talented; *(underworld)* a pickpocket.

Uas, *adj.*, **uas**-, *pref.*, *(someone or something)* outstanding, fine, great, excellent, top, superior, distinguished, noble, lofty; *al.* **uais**.

Many dictionaries derive **whiz** from *wizard*. But, gee **whiz**, there is nothing magical about **whiz**. A **whiz** like Einstein got his genius from study, practice, and hard work. Not metaphysics. (*DAS*, 577.)

> Irish-American **Whiz** Kids. (Jack Callahan, *Irish America*, 1995.)

> "Wonderful night."
> "It's a **whiz**."
> (F. Scott Fitzgerald, *This Side of Paradise*, 1920, 45.)

> Critics ... regard President Kennedy as a quiz-kid surrounded by **whiz**-kids. (*The Economist*, December 1962.)

Why-O (gang), n., a powerful Irish street gang in New York City in the 19th century.

Uathadh (*pron.* uəhah, uəhah, uəh-ŭ), *n.*, few, singular few; alone. I n-uathadh agus i sochaidhe, alone and in society.

The **Gopher** gang of the early-20th century saw themselves as the modern version of the old **Why-O** gang of the 1870s and 1880s. *I n-uathadh sluagh is sochaidhe*, having but few warriors and followers, the **Why-O** gang of Civil War veterans preferred a small force of the few to a large unruly street gang of the many.

Winona Club

Uathadh Nua (*pron.* uəhoo nuə), new singular few, new "few" club.

The **Winona** Club was the name of the Gopher gang's headquarters on West 47th Street in Hells' Kitchen. The **Winona** (**Uathadh Nua**, *pron.* uəhoo nuə, new singular few, [the] new few) Club was named in honor of the Gopher's underworld predecessors, the Why-O gang.

Whiskey, (*archaic; pron.* whiskybae), *n.*, aqua vita.

Uisce beatha (*pron.* ish-kə b'ahə), water of life, aqua vita. **Uisce** (*pron.* ish-kee), *n.*, water. **Beatha** (*pron.* b'aha), *n.*, life.

The archaic English spelling and pronunciation **whiskybae**, and its contraction **whiskey**, demonstrate how dramatically Irish shape-shifted into English. The slender Irish *s*, pronounced *sh*, in **uisce** (*pron.* ishkee, water) became the sibilant "s" of "whiskeybae" and "whiskey."

The Irish and Gaelic **uisce beatha** (*pron.* ishkee b'ah) lost its **beatha** (*pron.* b'ah, life) and the Irish word for *water* became the English word for *whiskey*.

Y

Yacking, *n.*, incessant talk; persistent conversation; *vn.*, chattering, nagging.

Éagcaoin (*pron.* éag-keen), *vn.*, complaining, lamenting.

> YACK: A syllable imitative of a snapping sound. (*OED.*)

Yell, *n.*, a loud shout; *v.*, to shout loudly.

Éamh oll (*pron.* éw'ol), a great cry, a loud shout, a loud call.

The *OED* derives **yell** from Middle Low German *gellen, gillen*, weak, Old English *galan* to sing.

Yellow, *adj.*, cowardly, craven. **Yellow**-dog contract. **Yellow** union. The word **yellow** was applied to an organization, policy, or person opposed to militant action by a trade union.

Éalú (*pron.* éalu), **éalódh** (*pron.* éaloh), *vn.*, secretly absconding, surreptitiously fleeing, sneaking away, slinking off, chickening out.

When you turn **yellow**, you do not turn color; you turn and sneak away like a coward.

> One of our noblest he-men, a regular fire-eater to hear him tell it, has turned **yellow** at the front. (J.M. Grider, *War Birds*, 1918, [1927], 264; *OED.*)

Index

Burns, Mary 11-12
Burroughs, William 87, 195
Bush, George H. W. 125
Butler, "Big" Dick 57
Butler, Hubert viii
Butler, Jerry 138
Buttons, Red 85
Byrne, Robert 210
Byrnes, Edd 203
Byrnes, Mamie 24-25
Byron, Lord "George Gordon" 94
Cagney, James xvi-xvii, 2, 157
Cain, James M. 132, 259
California Arts Commission 63
Callahan, Jack 292
Campaigns in the Rocky Mountains (Hildreth) 50
Cant, Alexander 111
Cant, Andrew 111
Canting Academy (Head) 102, 198
Capone, Al 234
Carny lingo 186-88, 277-78
Caray, Harry 180
Casey, Bowsie 258
Casey, Marion 181
Cassidy, Charles 46
Cassidy, Clare 1, 276
Cassidy, Daniel P. 270
Cassidy, Matty 6-7
Cat on a Hot Tin Roof (Williams) 128
Cattle Raid of Cooley (Tain bo Cuailnge) 177
Caveat (Harmon) 98, 136-37, 242
Census, U.S. 30, 37, 46, 68, 107, 240
Champollion, Jean-François xi-xii
Chandler, Raymond 142, 223
Chapman, Robert 275
Cheapjack (Allington) 195
Chicago (Algren) 155
Chicago Cubs 180
Chicago White Sox 68
Chronicles of England (Holinshed) 156
Circus Parade (Tully) 32, 201, 278
Citizen Hearst (Swanberg) 153
Citizen Hobo (De Pastino) 282
Civil War (US) 46, 130, 250, 259-60
Clann na Gael 18-19
Classical Dictionary of the Vulgar Tongue (Grose) 19-21, 86, 104, 125, 156, 194, 220
Cline, Massie 256-57
Clock Without Hands, The (McCullers) 115
Cobb, Ty 65
Cobbett, William 133
Cobden, William 134
Cochrane, George 121
Cockery, David 105
Cohan, George M. 211
Cohern, Gib 46
Coleman, Harry J. 169, 173
Colton, Henry 47, 176
Condition of the English Working Class, The (Engels) 12
Connolly, James 12, 130
Constant Sinner, The (West) 82, 152
Cooney, Celia 127
Cop slang, Irish origins of 18-20

Cordelia's Aspirations (Harrigan) 202
Cornell Daily Sun 115
Court Gamester (Seymour) 100
Cowboy slang, Irish influence on 33-35, 57, 133, 228
Cowboy Songs and Frontier Ballads (Lomax) 33, 35
Cowboys, Irish 8
Cowgate slum (Scotland) 11
Craps 47
Cribb, Tom 214
Criminal Slang (Monteleone) 178
Cromwell, Oliver xii
Cronin, Mrs. 34-35
Curley, James M. 114, 161-62
De Pastino, Todd 282
Dead Rabbits Gang 17-18, 232, 248
Deford, Frank 122
Dekker, Thomas 120, 144
Delano, Lefty 239
Demarest, William xvi
Dempsey, Jack 172, 186
Descartes, René 5
Desmond, Earl of 241
Detroit Tigers 65
Devery, "Big" Bill 91, 103
Diamond, Eddie 94
Diamond, Legs 94
Diary of Samuel Pepys, The (Pepys) 277
Dickens, Charles 172
Dictionary of American Slang 85, 116
Dictionary of American Underworld Lingo (O'Leary) 83, 157
Dictionary of Americanisms (Matthews) 189
Dictionary of Hiberno-English (Dolan) 1, 252
Dictionary of the American West (Adams) 34
Dineen, Patrick 50-51, 81, 252
Dinosaur Provincial Park (Alberta) 182
Disney, Walt 163
Dock Walloper (Butler) 57, 87, 90-91, 103, 106, 120, 126, 136, 164-65, 195, 206, 234, 246
Dolan, Terence Patrick 1, 252
Don Juan (Byron) 94
Donlevy, Brian xvi
Dorgan, Thomas "TAD" 184-85, 260
Dork of Cork, The (Raymo) 135
Douglas, Ann xv
Draper, Shane 47
Dreiser, Theodore 211
Drinking Life, The (Hamill) 213
Dublin slum (Ire.) 11
Dubliners (Joyce) 279
Dude, Irish origins of 55-58
Durante, Jimmy 268
Dwelly, Edward 121
Early History of Man (Taylor) 103
East River slum (NYC) 37
Easter Rising of 1916 12-13
Eastwood, Clint 79
Education of a Felon, The (Bunker) 286
Edward III (King of England) 202
Egan, Pierce 21, 195, 211, 213, 266
Egypt xi-xii
El Fey Club (NYC) 108
Ellington, Duke 63

AK Press
Ordering Information

AK Press
674-A 23rd Street
Oakland, CA 94612-1163
U.S.A
(510) 208-1700
www.akpress.org
akpress@akpress.org

AK Press
PO Box 12766
Edinburgh, EH8 9YE
Scotland
(0131) 555-5165
www.akuk.com
ak@akedin.demon.uk

The addresses above would be delighted to provide you with the latest complete AK catalog, featuring several thousand books, pamphlets, zines, audio products, video products, and stylish apparel published & distributed by AK Press. Alternatively, check out our websites for the complete catalog, latest news and updates, events, and secure ordering.

Also Available from AK Press

The first audio collection from Alexander Cockburn on compact disc.

Beating the Devil
Alexander Cockburn, ISBN 13: 9781902593494 • CD • $14.98

In this collection of recent talks, maverick commentator Alexander Cockburn defiles subjects ranging from Colombia to the American presidency to the Missile Defense System. Whether he's skewering the fallacies of the war on drugs or illuminating the dark crevices of secret government, his erudite and extemporaneous style warms the hearts of even the stodgiest cynics of the left.

Available from CounterPunch/AK Press

The Case Against Israel
by Michael Neumann

Wielding a buzzsaw of logic, Professor Neumann dismantles plank-by-plank the Zionist rationale for Israel as religious state entitled to trample upon the basic human rights of non-Jews. Along the way, Neumann also offers a passionate amicus brief for the plight of the Palestinian people.

Other Lands Have Dreams: From Baghdad to Pekin Prison
by Kathy Kelly

At a moment when so many despairing peace activists have thrown in the towel, Kathy Kelly, a witness to some of history's worst crimes, never relinquishes hope. Other Lands Have Dreams is literary testimony of the highest order, vividly recording the secret casualties of our era, from the hundreds of thousands of Iraqi children inhumanely denied basic medical care, clean water and food by the US overlords to young mothers sealed inside the sterile dungeons of American prisons in the name of the merciless war on drugs.

Dime's Worth of Difference: Beyond the Lesser of Two Evils
Edited by Alexander Cockburn and Jeffrey St. Clair

Everything you wanted to know about one-party rule in America.

Whiteout: the CIA, Drugs and the Press
by Alexander Cockburn and Jeffrey St. Clair, Verso.

The involvement of the CIA with drug traffickers is a story that has slouched into the limelight every decade or so since the creation of the Agency. In Whiteout, here at last is the full saga.

Been Brown So Long It Looked Like Green to Me: the Politics of Nature
by Jeffrey St. Clair, Common Courage Press.

Covering everything from toxics to electric power plays, St. Clair draws a savage profile of how money and power determine the state of our environment, gives a vivid account of where the environment stands today and what to do about it.

Imperial Crusades: Iraq, Afghanistan and Yugoslavia
by Alexander Cockburn and Jeffrey St. Clair, Verso.

A chronicle of the lies that are now returning each and every day to haunt the deceivers in Washington and London, the secret agendas and the under-reported carnage of these wars. We were right and they were wrong, and this book proves the case. Never leave home without it.

Why We Publish CounterPunch

By Alexander Cockburn and Jeffrey St. Clair

TEN YEARS AGO WE FELT UNHAPPY ABOUT THE STATE OF RADICAL journalism. It didn't have much edge. It didn't have many facts. It was politically timid. It was dull. CounterPunch was founded. We wanted it to be the best muckraking newsletter in the country. We wanted it to take aim at the consensus of received wisdom about what can and cannot be reported. We wanted to give our readers a political roadmap they could trust.

A decade later we stand firm on these same beliefs and hopes. We think we've restored honor to muckraking journalism in the tradition of our favorite radical pamphleteers: Edward Abbey, Peter Maurin and Ammon Hennacy, Appeal to Reason, Jacques René Hébert, Tom Paine and John Lilburne.

Every two weeks CounterPunch gives you jaw-dropping exposés on: Congress and lobbyists; the environment; labor; the National Security State.

"CounterPunch kicks through the floorboards of lies and gets to the foundation of what is really going on in this country", says Michael Ratner, attorney at the Center for Constitutional Rights. "At our house, we fight over who gets to read CounterPunch first. Each issue is like spring after a cold, dark winter."

YOU CANNOT MISS ANOTHER ISSUE

Name _____

Address _____

City _____ State _____ Zip _____

Email _____ Phone _____

Credit Card # _____

Exp. Date _____ Signature _____

Visit our website for more information: **www.counterpunch.org**

- ☐ 1 yr. **$45**
- ☐ 2 yr. **$80**
- ☐ Supporter **$100**
- ☐ 1 yr. email **$35**
- ☐ 2 yr. email **$65**
- ☐ Donation Only
- ☐ 1 yr. both **$50**
- ☐ 2 yr. both **$90**

Send Check/Money Order to: **CounterPunch, P.O. Box 228, Petrolia, CA 95558**
Canada add $12.50 per year postage. Others outside US add $17.50 per year.

A Bush & Botox World

By Saul Landau

Gore Vidal on Saul Landau: "Landau has opened many windows for the rest of us: parts of the world, where we are not usually allowed to know about except to be told how wretched they are."

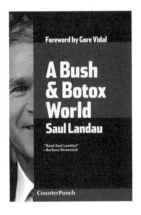

Bush & Botox World provides insight into the culture under which the Bush White House operates. It uses Botox as a metaphor for both the rapid technological change of the globalized world and its superficiality. Landau syncopates visits to modern Vietnam with analysis of the bizarre world of anti-Castro terrorists. He brings readers into the homes of corporate executives and into the street lives of African American kids on east Oakland's streets.

Between the prose pieces, Landau inserts pithy poems on aging, computers and a concert in Istanbul. He takes readers back to the horrors of the 1976 assassination of his friends and colleagues, Orlando Letelier and Ronni Moffitt on Washington, DC's Embassy Row and into the blood-filled streets of Falluja. The allegorical essays on Hearst's Castle and the Salton Sea stand as both insights into the contemporary world and warnings for the next generation.